CCURATA TABULA
BULA

Peter Freuchen's Book of the Seven Seas

Peter Freuchen

PETER FREUCHEN'S

BOOK OF THE

SEVEN SEAS

BY

PETER FREUCHEN

WITH DAVID LOTH

JULIAN MESSNER, INC.

New York

Published by Julian Messner, Inc.
8 West 40 Street, New York 18

Published simultaneously in Canada
by The Copp Clark Publishing Co. Limited

Jacket and frontispiece photographs by Philippe Halsman

Endpaper map, The World of 1690,
from DECORATIVE MAPS OF THE 15th-18th CENTURIES
by R. A. Skelton, courtesy of Staples Press Limited (1952)

Manufactured in the United States of America
Printed by Colorgraphic Offset Co., Inc., New York

Library of Congress Catalog Card No. 57-11723

THIS BOOK
IS DEDICATED TO
THE MEMORY OF
HANS ISBRANDTSEN,
A GREAT FRIEND AND A LOVER OF
THE SEVEN SEAS

Line engraving by Frans Huys after Pieter Brueghel the Elder

Contents

Illustrations

Foreword

A Spanish treasure galleon.

Foreword

I began really to learn about the Seven Seas in Greenland, although I was born and raised in a little port, Nykoebing Falster, in Denmark, and knew ships and sailors and stories about famous voyages all my life. But when I sat through the long dark nights of the Arctic winters at Thule for years, for many years indeed, I discovered the ocean in my imagination.

There was little enough of it that we could see. All winter long the ice stretched out for miles and miles in front of us, firm and solid. As soon as the sun showed over the horizon in spring, we had a wide outlook. But it would be months before the ice was breaking up, and then it was tantalizing to look out from the shore at huge icebergs drifting south in endless procession. When a fellow is sitting alone for months on end, as I was, he lets his imagination fly freely. So in my mind I followed those big fragments, broken off from the icecap, as they floated eternally to their doom. I thought of them sailing so majestically south until off Newfoundland, I knew they would turn east and meet the warm waters of the Gulf Stream. There they would die, swiftly and surely, for the Gulf Stream can finish off even a large berg in twenty-four hours.

Well, I wondered, from where comes this Gulf Stream, and why, and how does it happen to be just where it is? On the sails of my imagination still, I followed this mighty current to where it is born in the Caribbean. That took me to the waters of other currents, and to studying the winds and tides which play so great a part in the mysterious movements of the sea. Why, I asked myself, are the winds so steady in one place and so capricious in another and don't blow at all somewhere else? Why should the tide rise as high as a house on one coast and hardly at all on another? Why twice a day in most of the world, but here and there only once? And where, after all, does all that water come from in the first place?

Little by little it dawned upon me that there is a logical connection between everything that happens in that immense connected body of salty water that covers 71 per cent of the surface of the earth. The fact is that the ripples from a pebble thrown by a little child could be traced all over the Seven Seas if only we had instruments delicate enough to record them. There is, indeed, a grand pattern in all the wonderful phenomena of the ocean—its storms and calms, deeps and shallows, the animals and plants that live in it, the birds flying over it, its islands and volcanoes and caves, even the men and the ships moving about upon it.

Since those long, dark, lonely winters in Thule, I never have stopped wondering and learning about the Seven Seas. Why seven? was one of the first questions I asked myself, since I could name seven times seven which are called seas on the maps. For every answer, there were two new questions, because the majesty and the mystery of the sea are inexhaustible. Immense in their extent, irresistible in their power, unconquerable in their precision, the seas have inspired men through all ages with feelings of awe and mysticism and fear. Everyone feels himself weak and impotent when he faces their might. No one can halt the tides or fight the currents or control the waves. But everywhere men feel a compulsion to pit their strength against the sea, to explore it and wander about on it, to use it for their own ends and wrest its wealth from it.

Primitive people worshiped the sea out of fear of what it might do to them, and gratitude for the treasures which it washed up for them on its beaches. We know a great deal more about it than they did, but we still stand on the shore, humble in our insignificance as we face the waves rolling in from a turbulent ocean.

When gales whip the trees and rattle our windows or snow piles up outside so that no one wants to go for a walk, landlubbers snug in warm rooms are likely to tell each other how sorry they feel for all the poor sailors on a night like this. But they feel, too, a little wistful envy of the men who brave cold and storms upon the restless water. Then on a fine day the sight of foreign seamen or of tall ships from far away or of an exotic bit of merchandise from halfway round the world or even of an oddly shaped scrap of driftwood cast up on the beach gives any of us a pang of jealousy of the men who move about over the sea viewing the wonders of the deep. And it must be confessed that these wonders lose nothing in the seamen's telling of them.

The stories which these fellows bring to us are the stuff our dreams are made of. We may not believe the tellers of the salty tales for a minute, but in our secret minds we live them. We all are great heroes in our dreams. We drift endlessly in hot, dead calms while all on board but us are in despair. We baffle the most violent storms, conquer the bravest fighters, foil the most bloodthirsty pirates, bring home the richest cargoes from the most amazing voyages, wrestle with monsters, dive for sunken gold, see the strangest sights. Then, in the end, science takes over from imagination—and behold, there are even greater wonders than we dreamed.

This book is the result of my own imagination and curiosity. Here I have tried to set forth something of both the science and the dreams—the facts and the fancies which make the Seven Seas endlessly fascinating.

Noank, Connecticut
August 30, 1957

Peter Freuchen

The Seven Seas change their shapes all the time, but until comparatively recently the maps men made of them changed even more rapidly, although for a different reason. Sailors did not know where the seas began and ended. This chart was one of those drawn when science began to replace imagination among the map makers.

Part I

The Shape of the Seas

The Birth of the Ocean
The Changing Face of the Waters
The Magic Figure
A Glimpse of the Future

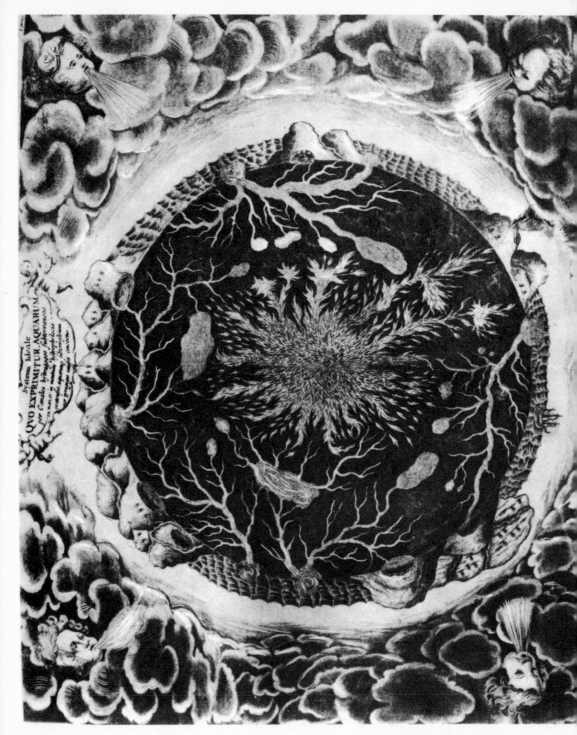

The ocean and the earth as a seventeenth-century geologist supposed them. Athanasius Kircher, a Jesuit scholar, worked out this relationship of the ocean, the land, the subterranean rivers and the fires in the center of the earth in 1664.

1

The Birth of the Ocean

The Greeks said that the world is a flat disk around which flows a great river wider than anyone could guess. Although all they could see of it was their own landlocked, island-dotted Mediterranean, they were so impressed by its power that they called it by the name of the father of gods as well as of men, Oceanus, the beginning of all things. At that, the Greeks probably got their idea of the sea from even earlier Babylonian thinkers, who imagined a universal sheet of water out of which rose a single round mountain, the earth.

The men of the Bible supposed that a watery chaos existed from the beginning of time until "the Spirit of God moved upon the face of the waters." According to this version, the actual formation of the seas was just one part of the Lord's work on the third day of creation.

So every people that looked upon the ocean gave it some supernatural origin. But the real story which modern scientists have pieced together from observation and analysis is even more wonderful. The truth, as their instruments and calculations have revealed it, is a stranger fairy tale than the most riotous imagination ever dreamed. In brief it is this:

Once upon a time, about two and a half billion years ago, a huge ball of flaming gases was thrown off by the sun and went whirling out into space. However, the sun did not lose all control over it, but kept the fragment spinning in a regular orbit around itself.

This sphere was the earth, an intensely hot mass revolving a good

21

deal faster than it does now because it has been slowed by age and a greater solidity. Of course it began to cool as soon as it got far enough from the sun, and eventually the hot gases became molten rock. An atmosphere of dark, thick clouds, as black as the heaviest rain clouds we ever see, extended upward for miles all around it. But there was no rain because the earth was so hot that any drops immediately hissed upward in steam like the moisture on a house-wife's finger when she tests the iron to see if it is ready to use.

The cooling of the earth was a very violent process, leaving great cracks and crags, basins and bulges rather than a perfectly round, smooth ball. The liquid rock was pulled back and forth in tides such as we see in the ocean now, but caused by the sun's attraction. These built up into enormous waves which swept across the earth without any solid obstacle to block them. They grew of their own momentum at the same time that they became thicker in texture. At one point, probably not long before the outer layer of rock cooled into a solid crust, this solar tidal wave of liquid rock achieved such a height and velocity that an enormous chunk of it was flung completely clear of the earth. That was the origin of the moon.

The rest of the earth's crust by this time was so nearly solid that it would not flow into the depression left when the moon broke away. Eventually the depression became the Pacific Ocean. The scientists mention as one proof of this the fact that the floor of the Pacific is basalt, which is the stuff of the earth's middle layer; while the floors of the other seas are granite like most of the rest of the outer layer. Furthermore, recent scientific calculations have meas-ured the mean density of the moon, and it is very like that of the earth's crust but much less than that of the earth as a whole. This indicates that the moon is made up of the same substances as the earth's crust.

As time passed, a million years or so after the sun had thrown it off, the earth cooled to something like its present consistency. This is a hot, still molten center, a middle layer which is only semisolid in its inner portion, and more and more solid the nearer it comes to the surface, and a relatively thin outer shell which is the bedrock of our world. The constant spinning sorted out these materials while they still were soft, so that the lightest are on the outside. The next heaviest, basalt, forms the middle layer. The heaviest of all, which is believed to be molten iron, is at the core, as hot as the sun or the most torrid hell ever imagined.

As soon as the crust was cool enough to retain water, it began to rain. The deluge is faintly described in Genesis, but instead of forty days and forty nights, it rained for more nearly forty centuries. It rained without letup and with the force of a tropical downpour. It rained until the clouds had dumped something like 300,000,000 cubic miles of water upon the bare rocks which was all there was on earth, for as yet there was not a grain of sand or bit of dirt, let alone a blade of grass or any other living thing.

At last the rain stopped and the sun shone for the first time upon the face of the earth, for until then the clouds were so thick they prevented any ray of light from penetrating them. The great cracks and basins left by the cooling process were filled with water, clear and fresh. The crags and bulges rose above it, nothing but clean, bare rock. The water was not quite as pure as rain itself because the deluge, rushing down the sides of the hills, had begun the interminable process of washing salts and minerals out of the rock into the sea. But at its birth, the ocean was as fresh as an inland lake, and spread out, covering about as much of the earth's surface as it does today, and roughly in the same places.

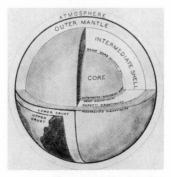

Courtesy of the American
Museum of Natural History

Table I

The Geologic Ages

ARCHEOZOIC (from Greek words meaning "ancient" and "life"). It lasted from the beginning of the world until about two billion years ago—in those oldest eras the geologists are willing to give or take a hundred million years or so.

PROTOZOIC (from a Greek word meaning first in rank as well as earliest in time). This was more than half of all the earth's history, about a billion and a half years from the end of the Archeozoic until about half a billion years ago.

PALEOZOIC (also from a word meaning "old"; the geologists, wishing to express the great antiquity of these early eras, are lucky that the Greeks had plenty of words for it). Here we get into time which can be measured more accurately because the rocks, sedimentary deposits, fossil remains and so on are preserved sufficiently. This last of the early geologic ages lasted for 300,000,000 years or so, until less than 200,000,000 years ago. Since it and the succeeding eras can be studied more completely than the two earliest, they are subdivided, the Paleozoic into six ages:

1. *The Cambrian* (from the old name for Wales; the earlier Paleozoic ages were studied in Great Britain and so got mostly British names) lasting from about 500,000,000 years ago to a little more than 440,000,000 years ago.

2. *The Ordovician* (the name of an early tribe in Wales) from 440,000,000 years ago to 360,000,000.

3. *The Silurian* (the ancient, pre-celtic people of Britain) from 360,000,000 years ago to 320,000,000.

4. *The Devonian* (named for the County in England) from 320,000,000 years ago to 265,000,000.

5. *The Carboniferous* (because it was the age in which the first great coal deposits were formed) from 265,000,000 years ago to 210,000,000.

6. *The Permian* (named for a Russian province where notable remains were found) from 210,000,000 years ago to 185,000,000.

MESOZOIC (from a Greek word meaning "middle" or "intermediate" because this was the Middle Ages of geology). It lasted for only 125,000,000 years, but it is divided into three sub-ages:

1. *The Triassic* (meaning "group of three") lasting from 185,000,000 years ago to 155,000,000.

2. *The Jurassic* (named for the Jura Mountains in Europe which were one of this age's most notable features, although our own Sierra Nevadas were formed at that same time) from 153,000,000 years ago to 130,000,000.

3. *The Cretaceous* (which means "pertaining to chalk" and as you might expect the white cliffs of Dover were formed at this time) from 130,000,000 years ago to 60,000,000.

CENOZOIC (from a Greek word which means both "new" and "common"). Although this has been going on for a mere 60,000,000 years, it is the era in which sea and land have taken pretty much their present form. Geologists divide it into two unequal parts:

1. *The Tertiary* (meaning third in rank or number) lasting up to a million years ago.

2. **The Pleistocene** (appropriately meaning "most new" and called *Quartiary* in Denmark and elsewhere) in which we live and which virtually has just started, a million years old.

2

The Changing Face
of the Waters

The ocean had hardly been formed when it, like the land, began to change its shapes and boundaries. It never stopped. Throughout the history of the earth the biggest changes have been largely the work of either the cracking and folding and exploding of the earth's crust or of the growth and melting of glaciers.

The earliest changes, and many of the later ones, were caused by the continual cooling of the earth. As the rock solidified, miles down, it shrank and the crust, deprived of that support, would collapse. But the shrinkage was not uniform, and when one huge section fell, it might push against another and thrust it up in piles and folds of rock. Land would emerge from the sea—one must imagine it taking place with such power as to pile up the biggest mountain ranges, the Andes and Himalayas and Rockies. Water would rush into the low places and into the deep cracks and chasms left by the upheaval.

The record of the shifting seas for about four-fifths of the earth's life, say for the first two billion years, is found only in bits and pieces. Water covered some areas and retreated from others, but erosion and the heat and pressures of later geologic eras erased most of the evidence and left the rest very hard to interpret. There still is some sedimentary rock dating from that period, but it is much distorted.

However, scientists believe that during these two billion years there were four major upheavals which changed the shape of the seas radically. Each of them threw up mountain ranges as high as any on earth today, although only traces of the third and fourth are left—the Laurentian range and some other rock in Canada, some roots of old mountains in the north central United States and southern Canada. Of course, each of these four upheavals had its counterpart in the ocean, making depressions probably several times deeper than the mountains were high.

All of these great ranges—and most of the later ones too—were eroded away and washed into the sea. Everything soluble, including some gold and silver and many other metals, added to the mineral content of the water. Because 85.5 per cent of the minerals are sodium and chlorine, the elements of salt, we speak of "salt water," and can taste it. Forty-seven other minerals divide the remaining 14.5 per cent. Actually the rivers bring down more calcium than chlorine, but calcium is only in fifth place among the minerals in sea water. The difference is accounted for by the animals which use great quantities of calcium, and which they take out of the water as fast as it comes in.

Everything which will not dissolve settles to the bottom, and the hardened layers of this sediment gives us our chief clues to the history of the ocean, and the world. But before man came along to be curious about them, those of the first two billion years of the earth were tilted up as mountains and then eroded away completely except for the few traces already mentioned. Since this geologic period lasted four times as long as all the eras since, there was plenty of opportunity for the erosion.

Just what happened to extend or diminish the area of the ocean through the melting or growing of glaciers also is obscure in these ages. That there was at least one great ice age in this time seems certain. Therefore a great part of the land was covered by glaciers, while at the same time the seas were smaller than they are now because so much water was frozen in glaciers.

Beginning about half a billion years ago, or a little more, with what geologists called the Mesozoic (or middle ages of life) era, the record is more complete. The layers of sedimentary rock and the fossils have been preserved. They reveal when the seas covered what is now land and for how long. Virtually every part of the earth has been under water at some time. In the slow procession of the geologic ages (see Table I), the ocean spread or shrank. The ice ages froze vast amounts of water into their glaciers, and the seas retreated from the land. Then, as the climate warmed, the land was uncovered on one side by the melting sheets of ice and inundated on the other by the advancing seas. Hardly any part of the world has been free from such an experience; toward the end of the Mesozoic era, glaciers covered even much of what is now the tropics in both hemispheres.

The big changes, affecting whole continents and seas at once, have been caused by the glaciers or by violent upheavals of the earth's crust. Smaller, although equally spectacular effects, are achieved sometimes by less earth-shaking forces—by the action of the sea itself, by volcanoes, by erosion, by the industry of living things. The results have considerably altered the shape of the seas, and of the islands and coasts, too.

The sea always is pounding away at its shores, and it almost never is quiet. Its waves can work up a power superior to any yet created by man, except perhaps for atomic energy if it is ever harnessed to something more constructive than a bomb. The force of the waves has ground away parts of the land, allowing water to flow into low places, or it has carved cliffs into interesting and slowly changing forms. Perhaps the most alluring of these sea-made phenomena are caves. All sorts of communities all over the world boast of the wonders of their caves, and the best known attract people by the thousands to gape at their pillars and frescoes, strange shapes and fantastic colors.

Most caves probably were carved out by subterranean rivers and springs washing a way for themselves through cliffs on their way to the sea. They dissolved some of the materials out of the hard rock. But many caves have been hollowed out by the waves, carrying sand and gravel to help in the grinding operation, as they dashed against a steep face of rock for thousands of years. The softer spots or veins were less resistant, and were worn away until great caverns were created, some of them leading deep, deep into the rock. Then very

27

often the coast was raised or lowered, and the openings may be well above or below the level at which they were formed.

These caves provide a weird and wonderful demonstration of the workings of the sea. One of the largest, and one of my favorites, although it has not been the great tourist attraction it deserves to be, is on the north shore of Santa Cruz Island, largest of the southern California Channel Islands. Santa Cruz is rugged and mountainous, some twenty miles long and five to six broad, lying about twenty miles south of Santa Barbara. All along the rugged shores, the waves have gnawed out caves, some mere slits in the stone, some with underwater entrances. The biggest of them, known since the early days of exploration, was called Cueva Pintada, or Painted Cave, by the Spaniards. The many sea lions who make a home here for part of the year when their migration brings them to these waters are the chief beneficiaries of the fact that people do not know it as well as they should.

The Painted Cave was found in 1542 by a daring Spanish sailor, Juan Rodriquez Cabillo. Its entrance is seventy or eighty feet high in the form of a great pointed Gothic arch flanked by two massive buttresses. Your boat floats through this grand arch into a vast chamber about 100 feet high, and you can see at once why it is called the Painted Cave. The limestone walls have been colored in the most fantastic patterns of green, red and yellow splashed by high waves depositing their salt upon a white background. As your eyes accustom themselves to the twilight of the cave, the patterns shimmer in a beauty impossible to describe.

Across the great chamber is a big black spot, right at the surface of the water enlarging and shrinking as the waves roll across the floor. It is an opening into an inner apartment of the cavernous system. Each wave almost closes this door to the interior, but as it recedes there is enough space for your boat to enter. The next wave, of course, nearly shuts the door after you. Inside, you are in an even larger chamber, entirely dark, and with a roof so high that your torch will not throw a beam high enough to get a glimpse of the ceiling. On the inner side, a great ledge slopes down to the water, and here in their mating season hundreds upon hundreds of sea lions live for some months.

As your boatman watches his chance to steer out of this interior apartment into the Painted Cave, the wonder of the colors will strike you even more forcefully as you come out of the darkness into the cathedral-like dimness of the outer chamber.

More varied alterations in the shape of the seas are caused by the erosion from the land and the building up of coral formations in the sea. Rivers deposit their silt and carve their channels in the borders of the ocean, while in all warm waters the industrious coral builds up reefs.

Volcanoes have furnished some quite different, but no less spectacular, changes in the sea. Some of them we can see as islands, thrust up above the sea, and of these we will have more to say. But most of the volcanic action under water causes only a passing turbulence of waves on the surface. As a result, there are countless high volcanic peaks, rising sometimes miles high from the ocean floor, and great fields and folds of lava which are completely invisible. Many of them have been located by soundings, but there must be a great many unknown because only a very small part of the world below the waves has been explored.

In fact such explorations are only a little more than one hundred years old. The first man who even attempted to find out how deep the open ocean might be was Magellan on his pioneer trip around the world. He had a line only 1,200 feet long, so it did not touch bottom. The first successful ocean sounding was made in 1839 by an Englishman, Sir James Clark Ross, in the Antarctic. He had made a special line for the purpose and finally lowered it to the bottom in an abyss 14,550 feet deep. He noted that this is almost as far below sea level as Mont Blanc is above it (15,781 feet).

For another hundred years men managed to make soundings here and there, learning that the ocean floor was by no means as flat and monotonous as people had believed. In fact, it is more rugged than the land, with peaks much higher than the Andes or Rockies and great gashes as deep and steep as the Grand Canyon. Nowadays soundings are taken automatically by a sonic device which measures the depths by the time it takes an echo to come back from the bottom. Ships carrying this instrument get a complete record of the depths over which they pass. But it will be many years before we have enough data, properly sorted, to map the ocean's floor as accurately as we do the land. We have learned a lot about it, and scientists are adding to our knowledge all the time.

It is now believed that there is almost no extensive flat area at the bottom of the ocean. There are some vast level stretches of what is called the continental shelf, which is almost an underwater extension of the land, floored with sand, rocks, and silt brought there by rivers or left by glaciers. In some of the Arctic it is 750 miles wide. Parts of the eastern United States have a shelf 150 miles wide, and in spots the shelf is only a few miles. Then the basins of the Seven Seas slope steeply down to the bottom, and at the bottom the topography is very rough indeed. The biggest flat area known so far is a plain stretching for several hundred miles on the floor of the Indian Ocean, southeast of Ceylon.

One feature of the ocean floor is that the deepest trenches are fairly close to land rather than in the middle of the ocean (see Table II). But some other odd topographical items keep cropping up. Only this year (1957), Dr. Maurice Ewing of Columbia University's Lamont Geological Observatory announced the tracing of a deep crack or trench which, starting in the north polar regions, runs down about the middle of the Atlantic, loops around south of Africa and Australia, with a branch running up through the Indian Ocean, and turns north through the Pacific, all the way to Alaska. The trench, about two miles deep and twenty wide, has a total length of about 45,000 miles.

Dr. Ewing's theory is that it is caused by the continents pulling apart as it were, creating strains which open up the crack. Earthquake zones are found all along it, indicating that the process is still going on, and on each side of the trench are high mountain ranges, up to seventy-five miles wide, with peaks rising 6,000 to 12,000 feet

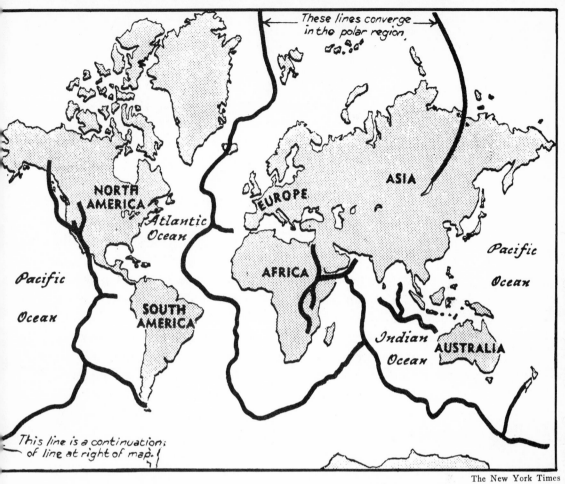

The great oceanic trench discovered only in 1957.

The New York Times

above the ocean floor but nowhere closer than 3,600 feet from the surface.

This theory squares with the existence of the most studied and longest known of the undersea mountain ranges, the Atlantic Ridge, which is part of the mountains Dr. Ewing mentions. Traces of the ridge were found by some of the early soundings a century ago, and by 1930 its main outlines had been established. It is 300 to 600 miles wide and runs some 10,000 miles along the route of the trench Dr. Ewing describes, beginning near Iceland and extending through the Atlantic until it curves around south of Africa and up toward the Indian Ocean. Most of it is 5,000 to 10,000 feet high, but in a few places it thrusts peaks up even higher, high enough to become islands—the Azores, the Rocks of St. Paul, Ascension, Tristan da Cunha, Gough and Bouvet. The tallest of all, Pico Island in the Azores, is 27,000 feet high although less than 8,000 feet show.

There are passes through these mountains, very much like those on land. The deepest is the Romanche Trench, cutting through the ridge from east to west about halfway down, near the equator. There are other features similar to topography on land—Wyville Thomson Ridge running between Iceland and Scotland which separates the Arctic from the Atlantic, Telegraph Plateau south of Iceland which made it possible to lay the Atlantic cable, the famous Challenger Ridge, and Dolphin Ridge, which some people believe is the lost island of Atlantis. All of these differ in one important point from the plateaus and ranges of the land: they suffer no erosion and so are unchanged as long as they are protected by the covering sea.

Yet the more the ocean's floor is mapped, the more it will be found to change because other forces than erosion are at work. Volcanoes and earthquakes constantly modify the shape of the basins at least as much as they alter the face of the earth.

Table II
Deepest Ocean Soundings

Ocean	Depth in Feet	Location	Date
North Atlantic	30,246	N. of Puerto Rico	1939
South Atlantic	26,575		
North Pacific	35,640	Marianas Trench	1951
South Pacific	34,884	Tonga Trench	1952
Indian	22,968		
Arctic	17,850	N. of Point Barrow	1927
Antarctic	19,266		

(Three other deep North Pacific soundings are the Mindanao Trench, 34,440; Kurile-Kamchatka Trench, 34,077; and Japan Trench, 34,038.)

3

The Magic Figure

Everybody talks about the Seven Seas, but hardly anyone can name them or tell just where one begins and the other leaves off. That is really not so surprising when you realize that the number is pretty artificial. It might as well be five, and might better be one. For in fact the whole ocean is a single expanse of water with the continents just islands in it.

"The Seven Seas" is a very old phrase and a very new one, too. In between nobody tried to count. The Ancients of the Mediterranean world knew seven large bodies of water, so they thought these were all the seas of the world. They thought, too, that the world was mostly land—six-sevenths, the men of the Bible supposed. For a long time people were content with this, but when the age of exploration began, they learned that the Ancients had made a little mistake. There was not only a lot more water than they believed, but men were going out and finding great new seas all the time, and giving them names. So the expression "Seven Seas" dropped out of use for many centuries.

It came back in 1896. That year Rudyard Kipling was looking for a title for a new volume of his poems. He selected *The Seven Seas*, and because he was a great man, and a popular man, the world had to make his words good. So the geographers figured out a way to divide the ocean into seven parts. It isn't a very good way, but we get along with it even if few of us can remember what the seven are. The whole thing is a triumph of poetry over reality.

On the map the world is full of seas. A chart of the Mediterranean, which altogether is not big enough to be one of the modern Seven,

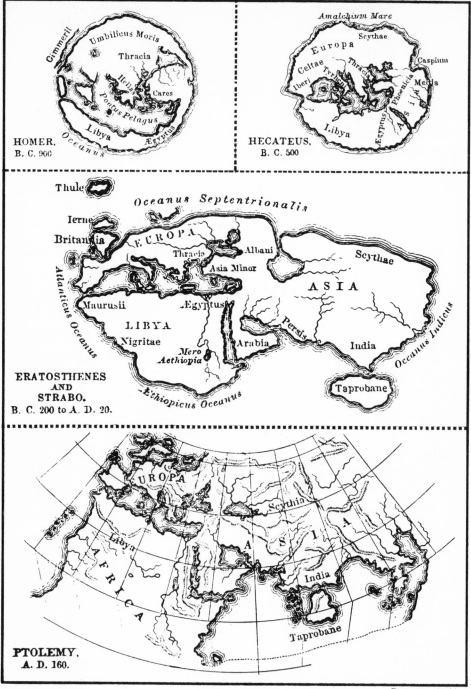

Maps show the state of man's knowledge about the Seven Seas. In Homer's time, the great river Oceanus was believed to encircle a round, flat earth. Hecateus still thought that, too, but the Mediterranean world at least was more accurately charted. By the time of Strabo, the Atlantic, Indian and Northern Oceans were recognized, with Europe, Asia and Africa in proper perspective. When Ptolemy expounded his theory of the universe, he knew the world was round, as the meridian lines in his map show. No one improved on Ptolemy for another dozen centuries or so.

shows five other seas within it. The even smaller Black Sea contains the still smaller Sea of Azov. So no geographer applies the word "sea" to his big Seven now; they are oceans. This is the way they compare with those of the Ancients:

The Seven Seas

In Antiquity	Today
Mediterranean	Arctic
Red	Antarctic
China	North Atlantic
West African	South Atlantic
East African	North Pacific
Indian Ocean	South Pacific
Persian Gulf	Indian

Up until the time of Kipling's poem, many people were quite happy with just one Pacific and one Atlantic. But in fact it is not as foolish as it seems to divide them in half. Nature already has done it, separating the two parts of each by the doldrums—a wide and rather shifting belt of calm air near the equator, between the prevailing wind and current systems of the Northern and Southern Hemispheres. North of the doldrums the movement generally is to the right or clockwise. South of the dividing line the movement is to the left, or counterclockwise. So, even before Kipling, people had spoken of the South Pacific or North Atlantic without suggesting that they were separate oceans.

In a way, each of the Seven Seas has its own individuality, and not just differences in size and shape. The North Atlantic, for example is the saltiest, on the average with 37.9 parts in 1,000 (although the saltiest separate bits of ocean anywhere are the Red Sea and the Persian Gulf—40 parts in 1,000—because it is so hot and dry there that evaporation is very fast). The Atlantic is what you might call the wettest ocean, too. That is, it gets, North and South together, about half of all the rain that falls in the world, not so much directly as by run-off from the rivers because most of the big ones drain into it. The Pacific, in proportion to its size, gets the least rain. The

ARCTIC
Greenland
Ellesmere Island
Amundsen G.
Devon I.
Melville I.
Banks I.
Victoria I.
Baffin Island
Bering Strait
ALASKA
North America
LABRADOR-C.
NEW FOUNDLAND
LABRADOR
KUROSHIO CURRENT
ALEUTIAN ISL.
SAN FRANCISCO
NORTH PACIFIC OCEAN
Hawaiian isl.
NEW YORK
GULF STREAM
Leif Ericssons Route
Strait of Denmark
ICELAND
AZORES
1492
Columbus's Route
SARGASSO SEA
ATLANTIC OCEAN
GULF OF MEXICO
ANTILLES
CUBA
NORTH EQUATORIAL
Cape Verde Islands
Doldrums
Doldrums
PANAMA CANAL
GALAPAGOS ISL.
Kon-Tiki Exp.
HUMBOLDT CURRENT
South America
BUENOS AIRES
SAMOA ISL.
Fiji isl.
SOUTH EQUATORIAL C.
Cook isl.
Tahiti
SOUTH PACIFIC OCEAN
Easter isl.
Fernandez isl.
SOUTH EQUATORIAL C.
1519 – 1522
Magellan's Route
Tristan da Cunha isl.
Cape Horn
Falkland isl.
ANTARCTIC

Peter Freuchen's Map of the Seven Seas

DENMARK

Europe

Asia

North

OYASHIO CURRENT

Mediterranean Sea

BATTLE OF SALAMIS (480 B.C.)

Africa

PERSIAN GULF

RED SEA

LEYTE (1944)

CEYLON

DRIFT

MONSOON

PHILIPPINES

SPICE ISLANDS

PACIFIC

Doldrums

INDONESIA

NEW GUINEA

BATAVIA

Timor

Torres Strait

COCOS Isl.

EQUATORIAL CURRENT

INDIAN OCEAN

Madagascar

Australia

Capt. Cook

Cape of Good Hope

CAPETOWN

SOUTH

PACIFIC OCEAN

OCEAN

route 1595

Arctic and Antarctic are the least salty oceans because they are always being diluted with melting ice and have no rivers to bring them salts from the land.

Even the Arctic and Antarctic, although both are cold and filled with ice in winter, have little in common. A lot of their differences are due to the fact that the Arctic is a great body of water almost completely surrounded by land, while the Antarctic is a great body of water surrounding a mass of land. Because of that, the Arctic was a place where people lived for centuries with no communications from outside, while no one but explorers and whalers ever has been in the Antarctic.

In the Arctic Ocean, great ice floes, usually from seven to thirteen feet thick, cover enormous areas in winter. The ice has no ground to fasten to, so the floes drift with the prevailing winds and currents in general from the northern coast of Siberia to the northeastern corner of Greenland, right across the North Pole. Nothing like it is ever seen elsewhere. Then the Arctic is the most isolated of the oceans. It has only one really wide connection with any other, the big space between Iceland and Europe where it joins the North Atlantic. Denmark Strait between Iceland and Greenland and Davis Strait between Greenland and North America are comparatively narrow, and Bering Strait between Alaska and Siberia, the Arctic's only link to the Pacific, is very narrow indeed, only thirty-six miles across. No other ocean is so nearly landlocked as this.

The Antarctic Ocean has no land barriers at all between itself and its neighbors, the South Atlantic, South Pacific and Indian. Over the South Pole and the land surrounding it, ice accumulates to a great thickness and much more uniformly than in the Arctic. When the icebergs detach themselves into the sea they often are of enormous size, 150 to 200 feet above the water, 1,200 to 1,500 feet below, and perhaps thirty miles long. The Antarctic Ocean is in the shape of a great ring or band of water around the polar continent. Only when the wind blows off the land, from the south, is there clear weather. The rest of the time great clouds of fog pile up. Since the prevailing winds are from the west, blowing in a great circle around the world at this point, this means mostly bad weather. Also, since there are no islands here to break the force of the wind, the sailors encounter the roughest—although not the highest—seas and the fiercest prevailing winds to be found in any ocean. Because there is little exchange of air and water with the other seas, despite their wide open borders, ice and snow are much more evenly distributed in the Antarctic than in the Arctic.

The Atlantic, named for the legendary lost island of Atlantis, has made up for its romantic origin by becoming through the last 400 years the most important commercial highway in the world. But people go on getting the romance and the business mixed up.

There never were any more businesslike fellows than the Spanish adventurers who first went to America seeking gold and silver. But very often their ships were becalmed, and as they exchanged notes they found that usually it happened when they were on the edge of the steady trade winds at about 30 degrees north or south latitude instead of in the path of the breeze. Now, calms are a blessing to passengers on steamships, but they were a deadly peril to men on sailing ships—worse than storms and shoals because these only killed you while in a calm you might literally rot slowly and agonizingly.

The sailing ships could carry only so much drinking water and as they lay becalmed under a hot sun for days, yes, even sometimes for weeks, the tortures of thirst were maddening. The first victims were the horses. When they died, or even beforehand if they were crazed with thirst, they had to be thrown overboard. Spanish caballeros thought very highly of their horses, even to the point of crediting them with souls. When they had to fling the poor beasts into the sea, they suffered much remorse, so much that they believed the ghosts of the proud war horses were haunting the scene. In their dreams, the Spaniards saw the restless spirits, and when they told of these dreams to the sailors, it was very real. Whenever they passed that way again, mariners would see in spray or mist or cloud the images of wild sea horses bearing down upon them. The badly frightened seamen called these broad belts of calm "the horse latitudes," and that is how they are known today.

For all its well-earned reputation for storms and violence, the North Atlantic has acquired more than its share of the legends of too much tranquillity. One reason is that the vast Sargasso Sea, a region unlike anything in any other ocean, is in the North Atlantic. Roughly a thousand miles broad and twice as long, its western edge stretches from a little north of Bermuda to near the Virgin Islands and eastward into mid-ocean.

Columbus was the first man to see the Sargasso Sea, and he noted that the water was covered with great patches of seaweed. In fact, the region takes its name from the weed, sargassum. The weed accumulates there because the Sargasso Sea is a calm pool in the great, complex streams of the North Atlantic winds and currents. On a gigantic scale it is like the placid water you may see between two swift currents of a river; the stream flows by on either side, but imparts to the pool only a lazy circular eddy in which a bit of twig or leaf may float round and round for days.

Winds avoid the Sargasso Sea. There is little rain, not many clouds. The sun beats down, warming the sluggish water, and the weed hardly seems to move. A lot of it grows there, and each year new patches are added, too. Sargassum, ripped from the rocks and reefs of Florida and the West Indies by hurricanes, gets afloat in the Gulf Stream. Carried north and then east, some of it drifts off from the edge of the Gulf Stream as it heads for Europe, and that weed comes to rest in the Sargasso Sea.

Fearsome are the stories sailors bring back from this quiet region, which they say is the graveyard of wrecked ships, brought there by the gods or devils of the sea for burial no matter where they died. More terrifying are the stories of ships caught in the weeds and doomed to sail slowly forever in wide circles, manned by the ghosts of their dead crews. No one can deny that every now and then seamen have come across ships floating derelict with the entire crew killed by an epidemic or by thirst or starvation. The tales grew in

Exploring the Sargasso Sea.

the telling, so for hundreds of years we heard in most horrifying detail of these spectral vessels trapped in the Sargasso Sea, sailing interminably to nowhere. Even steamships, their propellors enmeshed in weed, were said to have been caught. Actually there is not enough sargassum to entangle the smallest ship.

The Sargasso Sea is without land boundaries, but the North Atlantic has more almost landlocked seas than any other ocean—Mediterranean, Caribbean, Black, Baltic and so on—and islands in great profusion. The South Atlantic, on the other hand, has almost no islands, just a few lonely rocks, or any seas. Its wide base on the Antarctic, a front of 3,965 miles, makes it far rawer and colder than the North Atlantic.

The Indian Ocean has its own reputation for tranquillity, but a tranquillity of less terror. It is famous for its regular monsoons, blowing in the winter from the East Indies toward Africa and in summer in the opposite direction. Especially in its northern section, the Indian Ocean provides its share of adventure for men by working up into fierce hurricanes when the monsoons change.

That great navigator, Magellan, first European to sail upon the Pacific, gave it its name. After the storms of his passage out of the South Atlantic through the straits at the tip of South America, the calm, sunlit waters of the biggest of oceans seemed very mild and peaceful to him. He never found out how much bad weather could be worked up there. Even today, so great is the power of a name, the South Pacific especially is known for its beauty, for long and pleasant voyages and island paradises, rather than for its terrible storms.

The North Pacific has less glamour in legend, and for some people, in reality. It is the scene of the most earthquakes; the center of what is known as the earthquake zone is near the Bay of Tokyo, and here the average number of shocks is said to be four a day. Really serious ones happen only every six or seven years though.

Besides the damage on shore, big quakes make changes in the ocean, too. The one that caused the biggest loss of life was the one which destroyed most of Tokyo in 1923 and killed nearly 150,000 people. It also destroyed the fishing off the coast. The fish which used to go there moved their quarters more than a thousand miles to the north and went up to Korff Bay off Kamchatka. In 1938, the Russians had established eleven fishing bases in a bay which had none before the quake, and incidentally used the longest nets I ever saw. They rented three of the bases to the Japanese.

The South Pacific has the next biggest earthquake center, located in the deep ocean trench off Chile and Peru. Also it is known for the greatest deeps—the deepest off the Marianas is 35,640 feet or about a mile deeper than Mount Everest is high.

These are only the highlights of the qualities which give each of the Seven Seas its own character. But all of them are changing, and perhaps their characters will change, too.

Table III
Seven Seas Statistics

	Area (sq. miles)	Average Depth (feet)	Largest Island (area in sq. miles)
N. Atlantic ⎱ S. Atlantic ⎰	41,105,436	12,880	Great Britain—84,186 Tierra del Fuego—18,800
N. Pacific ⎱ S. Pacific ⎰	69,374,182	14,048	Honshu—89,009** New Guinea—316,861
Indian	28,925,504	13,002	Madagascar—228,642
Arctic	5,440,197	3,953	Greenland—840,000
Antarctic	—*	—*	Antarctica—unknown

*Included in Atlantic, Pacific and Indian as no fixed boundaries exist.
**Borneo, 290,012, and Sumatra, 167,620, are larger but lie in both North and South Pacific as the equator bisects them.

4

A Glimpse of the Future

Every once in a while one sees in the newspapers that some part of the coast is sinking into the sea or rising out of it. But it always is very little, and so hard to measure that we pay no special attention. We are right not to be alarmed, because these gradual changes are so slow that we have no trouble getting used to them. But the sea has other possibilities of change, and while we do not need to expect them to happen tomorrow, they are perhaps a bit more real than dreams.

Any great upheaval such as those that made the mountains is not very likely for another good many million years. The last one was just the other day, as geological time goes. The old earth seems to have to rest for thousands of centuries between its major reconstruction jobs, so there probably will not be another one in this geological age. But there are some interesting speculations involving other sorts of changes in the shape of the ocean which would affect human beings almost as much.

One, which many scientists think is going on now and could accelerate in the not too distant future, is the almost complete liquidation of the last ice age. A lot of the earth's water is tied up in glaciers, enough that even the melting of a substantial part would cause the ocean to rise about 100 feet. If it all turned to water—a very remote possibility—it has been estimated that the sea level might rise as much as 500 or 600 feet.

In the first case, most of the Atlantic seaboard of the United States, including all the big cities, would disappear; the shore line would move to the base of the Appalachian Mountains, with a few islands to indicate where several states used to be. The Gulf of Mexico would move halfway up the Mississippi, and on the Pacific the water would cover everything up to the beginning of the coastal ranges. Equal floods would wipe out great populous centers of western Europe, Asia, Africa, and South America. Thousands of islands would vanish and thousands more would shrink.

A rise of 600 feet would put the seas back to nearly the maximum boundaries they ever have achieved. Instead of 71 per cent, they would cover 85 or 90 per cent of the earth's surface. Then there would be almost nothing left of the eastern United States at all except for a chain of islands where the Appalachians now stand. The Great Lakes and the Gulf of Mexico would meet in the Mississippi Valley, and to the west only the high plateaus and the mountains would remain. Hudson Bay would become a sea covering most of northern Canada. There would be little left of European civilization as we know it. A few rocky islets would mark the sites of the British Isles, western France, Belgium, Holland, and the Scandinavian countries. The highlands of the Spanish and Italian peninsulas would be isolated in a sea which would extend down into Africa beyond the Sahara Desert. From the north the seas would roll over a considerable part of Russia. Similar changes would take place in the shape of the other continents and islands.

There is one big "if" to all this which makes the prospect less alarming. The melting would take thousands of years, and two factors would interfere to make the flooding less extensive than one might suppose. The land, relieved of the weight of the ice, would tend to rise just as a ship unloaded of its cargo floats higher in the water. The floor of the sea, unable to support the weight of the extra water, would tend to sink under the load.

If the glaciers were to reverse their present trend, and advance in a new ice age anything like some the world has known, they would drain so much water from the sea that all the great ports would become inland cities 100 miles or more from salt water. The great continental shelf, with its sands and rocks, humps and hollows, canyons and reefs, would emerge to view. Rivers would begin to cut new channels to the sea. England would become a part of Europe. Siberia and Alaska would join, and some island chains would become considerable masses of land.

To mankind the resulting changes in climate would be more important than the shrinking or expanding area of the land. With the great ocean extending its warm waters nearer to the poles and the refrigerating effects of huge ice masses gone, almost all the world would have the equable climate we associate now with the tropics. Fruits and vegetables would grow in soil which now has only tundra. It takes a large land mass to create the extreme changes of temperature we know in the temperate zone, and there would be no more land masses big enough to maintain the sort of weather we now have.

On the other hand, a new ice age would cover with glaciers much of the territory on which people live, and the rest would have to take lessons from the Eskimos on getting along with cold. Caribou would return to the shores of the Mediterranean, where relics of primitive man show that these animals once thrived in an earlier ice age.

Neither of these glacial extremes is altogether fanciful. In fact, both have happened four times in the last million years or so, in the Pleistocene age. While most scientists believe that the earth is in a period of melting glaciers, and that this must go much further before another ice age descends, there is no certainty. What does seem certain is that thousands of years must pass before major changes occur.

Another great sea change which could force man to remodel his way of life over vast areas would be a sudden alteration in one of the major ocean currents, or its destruction by an undersea earthquake. The current which affects Europe and the United States most is the Gulf Stream. It helps give both their special climates and rainfall. If it stopped its flow for any reason, hundreds of millions of people would have to get used to an entirely new environment. Similarly, the destruction of any other major current would convert fertile lands into deserts and deserts into gardens, lengthen or shorten winters, increase or diminish the rains.

A Glimpse of the Future

We know some of these effects because twice in recorded history the Humboldt Current, a broad stream of cold water running from the Antarctic up the west coast of South America, has been interrupted. Normally, when winds do blow inland toward the Andes— and the prevailing breezes are the other way—they are drawn upward and cooled by the altitude faster than they are warmed by the land, and the moisture in them becomes tangible only as fog. So, between the mountains and the Pacific Ocean, rain is almost as rare as snow in Florida. But once when the Humboldt Current failed, a warm current from the north, El Niño, pushed down along the coast and the winds were typical of the tropics, warm and heavy with moisture. They drenched the land with torrential rains, turning dust to mud, washing away clay houses which were never built to resist even a mild shower, and causing disastrous floods. The loss was equally bad at sea. The squid and crustacea which relied upon the cold waters of the current and the fish which feed on them died with the rising temperature. The seals and whales and great flocks of birds which created the famous guano islands starved or migrated. Things got back to normal when the Humboldt flowed again, but the revolution in conditions of life—the same thing happened in Africa when the Benguela failed, geologists say—gives us a taste of what might happen anywhere if an ocean current is destroyed, for every continental shore is affected by them.

Perhaps the next great sea change will not be the work of nature but of man. Russians have been discussing half seriously for some years a project which would make the northern wastes of their vast country a temperate and indescribably rich land. All they need is the machinery to warm the waters of the Arctic around the northern shores of Siberia.

Atomic energy offers the possibility of creating that machinery. The Russian theory, as I heard it when I was there years ago, is that if Bering Strait were dammed—no specially formidable undertaking for modern engineers—atomic pumps could draw the warm waters of the Pacific over the dam in a flow big enough to raise the temperature of that whole section of the Arctic. This would do for

Siberia what the Gulf Stream does for New Jersey. The great wastes, largely covered with ice and snow, would be converted into a lush and fertile land capable of supporting a large population. This probably would happen, too, to Alaska and northern Canada.

So far it sounds wonderful. But the effects would not be confined to Canada and Russia. The cold Arctic water, swelled by the ice and snow melted by the new warm stream coming over the Bering Strait dam, would have to go somewhere. The only place for it to go, with the Pacific exit of the Arctic blocked, would be the Atlantic. Most of it would come through the Barents Sea, past the coast of Norway. The flow would probably push the Gulf Stream out of its course, if not destroy it along European shores, and all the way from Scandinavia to Spain the land would be little better than a desert. The chill waters would dry the air so that fog would be unknown in London and rain a rarity. That hardly would make up for the destruction of European agriculture. Denmark could expect a climate like that of the northernmost tip of Labrador.

Of course, this may come to no more than a scheme worked out fifty or sixty years ago to dig a canal from the sea into the lowlands of the Sahara Desert and create a big inland body of water. The idea was to make a way to reach the riches of the interior of Africa which was then inaccessible for commercial purposes. At the time, the greatest opposition came from scientists who feared that the pressure of the weight of the new sea might cause volcanic eruptions elsewhere.

While the principal changes of the future are those in which the sea seems to operate on the land, there is one by which the land alters the shape of the sea. As rivers bring down silt and sand and rock from the mountains, the stuff is piled up in the shallow waters of the continental shelf. Eventually it gets so heavy that the ocean's floor may sag, resulting in deeper, rather than shallower, water. Sometimes, it is suggested, the load is so big that the earth's crust at this point collapses altogether, causing a tremendous but relatively local upheaval.

Such things are compensated for by the rising of the land. According to the Wegener theory, all the continents are moving almost imperceptibly to the west, which may account for the fact that the Andes mountains are growing, in certain places as much as thirty feet a year or more, in the same way that dirt mounts in front of a bulldozer. And in a place in Greenland where the Eskimos put up stone scaffolds to keep their kayaks away from the dogs, they have twice within my lifetime had to build new ones nearer to the sea because the land has risen. Maybe this is due to the land shifting its balance or maybe to the weight of the ice. Other places in Greenland submerged in the sea had in former times been above the water.

In all these changes, as in all the past since the earth was formed, the main basins of the ocean will remain as they are. They are immune to the influences of glaciers and currents. These basins have their own earthquakes and volcanoes, which seemingly open up big cracks or pile up huge mounds, but these events have only incidental effect upon the surface and can happen without man being aware of it in the least unless he has some very delicate and sensitive instruments. These basins are the most immutable physical features of the world and will be changed basically only in one of the great and very rare cataclysmic upheavals which would revise the shape of the whole earth's crust.

Courtesy of the American Museum of Natural History

Receding glaciers.

Tropical fish

Part II

Life in The Seven Seas

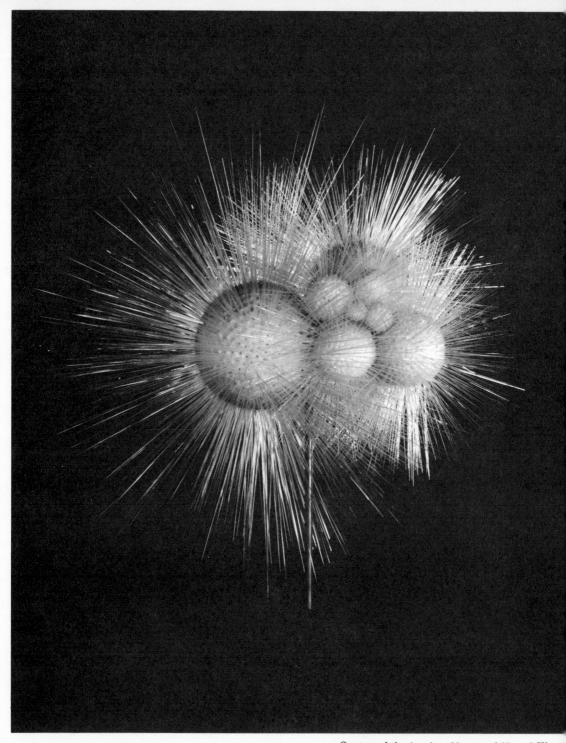

Life began in the sea with microscopic forms probably not much different from
this vastly enlarged model of a protozoan.

5

Genesis

Man is a conceited animal, and because he knew a little about the land long before he had much more than a few fearful superstitions about the sea, he likes to suppose that most of the life of this world is on terra firma. Yet any way one looks at it, there is more in the sea.

Of all classes of animal life, 94 per cent can be found in the sea and 44 per cent only on the land; and the biggest animals and the longest-lived animals belong to the sea. Finally, life itself began in the sea, and had developed to a fairly high order before a single living thing, animal or vegetable, appeared on the bare rocks of the land.

The basic mystery, of course, is how life started. All we really know is that it happened in the sea. Somewhere, somehow, in the friendly shelter of salt water, an organism, probably microscopic in size and composed of a single cell, appeared with the ability to reproduce. It has been growing and changing ever since.

Scientists infer from their fossils and other data that life appeared about two billion years ago. They know that half a billion years ago there was a rich sea life, for fossils of all the principal groups of invertebrate animals have been found dating that far back. Still there was no trace of life on land.

The scientists usually speak of the miracle of a one-celled living thing as taking place originally in a shallow sunlit pool. Their main reason for placing it there is that such a pool nowadays is more hospitable to these simple forms of life than cold, sunless water, and plants on which animal life depends need sunlight. But nowhere is the sea so cold or so dark that it cannot find a tenant. In fact, by the time of which we have any exact knowledge through actual remains, there was a wide variety of plants, of animals which grew shells, of worms and jellyfish and sponges and those sea anemones which, living in great colonies, become coral. A little later, and still before the land had life, animals with backbones appeared in the sea. Only about three or four hundred million years ago, in about the middle of the Paleozoic era, did some of these plants and animals first discover how they could keep alive on shore.

The main divisions of life, then, were established in salt water. Some of the earliest microscopic organisms managed to use sunlight to turn water and chemicals into food for themselves. They became plants. Others discovered the device of taking into themselves the first type of organism. They became animals. Later on the animals learned how to eat each other instead of just plants—and some of the plants began to feed on animals. That is when life began to be confusing.

It grew more confusing, at least to simple land creatures like man, because in the sea life goes on in three dimensions, while we generally know about only two. Land life is limited to going to and fro, except for the birds and they do not go very high, but all sea life experiences the problems of up and down as well. This perhaps is why there is so much more variety. But of course there is much more room, too, and more varied environments, part of it stemming from the third dimension. The varieties of pressure are much greater, for example. Any land animal with lungs and warm blood would burst under pressures which a whale or a seal, using the same general mechanism, finds quite harmless. There is, of course, plenty of sea life which cannot stand a transfer from one pressure to another. There is, therefore, the life of the surface, which is what most people know. Then there is a less crowded life at intermediate levels; and finally the rather sparsely populated deeps.

It used to be believed that nothing could live more than a few hundred feet down. But a century ago men found living creatures on mud brought up from as much as a mile deep. Since then it has

Courtesy of Buffalo Museum of Science

Life in the sea half a billion years ago.

been established that some sort of life not only exists almost all over the ocean's floor, but that there are species which live and even thrive mightily in the middle layers of the sea, swimming or drifting at a depth too great for light to penetrate, and yet well above the bottom.

On the other hand, there are animals other than seals and whales which can shift from one to another level with an ease which is hard to understand. There are some small shrimps, for example, which go down below the level of light by day, apparently to escape being eaten, and return to near the surface at night. In the journey they experience a difference in pressure of about 500 pounds to the

55

square inch. No land animal can come close to this, because on land there are no such pressure differences.

Scientists suppose that life emerged from the sea as the result of an accident—stranded by some sudden drop in the ocean's level or by a sudden rising of a stretch of land. They assume that the first successful switch from sea to land was made by plants, some species of seaweed which already had developed roots in order to cling to rocks, or some algaelike specimen which could get along in fresh water. It is argued that stranded animals with no plants to eat would have died unless they could reach the sea for food, and if they could have gotten back to the sea, they would have stayed there. Once plants had been acclimatized, stranded animals might be able to adapt themselves to the land, too.

Development of life in the sea did not stop with the departure of these emigrants, and in time the ocean even acquired some interesting repatriates from the land. Whales, for example, or their pioneer ancestors, originated on land. They roamed the earth not more than 150,000,000 years ago and probably less. They had legs, and the jaws and teeth of killers. It is presumed that their favorite hunting grounds eventually became the shallow waters at the mouths of rivers or off a level stretch of coast. Fish, both finny and shell, probably were more plentiful and easier to catch than meat, so these mammals spent more and more time in the water. Eventually they swam more easily than they walked. Millennia later they could do without legs altogether, and that was when they turned into whales. The forelegs became flippers used for steering. The hind legs shrank to mere traces, useless but still found in rudimentary form under the skin when a whale is cut up. In modern times, this has become not only the largest animal in the world but the almost undisputed king of the sea. Seals, porpoises and dolphins belong to the same family.

The strange, unpredictable forms which life took in the sea ran to fish with real legs, not just the remnants such as whales have. One of the oddest was a bluefish with four legs, known scientifically as coelacanth. Fossil remains show that they must have been extremely plentiful sixty million years ago, but then they began to slip in the race for survival. The last petrified specimen ever found had died an estimated eighteen million years ago.

Then, all of a sudden, in December, 1938, a fisherman netted one, alive and full grown, off Capetown, South Africa, in forty-five fathoms of water. That fish caused a sensation. It was five feet long, bright blue in color, and had a big head. The fisherman had never seen anything like it, which was not surprising because the species was supposed to have been extinct millions of years before human beings appeared in the world. Scientists gave it the name "Latimeria." They doubted that it could be the only one of its kind in existence, and a South African professor spent the next fourteen years trying to find another. He finally succeeded in 1952, near a little island northwest of Madagascar. Since then about twenty of these bluefish have been caught, and one was fed and kept alive in a tank for more than three months. Where had they been for nearly twenty million years? That is just one of the sea's unanswered riddles.

From the standpoint of elapsed time, it was not so mysterious a riddle as that of a mollusk which the *Galatea* expedition brought up from the deep Marianas Trench in 1956. The last previous specimen of this primitive mollusk was estimated to have been petrified four hundred million years ago.

While the oddities and realities of life down where life begins to fail have been studied only quite recently, the latest discoveries, including those of the strange bluefish and the mollusk, have led to a theory that in these regions we may find some new solutions to the riddles of evolution. One reasonable explanation I have heard, of why the bluefish never was seen in all these years, is that it had become a deep-sea dweller, living out of reach and out of sight of men. This, of course, does not tell us how the examples so recently found happened to stray up within our ken. But perhaps they were developing toward a form which would enable them to move into the realms of greater food supply nearer the surface.

At any rate, there is a theory now that studies of life at sea depths below those we have ever been able to reach before will turn up more animals known up to the present only by their fossils. It is true that most of the fish brought up from the deeps so far have not given much support to this theory. For the most part they resemble the species to be found at the surface, modified, of course, for life under great pressure and in total darkness or at best in deep gloom. It also is true that the greatest variety of forms has been found in the waters nearer the surface where basic plant foods grow.

Yet the exploration of deep water can hardly be said to have started—and the areas to be covered are enormous. Not only do they extend over most of the world horizontally, but they must be explored vertically as well, for distances down to five or six miles. And each level may present an environment quite different from the others.

Only in the last few years have we had the equipment for taking "cores" or samples from the deepest trenches, or cameras which can be used to photograph life under thousands of feet of water, or such devices as the bathysphere in which men have gone down a mile or more. So we are just at the beginning of the firsthand studies of deep-sea life.

Courtesy of the American Museum of Natural History

The "living fossil." This is a cast made for the American Museum of Natural History from one of the coelacanth "Latimeria" caught off Madagascar.

6

Population Problem

People who think India or China or a New York subway in the rush hour are crowded might be surprised by the amount of life to be found in what at first glance seems a placid, empty stretch of sea. Of course, there is no census available, but the inhabitants of the ocean are a great deal more numerous than the sands of the sea, an expression which used to be used to indicate an infinite quantity.

Like the land, however, the ocean has certain inhospitable spots that can scarcely support any life whatever. But where conditions are favorable, which is the case over areas much greater than is the case on land, the population pressures are tremendous. Here nature seems to have provided a complex sort of cafeteria where one species devours another in great quantity, apparently for no other purpose than to feed still another which in turn is the exclusive diet of a fourth—and so *ad infinitum*.

It is possible to trace the whole slow development of life through the various stages of this gastronomic cycle. At the base of the whole population, as they were the first, are microscopic one-celled forms which are called diatoms. They perform the function of translating water and minerals into food with the aid of the sun, and they wear a very thin and delicate but hard coat of mineral substance. In large areas of the ocean diatoms are so thick that a drop of water greatly magnified would look like a shaft of sunlight in a dusty room, full of tiny particles dancing and jostling each other in a cloud.

Diatoms are the attraction that draws the not much larger animals to those parts of the sea where the basic food is found, and oddly enough this is in cold and not warm water. Here a large population of little creatures, which look like worms or bits of jelly or flecks of fluff or undersized shrimps, collects to feast upon the algae and the tinier animals fattened by diatoms. All of them become so intermingled that I have seen them as a tangible, visible layer spreading over acres or even miles of water. The mass goes by the name of plankton, from the Greek word for wanderer, because none of the pieces which compose it have any independent motion of their own; the whole thing simply drifts with the winds and waves and tides.

Plankton seems to be the reason that the relatively shallow waters maintain the largest populations. On land the warm moist areas of the tropics have the lushest development of life, but at sea, with only a few exceptions, this is reserved for the cooler waters of more temperate regions. The tropical seas, of course, are well stocked but on the average they are not nearly so crowded. Life reproduces itself more rapidly in warm water and in great variety, but not so massively. The difference seems to be due to plankton, which is the food for everything that moves in the water, directly or indirectly, and in the tropics it does not grow in such large quantities.

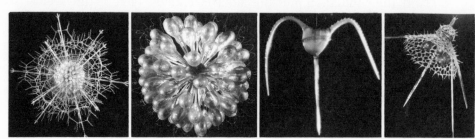

Courtesy of the American Museum of Natural History
Greatly enlarged models of protozoans and other components of plankton.

People, too, can get a nourishing meal from plankton. It has been tried in the high Arctic. I have seen it boiled; it turns red like a lobster and forms a sort of porridge which can be eaten with a spoon.

The growth of plankton in cool to cold water is based less on a liking for low temperatures than on the fact that the mineral content is higher in cold water, especially the nitrogen and phosphorus of which plants need so much. This makes it easier for diatoms to thrive.

Because plankton is so plentiful, the great schools of fish are found in temperate or even colder climates. Cod and herring, for example, are chiefly denizens of the North Atlantic and the Arctic, salmon of the North Pacific and Atlantic. When Charles Darwin was on his famous voyage aboard the *Beagle,* one of the strongest impressions he received was the sudden evidence of an enormous marine population the moment the ship passed from warm to cold water off South America. When tropic waters do teem with life, it is because of a cold current, as in the Humboldt off the west coast of South America, or the Benguela off the west coast of Africa.

The population of the sea maintains itself in a balance which man has not been able to disturb to the degree he has altered conditions on land. Although millions of tons of fish are taken every year for human food alone, fishermen have not succeeded in exterminating once plentiful species, as hunters have eliminated many animals and birds from the land. Regulations to protect spawning and breeding grounds—as of salmon and seals—have prevented this in some cases, but in others the sheer numbers of the fish have been their salvation.

An idea of the varied population of the ocean may be gained from the number of different kinds of some fish. There are more than one hundred different species of the herring family, for example.

The really dense animal populations of the sea are found in the top layer where the plants live. Since all plants need some sunlight in order to perform their miracle of transforming minerals into food, they can grow only in the upper few hundred feet of the ocean. Most of them are within 200 feet; and below 100 fathoms, even in the clearest water, the light becomes too dim for any plant to survive.

There are fish, however, which live out all their lives below this level. There are others which spend most of their time there, rising higher only to feed. The famous balance is maintained by other species, such as seals and whales, which come down into these plantless waters to eat shrimps or fish which have retreated there after getting their own nourishment higher up.

What with regular visits to upper levels and a certain amount of food which sinks as surface plants and animals die, the layer of ocean between the last of the plants and the last dim light of the sun maintains a great deal of life. Then, as one goes deeper, the density of the population declines abruptly. In the real deeps there are no forms which can move up to a higher layer and get back again. The basis of their food supply, much as they prey on each other, is the remains of dead plants and animals sifting down to them from above. They can get only what escapes the hungry hunters of the shallow and intermediate waters. That this is enough to keep anything alive is wonderful. Yet hundreds of species do it in numbers at which we can only guess, and even they leave enough for the little worms which live in the mud or ooze of the ocean floor, the animals literally at the very bottom of the heap.

Some extremely ingenious devices have been worked out in the evolution of these tenants of deep water. Where the light is very dim, some of them have developed enormous eyes with virtually telescopic lenses, very much like owls. Others, especially the fish who survive where there is no light at all, are quite blind but have developed long feelers which enable them to identify and collect any stray bit of food that may come within a considerable radius.

Others of the deep supply their own light. They have built-in torches which they can switch on and off depending upon whether they are pursuing or pursued. Or they have regular lamps, spots of steady light, which give a faint glow through the water around them. One deep water squid can squirt a luminous fluid which lights up the immediate vicinity, a neat variation on the "ink" ejected by his cousins nearer the surface to becloud and darken the water. It is supposed that about half of all the varieties of fish living in the dark depths have some power of illumination.

That there is plenty of room for expansion of the sea's already large population is obvious. As the mineral content of the sea rises, which it has been doing gradually all through the world's history, there can be more nourishment for plants and therefore for animals. As for actual living space, the ocean has about 300 times as much of that as the land.

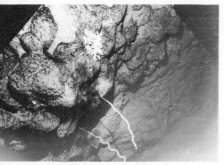

The white rope-like streamers are sea fans of the gorgonidae coral family, photographed 6600 feet below the surface of the Atlantic.

Life more than a mile down in the North Atlantic. The tracks in the mud are made by worms. Two "sea pens" are standing up below the most pronounced worm track at the right.

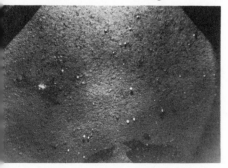

Sea-squirts, photographed 2100 feet down.

Courtesy of the American Museum of Natural History

Dwellers in the abyss.

The new techniques of deep-sea photography have made possible the detailed visual study of oceanic deeps. The pictures taken from the Lamont oceanographic schooner *Vema* are typical.

7

Feast and Famine

On land, man is in a class by himself when it comes to destroying other forms of life, but in the sea he has his superiors. The struggle for existence has been going on four or five times as long in the ocean, and more ingenuity has been developed. Beneath many a seemingly placid surface, there is a fierce and unending warfare.

The size of a fish doesn't seem to have much to do with the size of its favorite food. The biggest animal in the world, the blue whale, feeds on little shrimps that are only two inches long at maturity. Since a blue whale may weigh 100 tons or more, he consumes an incredible amount of shrimp. But the somewhat smaller sperm whales—they run to seventy feet long—go after larger game, especially the giant squid, which may be almost as big, up to fifty feet, measuring both body and tentacles. The sperm whale is a deep-sea fisherman, too, because he has to go 1,500 feet or so below the surface to find his prey.

On and near the surface, in the great plankton-producing areas of the sea, meals are quite regular for all life. Schools of fish browse on the plankton or other plankton-consuming animals like herds of cattle in a field. The ones that eat plankton have a filter mechanism which strains the food out of the water, and they can get their fill simply by swimming or drifting or creeping along with their mouths open. In these waters are the big commercial fisheries—man coming along to reap the final harvest. In waters too deep for plant life, food is more precarious, and here an alternating feast and famine is more common.

The sea has its deserts where scarcely any life can survive. These are as likely to be in warm as in cold water, the basic question being whether conditions are right for plant life. In mid-ocean, except where the currents flow, these conditions do not prevail.

One exception is the Sargasso Sea with its calm, warm, sunny waters filled with the sargassum weed, which is mostly a species of algae which goes on reproducing itself endlessly while being reinforced with an annual tribute of new weed brought by the Gulf Stream from the coasts of the New World. With this weed come some small animals to join the Sargasso colony. Some are the larvae of fish which hatch out in mid-ocean and have to adapt themselves to an environment far from the sandy or rocky bottoms to which their ancestors were accustomed. Others are little animals which normally cling to rocks or weeds or live on the bottom—shrimps and worms and spiderlike creatures. Over the centuries some of them have changed their appearance to make it easier to get food. There is a Sargasso sea slug whose progenitors crept along the bottom in search of food. The Sargasso variation has learned to make its way over patches of weed—it is helpless and will sink to the bottom if it falls off—and has changed color so that it blends with the weed. One of the most voracious of fish, known to science as Pterophryne, has developed a camouflage which makes its body indistinguishable from a bit of sargassum weed.

Even animals which have no digestive system manage to compete for the nourishment of the sea. On some European beaches a little flat green worm lives quite happily by giving algae a home in his body. Surviving on food which the guest manufactures, the host's share in the work is to creep up through the sand as the tide ebbs, giving the algae a few hours of sunlight needed for food production, and then burrow down again to safety for both of them as the tide comes in.

The strangest devices have been evolved to help the hunt for food in the sea. One of the oldest, but which strikes a modern fancy as something dreamed up by a space cadet, is the mechanism by which electric fish generate enough current to locate and then stun their prey. Electric eels do it best, and are able to produce enough power to knock out a horse, let alone a fish. Furthermore, by some electronic means which remain mysterious to man, the eel can locate its target twenty feet away.

The Portuguese man-of-war has developed another predatory device which makes him very unpopular at bathing beaches. The man-of-war actually is not a single animal but a co-operative colony of different beings each with its own functions for the common welfare, as well organized as a beehive and better than most human co-operatives. The principal members of the Portuguese man-of-war are those which form the tentacles and those which make up the stomach. The whole group looks like a lump of pale green or blue jelly which floats on the surface, kept buoyant by gas, with tentacles hanging down into the water like strings, sometimes as long as thirty feet. These strings are poison to any animal they touch except one (although not immediately fatal), and this is their contribution to feeding the group, for the colony lives on fish stunned by the tentacles. The food is distributed by the members who compose the stomach. These act like a well-trained gang of workers and join together to "swallow" the prey. The one animal immune to the poison is the little parasite fish with the technical name of *nomeus gronovii* which lives contentedly within the protection of the dangling strings.

The octopus uses his tentacles quite differently, actively reaching for his food instead of waiting for it to blunder into him. Each tentacle has a lot of little suction cups which can fasten firmly on any object, preferably edible, but have a muscle which enables them to break the suction at will. Food then is drawn to the mouth, which is a beak strong enough to crack a hard-shelled crab. It is said that the octopus does not care for human flesh and will not attack a diver. But he can defend himself; the giant squid sometimes leave scars on the heads of whales even when the whales have been victorious in their undersea combat.

In deep water where meals may be few and far between, some fish have adapted themselves very elastically in the literal sense of the word. A certain starfish, for example, can stretch himself to swallow

Portuguese man-o'-war.

a fish several times his own size, which then is digested over a long period until the next rare morsel can be encountered. The big blunt fish called grouper, which is a kind of sea bass and may be five or six times the weight of a man, is a handsome fellow in his coloring but has a mouth too large for real beauty. In fact, he sometimes seems to be all mouth because he can open it wider than his body is big around. Groupers lurk around rocks or reefs or wrecks and can catch quite a lot of fish simply by opening their mouths. James Dugan, who was a member of the Calypso Oceanographic Expeditions, tells of an authenticated case of a grouper who swallowed a man. The fellow escaped by crawling out through the beast's gill.

For voracity on a really large scale one must visit the seas where food is abundant. This calls for cold water near the surface, so that both plants and animals can thrive. This it what makes the food supply for the enormous schools of cod and herring and salmon, and which nourishes millions upon millions of seals and whales north and south, as well as schools of porpoises and flocks of sea birds. The only places within the tropics where this richness can be found are in waters which flow in from the colder seas, notably the Humboldt Current off the west coast of South America and the Benguela Current off the west coast of Africa.

The Humboldt produces such a wealth of food that for countless centuries some of the largest populations of sea birds ever known feasted there and deposited upon their nesting grounds the world's best supply of natural fertilizer. On these so-called guano islands off the coast of Peru, the deposits were virtually mined and in such volume that for many years, until we learned to make chemical fertilizers, the agriculture of a good part of Europe and America depended upon this source.

Strips of a plentiful marine food supply also exist along the edges of all the oceanic currents where they meet another current. The turmoil created by such a clash brings cold water up from the depths, for even in the hottest climates the water is near the freezing point a couple of miles down. The combination of rich minerals and sun starts off the cycle of feasting in the sea.

8

Beauties and Beasts

Submarine gardens and aquariums have become great tourist attractions because the sea produces beauty such as no one sees on land. Some forms of life too small to be seen themselves give loveliness to the water in which they live. But it must be admitted that the sea has hideous little monsters, too.

One is entitled to be terrified by the aspect of an animal with big glaring eyes, teeth like those of a big saw, a tail and fins armed with nasty looking spines. But strangely enough, even the ugliest and meanest looking creatures in the sea seldom are harmful to man, although they prey on each other viciously. And for every repulsive beast there are dozens which are beautiful or interesting to watch.

The bright colors of the parrot fish and the graceful agility as it darts among waving fronds of a coral garden are an endless pleasure. The magic of phosphorescence in the wake of a ship or gleaming in the froth of a wave is a delight and a wonder to travelers by sea who neither know nor care that it is due to luminous one-celled protozoa or great shoals of tiny phosphorescent shrimp or microscopic plants. A fish leaps from the water then flashes through a shower of sparkles like a fireworks display.

Just below the surface, the beauty of the ocean takes other forms. Especially where coral builds its weird, fantastic shapes, the undersea gardens produce some marvelous effects. The water, filtering out some of the sun's rays and modifying others, transforms the colors of flickering fish and waving fronds into shades which we cannot get in the clear air. The relatively new pastime of "snorkeling" gives

69

to the tourist a view of wonders which until a few years ago only professional divers ever saw.

One of the handsome blossoms, found in many colors and several varieties, is the sea anemone which attaches itself to rocks and stones between low and high tide. But despite its name and flower-like appearance, it is an animal, and is plucked only by the unwary or the uninformed. The sea anemone has tentacles with which it can sting, sometimes very painfully.

Many horrible stories are told about sharks. They are ugly fish, all 200 varieties of them, and carnivorous, so a screen of horror has been built up around them. Dangerous sharks are indeed to be found, mostly in Australia where the relatively small gray or Australian shark, in fact, takes its toll from bathers in spite of careful lookouts and warnings and nets. But many of the popular ideas about sharks are based on stories written by peaceful amateurs so far inland that they long for adventure at sea. In most of these yarns of terror and narrow escapes, "the black dorsal fin protrudes above the surface" to warn the hero or give the onlooker a fearful moment or embellish whatever emotion the writer wants to arouse. The fact is that a shark almost never shows its fin above the water.

Another common belief is that the shark turns upside down just when he is going to seize his victim. This is not true either. A shark's mouth is on the underside of its head, but the animal knows how to use it on upright keel, so to speak, and its teeth really are formidable. But sharks are the scavengers rather than the terrors of the sea.

They cannot be regarded as a menace to mankind when one considers how very few cases of attacks are recorded and how many sharks there are almost all over the sea. In Miami, Florida, about 300,000 people go swimming in the ocean every day during the season. In the last thirty years very, very few cases of shark attacks have been reported, and most of these very likely were made by barracudas. Barracudas are ferocious fish with vicious teeth and a habit of attacking everything that moves. They even will go for something floating motionless on the water if blood is to be smelled.

Most sharks are peaceful fish. The so-called man-eater is normally timid, attacking only when excited by the smell of blood. The most common hammerhead shark around Florida is outright shy and never puts up a fight even when harpooned.

Some sharks live close to the bottom all their lives, such as the Arctic shark, a most mild and lazy animal. The natives of Greenland catch them through the ice in winter on very thin, easily broken lines. Bait is placed on large hooks with a piece of chain just above the hook since otherwise the shark will swallow more and more of the line, which is nothing but double twine. The shark never will try to break it, and when hauled to the surface often is drowned. This happens because sharks have no gills, only lateral gill clefts. They have to swim forward all the time with open mouths so water, from which all fish get their oxygen, may pass in and run out through the gill clefts. If a shark can't move, it gets no oxygen, and that is the end of it.

They must have an extremely keen sense of smell. In the Arctic a bladder filled with blood is put on the hook. Small holes in the bladder allow the blood to seep out, and one can be dead sure of catching a shark in no time, because it will smell the bait from faraway.

But dangerous this shark cannot be called. Neither is the basking shark nor the whale shark ever known to attack men. Even if harpooned, they will not try to fight, yet these two sharks are the largest fish alive. The whale shark reportedly reaches a length of seventy-five feet. It then will weigh about seventy tons, more than two tons of which is liver, used for its vitamin-rich oil.

Most tales of fights with sharks are fantasy. No absolutely proven account, scientifically substantiated by witnesses, has been forthcoming so far about men being seized by sharks while swimming, and dragged under the water. But it is quite exciting for summer guests at the sea to experience the fear of this mysterious monster of the ocean supposedly lying in wait for everybody. In reality more than a thousand times as many people are killed driving to and from swimming beaches than by sharks while refreshing themselves in the ocean.

By any standard of looks, there is an arrow worm which is much more menacing in appearance than any shark. He resembles closely the pictures of the dragon which Saint George killed. He has terrific jaws and a tremendous appetite. If he were only a trifle larger, he might be the terror of the seas, but fortunately he grows no longer than a man's little fingernail.

Whales and seals are more interesting and less frightening to watch, and more mysterious, too. Both are warm-blooded, air-breathing mammals, but have a facility for deep-sea sounding which men have duplicated very seldom. Only those few human beings who have descended into the ocean abysses in bathyspheres have penetrated as far down as seals and whales can go in a matter of a minute or so in pursuit of a meal. They seem to defy two principles which govern all other similar animals.

First of all, like ourselves, they accumulate carbon dioxide in their blood. Like ourselves and all other air-breathing animals, they expel this gas when they exhale. If most such animals don't get rid of the carbon dioxide very quickly, they die—the record for a man holding his breath is about six minutes, and usually less is fatal. But a whale can stay under water for an hour. When he comes up, he lets out his breath in a great fountain of spray—the origin of the whaling call, "Thar she blows!"—and is quite comfortable. Obviously it is impossible to measure the carbon dioxide in the blood of a whale or a seal just before it surfaces, so no one knows just how it manages to tolerate the gas.

The second natural law which whales and seals seem to defy is their resistance to the pressures of deep water. Some men have been able to dive 200 feet without the help of apparatus to protect them, and they are as rare as men who can run a four-minute mile. Whales go down a mile as a matter of course, and seals 1,500 feet or more. At a mile depth, the pressure is some 2,000 pounds to the square inch. Much less ought to crush even a whale's ribs. That it does not may be due to the fact that whales (but not seals) have an adjustable frame. Their ribs are not attached to the spine, and can accommodate themselves to more pressure than ours. Seals seem to resist the danger by slowing their heart rates as they go down—from a normal 180 beats per minute at the surface to as low as twenty. This may be the way they avoid "the bends" which can cripple a human diver if he is hauled up too fast from not much more than one-tenth the distance seals manage without discomfort. One of the impressive sights of the sea is a whale zooming up from a deep dive and shooting on clear out of the water, topping the waves by the height of a two-story house, and falling back with a crash and splash like a small volcanic eruption.

Seals are as accomplished, if less spectacular, in the water, all except the babies of the species who can't go into the water at all until they grow new fur. At birth their hair is not water-repellent as is the skin which later in life will make them so valuable in the market. If thrown into the water, baby seals would probably sink and certainly freeze. This handicap seems to be due to the fact that the seal is the only animal which urinates while still in the womb. The mixture of urine and maternal fluid in which the embryo rests apparently has the effect of almost tanning the hair, and the baby is born unable to venture into the sea which will be his preferred environment later.

At the other end of the scale of marine life is the microscopic growth which is so abundant that it colors great bodies of water. A reddish brown algae is at times so thick that it gives names to the Red Sea and the Vermilion Sea. Other growths give the green or yellow or brownish hues to water which otherwise is blue from the reflection of the sky. Many fish, of course, adopt the color of their environment. So we might think the dwellers in the completely dark water half a mile or more below the surface would be black or colorless. Actually, the transparent animals, such as glass worms and colorless jellyfish, exist in water where there is light. In the great depths, while color can have little meaning, there are brown and violet fish as well as black ones, and other animals of rich scarlet or purple.

Marine birds are as striking a feature of the seascape as any fish. The gulls which swoop and hover over harbors and along the routes of ships live from the sea. They are only the most familiar of a great tribe of feathered fishermen. The biggest and the one capable of the longest flights is the albatross. The great auk, now extinct, was bigger and was an odd-looking creature like the smaller auks which still are found in northern waters. The sea duck, in appearance much like the land variety, sometimes is more richly colored, with a glossy green head, red breast, and black and white markings. Among the more efficient catchers of fish are penguins which can't fly at all, having converted their wings into flippers. In their full evening dress and with their peculiarly pompous waddling gait on land, they are the best clowns in the aviary, but in their native cold waters they are clever fishermen. The biggest of them, the emperor penguin, is about three feet tall.

For mournful dignity it is impossible to match the walrus. Of an imposing size—specimens twelve feet long and weighing a ton and a half used not to be uncommon—he is a kinsman of the seals. With his long tusks and mustache of bristles, his portly figure and sorrowful expression, the walrus is a gentlemanly and friendly fellow, but his oil, hide, and tusks all had commercial value, so he was hunted ruthlessly. A resident of the Arctic exclusively, he is as much at home on ice, which he climbs with the aid of his tusks, as in the water. Except to oysters and other bivalves, which are his food, he is as gentle and inoffensive as anyone could ask, at least until he is harpooned, when he can be very dangerous indeed.

Marine life is so versatile that it can turn legends into reality, or almost. The Greeks, for instance, were sure that somewhere there must be fish with the heads and backs of horses, just as mermaids and mermen were fish with the upper parts of humans, and centaurs, men with the limbs of horses. The Greeks called this horsefish hippocampus, and that became the dictionary name for the attractive little sea horses which haunt weedy, shallow waters. The head does look like that of a horse, and the tiny body tapers off into a rather long tail without the typical fin of most fish. Sea horses use their tails to wrap around and cling to the stems of weeds rather than for swimming.

The catalog of sea beauties and beasts could be extended almost

A New Zealand penguin couple.

indefinitely. For the lover of the Seven Seas, there is fascination in all of the rich and varied life, and just as on land, everyone will have his favorites. Even the octopus with his eight long tentacles studded with two rows of suction cups has his admirers who explain that it is a libel to accuse him of dragging down divers or swimmers; he doesn't care for man as a diet. Octopuses may be an acquired taste, but there is variety enough in the sea to satisfy all tastes.

Courtesy of the American Museum of Natural History

Sea Horses.

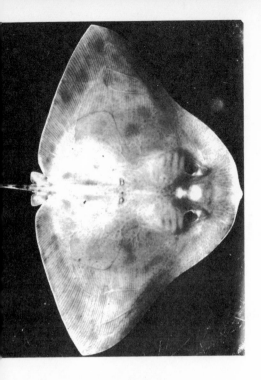

The Butterfly Ray.

The common starfish.

Two-headed dogfish. It is said, these,
and their bigger cousins, sharks, are
cowards, even when they have only
one head.

Giant squid, about which fearsome
stories have been told but which
divers say is quite a friendly fellow.

Beauties and Beasts.

9

Courtship in the Sea

The ways in which the animals of the Seven Seas manage to reproduce themselves are of a bewildering variety, and some of them seem to be designed to make it just as difficult as possible for the species to survive.

There are three basic procedures, however. The smallest of the organisms multiply by simple division, the tiny animals merely splitting in two. Among the great majority of the rest, the female lays eggs which the male then fertilizes. There are two classes within this group. One of them provides some form of parental protection for the offspring, which never are numbered in more than thousands. The other provides no protection, so the offspring of a single pair are in the millions at every breeding season. The third and least common method of reproduction is the fertilization of the egg within the female by the male, and strong parental protection for the offspring after birth.

By far the largest number of fish employ what strikes us as the most wasteful, haphazard method. The female lays millions of eggs in sea or sand, and the male spreads millions of sperm cells among them. Both parents then swim off about their business, and the survival of the offspring is left to chance and the conditions of life.

Some fish, such as the salmon, will go to a lot of trouble to get to their spawning grounds. Salmon go back to the headwaters of the river in which they were spawned themselves, fighting their way up waterfalls and strong currents for reasons which men never have understood. The Chinooks in the Pacific do the same, and so do the shad running up such rivers as the Hudson and the Connecticut.

Oysters, mussels, clams, and their numerous relatives take advantage of the tides for breeding as well as feeding. The tides bring them their food in the ebb and flow of the shallow waters, and these little animals spawn at the height of the spring tides. When the tides are at their highest, some animals will spawn on the sand, giving the offspring time to hatch in the sand before the next high tide comes along to wash them back to sea. The grunion of California, for instance, strand themselves between waves at the full moon's high tide. The female deposits her eggs; the male fertilizes them, all in the moment before the next wave dashes up. Breeding accomplished, the grunion flip themselves back into the ebbing wave. It will be a month before waves reach so far up the beach again, and by that time the developed grunion are waiting inside the eggs' membranes. The sand in which they have grown is roiled by the wave; the little fish burst from the eggs and swim out with the receding water.

The beaches play a big role in the breeding of many species. One sea worm which seems to do its spawning the hard way survives in spite of difficulties which it deliberately brings upon itself. The female buries her eggs in the sand, and the male has to go looking for them in order to fertilize them. He manages to do it, too. Another worm, dweller in cracks or holes in the rocks under water, breeds without leaving its shelter. These worms simply detach the part of their bodies containing the reproductive cells and let them float out to the surface. Here eggs and sperm spread over the water, sometimes in such quantities that great patches are discolored for a day or two.

This casual surrender of a part of the body is carried out by larger animals, too. The male octopus once a year grows a special sperm-bearing attachment on one of his tentacles. When it is ready, the female swims by and simply takes it away, tentacle and all, to the reef or rock where she will lay her eggs. She remains with them, spreading her "ink" over them from time to time. They hatch out in fifty days, and by then the male parent has grown a new tentacle.

The mammals of the sea, being more akin to corresponding forms

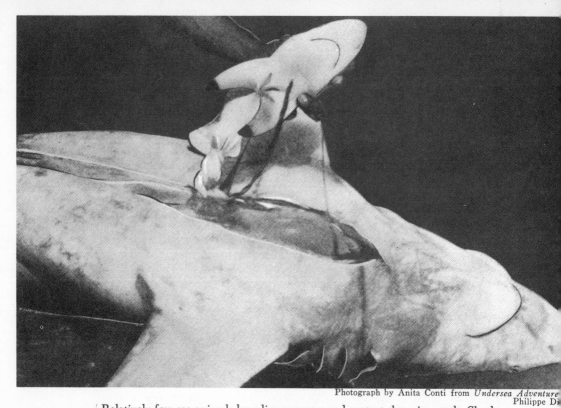

Photograph by Anita Conti from *Undersea Adventure*
Philippe Di

Relatively few sea animals bear live progeny and protect them in youth. Sharks, which otherwise have a bad reputation, are among the few. Here a mother shark is giving birth to her babies.

of life on land, have courting habits which seem less odd to those who have read about the behavior of elephants and elk. Seals and whales, like many of the largest land animals, are polygamous, the strongest males sometimes having large harems of cows.

Sea lions are fairly typical. They are like seals except that they have external ears, a longer neck, no claws on their flippers, which are entirely hairless, and a thin brown body hair which is valueless as fur. (They are killed by men to make leather out of their hides.) One of their favorite breeding grounds is the dark inner chamber of the Painted Cave of California. Every spring hundreds of male sea lions enter this big room—which at other times of the year is visited only by human tourists—and each one selects for himself a special place on the rocky ledge which slopes up out of the water all around the chamber. There they lie, resting until the females come along.

Immediately the peaceful, silent cave becomes a bedlam, the barking and roaring of the bulls echoing in thunderous waves of

Seal nursing young.

sound. Cruel fights take place, for no bull can have his harem too big, and the victors may be challenged again and again before the brief mating season is over. In the fighting, the cows may be injured, too, and by the time they leave, there will be few unhurt animals in the cave. The cows go first, swimming off to bear their young in peace, while the bulls, exhausted by their wounds and many fights, remain to rest on the cave's shelf until they have recovered.

Seals, who breed on the icy rocks of the far north and far south, are equally fierce in their competition for cows, and an old bull will be covered with the scars of years of combat, although some varieties live peaceful family lives. The hood seals, for instance, pair off, and parents and pup occupy without interference a separate bit of rough ice from the patch held by others. The walrus lives up to his appearance of being a philosopher by breeding only every three years. They make the most devoted parents of all animals in the sea, the females suckling their young for two full years.

81

10

High I. Q.

Fish aren't supposed to have much sense, and indeed their brain capacity is small, but perhaps one reason for our feeling about their intelligence is that we do not understand them. We think it is pretty clever of men to be able to predict high and low tide accurately. But when a grunion figures out just which wave of high tide will be the highest, we do not credit him with being bright, but say it is just instinct.

Now, in spite of this, it can be proved that fish will learn. A pike in a fish tank will quickly gobble up a little fish placed in the tank with him. But try the experiment of putting a clear piece of glass down the middle of the tank and then tossing the little fish into the protected end. After the pike has bumped his nose hard two or three times on the glass, lunging for his prey, he will let that fish alone even after the glass is removed. Toss another little fish, the twin of the first one so far as the eye can tell, into the tank and the pike will grab it in a flash. But he will never attack the first one, remembering his sore nose.

Of course, the stories of intelligent sea animals are told mostly about the higher forms, the mammals, and sometimes about the birds. Seals can be trained to perform all sorts of tricks and will put on quite a show in a zoo or circus. But the palm for exhibitionism in a state of nature must go to the porpoise. These graceful creatures, swimming easily faster than anything man ever puts on the sea, have been credited with a genuine liking for people. They gambol and circle around ships seemingly just for the companionship, for they eat nothing that is thrown overboard. Sailors have told almost incredible tales of porpoises guiding ships through dangerous rocks and shoals, and some of the stories at least have turned out to be true. James Dugan tells of one porpoise which became a pet and sort of volunteer lifeguard at Bondi Beach outside Sydney, Australia, one of the most popular and frequented bathing beaches in the world. Porpoises are great acrobats, able to perform the most astonishing leaps and twists into the air, and they enjoy showing off just for the applause. (Of course the reward of a fish will not be refused.) Says Mr. Dugan: "The mammalian orders which returned to the sea during the development of species—whales, porpoises, sea lions and other warm-blooded divers—would probably have been successes if they had stayed ashore. They have intelligences rivaling those of dogs or monkeys."

As navigators, fish and mammals and birds were well developed long before men ventured to sea at all—indeed, before men existed. Whales will cross an ocean to get from one feeding ground to another. The sea lions find their way back to the Painted Cave each spring, coming perhaps from thousands of miles away, as easily as if they were equipped with the most modern instruments. Birds which may scatter over a whole ocean for feeding return unerringly to one tiny island or another for their nesting, and steer a straight course through any kind of weather.

In fact, there is a widely held theory that men used the navigational skill of birds before developing their own ability to chart a course out of sight of land. The story of Noah finding land by sending out the dove to look for it has some more than legendary counterparts. Floki Vilgerdarson, the Norseman who discovered Iceland, is said in the saga to have been shown the way by a raven he took along for the purpose. In fact, he used three. The first one he released flew back the way he had come, so he knew that was the closest land. The second circled the ship and came back, so he knew land was still far off in all directions. The third took off straight ahead, so Floki followed and came to Iceland at last.

Courtesy of the American Museum of Natural Histo

Audubon's "Least Stormy Petrel," from an original print.

Similarly, the Polynesians are supposed to have colonized from one island to another by watching and following the migratory birds. According to this version, plover led the Tahitians from their island to Hawaii, while the cuckoo drew Solomon Islanders down to New Zealand. Either trip is well over a thousand miles, but of course it will be said that it was men who had the intelligence; the birds didn't know what they were doing.

Adaptability to environment may not prove intelligence, but some sea animals are clever at it just the same. The octopus can change color from brown to green to red to a dull purple. Lobsters have learned how to extract copper from sea water, a feat which men have not yet duplicated as successfully. Seaweed takes out iodine in the same way and sea cucumbers get out vanadium.

Whether or not it is intelligent to take the easiest way in life is debatable. Those who think it is might well pay a tribute of respect to a little round sea squirt, one of the *Tunicata*, which used to be higher upon the ladder of evolution than it is now. It had a backbone and a nervous system, although it was one of the lower Vertebrata, but then reverted to an earlier model. The sea squirt gave up its backbone and nervous system for an exceedingly placid existence in which all problems of survival are removed from its control. Its principal equipment for feeding consists of two holes with a sort of filter between them. Sea water flows in through one hole, is filtered for any food it may contain, and flows out the other hole. The clear layer of water near the bottom in some otherwise rather muddied waters is said to be due to the filtering work of sea squirts.

Many sea animals have had to become extremely "weather-wise" to survive. Harp seals, after their whelping on Arctic ice floes, realize just when the approach of winter will thicken the ice so greatly that they will not be able to keep open the holes through which they have been diving to catch fish. Just in time they start their leisurely progress south, although they can travel at fifteen miles an hour if they are pushed, with an uncanny knowledge of just which fields of ice it is safe to pass under and which must be circumnavigated. They have learned to ride the ice which is going their way, and leave it at the right time. By the end of December or early January, the herds of seals will reach southern Labrador, the Banks of Newfoundland, and the Gulf of St. Lawrence where they will spend the winter in rich feeding grounds. Before the first hint of spring they are off to the north again, the round trip often being as much as 4,000 miles, and they will reach their favorite ice floes for whelping at the end of February or early March, right on schedule.

Courtesy of the American Museum
of Natural History

Puffer fish do not swell from a sense of their own importance but to frighten an enemy or try to escape a danger. Here is one before and after puffing.

Line engraving by Frans Huys after Pieter Brueghel the Elde

A ship close-hauled on starboard tack.

Part III

The Sea in Action

The Tide
The Winds
The Currents
The Waves

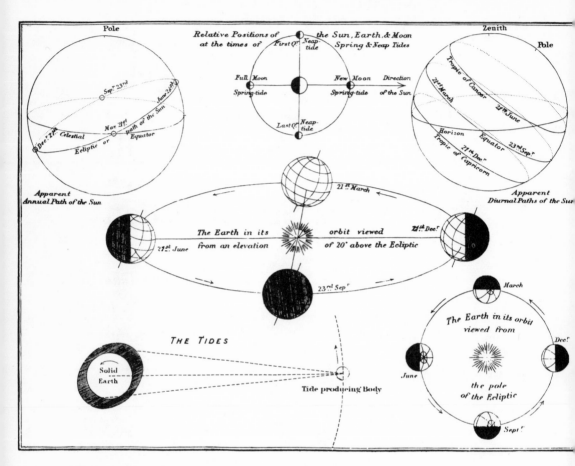

Diagram prepared by Sir Robert S. Ball, a leading British astronomer, to show how the sun, moon and seasons affect the tides. Top center, the chart shows how at times of new and full moon the pull of this satellite is in line with that of the sun to create the high "spring" tides, while at the times of the quarter moon it and the sun are pulling against each other to hold the seas to the lower "neaps." The path of the sun (traced in the charts at upper right and left) and the orbit of the earth (shown in the charts at center and lower right) demonstrate the seasonal variations which have their effect on the strength of the tides. This response of the ocean tide to any planetary attraction is charted in the diagram at lower left.

11

The Tide

No scientist will proclaim that the earth is too well known at present, and if that is true of the land, how much more so of the Seven Seas! In fact, oceanography only recently has been recognized as a science at all, and we are just beginning to learn something of both the obvious and the mysterious forces which move all that water.

Winds stir up the surface. Currents flow through it, perhaps moving only the top layers but in other cases creeping deep through the submarine canyons. Volcanoes and undersea earthquakes disturb the water to the farthest drop on the other side of the world. The very molten core of the earth heats some of it so that it rises from the frigid depths. All these forces work sometimes for and sometimes against each other, so that even such an apparently simple question as how long a drop of water takes to circulate from the beginning of its travels, say at the bottom of the sea, to the surface and back again to where it started, cannot be calculated. The span of 500 years has been mentioned, but it will take many observations and the work of many scientists before we really know even to what extent the heat from the heart of the earth radiates through the ocean.

Certainly, though, the greatest force which acts upon the water of the Seven Seas is the tide. Each small particle in the entire ocean, even in the deepest part of the abyss, senses the pull created by the attraction of the sun and the moon. Of course, so does each little particle on firm land, too. But these cannot respond by moving, as does the water. Actually the stars also exert a similar attraction, but it is so faint that it has no practical effect, and we can afford to ignore it.

Lofman-Pix, photographed for *Holiday* Magaz

High tide, Bay of Fundy.

The result of the power exerted by the sun and the moon is the tides. The moon is by far the main factor because while the force is proportioned to the mass of the attracting body, it is known to diminish in proportion to the square of the distance. So although the sun is twenty-seven million times the size of the moon, the moon is so much nearer to the earth that it is the main factor in the ebb and flow of the tides.

Everyone who has lived by the sea has noticed that the time of

Low tide, Bay of Fundy.

high tide is about fifty minutes later each day, which corresponds with the rising of the moon. Also the height of high tide will be seen to vary with the moon's monthly cycle so that twice each month the highest of all, called the spring tides, occur at new moon and full moon. At this time the sun, moon and earth are all in a line so that the pull of the sun is added to that of the moon throughout the ocean. When the moon is in its first and third quarters, it and the sun and the earth form the three points of a triangle. Then the pull

91

of the sun is working against that of the moon and the flow of the tide is relatively lower. These tides are called the neaps.

Local geographical conditions make very big differences not only in the extent of the tide at any one place but also as to its time. Because these conditions are never quite the same, the tides on any two coasts are never quite the same either.

Some of the contrasts are surprising. At the North Pole there is, of course, no tide at all; and at Cape Columbia, where Admiral Peary started on his trip to the Pole, the tide is only four inches. But in the Bay of Fundy, between Nova Scotia and New Brunswick in Canada, the rise in Minas Basin at the head of the bay is as much as fifty-three and one-half feet from low water, the highest in the world. Here the reason is quite clear. About one hundred billion tons of water is carried in and out of the bay twice every day.

One thing that helps explain the complications to which the tides are subjected is that the water is divided up among a great many basins, so to speak, the boundaries of which are determined by surrounding land above or below the surface and the uneven bottom of the ocean. In each basin the influences of gravitational attraction are always changing, and so are the currents flowing in and out, and the ebb from each previous high tide. All this can produce the most surprising effects.

For a long time the behavior of the tides at the island of Tahiti was a riddle to sailors and scientists. The fact is that there are marks on the beach which enable one to read the time with comparative exactness from the height of the water. High tide occurs at noon and midnight, low tide at 6 o'clock, morning and evening. One would think that the moon is entirely ignored at Tahiti and that the water there chooses to follow the sun only.

The explanation is that the island lies at the pivotal point in one of those basins I have mentioned. As in all these basins the water is set in oscillation by the pull of sun and moon, and the "swinging" of the water sends it all up and down. Now if you put water in a pan and tilt up and down gently, you will notice that the water in the middle remains nearly at the same level, while on the edges it will go up and down much more. It is like a see-saw swinging on its axis. Tahiti forms such an axis, and therefore the force of the moon is not felt. Only the sun works on the water here, so the time of the tides does not change as elsewhere by the fifty minutes which the moon's cycle departs from that of the sun every day.

If this seems strange, what are we to say of places which have only one tide a day instead of two? This happens in Norton Sound south of the Seward Peninsula in Alaska, and in parts of the Gulf of Mexico.

Tides are of the greatest importance in navigation. In the open sea, of course, the ebb and flow of the tides are not felt, but it is a different story when the ship nears port. The vast amount of water put in motion by the moon cannot be resisted by anything made by man. We have to submit to it, and where the tides are strong even the biggest ships must wait for an auspicious time to come in and out of harbor. The largest vessels afloat, for instance, sail to and from New York City, and although the harbor here is protected by The Narrows and most of the piers are built rather far up the Hudson River, the proudest liners wait for slack water so the tidal currents will not swing the ship right through its pier.

Certain big inlets with narrow entrances have a tidal current so violent that navigation is entirely out of the question except at slack water. One in Greenland named Soendre Stroemfjord now is seen by thousands of airplane passengers as it is one of the landing stations on the air route from the United States and Canada to Europe. To them the inlet looks rather like a smooth and friendly fjord, but out at the narrow entrance is a small island called Simiutak, which is Eskimo for cork. The inlet really is like a big bottle emptying and filling itself, and the island forms the cork, not quite closing the neck. Standing on this island, I have seen the tide rushing in and out like a furious river. For the big body of water inside the fjord must be sent out and taken in twice a day. In the early days, the Eskimos in their skin boats could only cross the water during about half an hour twice a day. Even now, in powerful motorboats, one has to be careful, although the boat may be able to face eight or ten knots of the current.

The same thing happens in other parts of the world, and not always in a fjord. When tide and wind work together many narrow passages can be very difficult to navigate. The best known one of the much traveled waters is Pentland Firth between Scotland and the Orkney Islands. Here the current running in and out of the North Sea is so dangerous that even today captains would rather make a longer detour further north than face the conditions which northwest winds of some force and an ebb tide can create. The heavy breaking seas of the Swilkie, as the Scots call it, are really to be avoided.

Many sailors have lost their lives here, and since the days of the Vikings, Pentland Firth has been feared. It is said to be haunted by ghosts howling and calling to seamen passing by on dark winter nights. On a modern ship today, when the strait is almost as well lighted as a city avenue and the engine throbs powerfully and steadily, everybody feels easier when Pentland Firth is left behind.

Sailing directions, those invaluable aids to navigation, are full of warnings about tidal conditions and tidal currents which sailors have learned about from experience. *The Alaska Pilot* tells captains that tides create the greatest dangers to be found in the Aleutian Islands.

In Alaska, too, can be found the so-called "bore," a very special tidal phenomenon. It builds up in a body of water called Turnagain Arm, in Cook Inlet, named for the famous English explorer. Cook Inlet has exceptionally high tides, often more than thirty feet above low water, and Captain Cook sailed into Turnagain Arm at high tide only to find his ship standing, if not high and dry, certainly embedded in the mud, and he couldn't get off for six hours.

Every bore (of this kind, anyway) is created by very unusual circumstances. The flood tide enters, not in a decent way, gently rising without any special movement, but in a single wave with a high front running along at a speed of twelve or thirteen knots. The inlet into which it flows must be a shallow river mouth or fjord with obstructions at the entrance sufficient to delay the flow. Combined with wind from just the right quarter, the tide will rise faster than it can pass over the obstructions. Only when it reaches a given height sufficient to surmount the obstacles does it break over and come rolling in with a steep, high front. The Alaska bore may have a crest of more than five feet, but in other places, I have heard, the wave may be as much as eleven feet high.

At Turnagain Arm, which is the only place where I personally have witnessed the rise and approach of a bore, it can be heard as a roar like the pounding of surf some twenty minutes before its arrival at any spot along the inlet. It does not cause too much alarm as people are prepared for it, but it can be dangerous to small craft drawn up on the beach in what is usually regarded as a safe place.

The tremendous power of the tides has long fascinated men of an inventive turn of mind as a possible source of energy, and one might wonder why all this strength has not been harnessed. Well, of course, it has been in some places. There are tide motors in use—I have seen them in England—but not on a scale to light a city or run a big factory. One method is to have floats which can slide up and down on a post. The incoming tide forces them up and at the ebb they go down, transmitting power in both directions. Another device is a tank with an opening into which the tide pours, turning a wheel one way as it flows in and the other way as it flows out.

For a great many years, engineers have studied the problem of how to harness the very high tide of Passamaquoddy Bay in Maine to supply electricity. As a matter of fact, the United States Government spent several million dollars on preliminary work but abandoned the idea, and so have some private companies. Engineers tell me that the difficulty is not so much to get the power out of the tide in the first place—they know how to do it without too vast expense—but that the pipes and machinery would be expensive to maintain in salt water, and Passamaquoddy is so far from any big users of electricity that cost of transmission makes the project uneconomical.

Still it is not at all improbable that in time men will put the tides in harness, and then they will be useful to man as well as a problem to navigators.

12

The Winds

"When wind comes before rain,
Sun comes soon again.

When rain comes before wind,
Get your small sails in."

These were some of the first lessons a young sailor got from his skipper who did not know too much himself about meteorology. But old people, through tradition and stories and their own experience, have gathered some knowledge about the winds. And because the wind often is the most important phenomenon of nature for sailors and fishermen, it is understandable that they were the first to try to predict what the weather, and therefore their own working conditions, would be. But the old verse I have quoted cannot, of course, be taken as an absolute fact.

Those who live on land, especially in cities and towns, must look at the smoke from a chimney or at the leaves of the trees to see if there is the slightest breeze. Very often the direction cannot be determined because it is changed by obstructions such as nearby buildings. At sea no obstacle stops the wind from running its course. It can easily be followed by the waves—even the slightest movement can be seen.

The word "wind" describes currents in the atmosphere. The wind is caused by two major factors. They are the rotation of the earth and the heat from the sun. The three main disturbances which create irregular movements in the atmosphere are the cyclone, tornado, and hurricane. These, of course, are easily distinguished from the trade winds, monsoon and other regular currents of air from breeze to gale.

A cyclone is a system of wind circulating around a center of low barometric pressure. There is a simple law, first worded by the Dutch meteorologist, Buys-Ballot. It goes as follows: In the Northern Hemisphere an observer standing with his back to the wind will have the low pressure on his left. In the Southern Hemisphere there will be a lower pressure on the right hand than on the left.

A cyclone always blows spirally inward toward the center and the whole system can travel at a rate of twenty miles an hour or more. The direction in equatorial latitudes is mostly from east to west, in higher latitudes, from west to east. Also, as is understood from the Buys-Ballot law, in the Northern Hemisphere, the rotation of the cyclone is counterclockwise and in the Southern Hemisphere clockwise.

A tornado is a very violent, stormy rotation of the air, fortunately seldom more than some few hundred feet in width and about twenty-five miles long. It is accompanied by a funnel-shaped cloud around which the wind revolves, spiraling upward, usually counterclockwise. Just as on land a tornado can pick up houses and uproot trees, so at sea it can suck up to a terrific height great amounts of water. This water eventually will be let down and ships have been swamped by it. Tornadoes are also responsible for the so-called "rain of blood" (from a red dust) heard of east of Australia, or the "rain of fishes and frogs," extremely rare but still vouched for by credible witnesses.

A hurricane is a cyclone with a very large diameter, sometimes 300 miles or more. The low pressure moves with a speed of from ten to fifteen miles an hour and the wind sweeps around with a velocity which has been measured at 140 miles an hour or more. Hurricanes usually move in low latitudes toward the west and southwest, only to change their course to north and northeast as soon as they reach higher latitudes. This is most fortunate for the North American continent, which is thus spared many hurricanes originating in the Caribbean. These storms now are very closely observed by meteorological stations—in recent years the weathermen have given women's names to hurricanes—and elaborate warnings are sent out—broadcasts as to speed, course, and dimensions. Those on shore can take precautions, and ships at sea often can escape if they are in the path of the hurricane.

Around the equator, or a little to the north of it, there is a rather narrow belt of low pressure. From there the pressure increases, subject to many variations, with the distance toward the poles. Therefore, north and south of this equatorial belt, known as the doldrums, which usually enjoy light or variable winds, an easterly wind blows. These are called the trade winds. At the surface of the earth, the wind almost always blows at an angle of 20 to 30 degrees into the

Diagram of the Winds.

low pressure, so that the trade wind on the north side of the doldrums is northeasterly while the trade wind of the Southern Hemisphere comes in a southeasterly direction.

The doldrum belt varies a little with the time of the year. It is somewhat north of the equator in winter, but in the northern summer the doldrums move even further north and consequently both of the trade winds follow.

Now the distribution of pressure in the Southern Hemisphere shows a belt of high pressure around the thirtieth parallel. This is of special interest for sailors as the barometric pressure usually is higher over the sea than over the continent. These belts are called the subtropical anticyclones. They can be studied much easier than similar phenomena in the Northern Hemisphere, where there is more land to interfere. (It must be remembered that the Northern Hemisphere is 60.7 per cent ocean and the Southern 80.9 per cent.)

As I have said, the wind blows with many variations. For instance, in the Northern Atlantic, the prevailing winds are westerly. But in the days of sailing ships, merchantmen bound for Iceland and Greenland or Newfoundland sometimes stayed over in the spring to wait for a so-called "Easter east wind." This was a strong breeze which would bring them to Davis Strait across the Atlantic easier and much faster than tacking against the west and southwest winds.

The Southern Hemisphere's strong westerly wind is more regular because very little land interferes, yet here, too, low pressure can produce intermittent but often terrible gales.

The subtropical anticyclone or the subtropical high-pressure belt, as it also is called, controls conditions in the Indian Ocean. In northern India the sun heats the air in summer so that it gets lighter and rises. As a result, over the entire Indian Ocean a very broad current of air produced by the continuous increasure of pressure from the subtropical anticyclonic belt of the Southern Hemisphere blows in over India as a southwest wind known as the southwest monsoon. During its several-thousand-mile journey, this wind has passed over the warm ocean. Consequently it reaches India as a warm and very damp current of air. Then it is forced up over the coastal mountain ranges where it cools and causes the annual deluge known as the monsoon rains. This will last until late September or early October.

In winter, the wind shifts the other way and the northeast monsoon blows in exactly the opposite direction. It begins to diminish in intensity during April. Then there will be a short period with variable winds, mostly light. Early in June the depression again is formed and the monsoon cycle begins all over again.

There have been many theories about the origin of cyclones. The

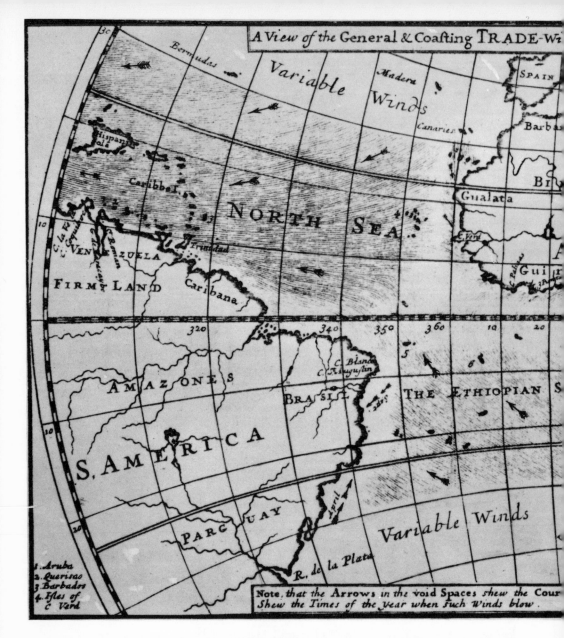

A View of the General & Coasting TRADE-Wi

Note, that the Arrows in the void Spaces shew the Cour
Shew the Times of the Year when such Winds blow.

A studious pirate, William Dampier was one of the early scientific observe
he made careful notes on his observations. In 1699 he publishe

most acceptable may be that of the Norwegian scientist, Vilhelm
Bjerknes, who explains that a cyclone starts with a warm core and
ends with a cold core. This is a result of two fronts meeting each
other. To give a rather general explanation—a cyclone should be
visualized as a wave on the front between cold easterly currents of

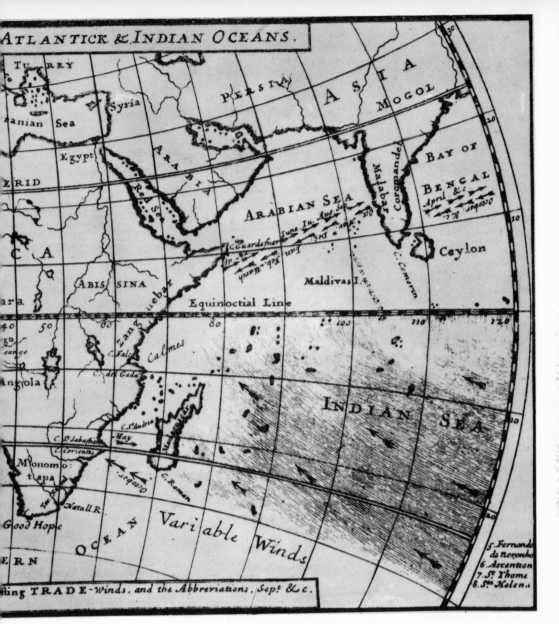

ATLANTICK & INDIAN OCEANS.

the winds. In the intervals of looting towns and capturing ships at sea,
"Discourse on Winds," for which this map was an illustration.

polar origin meeting warm westerly currents of equatorial origin. As
the polar air meets the equatorial air, something like waves of wind
develop along the polar front and these are of different specific
gravity. The cold air pushes beneath the warm until all the equatorial air is lifted above the ground, and then the mixing of the two

air masses will take place, but only if the air that goes up can be moved by a sufficiently strong wind. Unless this is the case, the air moving upwards from the lower layers is replaced by a flow of air from the surrounding areas and this will result in an increase of pressure instead of a cyclone. When there is a strong wind, the process of mixing the warm and cold air can begin, and the earth's rotation will increase the force of the wind waves. A cyclone most often forms in the northern crest of such a wave, although there are many variations in the actual phenomenon.

Very often the winds at sea are influenced strongly by land masses. The temperature of water changes much more slowly than that of the surface of the land, and the air above the different seas is affected in different ways. In our days, with meteorological stations everywhere, wind information is exchanged by international agreement all over the world. It is mainly for the benefit of fliers, but ship navigators benefit too, even if they are interested only in the lower part of the atmosphere. In most cases, gales can be determined many hours before they arrive, so ships can change course around the bad weather if it is menacing enough to justify a detour.

Looking at a map of the winds, one can see that the same laws that apply to currents in the sea also rule the atmosphere. As backwash is found in water, so is return-wind often seen along the borders of regular wind routes. If a passenger on a big ship observes the birds following the vessel, he will notice how, by spreading their wings, they can rest in the air without moving a muscle, taking advantage of the air that meets the high sides of the ship and is pressed up over it. The bird finds just the place where the updrift of the air and his own weight maintain a balance. The same thing can be seen between crests of big waves. Time and again the birds are seen following the furrow between crests, moving forward and sideways at the same time. They are not flapping their wings at all, which shows there is a separate circulation of the air between the crests.

The same principle has been utilized by gliders which take advantage of ascending currents and are able to stay up for hours.

The polar wind, from both the south and north, has an immense impact on the lower latitudes, even when it does not contribute to cyclones. Of course, we are most interested in the Northern Hemisphere, especially in the Atlantic, because it is the most widely traveled. North of the Atlantic is Greenland, covered with the biggest glacier in the north, and the weather in Europe, Canada, and the United States is often, so to speak, made in Greeland. That is why, during the last world war, the German General Staff made many and great efforts to obtain knowledge of the weather conditions there. No fewer than fourteen different expeditions were destroyed by the Allies, expeditions whose aim was to stay in Greenland and send news of weather conditions home.

The wind system here is generally this: As the air drifts in over the Greenland icecap, it is cooled off and thereby becomes heavier than the surrounding atmosphere. These descending currents blow out from the edge of the big glacier to both east and west. This has been observed by travelers across Greenland who have the wind against them while going up the glacier from either side and have hard packed snow to travel on. In the middle of Greenland they will usually find calm or very light, variable winds, and as a result, snow almost as soft as in the forests of Canada, although sometimes unforeseen winds may occur and upset all theories and calculations. Usually, however, the cold currents of air continue down over the North Atlantic, in one direction hitting Scandinavia, North Germany, and England with all their force, and in the other, Canada. Warnings sent three times a day from Greenland now advise not only air pilots and farmers, but all ships at sea about what sort of weather is coming.

The safety of ships with their passengers, crew, and cargo is more assured now than ever before. But this means only that mankind has learned to take precautions. The wind blows just as regularly as ever—strong or mild—bringing a contact between land and sea such as no other natural force can.

Table IV
Winds at Sea

The idea of more precise and concise terms than were commonly used in log books to describe winds at sea occurred to a scarred British Navy veteran, Francis Beaufort, in 1805. (At thirty-one years old, he had seen a lot of service; in one fight he was wounded by three sword slashes and sixteen musket balls.) Later as Hydrographer of the Navy and a Knight, he lived to see his scale of winds generally approved. It and the earlier but still widely favored table follows.

BEAUFORT SCALE			LOGBOOK TERM	
Description	*Miles per hour*	*Force*	*Description*	*Miles per hour*
Calm	Less than 1	0	Calm	Less than 1
Light air	1 - 3	1	Very light	1 - 3
Light breeze	4 - 6	2	Light	4 - 7
Gentle breeze	7 - 10	3	Gentle	8 - 12
Moderate breeze	11 - 16	4	Moderate	13 - 18
Fresh breeze	17 - 21	5	Fresh	19 - 24
Strong breeze	22 - 27	6	Strong	25 - 38
Moderate gale	28 - 33	7	Gale	39 - 54
Fresh gale	34 - 40	8	Whole gale	55 - 72
Strong gale	41 - 47	9	Hurricane	More than 72
Whole gale	48 - 55	10		
Storm	56 - 65	11		
Hurricane	More than 65	12		

13

The Currents

When people speak of the Seven Seas they usually know that there is a connection between them. What happens in a part of one ocean affects all of them. If one goes to a beach and throws a pebble into the water, it will be felt wherever salt water washes the beaches. We do not have instruments delicate enough, though, to register the movement caused in Australia when a child at Miami Beach plays with a toy ship or a fisherman draws a cod at Newfoundland.

The Seven Seas always are in motion, and as they are connected, every little particle of water which passes a certain point might come back. But will it take ten thousand years, or just a hundred years, or less? It is quite impossible to give an answer.

The many forces at work together or against each other form the currents which are found everywhere in the sea. There are strong, well-known currents, whose effects can be seen clearly, and small local currents which only fringe the bigger mainstreams and occasionally mix with them.

Now, how do such currents originate? The causes can be many, but here only a few of the most important will be mentioned.

A glance at a globe will show that nearly all the lands point south—Africa and the Americas as continents, Europe and Asia with the peninsulas of Spain, Italy, Greece, Arabia, India, Malaya, and Korea. Also California, Florida and Greenland are directed southward.

Around the Antarctic continent there is open space, and here the current produced by the spinning of the earth and the prevailing winds is flowing without hindrance, biting itself in the tail. The long fetch gives rise to high waves and nothing interferes with that current circling the world. It snows, it rains, and in the summertime ice melts. Also, huge icebergs are pushed out from the glaciers. All of this water needs an outlet, lest it rise up over the South Pole.

So the Antarctic Current broadens until it touches land to the north which, so to speak, scoops part of the Antarctic water towards the equator. Along the west coast of South America runs the Humboldt Current, bringing cold water to the north, keeping dry the part of the land that, in other tropical countries at the same latitude, has its yearly rainy season. The Humboldt Current brings cold water filled with minerals and small animal life from the higher latitudes to the south. The air over this current is cooled, so that when it comes in to the coast and is forced up over the Andes, it is already of such low temperature that it does not lose its moisture as rain, which is the case in so many other places in the world where air rises to pass high mountain ranges.

The Humboldt Current runs as far north as Ecuador. There it turns due west, hitting the Galapagos Islands and embracing the southern part of that group just at the latitude of the equator.

The current is bent out to the west because it meets another current coming from the north, El Niño. The two of them run parallel to the Galapagos. The influence of those two currents is reflected in the extremely different temperatures in the northern and southern parts of the Galapagos group, and in the big differences in the marine life.

The cold water running along and very close to South America's west coast has given a balance in nature. When strangers come here and stand on shore—or even inland, in Lima, for instance, where fog and cloud banks are seen each day—they will naturally predict rain. And yet less than one inch of rain falls in a year in certain parts of Chile and Peru.

Almost exactly the same thing occurs in the western part of South Africa. Here, too, the Antarctic sends a cool current up along the coast. It is called the Benguela Current, and its effect is similar to that of the Humboldt. The cold water keeps the air cool, and the

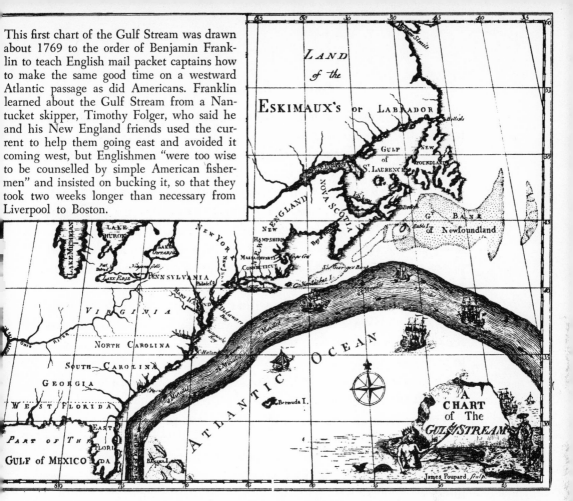

This first chart of the Gulf Stream was drawn about 1769 to the order of Benjamin Franklin to teach English mail packet captains how to make the same good time on a westward Atlantic passage as did Americans. Franklin learned about the Gulf Stream from a Nantucket skipper, Timothy Folger, who said he and his New England friends used the current to help them going east and avoided it coming west, but Englishmen "were too wise to be counselled by simple American fishermen" and insisted on bucking it, so that they took two weeks longer than necessary from Liverpool to Boston.

The first chart of the Gulf Stream.

rainfall on shore is less than half an inch a year in West Africa. Fog forms above the cold water running in over the coast but does not give any rain to nourish vegetation. In Australia as well, the Antarctic Sea sends a current along the west coast, and the result is desert and dry lands in western Australia.

The Gulf Stream is the most talked-of current on the globe because its warm water influences the climate of more inhabited lands than any other, and it is blessed wherever it is felt. The Gulf Stream has not been generally known for many years; only since 1769 when the great American, Benjamin Franklin, was Postmaster General. He had a map drawn showing a current running across the Atlantic. He was asked to do that because someone in New England

107

had complained that it took longer to sail from Europe to America than in the opposite direction.

Franklin investigated the problem and he soon found that an east-directed current, which he learned flowed as fast as three miles an hour, was well known to the whaling captains of New England. Now, time after time it has been found that skippers who are out for whales, seals or fish know much of nature which they never tell. They are not scientists and they are not interested in publicizing the places where they have the best catch. The competitors will have to find out for themselves.

But the whaling skippers knew that the current bending eastward from Cape Hatteras takes a due eastward course at the latitude of the Grand Banks, crossing the Atlantic Ocean. This current is easy to map as it can be recognized with the naked eye. The Gulf Stream has blue, dark water, while the Atlantic water, both north and south of the stream, is green and gray—filled with minerals and animal life.

The whalers did not notice this just for the sake of the color, but the fact was that no whales were ever found in the Gulf Stream itself—north of the current and south of it, yes. Therefore, many a time the whalers cruised back and forth across the clear blue water into the green, so their logbooks showed where it ran.

This Gulf Stream fortunately branches out and brings warmth and good conditions for vegetation to many places. First, a branch of it is sent along the west coast of Greenland, thereby giving that area such a contrast in plants, animals and men from the cold desolate east coast. Further on, branches are sent along the western part of Iceland, and the Gulf Stream washes the southern shore of this remarkable island. It is a token of the close connection with the Gulf of Mexico that one can find thick mahogany beams in the houses of poor fishermen along the southern coast of Iceland. These mahogany trees—possibly several hundred years ago—had fallen in water near Cuba or somewhere in the Caribbean. They had drifted up with the Gulf Stream, and were found by the fishermen in the treeless land. Today no mahogany trunks will be brought here—they are too carefully cultivated in the lands of their growth.

"The Gulf Stream" by Winslow Homer.

The Gulf Stream runs on its way although it has been slowed as it crosses the Atlantic. But it already has divided itself, spread out, sending currents due east and to the north and south. The northbound current runs along England and Scandinavia. It comes close to the long Norwegian coast and is bent around the Kola Peninsula where it turns around—after having thrown many odd things on shore. In a museum at Alexandrovsk, where open water, in spite of the northern latitude, can be found all year round, one can see what is actually brought up by the Gulf Stream—branches of all kinds of tropical trees, dead animals from the tropics, insects, utensils used by people there, and characteristic items thrown overboard from ships sailing along or across the Gulf Stream.

We have spoken of different currents, but it must be understood that the water goes somewhere and comes from somewhere, and therefore again we must go to the end of the world, as was the case with the Antarctic. As has been told, the South Pole is located in the interior of a big glacier-covered continent, surrounded entirely by sea; the North Pole is covered by the landlocked Arctic Ocean with only three outlets down to the southern waters. As was the case with the Antarctic, ice and snow in the Arctic, which melt in summertime, demand outlets. Besides, great rivers, mostly from Siberia and Canada, empty into the Arctic Ocean. This causes pressure of water so it flows down to the southern oceans via all three passages.

From Bering Strait, a current of cold water, the so-called Oyashio Current, runs along the coast of Kamchatka and the Kuriles Islands. It presses itself close to the east coast of Japan—between Japan and a warm northbound current—Kuroshio by name. On the east side of North America the cold Labrador Current runs down along the coast, pressing in between the Gulf Stream and the island of Newfoundland. It keeps the coast of Maine cool and the sea rather chilly for swimming until, further south, it mixes with the Gulf Stream—or submerges beneath it. The third big Arctic current goes along the east coast of Greenland. Thus all three big currents keep to the west, close to the east coast of those lands which they pass. (In the Arctic one always has the current with him when he has the land on the starboard side.)

The East Greenland Current is the mightiest outlet of the Arctic Ocean, bringing with it masses of ice—"storis"—which is carried around the southern point of Greenland, Cape Farewell. Here it meets a branch of the Gulf Stream. The combined currents turn north and bring ice and driftwood up the west coast of Greenland, sometimes almost as far as the polar circle.

If the ice is thawed here, much driftwood will be free of the embracing ice and wash ashore. The Labrador Current brings ice from Kane's Basin and Lancaster Sound, down along the east coast of Baffinland—the "vestis"—which sometimes, in bad ice years, unites with the "storis" coming from Greenland. Eventually this ice is brought down to the north of Newfoundland and Belle Isle Strait where, in the springtime, ice floes harbor a couple of million seals giving birth to their cubs.

Most of the East Greenland Current flowing through Denmark Strait between Iceland and Greenland will meet the Gulf Stream, going straight across its course. As the cool water is heavier than the

Icebergs drift south on the currents from the Arctic.

warm, it submerges and becomes a submarine current, and does not surface again until it reaches equatorial latitudes.

This current was first found by the great Norwegian explorer, Fridtjof Nansen. He had earlier, in Greenland, seen huge trees being carried across the Arctic Ocean and he knew that they came from Siberia. But which way? The American Jeanette Expedition perished in 1881, and during their efforts to reach the Siberian mainland the unhappy explorers left one of their boats and lots of their utensils on the ice. A few years later these were found by an Eskimo at Frederikshaab, in Greenland, having crossed the Pole or somewhere close by. They were then driven along the east coast of Greenland and more than a hundred miles up the west coast.

These facts led Fridtjof Nansen to start his famous expedition with the *Fram* (1893–1895). He sailed along the Siberian north coast and was stuck fast in the ice, expecting to be taken across the Pole itself. He did not reach further north than 86° 14′, but Nansen saw clearly a south-going drift of the ice which proved that he was right. Later on, Roald Amundsen thought that if Nansen had entered the ice further east than he did, he might have been taken

111

across the Pole itself, and he set out through Bering Strait with the *Maud,* but hit a more localized current which took him around and around—not bringing him anywhere for five years.

In 1937, the Russian explorer Papanin went by plane to the Pole and stayed on the ice until February of the following year. He had then drifted far south along the Greenland east coast, but at the same time he made many observations about the water beneath him. He found a warmer current running in the opposite direction of his own drift. Since then it has been found that on the bottom of the Arctic Ocean, which averages a depth of about 4,000 feet, a mountain ridge runs from the New Siberian Islands, across the Pole, to Greenland. It is called the Papanin Ridge, but never does it rise over the surface of the sea.

But the Poles are not the only sources of the prevailing currents. Sometimes one hears, more or less jokingly, the fear that Americans might change the Gulf Stream, thereby exposing Europeans to extreme cold which would prevail if the warm water did not flow there. This was very much discussed when the Panama Canal was planned. Originally the United States planned a sea-level canal instead of locks, so that it was thought the Gulf Stream might run out to the Pacific. One answer was that no man-made canal could take all the water of the Gulf Stream, which is almost 100 miles wide and a little more than one mile deep through the Florida Strait. As it flows with a velocity of almost three knots, it can easily be seen that it would take a canal more than 500 times the volume of the Mississippi River to absorb it. After all, the Panama Canal ended being a lock canal.

It must be noted that the speed of the Gulf Stream south of Florida results partly from the fact that it is flowing downhill. The easterly trade wind piles up the water in the Gulf of Mexico so that the level is about eight inches higher at the southwest tip of Florida than it is further out in the Atlantic. When it runs along the ocean, the water is about eighteen inches higher along the coast of Cuba than it is further out. This contradicts the old belief that the ocean is absolutely on a level. It is not.

The Currents

The general oceanic surface currents depend to a great extent on the prevailing winds, but other things must be taken into consideration. And here evaporation plays a very great part. This is easily seen, though on a smaller scale, in the Mediterranean. Just north of Algeria there is a place where it rains little, and usually is calm. Here the sun burns and as a result much water evaporates. What is left concentrates to a higher salinity, thus becoming heavier. The heavy water sinks to the bottom, but as there can be no hole in the surface of the sea, water must flow in from somewhere. The logical source is from the Strait of Gibraltar. Therefore, the current here runs from west to east. But going down to the bottom, it will be discovered that the water flows in just the opposite direction.

The same thing happens across both the Atlantic and Pacific oceans. The currents are to a great extent produced by a variation in the density of the water, which depends on varying rates of cooling, warming and evaporation. In each of the two big oceans there are two areas of maximum salinity of the surface water, one in the northern, the other in the southern tropical belt, separated by a zone of minimum salinity around the equator—then the salinity diminishes to the north. The belt of minimum salinity around the equator is caused by excessive rain and the upwelling of currents from Arctic and Antarctic waters. For instance, the East Greenland Current flows beneath the Gulf Stream only to reappear on the surface near the equator. Other currents have shown a tendency for cold water from the Poles to move toward the equator along the bottom. After having been heated, it flows back toward higher latitudes on the surface—to both sides.

The same thing which happens with the Gulf Stream can be found in the Pacific. Here it is the Japanese or Kuroshio Current which flows from the Philippines to the coast of Japan, there to be divided by the Oyashio Current, bringing cold water down. The Kuroshio runs to the east, crossing the North Pacific and, just as the Gulf Stream whirls around south in the Barents Sea, the Kuroshio does the same thing in the Gulf of Alaska. There are a couple of small islands here where a great quantity of articles can be found, originating from the Philippines and Japan, and lost or thrown overboard from ships in the vicinity.

The Kuroshio Current goes along the west coast of North America until outside California and Mexico it again joins the North Equatorial Current and runs back west, without obstacles, in the longest current known on earth—about 9,000 miles from Panama to the Philippines.

Since the main forces producing ocean currents are the prevailing winds, the trade winds produce a westbound current in each of the two big oceans, on both sides of the equator. The trade winds blow from the northeast and southeast toward the equator and this corresponds very well with the westward flowing current on both sides of the equator and an equatorial east-running countercurrent in the calm belt between them.

The North Equatorial Current in the Atlantic can be traced from the Canary Current coming down as a relatively cool current, being part of the Gulf Stream after it passes the west coast of Europe. Thus it is seen that the circuit is closed here. The currents follow a clockwise tendency, as everything does in the Northern Hemisphere. Over to the west the North Equatorial Current narrows a little, south of the Sargasso Sea.

In the Southern Hemisphere, in the Atlantic Ocean, the currents are a reflection of what happens in the north, only everything moves counterclockwise. The Benguela Current, with its cold water, moves along the African coast. It joins the South Equatorial Current flowing to the west until the eastern "hump" of the continent at Brazil splits the current in two. Lots of its water, maybe half of it, goes to the north along the coast and enters the Gulf of Mexico, thus joining the North Equatorial Current and contributing to the Gulf Stream. The other part goes south along the coast of Brazil—in fact it is called the Brazil Current—and outside of La Plata it turns east, joining the Antarctic Current, following it over to Africa and so closing this circuit.

Almost the same things happen in the Pacific. North and South Equatorial currents run from east to west. In between there is a countercurrent, yet it must be noted that it runs about fifteen degrees north of the equator itself. The North Equatorial Current does not receive contributions from the South Equatorial to the same degree as in the Atlantic. Also, other dissimilarities exist because there is no closed barrier as that which Central America offers. The Torres Strait, the Sunda Strait, and other waterways in the Pacific allow currents to pass through, but to the north and the south conditions are very similar to those in the Atlantic.

Some people refuse to recognize an Antarctic Ocean at all and one must admit that there is no border to point at. The prevailing west wind sends the current round and round. The counterclockwise current of the South Pacific joins it and the same thing happens as mentioned before.

The Indian Ocean has its peculiarities and does not follow the rules of the more disciplined oceans. The reason is that the Indian Ocean has no constant trade wind, but is governed by the more or less capricious monsoon which shifts east or west with the seasons and causes the currents to do the same. Although the Indian Ocean is much smaller than the Atlantic and Pacific, it is divided into two distinct and recognizable parts. In the southern part, the current runs counterclockwise, as would be expected in the southern hemisphere, east toward Australia, then northward where it not only sends some water to the Pacific, but also receives contributions from there. The current then runs westward until it reaches the African coast which it follows down to join the Antarctic Current again.

So we see the connection between all the seas, great and small. There is always movement, both horizontal caused by the currents, and vertical because of the difference in salinity. This is particularly so in landlocked seas such as the Baltic which receives a good deal of fresh water from rivers and has a shallow entrance, created by the Skagerrak and Kattegat. This entrance is hardly more than a sill over which salt water from the North Sea can barely pass. So the salt content of the Baltic diminishes rapidly from 2.5 per cent to 3.1 per cent in the Skaggerak at the west, to as little as 0.7 per cent east of Bornholm, and almost fresh water off Finland.

14

The Waves

Everyone has seen how, when smooth water is struck by wind, the surface immediately is covered with a ribbed pattern of transverse ripples. These ripples will be about one inch from crest to crest, and travel slowly in the direction of the wind. Most of the waves of the Seven Seas are products of just such wind pressure on water. There are other waves—so-called tidal waves which have nothing to do with the tide but are caused by volcanic eruptions or a sudden sinking of the ocean floor, and waves set in motion by glaciers pushing icebergs out to sea. But they are always irregular.

For the observer on shore, there is a big difference in the appearance of the waves, depending on whether the wind is blowing away from him or toward him. Only when they are coming in does he see them at their most majestic; if the wind is offshore he is seeing merely their birth.

Oceanographers have several terms they apply to waves. They speak of the "fetch," which is the distance a wave travels from the place it originates to where it meets its first obstacle. This may be thousands of miles. The wave's "height" is measured from the trough to the crest, and its "length" is the distance from its crest to that of the next one. When one speaks of the "period" of a wave, one means the time required for the crest to pass a point reached by the one ahead of it. The height, length and period all have a definite relation to the fetch, the power of the wind which originates the wave, to the water's depth, and to several other factors.

Up to a certain point waves grow in height according to the

strength of the wind that produces them. But when a wave becomes about one-seventh as high from trough to crest as it is from crest to the crest of the next wave, it will topple over and that is what makes a whitecap. Also if the wind reaches Force Nine on the Beaufort Scale, the top of the wave will be blown off.

These are some of the conditions which limit the size of waves in the Antarctic, for example. Here, where the westerly wind blows with terrific force, sending the waves in one direction without meeting land to disturb the strength or deflect the course, the seas, as sailors call them, are kept from rising interminably by these restraining influences.

In a severe storm the waves may grow higher after the wind has stopped and is followed by ground swells. These always are the most disagreeable to sailors, especially in sailing ships which need the pressure of the wind to steady the vessel's movements. A sailing ship with a big rig often suffers more from ground swells than from the gale. The ship cannot steer when there is no wind, and as the vessel rolls heavily from side to side, the heavy masts may be shifted by the slacking of the backstays and crack the decks or deckhouses. It has been known that the masts have been snapped in the roll.

A wave fortunately is not a moving wall of water advancing across the ocean. If it were, no ship could stand up against it, and very few coasts would be safe. The wave is an invisible force which itself moves and simply lifts the water as it passes along. Of course the movement of the water is not straight up and down. Each drop of water in the wave travels in a circular or elliptical orbit, but it ends up at almost the same place it started.

Waves can be traced halfway across the world, and sometimes they travel that far. Some of the rollers which break on the southwestern corner of England have come from Cape Horn, a fetch of more than 6,000 miles. But most of the waves of large size which we see on the shores of Europe or North America are raised in the North Atlantic storm area east of Newfoundland and south of Greenland and Iceland.

Modern ships are greatly affected by waves. Most freighters now are flat-bottomed so that they roll more readily than the sharper-keeled sailing vessels. But the amount and kind of movement is largely governed by the length of the ship. A little one which "goes on half a wave" very often acts much better in a rough sea than those which extend over a wave and a half or more. Such a little ship can keep its stability and just move up and down like a gull floating on the surface of the water. I have crossed the Atlantic many times in small craft in all kinds of weather when not a drop was splashed on deck and the sailors could walk along in slippers, even in high seas.

Measuring the height of a wave is easiest from such a small ship, too. She settles down into the trough, and if a sailor has taken a post high up on the mast, he can wait for the moment when he can just see over the crest of one wave to the crest of the next one as the ship reaches the lowest point. This, to be sure, is a rather primitive method of measurement, but it gives a good understanding of how high the waves are. Many observations have put the average height of waves during a hurricane in the ocean at around seventy feet.

No sailing ship can hold its course in such a storm. They must heave to, which means that staysails aft keep the fore part of the ship against the wind, and she just drifts. This requires ample space to avoid drifting ashore. When a sailing ship is hove to, everything is fine. The battle with the sails is over. The wheel most of the time is lashed, with only one man to stand watch, while as long as the ship battled the wind, two men were required to manage it. The heavy waves roll in under the ship, disappearing aft, and the movement is quite gentle.

Even the biggest modern ships must surrender to the waves once in a while and heave to. They turn their sterns up against the wind and waves, letting the propellor run slowly backwards so that the ship is kept up against the waves.

In the open sea, when the wind reaches and maintains a velocity of seventy-five miles an hour and upwards, which is hurricane proportions, the waves may roll with surprising regularity and impressive height. There is, of course, a simple relationship between the height of the wave and the velocity of the wind. One can figure, on an average, a height of eight feet for each ten miles per hour that the wind blows.

Ships will be affected variously according to their own length. A modern passenger liner, which stretches across two or three or even more waves, will not be affected at all so long as she runs directly across them. But if they strike her at an angle, it will be different. The ship, supported by its updrift in the water, suddenly loses its support on one side, falling sideways, only to be pushed up by the crest while the other side loses support to throw the ship in the opposite direction.

Ships not small enough to ride "half a wave," but too small to straddle several, may be in more difficulty. Several destroyers out on maneuvers once were running with great speed when they hit high seas. The destroyers measured about a wave and a half. Suddenly one of them broke in two, disappearing in a matter of seconds. Some thought that at one moment the hull was supported only in the middle by a wave while both ends were in the air. Built primarily for speed, the destroyer was unable to stand this unexpected strain. Others in the squadron supposed that at the moment of the disaster bow and stern had been supported by waves, leaving the middle in the air and causing the break. In either case, it was the length of the ship which was fatal.

The speed of the waves varies with a great many factors—for instance, if the wind is coming in squalls, the regularity of the waves will be disturbed—but they have been measured as moving ahead at about forty-seven miles an hour when the wind was fifty-two miles an hour.

As the waves roll along out of the stormy area which produced them, the height diminishes and the distance between the crests increases. Little by little they settle to a swell, moving ahead at an average speed of about fifteen miles an hour. To a sailor this swell when met at sea indicates the forerunner of a gale or that stormy weather has prevailed and is now abating.

Quite often the swells interfere with newer waves and the water is stirred into confusing patterns as it is agitated by two different wave systems. But a little experience enables the mariner to distinguish between the direction of the swell and that of the waves.

Modern observations have enabled men to tell where waves come from. The Antarctic Ocean, for example, sends its waves or swells far up in the Atlantic, Pacific and Indian oceans. Sometimes they can be followed beyond California, even up to Alaska.

Reports of waves 100 feet high have on occasion met with some skepticism. But they are by no means impossible. In fact, an even higher wave has been measured. Rachel Carson tells in her book, *The Sea Around Us,* of an accurate observation made in the Pacific on board the USS *Ramapo* which sailed from Manila to San Diego in February, 1933. She encountered stormy weather for seven days. Meteorological disturbances were reported all the way from Kamchatka across the Pacific, and over the continent to New York.

As a result, the fetch of the waves was several thousand miles. The *Ramapo* was running before the wind and with the sea. On February 6, a wind of sixty-eight knots was measured. One of the officers, standing on the bridge, saw a great sea rising astern at a level above an iron strap on the crow's nest of the mainmast. The *Ramapo* was in the trough of the sea on an even keel, so it was readily possible to calculate from the height of the bridge above the sea, the height above the deck of the officer's eyes, and the height of the iron strap, that the crest of the wave was 112 feet above its trough. This, so far as I know, is the greatest height of a wave ever measured with accuracy.

A good ship with able seamen never fears strong winds and heavy seas out at sea, but near shore it is different. The waves which can be resisted so merrily in the open ocean may smash a ship to pieces against the shore. The destructiveness of the water hurled in a breaking surf is beyond measurement. Stones hurled up through lighthouse windows 100 to 300 feet above the sea are proof of this. Huge concrete structures, stone breakwaters, can be smashed like children's toys.

The father of the great author, Robert Louis Stevenson, was per-

Lighthouse in the North Atlantic.

haps the first man to come close to measuring scientifically the force of a wave. With an instrument he developed himself, he reported that the force might be as much as 6,000 pounds to the square inch. Since then, this has proved to be an underestimate. Along many coasts, waves have shown their contempt for the strongest of man's works. At Wick on the east coast of Scotland a new pier weighing 2,600 tons was carried away.

At sea, rails of solid iron bars firmly secured on board ship have been twisted and bent like yarn by the force of water dashed onto the deck. Yet this force is less than that of the wave breaking on the shore. The famous old Eddystone Lighthouse, built in 1840, was supposed to be damaged by supernatural forces because the iron door to the tower, fastened with bolts, was broken open from within.

Little insignificant sand bars stand for centuries against the rolling waves, while acres and acres of land are removed at another place. For instance, Cape Cod loses more and more of its outer shore every year to the waves, and I have seen it estimated that in 8,000 years the Cape will disappear unless something happens to build up what is now being destroyed.

People living on a coast where waves roar incessantly never hear them unless they stop. This happened in April, 1946, on the beaches of Hawaii, where suddenly the eternal voice of the breakers was silent. This was the first warning of an earthquake off the island of Unimak in the Aleutians, 2,300 miles away. The sound stopped because the water ran out to sea, exposing the bottom for some distance, but soon a terrific rise rolled the ocean almost thirty feet above the normal levels of the tide, swept houses out to sea, and drowned many of their inhabitants.

The most surprising thing was that ships between the Aleutians and Hawaii noticed nothing unusual in the open sea. The waves created by the quake were only a couple of feet high and there was more than eighty-five miles between crests—the rules about proportion for wind waves do not apply—but they moved with such speed that they reached Hawaii in five hours, so they traveled at an average of 470 miles an hour. This is quite a difference from the fifteen miles an hour of an ordinary ground swell. These earthquake waves hit Valpariaso, Chile, in eighteen hours, a distance of 8,050 miles.

There is only one thing that conquers waves and that is ice. This often has been an escape from storms for sailors in the Arctic and Antarctic. Close to pack ice, the backwash of the sea can be most annoying, but as soon as the edge of the drift ice is reached, the crest of the waves is gone. The further the ship comes into the pack, the easier it is, until after a few miles the water between floes is as smooth as a little lake even though the wind may still be whistling in the rigging.

"Seascape" by P. von Kalckreuth.

"March—North Atlantic" by Frederick Waugh.

The challenge of putting on canvas the flow and movement of the waves, never the same in calm or storm, has always fascinated artists.

The square-rigged bark *Carradale*.

Part IV

Ships of the Sea

Eskimo kayaks.

15

The Pioneers

Just what sort of boats were used by the first people who ventured out to sea, as against those sailors who floated down rivers or made their way along protected coasts or fished in lagoons and lakes, has been a matter of much speculation. The outriggers of the South Seas, the skin boats of the Eskimos, the rafts of the American Indians are all types which these pioneers may have used.

It seems certain that men were making long voyages by sea many centuries before they ever could go more than a few miles by land. The ocean was a more friendly highway between one place and another than could be found through the rocks and forests and hills around the villages of primitive men.

The world has known so many types of boats that one has replaced another very quickly and the older ones are often forgotten. This was the case with the balsa raft, recently recalled to the memory of man by the Norwegian ethnologist and explorer, Thor Heyerdahl, who while studying old graves in the desert of Peru found the solution to an ancient riddle.

In these graves, even the very old ones, were long, narrow wooden plaques with an indentation for a handle in one end. They all were cut with great care from bone-hard wood, often the heavy algarroba tree, which must have been a strenuous job in days when no tools of iron or other hard metal were known. Many theories have been put forward at the museums which exhibit these boards. Sometimes the label reads, "symbols of rank probably used in processions." However, these mysterious objects always were found along with implements which concerned the sea, such as long oars, and were ornamented with obviously marine symbols.

Dr. Heyerdahl has proved, not only from the findings in the graves and in literature, but also from old drawings and his own experience, that these boards were neither oars nor rudders but centerboards used to navigate the large seagoing rafts of the Indians. This is also sure proof that the rafts had sails, since a centerboard naturally is useless on a craft without sails. So we learn that the sail was used on the coast of Peru a long time before the Incas were there, because the old graves all are pre-Inca.

In 1526, some Spanish explorers off Ecuador saw and took captive a Peruvian balsa raft with sails. This was before any Spaniards had seen Peru itself or knew about the Incas. In his report to the King of Spain, the master writes that "the raft had masts and rigging of very fine wood and well made, with cotton sails of the same design and type as our own ships." The raft carried a crew of twenty Indians and a cargo of more than thirty tons.

Other Spanish writers mention these sailing rafts as not much behind their own caravels in maneuverability. They wrote of rafts used to transport troops, for exploration, fishing and freighting trade goods. Often women were on board during long voyages along the coast. Some of the drawings made by these Spaniards show the long boards, but without any explanation. Furthermore, in these drawings there is no rudder or steering oar. But some of the Indians seem to be sitting in a position to manipulate the centerboards or "guaras" as they were called.

Dr. Heyerdahl has discovered the principle by which the raft could be managed, and it works just as well in tacking or beating to windward as any keel. The guaras, three or four yards long and a foot and a half wide, were placed vertically between the main timbers of the raft both fore and aft. By pushing some of the guaras deep into the water and lifting others up, the crew could go before the wind, luff up, tack, fall off and do all the common maneuvers of a sailing ship with keel and rudder. This invention then was unknown to most nations in Europe, but the Indians had mastered it.

Captain Thor Heyerdahl's *Kon-Tiki*.

When Dr. Heyerdahl planned his *Kon-Tiki* Expedition (see Chapter 22) in 1947, to prove that balsa rafts were capable of carrying people from Peru to Polynesia, he built a true replica of these Indian craft. Consequently he provided guaras fore and aft. But neither scientists nor sailors were familiar with guaras nor had much confidence in their value.

At first the sailors thought that the five guaras of the *Kon-Tiki* would only lessen deviation somewhat; that is, help steer the raft straight forward. They put the guaras in as deep as possible and fastened them securely. In this position they functioned effectively as a keel, so the raft could be sailed almost 90 degrees from the wind. More than that they could not do because the sail would fill from ahead and drive them backwards. The guaras also assured an even course when the wind was directly astern. Then the *Kon-Tiki* ran into a gale which loosened the guaras so that the raft drifted at the mercy of wind and current until it stranded in Polynesia.

While the guaras still were in place, but loose, it was discovered that no steering oar was needed. The raft could be steered and the course changed with the guaras alone.

Later, Dr. Heyerdahl studied old Peruvian and Ecuadorian documents more closely and found several old reports that balsa rafts had been seen sailing into the wind out at sea. He decided that perhaps he did not understand the old sailing technique. After consultation with other authorities, he built a new balsa raft on the exact principle of the *Kon-Tiki* but smaller. With that he put to sea and rediscovered the old Indian method.

The secret was that the Indians had established a system of balance, with the mast and sail as a fixed point, controlled by the pressure of the wind. One arm of the balance's lever was the raft itself astern of the mast; the other was the raft before the mast. If the guaras ahead of the mast were stronger, the stern followed the wind. If the guaras astern of the mast were stronger, the front part of the raft would follow the wind. The guaras nearest to the mast had less effect because of the proportion between the lever and the pressure.

These keen sailors on the new expedition soon learned just how high or low each guara should be for the desired effect. They could take the raft right up to the wind so the sail was dead or go to either side of the wind. They learned something, too, which might be useful to us in the twentieth century. For instance, by placing guaras or a similar device on the usual life rafts carried by ocean liners, we could make them fit for handling on the sea. The people on board them would not be entirely dependent upon being found by rescuers.

Thor Heyerdahl has become rather an enthusiast of the raft, and not only because of his own great success in the *Kon-Tiki*. He is a serious, conscientious scientist, and he contends that the Indians might have known regular boats in the pre-Inca civilization. But they abandoned them because rafts, being self-bailing, had many advantages. A boat could fill with water from a single wave and sink or have the cargo spoiled. All the water a raft can ship would run off by itself, and if the cargo is packed in water-resistant packages it will not be damaged. Since the raft sails as well as any boat then known, it was as easy to maneuver.

This advantage may have been the origin of the straw boats found in Polynesia and South America. Some places, of course, lacked suitable wood, too. But in any case, several places in the Pacific have boats, often quite large and shaped like ordinary ships, made of braided hollow grass. Their advantage is that any water coming from above will run out by itself. Of course, a boat of straw never can carry as big a load as a balsa raft.

Observing these wonderful rafts of South America, one realizes what a debt the builders owed to the balsa tree which provides such an extremely light but strong wood, unlike any other. Without this it would have been impossible to build and manage such big rafts for long voyages. This becomes clear if we compare them with the large, clumsy rafts one sees, for instance, on the Lena River in Siberia.

The rafts on this, the fourth biggest river of the world, are built on the ice. Dwellers in the "taiga," the immense Siberian spruce forest, spend the winter cutting down trees and bringing the logs down to the ice on the river. Here huge rafts are built to float down to the lumber market, the logs tied together in quite an ingenious way, and with houses, even having stone fireplaces, on the deck. Often two rafts are joined together, and each may be as much as 100 yards long.

When the ice melts, the rafts are afloat, but the steering is difficult and at times impossible. Their crews explain that strong winds which often blow up in the Siberian lowlands can push the raft aground on one bank or the other, while sand bars are always a hazard. These rafts have two steering oars aft, each handled by four men. Often, when an unexpected obstacle is sighted ahead, everyone on board works at the oars, or they put out in small boats, towing and tugging to change the course of the unwieldy craft. It takes three or four months to bring the rafts down the river. Looking at these, one

An outrigger.

must admit that the elegant balsa rafts of the Indians bear off the prize for both beauty and maneuverability.

On the other side of the Pacific from Peru, the South Sea Islanders developed a very clever safe means of travel by water. They were the people who invented the outrigger, a device which keeps their canoes virtually unsinkable and uncapsizable. Some of these could hold as many as forty or fifty people and a fair amount of cargo.

The outrigger was an excellent boat for travel between the islands, and it is believed that very great migrations were carried out in prehistoric times in these craft. When the canoe was made with a double hull it was particularly seaworthy and roomy. The hulls were simply hollowed out of great logs, sometimes with the sterns curved up quite high and crudely carved. The outrigger was a smaller log with several stout sticks to hold it firmly to the hull. Sometimes there was a sort of platform built upon these sticks between hull and outrigger. The canoe was kept on her course or manipulated by a steering oar, and the crew used short paddles.

Until one has tried to paddle an outrigger oneself, it is hard to realize how much skill it takes to overcome the tendency of the outrigger to act as a pivot on which the whole craft revolves so that it simply drifts around in a circle. It looks easy as the islanders come dashing out to meet a ship, but the quick twist of each stroke is hard to learn. Outriggers are drawn up on the beach when the crew lands, like the galleys of ancient Greece. The steersman holds the canoe off until he sees an especially large wave coming; then the paddlers race in on top of this wave to drive their craft far up on the beach.

Courtesy of the Mariners Museum, Newport News, Virginia

16

Civilization and Navigation

It cannot be considered an accident that the early civilizations which we admire all developed in and around seaports. In those days it was from their voyages, mostly for trade, that men learned about the rest of the world. Knowledge, new ideas, and better implements with which to work came to many peoples across the sea.

The Greeks and the Phoenicians carried the culture of their Mediterranean world to others. The Vikings, who got their education on the sea and learned to sail ships as no one before them ever had, brought back to their own country the civilization of more highly developed nations. Only when they forgot their origins in the sea did they lose their power and their influence. Only as they kept their skills as shipbuilders and navigators did their descendants continue to progress.

Yet it is true that the sailors who were so important in improving the lives of nearly all other people did not carry away the lion's share of the benefits. For life at sea was hard and, although writers from the land often speak of the seamen as extremely brave fellows who were pursued by adventure wherever they went, it was mostly a very dull life too.

From the time ships sailed out on the open ocean to be gone for many days, even many months without contact with the land, the conditions for most sailors were miserable. It must be admitted that their homes were none too pleasant either. The difference between the small dark dwellings in which most common seamen lived ashore and the forecastle of a ship was not great. The food of their families,

Piraeus, Old Port of Athens.

at least in northern countries, was not much better than the ships carried—salt beef or pork most of the time if they had meat at all, and moldy flour infested with parasites for a great part of the year. Drinking water in the small ports was never very good and hygiene was definitely very bad. All this was true even as recently as a century and a half ago.

Of life at sea in sailing ships many of the greatest authors in the world have written. From them we know what it was like to be on a clean and happy ship, on a dirty and slovenly ship. They have told us how it was when the captain, the most authoritative of all dictators when he so desires, was a greedy man or a cruel man or a wise and thoughtful man. This is all a proud part of the literature of every nation which has sent ships across the seas. So there is no need to tell these stories here.

But the ships that sailed the Seven Seas had a civilization of their own. It was a way of life for officers and men, and it was like nothing they could have experienced on shore. The great thing about the routine of shipboard was that every man had his place and his work, knew from whom he took his orders, and at the same time could have a very good understanding of just how important he was in the little world which was bounded by the rail of his ship. For every man was important.

No matter how much ships changed, this fact remained. When the nimble fellows who climbed the rigging of the old sailing ships were replaced by stokers sweating and straining far below the deck, the rules of life at sea were just the same. And today when it is possible to run a ship's engines very well just by pulling switches and turning handles, the essential civilization of shipboard is what it always was.

But in the development of this civilization, there has been one factor as important as the progress of the shipbuilders. That is the advance of navigation, and its history is as full of noteworthy discoveries and inventions as that of any realm of knowledge. Nowadays, of course, navigation is an exact science, but through most of time it was not so accurate. In fact, dictionaries call it an art rather than a science, the art of locating a ship's position and directing its course from one place to another.

The first navigators steered by the stars whenever they were out of sight of a familiar point of land. The only exception we know about were the sailors who went back and forth on the Indian Ocean. They could use the monsoons to tell their direction. It is difficult to say whether one should marvel more at the courage of men who would undertake to find their way to a distant port with no more help than this or at the skill with which they did it. No wonder that there were few captains who wanted to get very far from the coast.

The first important instrument to help sailors find their way across the ocean was the compass. This is supposed to have been invented by the Chinese, and Arab trading ship captains seem to have borrowed it from them some time before the thirteenth century. Europeans learned about it during the Crusades, and the modern

Sixteenth-century navigator using compass, a magnetized needle
on a straw floating in a bowl of water.

skipper of that day had his needle, magnetized by rubbing it on a
loadstone, floating on a straw in a bowl of water and pointing miracu-
lously north.

It is supposed that the astrolabe, an instrument which can measure the altitude of the sun, was learned from the same source at
about the same time, but it did not come into general use until much
later, after the discovery of America. However, some unknown
genius invented what was called a cross-staff, by means of which the
navigator could calculate the distance between the moon and a fixed
star and thereby get some rough idea of his position.

In 1530, an ingenious scholar named Frisius of Louvain hit on
the trick of using a watch to supplement observations obtained by the
instruments of the day and a quadrant, which is an arc to measure
angles.

These were the instruments which most captains used up to the
American War of Independence. They were good enough for them
to know their latitude fairly well, but the longitude could not be

fixed as accurately. It was done at all only by estimating the run and course of the ship. Since the speed of the vessel could not be measured exactly, and the course of a sailing ship was seldom on a straight line, the best of skippers was likely to be rather far off after a while in figuring longitude. The rough method they used was called "dead reckoning." Meanwhile the introduction of the use of trigonometry and logarithms to the art of navigation made every captain something of a mathematician. This happened early in the seventeenth century, and it was more than a hundred years before two notable inventions enabled the mariner to be sure of his position on the ocean.

The first of these was the sextant, an improved instrument for measuring the altitude of sun, moon or stars and the angles at the same time, which came into use in 1731. Only four years later came the chronometer. The sextant, which gave rise to the expression "shooting the sun" when the navigator was determining its altitude, provided a far more efficient method of figuring latitude. The chronometer, which is an adaptation of Frisius' watch, is suspended so that it stays horizontal no matter what the movements of the ship. With this, the calculation of longitude, or the distance east or west of Greenwich, England, was sufficiently exact that a competent navigator could determine where he was within a couple of miles, or even closer if several observations could be made and checked against each other. Of course, navigators are very much like other people and are slow to accept new ways. But by about 1775, virtually every ship that sailed the Seven Seas, from a European or American port anyway, had a chronometer and kept Greenwich Mean Time always. One help in getting the new wrinkles in navigation adopted was publication of all the necessary trigonometric tables and textbooks which made the mathematics of locating the ship's position relatively easy. The *Nautical Almanac*, for example, began publication with these tables in 1767.

Along with the improvement in instruments came better charts and sailing directions. For a long time the best charts were those based on a map of the world drawn by Gerardus Mercator (his real name was Gerhard Kremer) in 1569. The famous Mercator Projection enabled him to transfer the globe to a flat surface on which a ship's captain could chart his compass course in straight lines. The very great exaggerations his method required when he got near the North and South Poles were not troublesome to the navigators because they were not going there anyway.

Once the mariner knew where he was, the next important item was to find out what obstacles were in the vicinity—rocks and reefs, shoals and shallows. The slow gathering of knowledge about these and the plotting of their location on charts went on through all the centuries of sailing. Early charts included such dangers as sea monsters and devils and huge, nonexistent whirlpools, but eventually sailors saved their fantastic tales for other subjects, and the charts became as factual as a table of logarithms.

Navigating so as to take advantage of winds and currents, although practiced on a hit-and-miss basis for centuries, became scientifically exact about 100 years ago through the researches of a United States naval officer, Matthew F. Maury. The first modern textbook on oceanography was his *Physical Geography of the Sea.* Earlier he had achieved fame when he issued sailing directions based on wind and current charts which, he predicted, would cut as much as ten to fifteen days from the average sailing time between New York and Rio de Janeiro. This was in 1851, and he was proved right. On the basis of his work an international conference in 1853 adopted a uniform system of recording data in this field.

It was even later that the first international "rules of the road" were adopted at sea. This was done at a conference of all the maritime powers at Washington in 1889. They have been revised from time to time at other conferences, and they are modified in territorial waters by local conditions and laws. The purpose, of course, was to prevent collisions at sea; while they cannot be said to have been entirely effective, they certainly have reduced the great loss of life which was almost commonplace in earlier years.

In our own times, many more aids to navigation have been invented—the radio by which ships talk to each other and the shore, automatic pilots, electronic beacons to keep a vessel on her course. The bridge of a modern ship looks more like a scientific laboratory than the simply furnished, austere centers of command which were paced by so many heroes of fact and fiction. But it is not demonstrated that, for all the extra safety and convenience of the modern instruments, the skipper of today can find his way from port to port any more accurately than his predecessor in the days when sail was the only power for a ship and the captain's knowledge of the art of navigation her only assurance that she was on her proper course.

From *The Sea, Its History and Romance* by Frank C. Bowen. Halton & Truscott Smith, Publishers.

Gerardus Mercator.

17

Manpower

When Europeans think of manpower to send a ship through the water, they are likely to have in mind the galleys of the ancient world or the medieval warships. But there are many other forms of oared vessels which were more important to the people who used them.

Up until four hundred years ago, even the most civilized countries used oared ships for fighting because, until the invention of the steam engine, oars were the most reliable way of getting a vessel in any direction one wanted. And of course in those days nobody fought in very rough weather.

The classic manpower ships were the Greek biremes and triremes, two or three banks of oars on a side. The Greeks talked of larger figures, but when they referred to the number five or six they seem to have meant the number of men to an oar rather than the number of banks of oars. From the earliest times, the galleys had sails, but they were only for auxiliary use when the wind was just right. Later on, the Mediterranean galleys were manned by slaves—the Turks and Arabs used Christian slaves when they could catch them; the Christian countries also used Moorish slaves but more often convicts. In fact they kept the galleys in France just to serve as convict ships long after there was any real employment for them.

But manpower in ships is seen at its best when it is the main and even the only form of sea transportation a people has. These are the outrigger canoes of the South Seas, the great bargelike craft of some Eastern potentates, the canoes of the American Indians—although these last two were not very often ventured at sea. But in many ways the prize for efficiency and ingenuity must go to the Eskimo skin boats.

Nobody knows exactly where the Eskimos came from or when they first reached the Arctic coasts. But they must have lived further south at one time. They are great people for continuing their old traditions, and their stories are handed down unchanged from generation to generation, which makes it possible to understand some things about them that would be a puzzle otherwise. They tell stories of such animals as snakes and frogs and other creatures which certainly do not exist where the Eskimos live now. So it is presumed that they were pushed north by somebody, probably the Indians with whom, it is known, they had terrible fights in former days.

But no Indian could follow the Eskimos north of the forests for long. An Indian needs wood for his house, bark for his canoe and toboggan. The Eskimo taught himself to build his house of snow and cover his vessel with skins of animals. He also was able to roll skins together and let them freeze in the shape of sledge runners, using frozen salmon or pieces of meat for crossbars. Thus he was entirely independent of the forest itself; the big ocean and the rivers always would bring sufficient driftwood to his beach for his harpoons and the rigid parts of his boat.

The Eskimo kayak is famous and so has been the skin boat in which these people master heavy waves, transporting big loads. The skin boat—or "oomiak" as it is called—has been known wherever Eskimos live. Nowadays, in some places—Greenland, for instance—they substitute wooden boats and motor craft, mostly because sealskins are not to be had as readily as they once were. Yet in Alaska, where the oomiak is in some ways more highly developed than elsewhere, they still make them covered with walrus hides split in two by the clever women. Such a walrus hide is resistant to wear, and you see oomiaks now proudly bringing the hunters out to sea and the game home to the camp, driven by outboard motors.

A most important feature of these skin boats is, of course, the sewing, as the seams are the most vulnerable part of the boat. There is a difference between east and west and different tribes. Some are content with one seam while others overlap the two edges of the skins as is done by modern sailmakers in the civilized world.

The same thing is true of the covering for kayaks. In Greenland and formerly in Baffinland—in fact among all eastern Eskimos—the skins of the big bearded seal were used much more than walrus hides to cover both oomiak and kayak. This again made it essential to renew the cover at least every other year, and where the kayak was used each day, a new cover was needed every spring. Many hunters have lost their lives from being too economical and hoping that the old cover would last still longer.

An oomiak is built on a framework of wood. This can be many different small pieces except for the bottom timber which must be one piece so the ribs can be fastened to it. Not a single nail is used in an oomiak. For one thing, the original Eskimos never had any nails. Secondly, after they did have such things, they avoided them lest they rust and rot the skins. Therefore, every bit is carefully tied together with sealskin thongs—very carefully indeed, as a single binding too loose or too tight would cause the frame to bend and render the vessel impossible to steer. Around the gunwale runs a bar to which the ribs are fastened; the skin covering the entire boat is sewn and attached to this bar with thick, strong sealskin thongs.

On the bottom, several boards are placed crosswise so nobody will step on the skin and put his foot through it. The rowers sit on thwarts which very often are narrow boards, sometimes only thick sticks if nothing else is available. Each time the rowers take a stroke they rise up from their seats and sit down again, as did the oarsmen in an ancient galley. The oars are usually very short with very broad blades, and the steering is done in the stern by a man sitting with a special steering oar always fastened on the starboard tide. When the sun shines back of such an oomiak, it looks very beautiful because you can see the rowers through the transparent skin.

In Greenland oomiaks always were called "women's boats" because no man with a bit of dignity would ever touch an oar in an oomiak. The owner steered, but otherwise a man could only be a passenger and the women did the work.

143

In early days when all traveling along the coast was done in oomiaks, a couple of kayaks always accompanied the bigger ones. Not only was that the only way for men to travel but during the day they hunted seals or birds with their spears. Also it was essential to have the kayaks along when the boats were passing promontories and came out in a rough sea. Then the kayaks rowed up and placed themselves to windward of the oomiak, taking the spray from the waves which otherwise would fill the skin boat. Swells did not bother the oomiak, which was buoyant as a bird on the water.

Those were beautiful days. No matter how fast one travels now, by motorboats or in planes, never will such days return as when skin boats passed up and down the coast. The girls sang as they rowed out of or in to stopping places, and most of the day they kept up their laughing and singing while they plunged their short, jabbing oars into the water with quick strokes.

Each one had needles in her topknot and sinew was always handy to repair any little slit in the skins. A piece of blubber, of course, was carried to smear and tighten the mend. When, in the evening, they arrived at a place where the grass was green and soft near the beach, the whole party went on shore; the boat was hauled up and turned upside down to form a wonderful shelter under which to sleep or shelter them from bad weather. At the same time, of course, the skin dried. Driftwood, always found along the beach, fed a bonfire over which to cook seals or birds caught during the day. The girls were always gay and happy; when one saw them dancing and playing at the camp, nobody would think that they sometimes had put in thirteen to fourteen hours rowing during the day.

Kayaks reached their highest development in East Greenland. The Eskimos here are not good sledge drivers but they certainly know how to handle their kayaks and two-bladed oars. The tipping-over, which tourists enjoy watching, has developed to a sport with tricks that impress the onlookers, but the art of turning upside down in a kayak is not so difficult as it looks. The vessel, of course, must be adjusted to the man himself, and as the owner and builder are one and the same person, he understands his own requirements.

The first thing is that the kayak must be absolutely straight lest it turn to one side or another while rowing. Around the cockpit the hem of his coat is tied watertight. Also around his wrists and his face the hairless sealskin coat is sewn very carefully and fits so well that no water can come in. Here the round, heavy face of the Eskimo, with his apple cheeks and no beard, is a great help. Short chin whiskers will allow water to penetrate. The first thing a man does, when he goes out in a kayak, is to put his arms and face in the water so that the skin of the coat is not too dry, which would allow water to seep in.

A kayak man learns to tip over not for sport but for safety in rough weather. He sits very low in the kayak, not more than a couple of inches above the surface of the sea, and if a big wave breaks over him, it will fracture his spine. So he must turn over at the right moment and take the break of the wave on the keel. Now it may be said that an Eskimo should stay on shore when bad weather is coming, but the fact is that at certain places it is much easier to come close to the seals in a high sea than in smooth water.

The types of kayak are different in different places, but East and West Greenland people have closed kayaks with a short paddle and light hunting gear. Only in North Greenland—that is among the polar Eskimos—is the open kayak used and the bottom is never sharp-keeled as is the case in the south. The reason for this is that kayaks up here are used for walrus hunting. As the harpoons and spears here are heavy and clumsy compared with the southern models, the hunter has to row close up to the walrus when putting his harpoon in the animal. Now the walrus is a huge, powerful beast and is very fast in the water. The moment a walrus is struck, he will always rise up in the water and try to avenge the pain with his terrible tusks, and many times he will manage to hit the end of the kayak. In a closed kayak the hunter would have to wriggle and struggle to get out. In the open kayak, a push with his hands will free him and the walrus will continue to fight the kayak; the hunter hopes to be picked up by his fellows.

The walrus hunter makes his kayak rounded and flat on the bottom so it is easy to turn. When he comes close to the walrus, his very last stroke before he hurls his harpoon turns the kayak away so he can paddle off fast. The harpoon point is attached by a line to a bladder placed on deck behind the hunter. The walrus, when diving down in the water, drags the bladder off the kayak. The buoyant poke prevents him from getting away or diving deep down. When the walrus comes up for breath, the hunter and his fellows swarm around, spearing him but always trying to keep out of range of his tusks.

Those kayaks are broader than the models in South Greenland. They are rowed with a much longer oar. As it would be too heavy for the man to lift all the time, he works it by placing it across a wooden rest a little like the horn on a western saddle, which is just in front of him, a most ingenious way of taking the load away from himself.

A kayak or an oomiak must be taken on shore as often as possible and treated with oil to keep from cracking. High scaffolds built of stone hold the skin boats aloft, away from the dogs.

In the south of Greenland and Labrador, where little or no winter ice forms to prevent the Eskimos from kayak-hunting the whole year round—or most of it—they usually stay at the same place all year. If they move, it will always be because certain animals show up at other places. A typical summer home for people with skin boats will be a low point of land jutting out in the sea, where the boats can easily be pulled up on shore every night. This gives the hunter a working field on three sides, while, if he stays in the head of a fjord, he only faces the sea in one direction.

The big danger for both kayaks and oomiaks is fresh-water ice. Ocean water in the Arctic always will be at its freezing point, which is lower than that of fresh water, so if it rains during the summer on a smooth surface where no waves mix the rain with the salt water, the downpour freezes instantly and forms extended sheets of thin but extremely sharp fresh-water ice. A kayak man very often cannot see the ice because of dark rain clouds, so he may row into it unaware of the danger until he feels water streaming into his kayak. No Eskimo can swim well, and very often when his kayak is pierced he

Eskimo hunter.

knows his fate is to drown. In our days, the baptized Greenland Eskimos are afraid of not being buried in a Christian graveyard. Such a fatalistic man immediately ties himself to the kayak with the hunting bladder so that his body will be found.

This known peril of fresh-water ice has been used on some occasions to cover up murder. Since modern times forbid private revenge with harpoon or spear, men have been known to cut the kayak skin of a fellow hunter with a knife. The murderer is safe, as it can never be seen whether the damage has been done by the ice or a knife.

The Eskimos, though bravely fighting nature when necessary, are always cautious when traveling along the coast. Time and again it has annoyed passengers that an oomiak follows every little bend in the coast, never crossing from one point to another. One reason may be that they do not want to miss something which may have drifted on shore. But often they will carry the oomiak and kayak across narrow stretches of land, the deep fjords in Greenland rather often being but short distances apart. It goes without saying that a narrow kayak is not able to carry much more weight than the hunter himself, but if some sticks or oars are placed across two or three kayaks together, quite a heavy load can be carried.

A man with his kayak on his head is not an unusual sight, for the light weight of the boat makes it easy. He usually is going to a lake for fish or birds. At one time swans were numerous in Greenland. When they were molting and could not fly, the natives carried kayaks to the lakes and hunted them, eventually to extinction.

To be a good kayak hunter, one must start very early, and a father makes small kayaks for his boys when they are four or five years old. He then goes out with the boys fastened to his own kayak so that it cannot tip over, and teaches the little hunters all the tricks. In our days, kayak rowing and tipping is taught in many of the schools.

Now that seals are getting scarce in southern Greenland, mostly because of the change in water temperature, kayak skins are hard to come by. But as the kayak is still a most practical craft for many fishermen, it has been found that the frame can be covered with canvas instead of skin. The canvas must be prepared and painted to keep it watertight.

Moving from Greenland westward, the kayaks get more and more clumsy. In many parts of the Eskimo world they are entirely abandoned, in other places only rarely used by the most industrious. But they are known, and the hunters still are very clever at building a kayak with very little wood. Ribs of walrus, caribou horns, and other available materials are often shaped and lashed together in an amazing way.

In Alaska is found the two-man kayak, one cockpit in front of the other. They are rowed with the one-bladed oar, and are so large that people can crawl down and sleep inside them. The coat which the man wears resembles, more or less, a woman's long dress, the hem of which is fastened around the cockpit. When the man wants to tip over, he crawls down in the bottom of the kayak, head and all, and only his oar sticks out so he can bring the whole craft on keel again. When the kayak is upright, the man crawls out and, by lifting the folds of his coat, bails out the water and goes on. These craft are very little used nowadays and are not very handy, although the two-man kayaks are regarded by some scientists as the forerunner of the one-man type.

For the work it is to do, a well-made kayak is the most exquisite product of the boatman's art. Its only rival in this respect in the history of oared vessels was the galley of cedar planks, caulked with bitumen, which was invented by the Phoenicians and used by the Greeks in the days of their greatest glory. Of course there was an auxiliary sail on such a ship, but the square of brightly colored linen, or even silk, often was more decorative than useful except in taking advantage of the pleasant breezes of the Mediterranean. For all the clever craftsmanship of its builders, the bireme or trireme had to depend more upon men's muscles than their skill to propel the vessel to its destination. That was not good enough for later generations of sailors, nor practical for voyages on the open ocean.

Official Mystic Seaport Photograph by Louis S. Martel

18

Wind Driven

Every student of ships and the sea has noticed how the development of different types of vessels took place according to the country of origin; its need of a new ship for a new use. It has been repeated time and again that sailing vessels evolved through the centuries from a floating log to a bundle of reeds or raft to the hollowing out of the log to make a crude boat. Nobody knows exactly when it was found that the wind, which meets no obstacles over water as it does on land, could be used to give more speed with less work.

The fact is that sailing vessels, which ruled the Seven Seas for most of the history we know, were perfected slowly over the years. They reached their finest in the last of them, and one type almost forgotten after its short period of existence were the opium clippers. These beautiful little ships with wonderful lines sailed so fast they managed to play a very important political role in opening trade between China and the outside world.

The opium clippers have their special history, and Basil Lubbock has written a book about this short but brilliant chapter of sailing ships. Furthermore, the Marine Historical Association in Mystic, Connecticut, has published a series of letters written by one of the most daring of the opium captains which give us an inside story of the trade. The American and European smugglers hardly played a commendable part in the expansion of commerce. The letters show how they entirely disregarded the moral aspects of their trade. They took terrible chances simply to earn great sums of money, not only for the big firms on shore which owned their ships but for themselves and their crews, who actually risked their lives.

150

Wind Driven

The Portuguese with their own trading port at Macao brought the first opium to China, and a Cantonese merchant began importing it from India in 1760. Used at first as a medicine, abuses developed, of course, so that by 1800, the Chinese Imperial Government forbade importation. Meanwhile, the British East India Company had discovered this profitable trade in 1780, buying 2,800 chests in Bombay from the local government the first year. The Company technically obeyed the prohibition order; that is, it allowed Indian merchants to take over the trade and rented ships to these smugglers.

In India the sale of opium was a government monopoly, and by 1826, smugglers ran 34,000 chests of the drug into China from there. It was estimated that the British opium profits in the first half of the nineteenth century averaged over $6,000,000 a year, which was more than the total annual revenues of the United States Government before 1800. French, Danes, and Swedes were in the trade, too, and the Americans, who seemed to have the best and fastest ships at that time, saw no reason to leave all this lucrative traffic to others. The first American to try it brought 124 cases from Smyrna, Turkey, to Canton in 1805.

Since 1745, by Imperial decree foreigners were allowed to trade only at Canton on the Pearl River. In fact, they had to anchor at Whampoa, twelve miles below Canton, and transfer their cargo to Chinese junks. By 1825, the mandarins had so tightened their blockade of the port that the smugglers avoided Whampoa and unloaded further south.

Great firms flourished on the opium trade. Houqua, the most fabulous of Chinese merchants, owed much of his wealth to it. So did highly respectable English and American families, and Indian princes and Parsee financiers. The combination of danger and mystery attracted bold adventurers as well as greedy blackguards. Most of them had one morality, a loyalty to their employers.

Most of the English opium ships were commanded by former naval officers, most of the American by young seekers of adventure from the well-to-do families of New England. Their crews were a melting pot, drawn from Calcutta, Bombay, Marseilles, London,

151

Canton, and the Philippines. In the 1830's and 1840's, American, English, and Indian ships raced each other with their forbidden cargoes, and thanks to the new clipper design, the Americans were winning.

The first clipper, the *Ann McKim,* was built in Baltimore in 1832. She was 143 feet long, and drew 11 feet forward and 17 aft. Her cargo capacity was limited to give her greater speed, and after a few years in the tea trade, she turned up on the opium run. Tea, slaves, opium, and later the California and Australian gold rushes were the reasons for the clippers—tea because it deteriorated in the hold on a long voyage, slaves and opium because they were illegal, the gold rushes because miners were in a hurry.

John W. Griffiths, the first American ship designer who did not build his own ships, drew plans for *Rainbow,* first of the "extreme" clippers, in 1845. She was launched with hollow water lines and a general drawing out of the forward body, bringing the greatest breadth aft while rounding out the ends at the stern. She was so slim and rakish that Griffiths' friends were afraid she couldn't possibly be safe, but only a few other sailing ships ever beat her speed, and they were clippers too, most of them designed by Donald McKay of Boston.

These men and their rivals were building ships especially for the opium trade. James Hall of Boston, outclassed only by McKay as a builder of speedy craft, delivered three to the Forbeses for this traffic; Brown and Bell built at least that many more in their busy shipyard on the East River at the foot of New York's Houston Street. Their activities were stimulated by the Opium War of 1839–1842. This struggle between China and Great Britain began when the Mandarin Lin at Canton decided to enforce the orders of the Emperor and had opium ships seized. The British won in battle the right to smuggle opium again, although the Chinese did refuse to make it legal. The British also obtained Hong Kong as a base for their operations. While the fighting was going on, the Americans did very well as they had the trade pretty much to themselves.

Indiamen at Whampoa.

Opium clippers were sent east to stay, and were not very big ships. The *Mazeppa*, which served sixteen years as a smuggler until she was swallowed in a typhoon, was 92 feet long, of 175 tons.

The chief dangers were shipwreck and pirates. There was a double hazard in the wreck; if the men survived monsoon or rocks, they might be picked up by Chinese patrols and were lucky to be freed after only a few months of torture. Half the crew of the *Merbudda*, which ran ashore on Formosa, died under the torture, and all but nine of the men from the brig *Ann*, wrecked there in March, 1842, were executed after being tortured for months.

A grounded or becalmed ship was also in danger from the pirates who especially infested Indonesian waters and the Straits Settlements. In any kind of a breeze, the clippers could laugh at the clumsy junks or best them in fair fight. Augustine Heard of the American clipper *Emerald*, meeting a black-hulled pirate craft which was armed with the guns of four foreign ships it had taken, simply rammed and sank the vessel. He refused to pick up a single one of the pirates screaming and dying in the water, but he had lived up literally to the opium smuggler's often repeated motto:

153

"Always go straight forward, and if you meet the devil, cut him in two and go between the pieces."

Battles did not always go to the smugglers. In 1842, the *Mavis* was taken by pirates and never seen again. The same year the *Christiana*, bound from Macao to Bombay, was captured. This was learned for certain only two years later when her sextant and chronometer were offered for sale. The $150,000 in silver coin she had carried for the purchase of opium was recovered, but not restored to the owners.

Because of the illegal nature of the trade there are few records of it. That is why the recently found letters of Captain James S. Prescott to his brother in New York are so interesting. The first was written in April, 1843, and the whole collection numbers twenty-two, a fine running commentary on the activities of the opium clippers.

Prescott came out in command of the brig *Antelope*. Although she was only 370 tons, she had a crew of sixty-five to beat off the pirates, and this was done several times. Prescott, however, was so little impressed that he mentions these fights in a few lines as a little trouble with pirates who attacked in the night when there was too little wind to get under sail. He speaks with greater interest of some of the clippers from America, which all sailors admired, and of Canton and its ways.

He talks of the *Ann McKim*, the first clipper, but more of the *Houqua*, named for the famous Chinese merchant and built by Brown & Bell in New York. The *Houqua* was brought out by Captain "Nat" Palmer of Stonington after he had spent some time in the trade with the medium clipper *Paul Jones*. Captain Nat as a boy skipper had been the first man to see the Antarctic Continent, and Palmer Peninsula is named for him. Prescott speaks of the *Houqua* as the finest clipper yet built even if she was launched on a Friday, put to sea on Friday, and arrived in Hong Kong on her first voyage on a Friday. Palmer apparently was not superstitious.

The world in which Prescott moved was very different from that of bustling New England. Canton, situated on both sides of the Pearl River, was a labyrinth of winding lanes and bamboo dwellings.

Along the river was a long row of "hongs," warehouses or "foreign factories" of the various agents, each of whom was licensed by the mandarins. There were British, Dutch, French, Spanish, Danish, Swedish, Indian, Greek, American—and others. The houses were attractive, mostly two stories high with whitewashed walls. The lower floors were the warehouses proper; upstairs were offices and living quarters, while for security reasons covered galleries connected the hongs with each other.

On the open square between the warehouses and the river, a market place had grown up, colorful with booths and peddlers and beggars and street performers. Nearby were the few streets with shops where "foreign devils" were allowed, including the narrow thoroughfare Hog Lane, the locale of all manner of taverns, brothels, and gambling houses.

Captain Prescott was more interested in his profits than in the color of his surroundings. The opium trade was a big money-maker; an English author, William C. Hunter, who was a passenger on the clipper *Rose* in 1837, describes how she netted a $300,000 profit on 300 chests of opium. "I am doing damned well," Prescott informs his brother in one letter, and in another, "I am doing so well that I hope to have $10,000 before the year is out." Then in January, 1845, he writes a long letter to tell his brother about "a little transaction" which took place recently and of which (although he does not say so) he was the ringleader.

The opium clippers were not allowed to lie within three or four miles of Woosung, he explains, according to the settlement after the Opium War, so that they were exposed to gales and liable to run ashore because there was no shelter from the elements. Prescott, forced by a gale, went closer to Woosung, although he knew he was not allowed there, because there was a fine anchorage in a good harbor. Six other ships followed him. The Chinese authorities went to the British Consul to try and have them driven out, but the Consul had no jurisdiction over American vessels, so the Chinese decided to use force.

"But," Prescott writes, "we decided to stick to and protect each

155

other to the last. We smugglers are always well armed and manned, and calculate to protect ourselves in all cases!"

In this case, the seven American ships, led by Prescott, fought off the Chinese harbor police, and he never mentions any unpleasant consequences. Rather he asks his brother:

"How would you like to be a smuggler? What do the people at home think I am up to here? What a pity you had not come out with me. You might now be a smuggler—have a fine command and be making your fortune!"

With equal enthusiasm he writes about the arrival of the *Rainbow* clipper, "the greatest ship that ever came to China." In spite of bad weather, she arrived ninety-two days out of New York. She unloaded and loaded cargo, and made the return trip in eighty-eight days, so fast she brought the news of her own arrival in Canton to New York.

Prescott was always toying with the idea of giving up the sea, as some of his companions had done. One of them was Warren Delano (great-grandfather of Franklin Delano Roosevelt) who, after several profitable years in the opium trade, went home to join the famous firm of Russell, Sturges & Co. Through him, Prescott also had a chance to be associated with this company on shore, but he always wanted to make just one more run.

"I am getting tired of sailing about," he wrote, "and I think two or three years at the most will do me here. I get uncomfortable."

Well, two or three years later he still was there complaining in December, 1847, that "everything about the East has become dull and stale and I feel more and more homesick every day. Many of my old acquaintances have gone home or are dead. The great changes that have taken place, even in this country, make me sick. I sometimes, when alone at sea, get the blues dreadfully. That is, when I am without a passenger. I never talk with my officers. It consequently is dull music."

In that last passage is revealed the essential loneliness of command in those days. It was believed then that it would be impossible to maintain discipline if the Captain did not isolate himself from

The *Emerald*.

The clipper *Lightning*.

everyone. He never talked except to give orders. He ate alone in splendid isolation, had his own waiter, was entirely out of touch with life on his own ship. Perhaps this explains some of Prescott's gloom, for his entire life was a long voyage at sea under these conditions.

He was sure he was going home for good in 1848, but in May he collided with a steamer "somewhere in the China Seas" and his ship was badly damaged, although Prescott brought her in safely in spite of the accident. But his letters indicate that the enthusiasm of his youth was dimming. There was an alarming increase in attacks by Chinese pirates—some of their junks carried more than 600 well-armed men—and in spite of British men-o'-war sent to clear the coast, the clippers *Omega* and *Carolina* were surprised at the anchorage in Chimmo Bay, close to Foochow. Officers and crew were killed and the cargo stolen.

Actually the days of the opium clippers were coming to an end, and one by one they were disappearing. The *Sylph* left Hong Kong for Singapore and never arrived, intercepted by pirates, it was presumed. A fleet of pirates boasted of capturing no less than five of the best-known clippers. And Captain Prescott wrote his last letter on February 20, 1849. In August he left Shanghai for Hong Kong as master of the bark *Coquette*. Another clipper, the *Gazelle*, was crossing the China Sea at the same time and her log shows that a typhoon roared upon her at about the place where the *Coquette* would have been. The *Gazelle*'s captain wrote: "Vessel buried in sea, cut away mainmast, but could not get lee rigging from being under water. Wreck of mainmast got under stern, carried away rudder. Shipping large quantities of water through cabin. Everything nearly washed off deck. Pumped and bailed."

The *Gazelle* survived, but the *Coquette* and her captain never were seen again. So, in the fury of a typhoon, Captain Prescott made his last gamble and lost, a very special skipper of a very special kind of ship.

Sail as a means of locomotion was nearing the end of its supremacy, the closing chapter of a development which goes back further than history. For the very first people who left records already had sailing ships. The earliest of which we know were Egyptians, who made a hollow hull of pieces of wood carefully fitted together because they had no big timbers. These craft were flat-bottomed, and flat at bow and stern. The one sail could carry them before the wind, but they had no keels and could not be brought into the wind at all.

Other peoples knew about keels and sails as early as they left records, and of the ancients the Phoenicians were the most accomplished sailors. It was they who developed the keel, gave the old tublike boats longer and slenderer lines, covered over the decks, and supplemented their oars with linen sails dyed in brilliant colors. They were the first great commerce-carrying nation, and they went as far as England. It was trade, not adventure or war, that led to their improvements in the design of sailing ships. It was their King Hiram whom Solomon employed to bring him gold and ivory, apes and peacocks, cedar and fir, this last for the building of the Temple.

By the time Rome ruled the Mediterranean, and what her citizens thought was all the world that mattered, the sailing ship was by and large the vessel of trade and the oared ship the man-o'-war. There was little improvement in design for many centuries after that in this part of the world, but further north the race of Vikings were adding sail to their open ships, although they still used the oar, too. They were fighting and raiding and trading all the time, so they often used the same craft for all three.

The modern sailing ship really began about twenty-one years after King John of Portugal married an English princess. They had a younger son, Henry, who became so devoted to the sea as a boy that he dedicated himself to improving the design of ships and the methods of sailing them. He was born in 1394, and in 1416, he founded a school for mariners to which he invited everyone who could help him—Arab mathematicians and map makers who knew how to use the crude compass of the day and could improve it, Jewish astronomers, Italian and Spanish sailors. He wanted ships which could make long sea voyages without having to hug the shore, and to him the world owed development of the craft which

159

made oceanic exploration possible—the caravel which was longer and slimmer than anything yet made, carried more sail and was tough enough to withstand gales and waves at sea, and the carrack, slower but capable of carrying more cargo. Prince Henry never went to sea himself, but he lives in history as "Henry the Navigator."

Then began the day of the seafaring nations on the ocean and the end of Mediterranean supremacy. Ships were developed for special purposes and to meet special conditions. The sailors of Portugal and Spain, then of England, France, Holland, and Scandinavia became the masters of the Seven Seas. Americans got into the trade before the War of Independence, and afterwards held their own in sail for generations.

By the nineteenth century, boys in any port on either side of the Atlantic could identify the various types of ships as far as they could see. There was a bewildering variety. The New England shipbuilders and shipmasters were famous, but New York was their equal and except for Donald McKay of Boston, perhaps their superior. The biographer of William Henry Webb, one of the leaders of his day, says that between 1807 and 1865 the scant mile of East River front from Grand Street to Thirteenth contributed more to the development of shipbuilding than any other place on earth except perhaps the Clyde. In the space of which he writes were Webb's own yard, Brown & Bell, Smith & Dimon, W. H. Brown, the Westervelts—all great names in shipping.

Boston, though, carried off the blue ribbon. Here Donald McKay established his shipyard after learning the business from Jacob Bell, and on his ways the finest development of the sailing ship was achieved. McKay launched his first clipper, *Staghound*, on December 7, 1850. The next year he built *Flying Cloud*, which twice made San Francisco from New York around the Horn in under ninety days—a feat equaled only by one other ship. Others of his ships hold all-time speed records for sail. His lovely *Lightning* made the best day's run ever recorded under sail, 436 miles for a shade better than an eighteen-knot average. In fact, only twelve runs of more than 400 miles a day are recorded for sailing ships, and ten of them were

The *Antelope*.

The *James Baines*.

by McKay clippers. His *James Baines* set the sailing record for the fastest transatlantic voyage, twelve days six hours from Boston to Liverpool, and for a voyage around the world, 134 days. When he built the *Sovereign of the Seas* in 1852, she was so big, 2,421 tons, that no one would order her from plans, so McKay built her for his own account and sold her after she proved herself. Then in 1853, he built the *Great Republic*, biggest sailing vessel yet, 4,555 tons, 334½ feet long with her main skysail truck more than 200 feet above her deck.

In those days, opium clipper races were followed only by people in the East, but the whole world was breathless over the drive for speed to California, and then a little later bets centered on the tea clippers. London tea merchants offered a prize for the winner of the race each year, and it was a big feature of the time in shipping circles. The clipper *Cutty Sark*, which won in 1869, made the best day's run recorded for a ship in that trade, 363 miles. The American tea clippers were in equally keen competition, of course. *Rainbow* set their first record with 109 days from Canton to New York, and the doubtful honor of the longest trip went to the *Eagle*, 166 days from Woosung to Boston.

The sailing ships developed for other special purposes are too many to take up in detail. The fishing fleets, the whalers and sealers we will discuss later. But almost every trade, honest and dishonest, gave something to the progress of ships, even the opium smuggling as we have said. But it is perhaps least well known that the first oil tankers were sailing ships. When people began to use petroleum in quantities, it was thought that steamships would be too dangerous because of the fire hazard. They clung to this idea pretty much until 1886, when a tanker of modern design was built. The very first vessel equipped to carry oil exclusively was the sailing ship *Charles* into which her owners built fifty-nine iron tanks (leaky ones, too) which filled her hold. The *Charles* and quite a few other sailing tankers were burned at sea.

But the sailing ship's great days were drawing to an end except for sport and romance. In 1880, half the tonnage built in the world

still was sail. By 1901, only one-fourth was sail, and the proportion
rapidly dwindled to a negligible figure. All the same, there were a
few late triumphs for wind-driven ships. One of the most interesting,
I think, was an iron ship which began her career in 1866 as a screw
steamer, the *Pereire,* and served twenty years carrying mails and
passengers for the French Line between Paris and New York. Then
her French owners sold her, and the new ones ripped out her engine
and boilers, converted her into a four-masted sailing ship, renamed
her *Lancing,* and put her in the New York-Melbourne trade. She
was faster that way, too, than she had been with steam. Her log
credited her with spurts of twenty-two and twenty-three knots, but
not even this iron ship could hold her own forever, and she joined
nearly all the other sailing vessels at last. In 1925, she was towed to
Genoa and broken up for scrap.

Official Mystic Seaport Photograph by Louis S. Martel

19

Steam

In 1809, the first steamship to venture into the open sea, the *Phoenix,* made a successful run from Hoboken to Philadelphia. That was only two years after Robert Fulton piloted his *Clermont* up the Hudson River from New York to Albany. One hundred and fifty years later the steamship has swept sail from the Seven Seas except for sport, pleasure, training, and a little trade in out-of-the-way places. But the steamship itself is nearly as obsolete as the galleon.

In this short period of its rise and fall, the steamship transformed the world. The big thing, of course, was that it made ocean voyages independent, or nearly so, of the winds and in time bettered the speed even of that wonderful clipper, *Lightning.* It is significant, too, that the age of steam and the age of iron came to the Seven Seas together.

At first there wasn't much respect for either. The "floating teakettle" was thought to be all right perhaps for the protected waters of a river or inland lake, but how was it going to stand up under the buffeting of storms at sea? What would it do when it ran out of fuel? As for iron ships—well, everybody knew iron wouldn't float.

Builders and navigators who believed in steam weren't so foolish that they used it at first for anything but auxiliary power, so that their ships carried plenty of sail in the old way. And they knew iron would float if designed properly. On this they proved their point to even the most irreverent scoffers when the *Garry Owen,* a new iron ship, went ashore in a gale in 1834. Right down the beach from her a wooden ship was stranded, too, in the same storm. The wooden

The first steamboat—Fulton's *Clermont* passing West Point, by Saint-Memim,
only known contemporary view of the ship.

ship broke up completely; the *Garry Owen* was able to get off almost
undamaged.

Twenty years later the lesson of the *Arctic* was even more com-
pelling. The *Arctic* was one of four sister ships of the Collins Line,
biggest steamships yet built in America, 282-foot, 2,846-ton side-
wheelers. (The *Pacific*, which disappeared at sea in 1856, held the
Atlantic crossing record for five years.) Speeding through fog across
the Grand Banks of Newfoundland, September 27, 1854, seven days
out of Liverpool, the *Arctic's* side was rammed by a little iron
freighter, the *Vesta*. The iron ship made port; the wooden hull of the
Arctic was so badly pierced that water soon flooded the boilers and
she went down with 322 men, women and children, mostly passengers. Panic among the crew increased the loss of life, but the wooden
hull got its share of the blame, too.

By this time steam was in unquestioned command. In fact, only
ten years after the *Phoenix* showed the way on the ocean, an American packet, the *Savannah*, was built in New York's East River es-

pecially to cross the Atlantic. A 300-ton, fully rigged ship, 98½ feet long, she was fitted with a steam engine which drove demountable iron paddle wheels. She sailed from the port she was named for on May 22, 1819, and reached Liverpool twenty-six days later. The first steamship to cross the Atlantic used her engine only eighty-five hours on the voyage or an average of about three hours a day, but she used up all her coal. She came home under sail alone. The first vessel to use steam going west was the 428-ton *Rising Star* built at Rotherhithe for the Earl of Dundonald. In the winter of 1821-22, she sailed and steamed from Gravesend to Valparaiso, Chile.

After that, ocean-going steamships were on their way, although it would be another sixty years before they passed sail in total tonnage built in any year. Long before then speed and dependability had taken the best trade way from sail, in spite of the speedy clippers. It was said the industrial revolution had come to the sea. It was a revolution for the sailors, too, and gradually the power of steam made it possible to provide better conditions for crew as well as passengers.

Sailors like myself who grew up in sail had great scorn for the men on steamers. We thought we were the only ones who really knew the sea. But some of us changed our minds. The first time I shipped out on a steamer and got soaked in a storm, I just took off my wet clothes, stood my sea boots next to my bunk, and turned in as I always had. When I went on watch again, I had to put on the still damp clothes, but that was one of the discomforts we put up with in sailing ships where in bad weather everything was a little wet.

"Why don't you hang your stuff to dry over the boilers?" a wiser shipmate asked.

I had not thought of that, and it was wonderful to be able to have dry clothes no matter how hard the wind blew. Right then I said to myself that I never would go to sea again in anything but steam.

The tradition of sail died harder among builders than sailors, if only in the keeping of masts and spars long after they were no longer used. The first of the so-called luxury liners, the White Star Line's *Oceanic*, built in 1871, was rigged as a four-masted bark, although she had a speed of nearly fifteen knots without sail, which would

Collection of Walter Lord

The *Arctic.*

hardly have helped the 3,700-ton ship anyway. And before that the biggest ship ever built until the twentieth century was fitted with no fewer than six masts—and almost never used them.

This giant was the *Great Eastern,* designed in 1851, launched in 1858, scrapped in 1889. Her displacement tonnage, 22,500, exceeded anything on the seas until the *Lusitania* was launched in 1906. With a length of 693 feet and a beam of 120, she dwarfed everything afloat in her own day, and not very many bigger liners have been built since. But she was a hard luck vessel from the very first, and piled up a long record of men killed and maimed, sponsors bankrupted, and a name remembered chiefly because it is given to a rock on which she ripped her bottom at the eastern entrance to Long Island Sound. Her only unqualified success was as a cable ship. James Dugan told her story a few years ago in a book called *The Great Iron Ship.*

In her own time the *Great Eastern* was one of the wonders of the world, before she went to sea anyway. She was bigger than Noah's

The *Savannah*.

Ark, as Isaac Newton once calculated the size of that early venture in shipbuilding. She was designed to carry 4,000 passengers, but seldom was fitted out for more than a small fraction of that number. She was the dream of one of the most famous engineers of the century, Isambard Kingdom Brunel, and she proved to be so expensive that she went through three financial reorganizations before she put to sea. On her trial run in 1859, an explosion in one of her funnels killed five men and, it was said, Brunel, when he heard the news.

The poor *Great Eastern*'s first earned money came not from a proud voyage across the ocean but from charging admission to sightseers. Her bad luck extended to her first skipper, Captain William Harrison, drowned when his gig overturned taking him ashore. By the time the *Great Eastern* sailed from Southampton for New York on her maiden voyage, she had cost at least eighteen lives.

On June 17, 1860, the biggest ship afloat left Southampton manned by a crew of 418 and with thirty-five paid passengers—first class fare was $125. Her new master was John Vine Hall, who held the first steamship captain's ticket in England. She reached Sandy

Hook on the morning of June 28 although she had been billed as the fastest vessel afloat. At that time the record for a transatlantic crossing was held by the *Persia*, nine days, one hour and forty-five minutes, set in 1856.

But if the *Great Eastern* was not very fast even with her engines totaling 11,000 horsepower driving two 58-foot paddle wheels and a 24-foot propellor, she certainly was big, and New York gave her a great reception, more like a fair than a welcome. It was estimated that half a million people watched her come in, and in four weeks 143,764 paid admission to come aboard. She also made two excursion trips, the first attracting about 2,000 people who found there were sleeping accommodations for only 300 and almost no food for a voyage of two nights, while the second drew only 100. After two months in America, earning about a fifth of what her owners hoped, she sailed for England with 100 passengers.

The *Great Eastern* was too big for any dock, so they beached her over a grid for the winter—she was much too cold for travel—and took her off only with the high spring tides. Her second voyage got her to New York a month after the Civil War started, and the sightseeing business was bad. This time the ship carried 194 passengers back, and 5,000 tons of wheat. She turned around fast in England because the government had chartered her to carry 2,144 troops with 473 of their wives and children to Canada—the largest passenger list she ever had. In September, 1861, she embarked the largest number of passengers paying fares yet, 400 of them.

Three hundred miles west of Ireland, the *Great Eastern* ran into a heavy gale whipping up huge waves, and the world learned all over again that man cannot make anything strong enough to resist the sea at its mightiest. The huge paddle wheels went and then the rudder posts, so that the rudder began banging against the propellor. The engines had to be stopped, and the big ship rolled and pitched helplessly in the storm. One attempt to set a sail and bring her into the wind failed when the wind tore the canvas away. For two days the waves battered the ship, smashing furniture and dishes, breaking through skylights to drench the interior, destroying lifeboats and baggage and cargo, killing the livestock which all ships carried if they planned on fresh provisions. At last a civil engineer among the passengers devised a plan for securing the rudder, and with that under control the big ship managed to get back to Queenstown, then on to Milford Haven for repairs.

It was said, though, that no other ship afloat could have survived such an experience. Those were the days of frequent wrecks and large loss of life. Between 1856 and 1866, ten vessels were lost at sea with 250 lives or more apiece. In the next ten years there were only four of that magnitude and in the next ten, five.

James Dugan thinks the big ship could have paid her way by carrying emigrants from Europe to America and bringing back wheat—her 5,000 tons on her second westbound passage was then a record amount of cargo. But her owners kept her in the regular passenger and cargo trade, and she did not do too badly at it for a couple of voyages in 1862. But then Captain Walter Paton, with such a heavy load aboard that his ship drew thirty feet, decided he couldn't risk the usual Sandy Hook route and headed for Flushing Bay by way of Long Island Sound. In the channel, she scraped on an uncharted rock, called Great Eastern Rock ever since, and tore a hole in her bottom eighty-three feet long and nine wide. Fortunately she had an inner hull, so that no water came in, but Captain Paton did not dare risk a voyage home on the chance the inner hull would hold.

There was no drydock big enough for her, and she had a flat bottom so she could not be careened on a beach for repairs. At last a pair of ingenious American brothers, Edward and Henry Renwick, offered to do the job with a cofferdam, a shell which could be sunk under the ship, brought up to fit tightly against her hull so that the water inside could be pumped out and new plates put on from inside. It was a masterpiece of makeshift, but it worked, and in four months the *Great Eastern* put to sea.

What with repairs and heavy costs of operation, the company which owned the big ship couldn't pay its debts, and in 1864 she was put up at auction. No bidders. By the time she was put up again, one of the directors of the old company arranged with Cyrus Field to

The *Great Eastern.*

charter her to lay the Atlantic cable. The director bought her in for $125,000—she had cost $5,000,000.

Field had been trying to lay his cable since 1857. He had done it once, but it parted in three weeks. Now in July, 1865, the *Great Eastern* started laying cable out from Ireland along the Atlantic's Telegraph Ridge. When 1,186 miles of it was down, after several stops to fish up miles to cut out faulty parts, it broke and was lost despite days spent in grappling for it. The *Great Eastern*'s bad luck was holding. But the next year she succeeded in not only laying another successfully, but returned to the spot where the first one was lost, which had been marked with a buoy, and fished it up.

Her next job was not so good. A French company chartered her with the grandiose idea of fitting her out to carry the 4,000 passengers for which she was designed from America to the Great Paris Exposition. Actually berths were fitted up for 3,000, but when she got to New York there were only 191 passengers for her. The French company defaulted on a good many of its obligations.

The *Great Eastern* went back to her one success—cable-laying. Chartered by Baron Reuter, the founder of the news agency, she carried a line from Brest, through the French islands of St. Pierre and Miquelon, to Duxbury, Massachusetts. Then she was chartered to help lay a cable to India, and when she sailed in November, 1869, she was the heaviest object ever floated. She drew thirty-four feet, displacing 34,000 tons with her heavy load of cable and fuel. She laid the wire from Bombay to Aden and then through the Red Sea to link with one coming east. But the big ship was retired from her best business when specially built cable ships appeared in 1874. For years she lay at Milford Haven while all sorts of wild schemes were hatched to use her, but none of them came to anything until in 1885 the managing director of Lewis' clothing shops in Liverpool, Louis S. Cohen, thought of making her a monumental advertisement for haberdashery. He was outbid—£131,000—by a company organized to make the *Great Eastern* a coaling hulk at Gibraltar, but the new owners had trouble getting a license for the proposed hulk, so she was chartered to Lewis' for a year. Back in her old port, she was a sad sight. Great advertising signs, some in letters thirty feet high, were painted all over her. Sideshows, freak shows, vaudeville shows, and assorted refreshment bars attracted crowds of visitors on board. Mr. Dugan estimates "half a million visitors had a whacking good time." The company that had bought her went bankrupt trying to repeat the success on their own in Ireland and Scotland. Failing to dispose of the *Great Eastern* at auction in 1887, they sold her for $80,000 to a firm of wreckers who took her back to Liverpool to be broken up. Troublesome to the last, the *Great Eastern* proved to be so well put together that they had to invent the wreckers' iron ball, seen now when big buildings are demolished, to get her apart again.

The *Great Eastern* was thirty-one years old then, and less ambitious but more efficient steamships had proved almost everything that the enthusiasts for the early teakettles on rafts had claimed. Three years before, in 1886, the first tanker of modern design had been built. In 1869, the opening of the Suez Canal doomed the clipper ships because steam vessels now could cut off the long voyage around Africa. Design was greatly improved, so that bigger cargoes could be carried per ton of ship. In the last half of the nineteenth century, the British merchant fleet grew by only one-half in registered tonnage but by seven times in carrying capacity.

One great effect upon America was to make the United States

indeed a melting pot. Only big steamships could bring in the many millions of immigrants in the last years of the nineteenth century and the beginning of the twentieth. The owners of the *Great Eastern* had not liked the idea, but other companies were not so particular, and the emigrant ship was a big feature of ocean travel.

Engineering improvements all this time made it possible for the builders to combine some of the good qualities of the *Great Eastern* with efficiency of operation, so that regularity of routes could be maintained, and even little trading steamships in far oceans puffed their way along remote shores and up to isolated islands on schedules. But that same engineering progress was perfecting the steamship only while her destined successor was being made ready.

20

The Motorship

When Dr. Rudolf Diesel of Germany patented an oil-burning engine which we call by his name, the stokers of the world should have given him a medal, or anyway a vote of thanks. There was hardly any work on earth—certainly none on the sea—as hard as that of the men who fired boilers in the stoke holes of steamships. Dr. Diesel made the engine room a clean and pleasant place where a man can work in a white coat if he wants to.

The good doctor took out his patent in 1892, but it was nearly twenty years before his invention was used on the ocean. The Nobels built a motorship called the *Wandal* for traffic on the Caspian Sea in 1903, but not until 1911 was the first ocean-going craft of this kind constructed. That was the *Selandia*, built in Denmark to the order of H. N. Andersen, head of the Danish East Asiatic Company. She was 370 feet long, rigged as a three-masted schooner, and she astonished the beholders by having no funnel. The *Selandia* cruised at eleven knots, and almost at once she proved for all time the superiority of the motorship over the steamer.

The man who had the imagination to order her knew the Seven Seas very well. I remember H. N. Andersen in his fine clothes as one of Denmark's most respectable figures, but long before I knew him he had settled down from an adventurous life. He went to sea in the first place as a ship's carpenter. During one voyage, the second mate was disabled, and the captain promoted Andersen to be mate, which got him out of the forecastle into the cabin. Then he spent a long time in the Far East. He built a yacht for the King of Siam, and finally came home to Denmark to head his own company.

The Motorship

He was a smart man who foresaw the great advantages of the motorship before many men of his time. The diesel engine, which burns crude oil quite slowly so that there is no explosion in the cylinders as is the case with the gasoline engine, could save the shipowner in lots of ways. The coal bunkers of a steamship, especially on those long voyages to the Far East, took up a great deal of room which could be given to cargo. The engine itself and the huge boilers needed some of the best space amidships. A diesel operated more economically, and its fuel could be stored in tanks built into the hull. The engine itself could be placed aft, avoiding the long shaft running back to the propeller. It did not need the big crew of sweating stokers and their helpers.

My own enthusiasm for the motorship comes from the days I spent as a stoker on a steamer. There was nothing one dreaded so much as being forced to crawl into the narrow space of the boilers to clean out the soot, which had to be done periodically, and was assigned as punishment because it was so difficult and unpleasant. I myself fainted more than once at the job. In the engine room of the modern motorship, the men simply have to turn handles, and the fuel pours in—no more careful spreading of heavy shovelfuls of coal over the thick glowing beds of embers under the boilers, which required skill as well as strength to keep a full head of steam.

There are virtually no more steamships built nowadays. The only steam engines constructed for the sea are those which the liners now use for heating the ship and the small ones which all ships carry to work their winches. A motor-driven winch works more jerkily than steam, and the operator cannot ease into his power as with steam.

Perhaps because of the head start which H. N. Andersen gave them, the Danes today build the finest marine diesel engines, and they make some forty per cent of all the diesels used at sea. They would have an even larger share of the market if the United States Government did not require all American ships getting a subsidy to use domestically made engines. In the era of the motorship, the United States has become the world's first nation in merchant tonnage, passing England during World War II.

175

The tremendous growth of the world's merchant marine has been due to the improvements in ships and the growing needs of people, too. When World War II broke out, there were 12,798 merchant vessels of 58,000,000 gross tons registered for all countries. A couple of years ago there were 14,793 but the increase in tonnage was more remarkable, having expanded to 89,000,000, and almost a third of it was American. The growth in the size of individual ships since the days when steam first was introduced can be seen from the fact that the figures as collected are only for vessels of 1,000 tons or more, although of course the work of smaller craft is not negligible. The change in the maritime powers can be seen from some simple figures on the first six nations now and then.

Leading Merchant Fleets in 1939

Country	Ships	Gross Tonnage
Great Britain	3,319	17,771,000
United States	1,379	8,126,000
Japan	1,180	5,102,000
Norway	1,072	4,499,000
Germany	854	3,916,000
Italy	667	3,178,000

Leading Merchant Fleets in 1955

Country	Ships	Gross Tonnage
United States	3,346	25,483,000
Great Britain	3,046	19,527,000
Norway	1,056	6,559,000
Panama	519	3,935,000
Italy	581	3,634,000
France	589	3,540,000

The next step in the future of ships, of course, is the atomic powered motorship. So far we have known only submarines, but the first surface vessels to be planned for atomic energy are already under construction. I have read that the British may launch their first, a huge tanker spoken of as being perhaps 80,000 tons or nearly as large as the *Queen Mary*, by 1960. Russia is building an atomic icebreaker in Leningrad, a great, broad ship more than 400 feet long.

She is to be called the *Lenin*, naturally, and the Russians are so proud of her that they have permitted pictures of her to be published as she looks in the shipyard. In Sweden, they talk of producing, perhaps by 1965, a tanker as big as 100,000 tons driven by atomic energy at a speed of thirty knots. The Swedes already have signed a contract to have their first atomic tanker delivered in 1963.

The first atomic general cargo carrier is not likely to be designed as a profitable venture. The United States, according to present plans of the Atomic Energy Commission and the Maritime Administration, will lay down such a ship next year, and the plans for her are well advanced, even to having artists make drawings.

A long, streamlined hull—nearly 600 feet with a beam of only twenty-eight—will have virtually all of the superstructure aft of midships, and there will be cabins for perhaps sixty passengers. She is being designed to carry about 9,000 tons of cargo, and will be rated herself at 21,000 tons.

Of course the engine is the most interesting feature. Most people think of atomic power as being possible with about a spoonful of fuel, but the engine of the atomic ship will take up more space than this would indicate, probably ten per cent of her whole length from deck to keel. The reactor, which will power turbines to turn the propeller for a speed of about twenty knots, will be enclosed in a 210-ton steel casing which will be further protected by steel and wood shields. The engine space is estimated as fifty by thirty-five feet. The horsepower is estimated at 22,000. The ship will cruise for 350,000 miles or nearly three years on one charge of fuel.

Costing $42,500,000 to build, it is not supposed that this ship will be commercially profitable. When she takes to the seas in 1960, if the present schedule is followed, the Maritime Administration expects to put her through an extensive series of tests and then send her on a demonstration cruise throughout the world. Finally she will be leased to a commercial operator.

With all these experimental ships in the works, it is probable that before many years have passed, the atomic ship will be a commonplace of the Seven Seas.

21

The Submarine

The most famous submarine in the world is one that never existed. It was the *Nautilus* of Jules Verne's *Twenty Thousand Leagues Under the Sea,* which is deeper than anyone ever has been. This was a wonderful craft for exploring and peaceful voyaging, but actually submarines have been used chiefly for war. Only in the last few years science has been able to devise an underwater ship that could do what Verne imagined.

It is said that the first venturer in a submarine, only it was more like a diving bell, was Alexander the Great about 2,300 years ago. The story goes that he used to have himself lowered several fathoms in a glass barrel, called a *Colimpha,* staying down as long as the air lasted. Once a whale came along and tried to find out what the curious object was, but Alexander was a brave man and simply waited until the beast went away. At least that was the version he or someone else gave. It accounts for one feature of an artist's conception of the world conqueror's adventures which was drawn many centuries later to illustrate a German book about his exploits.

There were other legends of undersea boats, and Leonardo da Vinci, the universal genius of the Renaissance, designed one. Then in 1626, a Dutchman named Cornelius van Drebbel is said to have made in England a watertight hull which could stay under the water for three hours and could be propelled by oars, twelve on each side. He died, though, before he could tell anyone else how he did it.

The first submarine that we are sure worked at all was the invention of an American, and it gave the tone for almost all the later

Alexander the Great in his glass barrel, as a medieval German illustrator imagined him.

models because it was a weapon of war. David Bushnell was a Saybrook, Connecticut, boy and a Yale man who was thirty-three years old in 1775, when the British were occupying Boston. He thought of a way to sink British warships with an undersea boat which would attach a torpedo to their hulls. He actually got one made by June, 1776, shortly before the battles in which the Americans lost New York.

It was shaped like a turtle, so much that it was called the *Turtle*, and was just big enough for one man. A water tank could be filled to get the craft under the surface, and a propellor was turned by hand from inside to move her along. Outside she carried a crude torpedo, 150 pounds of gunpowder in a wood block, which an ingenious arrangement permitted the operator to attach by a spike onto the hull of a ship. The charge would be exploded by a timing device, enabling the submarine to get away before the blast.

Bushnell found a daring army sergeant, Ezra Lee, who was willing to take a chance in the thing, and one June night he set off for a 64-gun English frigate, the *Eagle*, which was anchored off Governor's Island. He actually got to his target, too, but when he tried to hammer the torpedo spike into the hull, he found he was up against some metal sheathing. Before he could slip along to wood, the tide swept him away and he had to release the torpedo which exploded harmlessly. No further attempt was made, although George Washington said after the war was over that it was "an effort of genius."

The next almost practical submarine also was the work of an American, Robert Fulton. This ingenious man had gone to revolutionary France in 1797, and became convinced that the obstacle to Utopia was the restrictions on free trade set up by the British Navy, then blockading the French Republic. Fulton invented a submarine to destroy that navy. His vessel was something like Bushnell's except larger, and he did not get it built until 1800. He called it the *Nautilus*, too, that being the name of a snail-like mollusk with a beautiful shell, which no submarine has.

Fulton's *Nautilus* was longer than Bushnell's *Turtle*, shaped like a modern submarine, and she could sail on the surface. When she submerged, the mast was unstepped, and a tank of compressed air enabled the crew to breathe. She was twenty feet long and carried three men, two to turn the handles that operated the propellor while Fulton steered. In September, 1800, Fulton set out to sink two blockading British brigs a few miles off the coast. He got just within sight of them on the surface, then submerged. But his progress under water was so slow that he needed the tide to carry him to his target, and before he got there the tide turned. He had to wait six hours, submerged all that time with the candle blown out to save oxygen, then tried again. By that time the brigs had moved on and he couldn't find them.

Napoleon, who had hoped Fulton was right about destroying the British Navy so he could invade England, now lost interest, perhaps because his Minister of Marine didn't like the idea of sinking ships without giving their crews a chance to fight. Piratical, he called it. So Fulton came back to America to invent a more important ship.

A Frenchman, one Dr. Payerne, devised a submarine for something other than war in 1846, and it was used principally in the construction of a breakwater at Cherbourg. But the peaceful uses of this type of craft did not commend themselves to practical people, and experiments for war continued. America must be given credit (or blame) for the first successful sinking of a warship by a submarine. The attacking craft, built by Confederates, was called the *Hunley* and carried a crew of eight or nine men—accounts differ— to turn the crank which worked a propellor. Like Fulton's machine, she carried a tank of compressed air, and like Bushnell's, she was designed to attach a torpedo to the hull of a warship under water. On February 17, 1864, she sank the new Union wooden frigate *Housatonic* off Charleston harbor. The frigate saw the submarine coming and slipped her cable to get away, but seems to have bumped the *Hunley* in attempting to escape. The torpedo exploded and both ships sank. All eight men on the *Hunley* were killed; the crew of the *Housatonic* was saved except for two officers and three men. Several years later, divers found the two vessels lying side by side on the bottom.

In 1872, the United States Navy ran a number of tests in a submarine which was nicknamed *The Intelligent Whale,* and the New York Navy Yard in Brooklyn still preserves it. But the modern undersea boat stems from the work of John P. Holland, an Irish schoolteacher who came to America, and Simon Lake, a naval architect who was inspired by Jules Verne. Holland started building submarines in 1875, and had completed five of them when he formed the John P. Holland Torpedo Boat Company. His first, which the government thought successful enough to buy, was produced in 1898, and George Dewey, the hero of the Battle of Manila Bay, thought it was a wonderful job. Meanwhile, however, Lake launched a workable craft in 1895, and in 1897, built the *Argonaut* which was the first submarine capable of operating in the open ocean.

After that the progress of the undersea boats was entirely warlike. Of course, it was World War I which saw them promoted to a major naval weapon. But even Germany, which first used them in quantity, had only thirty when the war broke out in 1914. In all navies they were so uncomfortable and dangerous, with bad air and worse food and a permeating damp cold all the time, that they were called "pigboats." The harm they could do was first made clear to the world when the Germans tried to break the British blockade and interrupt British supply lines with their U-boats. (They got this famous name because the Germans designated each one with "Untersee" followed by a number and expressed U-21, to give the title of the submarine which drew first blood.)

By this time the periscope, through which ships could be sighted without coming to the surface, and torpedoes which propelled themselves, had been invented. The war was only a few days old in August, 1914, when the U-21 cruised out into the North Sea. Her skipper, Lieutenant Commander Otto Hersing, was at the periscope when he saw a British cruiser steaming toward him. Surface ships had not learned to zigzag to avoid submarines; the cruiser was holding a perfectly steady course, and made a perfect target. She was the *Pathfinder,* and the U-21's first torpedo struck her just under the forward stack. The fore part of the ship was blown to pieces; fire swept the rest, and in a few minutes she was gone. Only a fraction of her crew was saved. She was the first warship the British lost in the war.

It took some weeks for the commanders of surface vessels to begin devising means to avoid the submarine. They thought about it very seriously when on September 22, 1914, the U-9 bagged three British cruisers, the *Hogue, Aboukir* and *Cressy* (named for impressive English victories) all at once. When the first was hit, the other two stopped to pick up survivors and were sitting ducks for the U-9's torpedoes. After that, sailors learned to zigzag their ships to present a difficult target, never to stop for rescue work, to set extra lookouts for submarines and try to ram them, to travel in convoys protected by fast destroyers which could attack submarines with depth charges, to trap U-boats by disguising warships as merchant vessels, and eventually to use the wonders of electronics to locate the submarine before it came within range. This last, of course, was partly defeated by other scientists learning how to evade the electronics. During this war, Germany built nearly 600 submarines and lost 178 of them. Toward the end, the design was so improved that the new ones could remain at sea for as much as three months. In the one year of 1917, U-boats sank 1,264 ships of 6,371,000 tons.

The year before, though, there had been a hint of other uses for submarines. Germany sent the U-boat *Deutschland* on two trading voyages to the United States, and while this was not a very cheap or efficient way of moving cargo across the seas, it was said to be a portent of the future when submarines might be employed on such peaceful missions as Jules Verne described.

There wasn't much desire to follow up this hint, though, and most of the work on submarines between the two wars was to find out how to make them more efficient destroyers of other ships. One exception may be mentioned. My old friend, Sir Hubert Wilkins, who had been flying over the polar regions, hit on a fantastic plan for going to the North Pole in a submarine under the Arctic ice. I remember that at the time I gave a lecture in which I said his idea

Fulton's submarine was driven by sails on the surface and human hands under water.

Its namesake, the U. S. Navy's *Nautilus,* the world's first vessel to be driven by atomic energy.

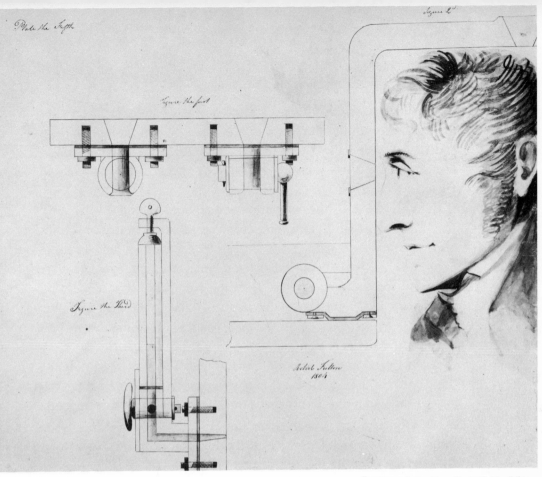

Fulton's self-portrait at the periscope of his submarine.

An officer making the same sort of observation on the newest *Nautilus*.

was perfectly feasible. He had a United States Government boat for the trip, on condition that he scuttle it when he was through with it, and it was called the *Nautilus,* that favorite name in submarines. Unfortunately, three days out of New York the craft was wrecked and had to be towed back to shore.

In World War II, the submarine was an ocean-going ship of some size. More than 1,000 tons, and constructed so that men could live quite a while on board, even submerged, they had long cruising ranges even if they did not match the Jules Verne model. Air conditioning for the men and refrigeration for the food made life on board tolerable if not always pleasant. Millions of tons of shipping were sunk by these vessels, German U-boats again taking the greatest toll, proving their efficiency in spite of all the devices for detecting them. England alone lost one-third of her merchant marine, more than 8,000,000 tons, in the first two years of the war. There was enough know-how to bring about the day of the cargo-carrying submarine, but except as sometimes one of the big ones was used to bring supplies to smaller ones at sea, this did not come to pass.

Now, as a result of still further development of the undersea craft's potential for war, there is a possibility that it may be diverted to peace as well. This opportunity is in the submarines powered by atomic energy, and we are allowed to know enough about them to be able to appraise their capacity for travel.

The first one was launched on January 21, 1954, by the United States Navy at Groton, Connecticut, and named, of course, the *Nautilus.* It was nearly a year before she was ready for trial runs, but on January 17, 1955, she went out for a week-long series of tests, diving dozens of times and cruising for 1,000 miles. So now there is a submarine capable of long and fast voyages under the water. It is said that the atomic-powered vessel can keep up with the fastest units of the surface fleet even when submerged, and outdistance them in bad weather.

Not even the largest and most powerful vessels, whether proud liners or mighty battleships, can resist successfully the worst poundings of the wind and waves. It is not likely that even atomic energy could drive a ship against the force which nature can raise, for no man-made materials could stand the strains. But at the depths where the new submarines can cruise quite comfortably there is so little effect from the strongest winds and highest waves as to be negligible. The submarine then is the one vessel which can be entirely independent of the elements.

The cargo-carrying and even passenger-carrying capacity of a vessel like the newest *Nautilus* is considerable. I suppose that the costs of building and operation are still excessive, but as science develops, this will be less and less true. One day in the sea, as has happened in the air, the technologists will finally catch up with Jules Verne.

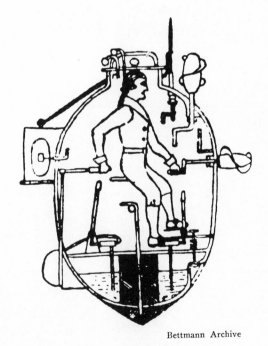

Bettmann Archive

Bushnell's "Turtle."

Oil painting of Columbus by Sarolla.

Part V

The Great Voyages

Planning the *Kon-Tiki* expedition at the Explorer's Club in New York. Left to right: Chief of Clannfh
ghuis, Herman Watzinger (first crewman recruited), Thor Heyerdahl and Peter Freuchen.

22

The Kon-Tiki

When one speaks of the great voyages which men have made to explore the Seven Seas, one thinks of the Ancients of the Mediterranean world, of Columbus and Magellan, of the Vikings in the Arctic and North Atlantic, of Peary and Amundsen discovering the Poles. Of all these we have records, complete or incomplete, and know something of the perils they faced and the difficulties they overcame. But of the pioneers who preceded them there is only so much as scientists have been able to deduce from other than the written accounts of the explorers themselves.

Yet it has been proved that some of the peoples we call prehistoric, because they left us no written record, made long and difficult voyages before they knew anything about keeled and decked boats or had other instruments for navigation than their naked eye observations of the stars and winds and currents.

Now in our own times such a voyage has been duplicated, and from it we have learned a great deal about the wonderful craft in which it was possible for these people to cross thousands of miles of open ocean. It has told us more than we knew before of how parts of the world were settled, and so any account of the great voyages of mankind should begin with this adventure, the most recent of them all in actual time but the most ancient in equipment used.

It is altogether fitting that this first and last of our great voyages should have been planned and led by a Norwegian. For it is well known that the greatest seafaring nation in the world is Norway. If one compares the size of the population with the merchant fleet fitted out here, exceeded only by the United States and Great Britain, it will be understood that this industrious people have recompensed themselves for the poverty of their soil with the richness of the sea.

No wonder that this country has furnished some of the greatest explorers at sea known to the world. They found Iceland and Greenland and were the first Europeans to put foot on the American continent. In later times, names like Fridtjof Nansen, Otto Sverdrup, Roald Amundsen, Riiser-Larsen are associated with our growing knowledge of the globe. But all of these went toward the Poles.

Then came Thor Heyerdahl, also a Norwegian, a young man, excited about a plan he had, and possessed of a will to show that his controversial theory could be proved by practical demonstration. Thor Heyerdahl is a scientist, an ethnologist, as well as an explorer. Like many others he was mystified by the people living on the Polynesian Islands.

When the first Europeans crossed the greatest of all oceans, they were amazed to discover a number of small islands and flat coral reefs isolated from one another and from the rest of the world by vast areas of ocean. Every single island already was inhabited by tall, handsome people who met the newcomers at the beaches with dogs, pigs, and chickens. They talked a language no one else knew, and they had villages with temples. Some of the islands actually could show old pyramids, paved roads, and stone statues as high as a four-story house. But no one knew who these people were or from where they had come. Each scientist had his own theory. Malaya, India, China, Arabia, Egypt, even Germany and Scandinavia have been seriously mentioned as the Polynesians' original homeland.

Some of the most mysterious things were huge stone monoliths on Easter Island. These and other relics of unknown origin gave rise to all sorts of speculation. Several observers noted that these statues in many ways resembled relics from a prehistoric civilization in South America. Then ethnologists put forward a useful theory about a bridge of land across the ocean which had sunk.

This theory of a land bridge was popular for quite a number of years, accepted by specialists in ethnology. But unfortunately these specialists knew nothing about geology and soon the geologists found that there never could have been any land bridge across the Pacific Ocean. Moreover, zoologists joined the geological condemnation of the land bridge theory by studying insects and snails in the South Sea Islands. They proved that the different islands always had been just as isolated from one another and from any continent around them as they are today.

But, of course, the Polynesians must have come to these remote islands from somewhere, either willingly or unwillingly. Further study showed that it is not millennia but only centuries since the Polynesians arrived. They have the same language on the different islands, yet the ocean over which they are scattered is more than four times as large as the whole of Europe. From Hawaii in the north to New Zealand in the south, from Samoa in the west to Easter Island in the east, there are thousands of sea miles, and if a long time had passed since the individual islands were first inhabited, it would not have been possible for them to maintain the same language without evolving various dialects.

Writing was unknown to those people. But they did have schools. Teaching history was the most important function of these schools because history always was related to poetry, which was the same as religion for these people. They worshiped their ancestors and every island had learned men who could enumerate the names of all the chiefs of the island since it had been first inhabited. These teachers used a very complicated system of knots on twisted strings to assist their memory. This was exactly the device the Incas had employed in Peru! Modern linguists collected these local genealogies from the different islands, and to their great astonishment they found that these names and numbers of forefathers listed corresponded exactly to each other. In this way it has been established that the South Sea Islands were not inhabited before about A.D. 500. This date has been reached by estimating twenty-five years as an average for a Polynesian generation.

These first people did not last very long. A new culture was brought in by another immigration to the same islands about A.D.

1100, and nobody knew from where such a late migration could have come. The Polynesians who met the first European explorers, though highly cultured in many ways, still lived in the Stone Age. They were intelligent and socially well organized, yet like the Indians of the American continent, they were Stone Age people, totally ignorant of any use of iron.

For Heyerdahl, that fact eliminated India and China as the place of their origin, and of course, the Near East or Europe.

Now, when the Spaniards first came to Peru, they were shown huge monuments that stood deserted in the jungle. Remains of large cities that had not been inhabited in historical times were found. The Incas described the former inhabitants who left those wonderful architectural monuments as wise, peaceful instructors who differed from the Indians by having white skins and long beards. They were also taller and it was said that when the Incas took over the country, the white, bearded people fled westward across the Pacific. Europeans exploring the Polynesian Islands were surprised to find that many natives had almost white skins and were bearded, their hair varying from reddish to blond. They had blue-gray eyes and hooked noses. On the same islands the genuine Polynesians have golden-brown skin, raven black hair and flat noses. These facts were the first hints to Thor Heyerdahl that there might be a close connection between South America and the Polynesians.

As he is a man with great imagination and practical skill, it occurred to him that balsa rafts could have carried people from South America across the ocean to the scattered islands. In defense of this theory he went through a purgatory of skepticism. Learned scientists in high, responsible positions at museums and universities told him to spend his time in more useful ways than by opposing well-established facts. The Incas had no boats, they said, and without boats how could they cross an ocean?

"They had rafts," Heyerdahl said stubbornly.

The derisive answer was that he should embark on a balsa raft and go out on the Pacific himself. Then he would be sure to drown himself and not bother serious people with his ideas.

So Heyerdahl did just that, all but the drowning. With five companions just as enthusiastic as himself, he faced all the difficulties. They went into the Ecuadorian jungle, felled some of the giant balsa trees and brought them down the river to the Pacific. With these they built a raft in Peru. Heyerdahl used all the patterns of the old Indian rafts as described by the early Spanish explorers who had seen them in actual use.

Nine big balsa logs were lashed together with hemp ropes—no nails nor any metal anywhere. Like the Indians' rafts, the *Kon-Tiki*, as the vessel was called in memory of an Inca god, had an open bamboo cabin and two masts with a square sail between.

The six men left on April 28, 1947, from Callao, Peru, towed out by a Peruvian naval tugboat until they were about fifty sea miles from land in a northwesterly direction. They were now in the Humboldt Current which carries the cold water up from the Antarctic until it swings west just below the equator. This was the major factor on which Thor Heyerdahl depended. Here, fifty to sixty miles at sea, sixteenth century Spaniards had met the Indian rafts tuna fishing and catching dolphins.

The wind is quite regular here. All day long an offshore wind took the old rafts out, while in the evening the regular west wind would bring them home. So it was in 1947. A wind came up, blowing gently and steadily from the southeast. The sail filled and the steering oar, which according to their Norwegian idea of sailing they had rigged up, was put in use. It was not until later that Heyerdahl learned to steer the raft with its "guaras." This wind gave the six men their first assurance, because they had been warned about several little known crosscurrents that could fling them right in on the rocks along the coast.

Late in the afternoon of the second day, the trade wind blew at full strength. It stirred up the ocean into a roaring sea which swept against them from astern and they now experienced the facts of life on board a raft. They saw with great relief—and triumph—how the wooden raft rode over the first threatening wave crests that came foaming toward them. The *Kon-Tiki* swung her stern calmly upwards when a threatening wave towered high behind them. But each time the masses of water rolled along her sides, the raft sank down again into the trough of the waves, waiting for the next big sea.

As they sailed, the troughs of the sea gradually grew deeper and they understood that the sea was increased by a current and not simply raised by the wind. The water was green and cold, and they certainly felt it as the water was all over them. The splashing and spray soaked everything, and the first night at sea was quite uncomfortable. They were not prepared for the low temperatures which they were now encountering.

The men had to be careful. With no gunwale, and the deck only a foot above the water, the two men at the steering oar had to jump when a wave broke and cling to a bamboo pole from the cabin roof until the deck cleared again. It was soon decided that nobody was to take watch at the steering oar unless he was tied with ropes so that he would not be washed away.

They had calculated that they would swing west with the main current before going as far north as the Galapagos. The wind still was blowing straight from the southeast, and although the sea ran high in the days that followed, they kept their sail hoisted. Afterwards the waves came hissing along from the southeast with more regularity and greater space between them, and the steering grew easier. After a while they found that they were going more northwest and sailing so quickly that their average run was fifty-five to sixty miles a day with a record of seventy-one miles.

Thor Heyerdahl and his friends had a chance to make many observations. The first, and maybe the most exciting, was that the raft was drawing a little deeper in the water after a few days. What was the matter? Heyerdahl himself noticed that the balsa wood was soaked with water so he took his knife, cut out a chip, examined it and threw it overboard. It sank and disappeared. He didn't say anything but later noticed that two of the boys separately had done the same thing. If this condition continued, the entire raft would go to the bottom before they were halfway across.

They talked it over and decided to cut deeper into some of the

The *Kon-Tiki* in Callao harbor before setting out on her version of the great pre-historic voyage.

logs. To their great relief, they found that about an inch deep the wood was fresh again and no salt water had penetrated. Later on, the Norwegians realized that they had been most fortunate in listening to advice that they use fresh, sap-filled balsa logs.

Heyerdahl also had done well to imitate the old Peruvians in putting the raft together. He had remained deaf to well-meant advice about using wire to tie the logs together. People told him that the old raft sailors had used hempen ropes only because they had nothing better. Hemp might rot, might slacken; to be absolutely safe, wire was the thing.

Now when they were at sea and the raft was moving up and down, especially during the two stormy periods, all the pressure was taken by the ropes. They were always creaking and groaning, chafing and squeaking. In fact, the ropes furnished a sort of underlying

197

music to everything that happened or was said on board. Every morning they examined the ropes, tightening them. And the ropes held. If Heyerdahl had listened to the cunning men and lashed the logs together with wire, in no time the movements between the logs would have cut the soft balsa wood to pieces.

After a week or so, the sea grew calmer and they all noticed that it gradually became blue, rather than green. This was the first sign that they were out of coastal currents and in a position to be carried out to sea. That also was evidenced by the animal life they encountered. The second day out, they went right into a thick shoal of sardines. It was almost as if there were no water, just sardines. But that indicated that they were still in the Humboldt Current. The next day they were visited by tuna fish, bonitos, and dolphins, while endless schools of porpoises tumbled around the raft.

The closer they came to the equator the more common flying fish became. Flying fish are attracted by the light, and large and small shot over the raft. Every morning the men collected them on deck and fried them for breakfast. In the beginning they were received with enthusiasm but later on they became somewhat annoying. Time and again a flying fish smacked right into the naked chest of one of the men, or even in their faces.

One day they even caught a snakefish in a most unusual way. One of the men, Herman, woke up with something long and wet wriggling in his sleeping bag. It was a dark night and Herman was disgusted. When they got a light on, they saw what no man alive had ever seen before, a living *Gempylus* or snake mackerel. A few skeletons of this fish had been found on the South American coast, but this one was alive and fighting.

Not a day passed but the *Kon-Tiki* met many different animals. Whales, shiny little shrimps, and sharks visited them now and then. Even a whale shark, the largest shark and the largest fish known in the world today, swam in circles around the raft. The whale shark often has a length of more than fifty feet and zoologists figure the weight at fifteen tons. A small, baby whale shark once had a liver weighing 600 pounds, and no fewer than 3,000 teeth in each of its jaws. The *Kon-Tiki's* crew were none too happy as they watched their visitor, its head visible on one side of the raft while the whole of its tail protruded from the water on the other.

The monster continued to circle for about an hour, until one of the men got so excited that he thrust the biggest harpoon on the raft deep into the whale shark's head. For a couple of seconds the sea giant hardly understood what had happened, but then it took action. The harpoon line rushed out over the edge of the raft as the shark plunged into the depths. Fortunately the thick line, which was strong enough to hold the boat, was snapped at once like a piece of twine, and the only thing they ever saw of it was a broken-off harpoon shaft that came to the surface quite a distance away.

The *Kon-Tiki* was caught up by the South Equatorial Current about 400 sea miles south of the Galapagos, and from there moved in a westerly direction. The water was blue and the sea grew calmer; turtles were seen, and often caught; the raft bobbed quietly up and down over the long, rolling swells with little white-crested waves. The trade wind held the sail steadily filled toward Polynesia.

In olden days travelers on rafts, of course, had to bring provisions along. The men on the *Kon-Tiki* had taken dried meat and sweet potatoes, but the most important thing, of course, for them as for their predecessors was an ample supply of water.

The old Peruvians did not use clay vessels for holding water. They generally used the giant bottle gourds, but also, and especially at sea, the thick canes of giant bamboo. They perforated all the knots in the center and then poured water in through a little hole in one end. This hole they stopped with a plug of pitch or resin.

Thirty or forty of these bamboo canes could be lashed along the raft under the bamboo deck where they lay shaded and cool with fresh sea water washing about them. A store of this kind could contain twice as much water as was needed on the whole voyage, and still more could be taken along simply by lashing more bamboo canes in the water beneath the raft. They weighed nothing and occupied no deck space.

The Norwegians found that fresh water had a bad taste after a couple of months but sometimes they had a heavy rainfall, and they rationed themselves to a quart of water per man per day. The ration was not always consumed.

Now even if they had not had adequate supplies they could have managed well enough as the sea was full of fish. There was not one day on the whole voyage when they did not catch fish and could have had more. What early raft voyagers knew quite well—and many shipwrecked crews never thought of—chewing raw fish will quench thirst. One also can press fluid out by twisting pieces of fish in a cloth. Or, if a fish is very large, it is a simple matter to cut a hole in its side which soon will be filled with liquid from the fish's lymphatic glands. It does not taste particularly good, but is better than dying of thirst and the percentage of salt is so low that thirst is quenched.

One of the Polynesian traditions is that their forefathers, sailing across the sea, brought along certain plants the leaves of which, when chewed, eliminated thirst or enabled the chewer to drink sea water without getting sick. No such plant grew in the South Seas and therefore they could not tell much about it, but it might have been the coca plant which contains cocaine and is still used by the Andes Indians. Another plant which it is supposed these earliest immigrants brought to Polynesia was the coconut, which is a cultivated crop and played a great part in the history of the Pacific. The *Kon-Tiki* expedition had about 200 coconuts. They were good to eat and the milk refreshing to drink. But several of them began to sprout after ten weeks at sea. In fact, when the raft reached Easter Island half a dozen were small trees a foot high with green leaves.

It is an old belief that a coconut, protected in its thick shell, could spread over the ocean without the help of men. To prove or disprove this theory, Heyerdahl had placed a dozen good, edible coconuts below the deck with the waves washing around them. Every single one of these was ruined by the sea water. As no coconut can drift faster than a balsa raft moves with the wind behind it, this was regarded as proof that the coconut had also been brought to Polynesia by men.

As the *Kon-Tiki* drifted along, guests came on board, to the great

200

surprise of the crew. There were the small pelagic crabs which crawled up from the sea. The first ones they saw as they passed a floating bird's feather. Two or three small crabs sat on it, sailing along before the wind. These crabs, which are a sort of sea-surface scavenger, soon were all over the raft, filling themselves with everything edible on board. At one point eight or ten of them were seen helping themselves to a flying fish. The crabs would eat anything, and if a scrap of biscuit or bit of fish was thrown before them they would come right out of their hiding place, pick at it with their claws, and run back into shelter like a schoolboy.

The distance to the South Sea Islands from Peru was estimated at 4,300 sea miles, and the *Kon-Tiki* was about halfway when her crew finally discovered the ingenious but long-lost system of using the centerboards or "guaras," pulling them up or down to steer.

It was too much to expect that they could cross the Pacific without a real gale, and they got one. It began July 21 with the wind suddenly dying away. The day was oppressive and absolutely still, and they all knew what this might mean. They were right enough, because after a few violent gusts from all directions, the wind freshened up to a breeze from the south and it grew and grew and for four whole days the weather varied between full storm and light gales. The sea was churned into white valleys filled with smoke from foaming gray water blowing down from mountains which towered high over the mast of the raft.

They were five days without sleep and when finally they came through the gale, the sail was rent, the steering oar smashed, and the centerboards hung loose because all the ropes were stretched, but the six men and the cargo were completely undamaged. They could not help but be cheered by the fact that the more leaks there were in the deck, the faster the water emptied itself. The main task now was to tighten the ropes, bring everything in order again, and all was well.

Until a good thousand miles out from Peru they had noticed small flocks of frigate birds, but these had been left behind. Then on July 3, the frigate birds reappeared at 125 degrees west longitude, and from then on small flocks of them were seen very frequently. They are clever hunters, shooting down over the wave crests to snap flying fish which take to the air to avoid dolphins in the water. These birds always approached the *Kon-Tiki* from the west, so the sailors were sure their home was in that direction.

On July 17, the raft was visited by two large boobies coming from the west, circling over the mast and disappearing again to where they came from.

More and more birds flew over them, and finally on the night before July 30, they saw land, the little island of Puka Puka. They lowered the sail, but next morning found that the raft had been carried along by a northward current during the night, and they had lost their chance to reach the shore.

Actually, the expedition was not too sorry. It was evident that they had crossed the Pacific Ocean to the Polynesian Islands by a raft, and they knew that sooner or later they would run up against land again. For three days they went on, and then out of a cloud emerged Angatau Island.

Exactly ninety-seven days had passed since they left Peru. This, Thor Heyerdahl had calculated, was the absolute minimum of time to reach Polynesia. This tells better than many words what a man Dr. Heyerdahl really is. He knows his maps, his currents; he knows everything. And he had with him the right crew. To pick such men may be, after all, the most difficult task.

From now on the expedition had some of its most interesting days. They were wrecked and had narrow escapes, as Dr. Heyerdahl has told in his own book. The big thing is he proved his theory, as well as the fact that Norwegians still are at home on the sea, and the old spirit of the Vikings has not died out.

As always, when something great is done, critics put forward questions difficult to answer. In this case, a practical objection was raised. Some Frenchmen under the command of a noted explorer, Captain Eric de Bisschop, argued just the opposite of the Heyerdahl theory. They agreed that a relationship between South America and Polynesia exists, but it was the other way round. People came from the west to invade the mainland.

This is not the place to discuss why the French refused to agree with the Norwegian; it is enough to say that Captain de Bisschop decided to prove his point as Dr. Heyerdahl had. He fitted out a raft of bamboo, fourteen feet broad and forty feet long. With four Frenchmen and one Chilean, he left Tahiti on November 6, 1956, on the 10,000-mile trip to Chile. After 194 days the raft *Tahiti Nui* ran into a severe gale about 900 miles west of Chile and about 300 miles west of "Robinson Crusoe's island," Juan Fernandez. The crew radioed for help, the raft being in great distress, surrounded by sharks and with countless mollusks clinging to it so that navigation was difficult.

Captain de Bisschop relied on the west wind drift, far south of the *Kon-Tiki's* course, and the South Equatorial Current to bring him east. It would seem that Dr. Heyerdahl's balsa raft was more seaworthy than the bamboo one. But it also might be a question of how each was built and what winds they were up against. Both *Kon-Tiki* and *Tahita Nui* did what they set out to do, and showed that rafts can bring people in both directions. Perhaps this actually was the fact in days of old before historians wrote things down.

Courtesy of the American Museum of Natural History
Flying fish.

23

South to Africa

Of all the stories sailors tell about their voyages I think none is more wonderful than that of Hanno, a Carthaginian who must have died at least 2,500 years ago. His is the first great exploration of which we have any sort of firsthand account, and it carried him further from the Mediterranean world than any other navigator was to go for almost 2,000 years.

We know about this adventure from a Greek translation of what is said to be an inscribed tablet from a Carthaginian temple, although the tablet has never been found. The translation, known as "the *periplus* of Hanno," describes a voyage around the west coast of Africa almost as far as the equator.

It may be that in the sixth century B.C., when he was preparing his expedition, Hanno had heard of a voyage which some Phoenicians were supposed to have made a century earlier out of the Red Sea all around the continent of Africa and back into the Mediterranean through the Pillars of Hercules, the Strait of Gibraltar. The city of Carthage, where Tunis now is, had been founded by Phoenicians, and the Carthaginians inherited much of the Phoenician trade and of their skill with ships. The story of the Phoenician trip around Africa is told by Herodotus, but he didn't believe all of it because he says the returned voyagers said they saw the sun in the north when they got down toward the end of the continent. However, this is just what makes modern readers think that maybe the Phoenicians accomplished what they said, because how else would they have known that the sun really is in the north at noon below the equator?

No one else ever had been there before. Whether or not Hanno had heard of this when he left Carthage about the year 570 B.C., he was going in the opposite direction, and the beginning of the Greek translation, apparently a sort of caption for the story, reads: "It was decreed by the Carthaginians that Hanno should undertake a voyage beyond the Pillars of Hercules. He sailed accordingly with sixty ships of fifty oars each and a body of men and women to the number of thirty thousand."

The rest of the narrative is in the first person. It tells of founding several colonies along the Atlantic coast of Africa. Then the expedition came to "a lake lying not far from the sea and filled with abundance of large reeds. Here elephants and a great number of wild animals were feeding." The people they met—Hanno or his scribe calls them "Ethiopians"—were hospitable but as they went further south, everything changed.

At what seems to have been the mouth of the Senegal River, the natives were wild men dressed in the skins of animals, and they prevented the Carthaginians from landing by throwing stones. They sailed on and when they came "to an immense opening in the sea," they saw fires burning on the land on either side and heard a frightening noise of "pipes, cymbals, drums and confused shouts." The fires grew larger, apparently forest fires, until: "We passed by a country burning with fires and perfumes and streams of fire supplied thence fell into the sea. The country was impassable on account of the heat."

The Carthaginians had taken some natives from further up the coast as interpreters, and these now said that a blazing mountain on the shore was called "Chariot of the Gods." The expedition by this time had rounded Cape Verde, the westernmost part of Africa. The fires and the noise drove them on, for the writer of the account admits they all were "much terrified," but Hanno kept the expedition going along the coast.

At last they came to a place where it seemed safe to land. It is supposed they were only about ten degrees, or perhaps less, north of the equator, into what now is French Guinea or Sierra Leone. They were amazed to see on shore a strange, savage little people "the greater part of whom were women, whose bodies were hairy and whom our interpreter called Gorillae." Actually they probably were chimpanzees, from the description. The "men" fled over precipes, clinging to holds which no man dared attempt, and when the Carthaginians got close to them, they threw stones. They were unable to catch any of these "men" but they did take three of the "women." The strange creatures seemed not to know they were captives, and continued to fight and bite and scratch until at last the Carthaginians killed them, flayed them and brought the skins on board ship to take back to Carthage.

The story does not tell us how long it took to get back home nor how many of the expedition were lost or were left as colonists. The secondhand accounts of earlier long voyages indicate that the expeditions were prepared to land long enough at a favorable place to plant and harvest a crop. That is what the band of Phoenicians who had sailed around Africa had done. They took more than two years to make the trip.

It does not seem probable that Hanno was obliged to do this. Since the natives were friendly until fairly close to the furthest point he reached, he could have traded for food or even gathered it in the forest. On the way back he might have been provisioned by these natives or even by the colonies he had planted on the way out.

We can speculate, too, on why his voyage was not followed up. It would seem that the sailors of that day, like those who came after, were looking for good trading opportunities, and Hanno's short account does not seem to have encouraged the business people to brave all the terrors of the Atlantic plus the dangers of the African coast.

So, for many hundreds of years, the daring explorers turned toward the East. From there came great riches, silks, and jewels, and above all, spices, which were absolutely necessary to make meat eatable if it was not preserved by salting. The explorers were looking toward the trade of Arabia and Persia, of India and Cathay. The regularity of the monsoons, it is said, was discovered by a Roman tax collector who was blown straight across the Indian Ocean from somewhere around the Gulf of Aden to Ceylon. He was told that if he would just wait a few months, the winds would surely change and carry him back where he came from, and that is just what happened. After that, all the great seafaring countries of the Mediterranean, right through to the days of Marco Polo and the most prosperous days of the Venetian Republic, sent their ships to the East.

The pioneering of the Phoenicians and the Carthaginians in the Atlantic was not fruitful to their successors. Maybe they had been too secretive about what they had discovered, for like many businessmen after them, they hated to tell anyone else about the secrets of their trade. The next sailors who went out into the Atlantic as a matter of course were men of the North, not objecting to trade if it came their way but with a reputation among the other people of western Europe as pirates and raiders and warriors. They never had heard of Phoenicians or Carthaginians, and so they were not able to take to the old route which Hanno had followed. But beginning where the Phoenicians left off in the colder seas, the Vikings did their own pioneering.

Official Mystic Seaport Photograph by Louis S. Martel

24

First to America

So far as we know, the first European to see America was a young Viking named Bjarni Herjulfson. He came originally from Norway, and not long before the year 1000, he sailed out of Iceland to visit his father who was in exile in Greenland. This big island had been settled only about ten years before by an adventurer and fighting man, Eric the Red, but the route was not always easy to find in those days, and Bjarni sailed too far south. Then, drifting in fog and a snowstorm, he was carried a long way to the west.

After many days he saw another island of low hills, heavily wooded, and then mountainous country very forbidding with glaciers and snow. It was the coast of Labrador, but Bjarni did not let his men land. He knew he was too far west, so he made all possible speed toward the east and after some days came safely to Greenland.

As all sailors like to do, he talked of his hard voyage, but almost the only person who was much interested in his story of new lands was one of Eric's sons, Leif, a navigator of great skill, a very handsome man, according to the sagas, and popular. He had no trouble recruiting thirty-five adventure-loving fellows to sail with him to see what manner of country it was that Bjarni had discovered.

This was about the year 1000, and by then the Vikings had mastered their wonderfully built ships, long and graceful with a single square sail and half a dozen or more long oars on a side. They took their proud name from the Norse word for a fjord, "vik," and they made it synonymous with daring at sea. The oarsmen on a Viking ship were no slaves; they were fighting men who lined up

208

Leif Ericson, statue from Iceland.

their shields along the gunwales while they rowed, and were as stout warriors as any landsmen. They were the hardiest of sailors. There were no decks to a Viking ship; in bad weather the men sheltered themselves as best they could by using their leather sleeping bags as tarpaulins. They could get along for days on very little food and drink, and tug at the long oars, two or three men to an oar, as steadily as any galley slave, and with more power. They sometimes rigged a sort of tent amidships, but it was not much use in really bad weather, and the Vikings never stayed at home because of a storm.

Leif and his thirty-five men steered southwest, and came to the land Bjarni had seen. It was a forbidding coast, an icy shore with ice-covered mountains or glaciers behind, as they described it. But Leif insisted on anchoring and going ashore to see if it was as inhospitable as it looked. It was, and he called it Helluland, or land of flat stones. It is Labrador on the maps now, but just as rugged, especially in winter, as Leif found it.

Further south the Viking ship passed west of Newfoundland into a gentler climate. Here they found trees and beaches of white sand, for they were in Nova Scotia, and an island with plentiful grass, which seems to have been Prince Edward Island. Leif named this part of the coast Markland, or land of woods, and in the sagas it is described as a place of wonderful pasture, so mild in climate that cattle probably would not have to be sheltered in barns over the winter.

The explorers seem then to have sailed right around the coast of Nova Scotia until they cleared Cape Sable. Leif still wanted to know what lay further west, so they struck out across the sea and this time they reached Cape Cod; at least most historians think so from the description in the sagas. The place was covered with wild grapes, so Leif called it Vinland, and decided that he and his crew would winter here. The grass was just as lush as on the island further east.

If they saw any natives about, the sagas are silent on the subject. But they were delighted with the trees, great oaks and pines which would be among the treasures of the New World for English ship-builders many years later. Greenland has no such woods, and this

210

forested shore was much closer than Europe, so Leif prepared to take back as much fine timber as his ship could carry. He and his crew built substantial houses, too, but they thought the winter rather mild, not at all what they were used to in Greenland.

When they got back to Greenland in the spring, their stories of the comforts of this new world and their fortunate voyage won for their leader the nickname, which history gives him, of Leif the Lucky. They also inspired another Greenlander named Thorfinn Karlsefni to plan a Viking colony in this paradise. While he was getting his people together, some other voyages were made to the western coast for timber, at least one of them by Leif's younger brother, Thorvald.

In about 1003, Karlsefni was ready to take off. He had assembled a company of 160 men and five women, and they even embarked a few of the hardy Norse cattle on their open boats. This they did because of the reports Leif had brought back about the wonderful pasture in Vinland. It was no easy job to transport livestock in these open boats across the North Atlantic, but the Norsemen were skillful enough sailors to manage it. Also, it is not likely that the expedition to establish a colony in the land which Leif had described, according to the saga, as "Vinland the Good" would be using the typical long fighting ship of the Vikings, with its narrow beam and high curving and carved prow and stern.

The Norsemen had ships for trade as well as war, and built the two quite differently. Apparently the labor problem was not unknown; at least the merchant vessel did not use and probably did not need the help of oars. These were provided to make the fighting ship maneuverable and speedy. The cargo carrier of those days was not in a hurry and did not have to maneuver. So the Norse trading ship was entirely propelled by sail rigged on a single mast. Furthermore, it was more rounded than the fighting or "dragon" ship, which got its name from the fact that usually its figurehead was some sort of monster.

These trading ships were roomier and more comfortable for a long voyage, and probably they took much longer, too. There were a

Leif Ericson off the coast of Vinland.

number of them which went back and forth between Greenland and Iceland or Scandinavia. They carried the cattle and the walrus tusks of the settlement to the homeland and brought back goods which could not be made on the island. So among the Greenlanders of that day were farmers as well as warriors and sailors. It was from among these that Thorfinn Karlsefni drew his colonists, for it was they who had been most impressed by the talk of what rich pasture was available for the taking.

There must have been several ships in the expedition, but we do not know exactly how many nor how long their voyage took. However, they arrived safely with their cattle, and if they suffered any losses, they did not tell the men who sang the sagas of their achievements.

At first the colony in Vinland was prosperous. It was spring when they arrived, and they had a good summer of planting and building before winter set in. Apparently both they and the cattle did well.

They discovered what the first Viking explorers had not, that the new lands were inhabited. The Indians, however, seemed friendly enough and wanted to trade. They had furs which the Norsemen recognized as very fine, and were happy to exchange them for milk and cheese, delicacies which were unknown in this part of America up to then, and would not be seen again until the days of the Pilgrims.

So the first winter passed off peacefully, and the sagas report that the little colony was increased by one. Karlsefni's wife, Gudrid, gave birth to a son, the first white child born in America. The boy was named Snorri.

The Karlsefni group, having come as colonizers rather than as traders or conquerors, might have opened the door to Europe for America if they had not been more peace-loving than the Norsemen are supposed to be in song and story. During the second summer, their leader began to be alarmed at the attitude of the natives, whom he and his people called Skrellings. For protection he had a stockade built around the houses and barns—the careful Vikings had not taken too seriously the glowing report that cattle wouldn't need winter shelter in these favored lands. The Skrellings, it seems, were not always satisfied with milk and cheese in return for their furs. They wanted some of the metal weapons which the newcomers carried.

By the second winter, the hostility of the Indians was so plain that Karlsefni established a rule that none of them was to be allowed inside the stockade. Trade was conducted over the wall, but finally even these precautions could not keep angry men from coming to blows. An Indian was killed, and of course the band that had come to trade went into the woods to collect their whole tribe to fight. It is said there was a homeric battle, with the Norsemen beating off the natives, but these Indians were clever at harassing the colonists, and by the time spring came the whole party was quite willing to give up and go home. So the first white settlement in America lasted for about two years, and left no traces of which anyone can be absolutely sure, although every now and then some remains are discovered.

So little impression did the Norsemen make upon the American scene, it may be added, that there is not complete agreement as to just where this colony of Vinland was. While Cape Cod and Long Island are among the places usually mentioned, there is a very respectable body of opinion which places the colony from the description in the sagas on the shores of the Gulf of St. Lawrence. One reason for the confusion is that the sagas were not written down for 300 years, and in that time details were mixed up although the main line of the story was not changed, it is believed.

It seems that for several hundred years the men of Greenland continued to visit the North American coast in search of timber and furs. The last voyage mentioned in the sagas was about 1357, and the fate of the Greenland people themselves is obscure. If any Norsemen survived in Greenland, all communication between them and Europe ended long before Columbus made Leif Ericsson's discovery of America official.

Official Mystic Seaport Photograph by Louis S. Martel

25

Westward the Course

There are two things about that redheaded, hot-tempered Genoese sailor, Christopher Columbus, which set him apart from the other explorers before and after him in what has been called "the great age of discovery." First, he was the man who dared to head out across the open ocean with full faith in his theory of geography, instead of following a coastline or hopping from one island to another. Second, his voyages opened up the New World and gave the Old World a push which set it on the road to modern progress, as Leif Ericsson had not done.

It does not detract from this great achievement that Columbus didn't know what he was doing. His theory of geography was so far off that he supposed Japan to be not more than 2,500 miles west of the Canary Islands. He died believing that he had reached the East Indies, never knowing that he had discovered America. But if he was wrong in detail he was grandly right in essential facts, and it is quite proper to date the modern era from him.

He became so famous that almost as many places claim him as claim Homer. But he seems to have been born in Genoa in 1451, the son of a weaver, and to have begun sailing on ships at about the age of twenty. Most of his seafaring was in the Mediterranean, although later he indicated that he had wider experience, including a northern voyage as far as Iceland, and had been going to sea since he was a small child. However that may be, in 1477, he was on a vessel which was wrecked in Portugal, and he settled there. It was the best country for a sailor, since the influence of Prince Henry the Navigator still

Colombo

Christopher Columbus, painted from two miniatures in 1542 by Sir Antonio Moro.

was strong. Portugal sponsored the most daring voyages of the age, and was getting rich from pepper to preserve food, and gold and ivory—all from Africa.

About 1484, Columbus developed his theory that the even richer trade of the Indies could be reached by going west. He was not unusual in believing the world to be round—all educated men knew that—but he calculated the size of the globe at only about two-thirds of its actual mass. That is what led him to suppose that Japan would be found so close to Europe; his figures did not allow space for North America or much of the Pacific Ocean. He had a hard time convincing anyone, because more skillful mathematicians than he knew how big the world was, and thought the voyage west to Asia was much too long to be practical.

While he was elaborating his theory and asking royal backing for an expedition to prove it, a Portuguese navigator, Bartholomew Diaz, discovered the southern end of Africa and pointed a way to the East. His voyage lasted two years, between 1486 and 1488, and he had been so impressed by the bad weather at the southernmost point he reached that he called it Cape of Storms. His king, however, who had not suffered any of the hardships of rounding this difficult land, looked toward the possibilities of trade, and named it Cape of Good Hope.

Unable to interest the Portuguese in his plan, Columbus went to Spain, where two royal commissions advised against his project on the ground that he had badly miscalculated the distance from Europe to Asia. So he had, but in the end Queen Isabella decided on intuition rather than information that this eloquent sailor might just possibly be right. He was a very convincing talker, this Master Columbus, and the Queen was a shrewd woman. She knew that it would not cost much to finance the expedition, and if anything came of it, the profit would be enormous.

Neither of them were impractical dreamers. The agreement which Columbus signed on April 17, 1492, assured him the use of three ships, gave him the rank of Admiral, promised him that he should be viceroy of any lands he discovered, and allowed·him to keep one-tenth of all treasure or goods he found. The three ships were the relatively new design of caravels, much more seaworthy and handy than anything known before, especially for ocean voyaging, although they seem very high and clumsy to us, with the decks built up high fore and aft. The square sails on the three masts could not bring the caravel closer than about 60 degrees into the wind, but it could take a great deal of rough weather.

Columbus' ships were the *Santa Maria,* his flagship, about 100 tons with a crew of fifty-two men; the *Pinta,* 50 tons and eighteen men; the *Niña,* 40 tons and eighteen men. This little fleet left the port of Palos on August 3, 1492, for the Canaries, as Columbus had decided to sail straight west from there.

That he may not have been the first European to go that way is suggested by a map which was discovered only in 1954, although drawn by a Venetian in 1424, and part of a collection assembled by an Englishman, Sir Thomas Phillipps, who died in 1872. This map showed four islands in about the position of the West Indies, which the Venetian called Antillia. Until 1954, this was supposed to be purely mythical; since the map turned up one cannot be quite so sure. Columbus may have heard of the Antilles either as fact or fancy.

The three caravels left the Canaries behind on September 9, and unlike most pioneering ocean voyages, enjoyed pleasant weather and easy sailing. But the sailors had time to get frightened at the distance they were getting from known land, and on October 10, thirty-one days out, there was an hysterical mutiny, but Columbus persuaded the men to keep at it for three more days. The very next morning they saw branches of trees floating in the water and knew land must be near.

"On the thirty-third day I came into the Indian Sea where I discovered many islands inhabited by numerous people," Columbus wrote on his way home.

The honor of actually sighting land went to Rodrigo de Triana, lookout on the *Pinta,* early on the morning of October 12. The place where Columbus first went ashore, after getting himself carefully

The *Santa Maria.*

dressed in his best clothes—dark green velvet suit, white ruff, violet stockings and red coat—he called San Salvador, and is generally believed to be what is now known as Watling Island, one of the Bahamas. Because Columbus thought he had reached the Indies, he called the natives who came to meet him Indians, although he was puzzled by how different they were from descriptions of Chinese brought back by travelers. He had no trouble with them because they, as he wrote, "believed that I have come from heaven."

He was a puzzled deity because he couldn't understand why the islands he saw fell so far short of Marco Polo's descriptions. He cruised through the Bahamas to Cuba and across the Windward Passage to Hispaniola. Here the *Santa Maria* ran aground—her anchor is a treasured Haitian possession—so Columbus built a fort out of her timbers and garrisoned it with most of her crew. He himself transferred to the *Niña,* and early in 1493, set sail for home.

219

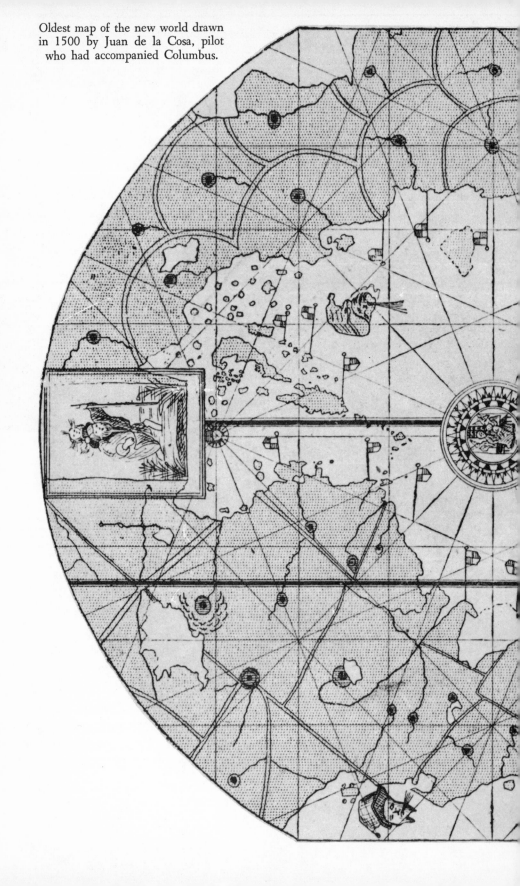

Oldest map of the new world drawn in 1500 by Juan de la Cosa, pilot who had accompanied Columbus.

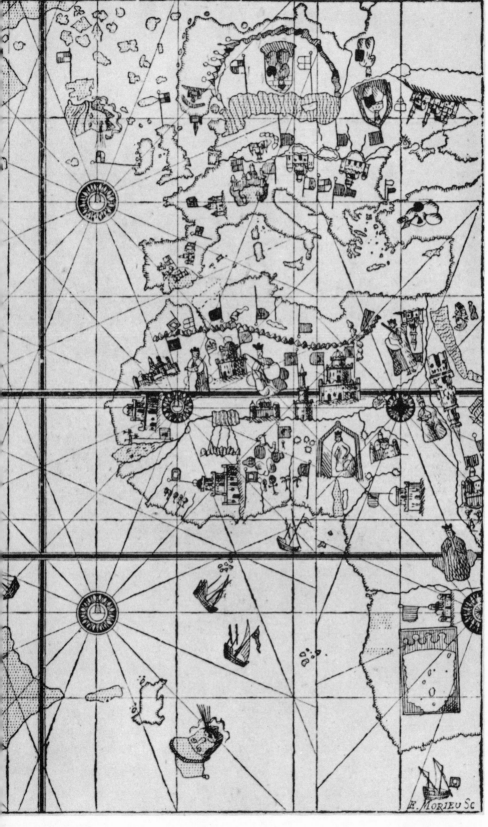

Columbus proved his skill as a navigator more on the return than on the outward passage. He took his two ships north until they were in the path of the regular trade winds which blow from west to east, and then had a fair run to Spain. However, two fierce storms were encountered, and the caravels had to be handled in masterly fashion to survive. Four of six Indians he had brought along died, and most of his crew were sick and weak by the time the *Niña* and *Pinta* sailed into Palos harbor on March 15, 1493.

Columbus made a very imposing appearance at the Spanish court with his remaining two Indians, a collection of New World plants and animals, and his own impressive getup as Admiral of the Ocean Sea. Although he couldn't explain just how he came to miss the fabled cities of the Far East, he did say: "The gate to gold and pearls is now open." He had brought back a few pearls and some gold, but had not located either the pearl fisheries or the gold mines.

It did not seem to anyone in Spain that there would be much difficulty in correcting these slight faults. After six months as a hero, Columbus sailed again in command of a splendid fleet of seventeen ships and 1,500 men, all eager adventurers. He discovered a great many islands, but from the standpoint of everyone concerned, the expedition was a failure. Columbus wanted to set up colonies—the one group he had left on Hispaniola had been destroyed—but his men wanted to find gold, and got into all kinds of trouble with the Indians whom they tortured and cajoled to reveal secrets of fabulous mines which did not exist. A great man at handling a ship, Columbus was not as good an administrator on land, and in 1496, he sailed home after a few of his men had anticipated his action by slipping off in some of the ships to complain about him and his brother, Bartholomew.

These complaints, probably justified in large part, and the failure to bring back great treasure made a big difference in the reception which Columbus received this time. He didn't seem such a great man at court, and it took him a solid year of arguing and persuading before the government would let him have six ships for a third voyage. He got few volunteers, and most of his proposed colonists were convicts.

On this voyage, in 1498, Columbus discovered the mainland of South America, and on his final voyage in 1500, with only four ships, he coasted along the shores of Central America looking for the passage to India. As a navigator and ship's master, he was unsurpassed; his tragedy was that he had to act as a great man on land, too, and for this he was not fitted. He came back to Spain in 1504, from his last voyage and died there, in not much better circumstances than he had been born, in 1506.

Meanwhile another explorer, this time Portuguese, eclipsed him in the popular fancy of the day. Following up on the discovery of the Cape of Good Hope by Bartholomew Diaz, the King of Portugal dispatched Vasco da Gama with four ships to open up trade with the Indies by sailing around Africa. Starting at about the time Columbus returned from his second voyage, da Gama in three years pioneered the route which remained for centuries the shipping highway to the Orient, around the Cape and across the Indian Ocean. His greatest contribution to navigation was to take a leaf out of Columbus' book and brave the open sea, sailing in a great arc from the Cape Verde Islands to the tip of Africa instead of following the coast all around the "hump" and down the dangerous western shores, as Diaz had done.

Meanwhile, too, an expatriated Italian seaman like Columbus was trying to find the route to Asia by way of the northwest. This man was John Cabot, born in Genoa, naturalized in Venice, settled as a merchant in Bristol, England. In May, 1497, he sailed in the *Matthew,* smaller than the smallest of Columbus' ships, with a commission from King Henry VII to take possession of any lands he might find, and enrich himself with a share of any treasure and the governorship of any new provinces. For fifty-three days, twenty longer than Columbus, he beat doggedly to the west and finally reached the neighborhood of Cape Breton Island. The cod fishing there was very good, and the spruce trees on shore appeared to be valuable, too, but there was no gold and no passage to India. John

Cabot and his son, Sebastian, made other voyages and found Nova Scotia. The father was rewarded with a pension of ten pounds a year from the King, but for longer than a man's lifetime, no Englishmen attempted to follow up on the Cabot discoveries.

The discoveries of Columbus and da Gama were more promptly exploited. Columbus didn't exaggerate when he boasted—for he was not a modest man—"I have placed under their Highnesses' sovereignty more land than there is in Africa and Europe." Men as daring as he and even more ruthless followed across the sea and the great Spanish Empire, largest the world ever knew, was the result. The Portuguese took the da Gama route, with the result that in a few years they had the virtual monopoly of Far Eastern trade. The whole world began to move at a faster pace toward greater progress and increased knowledge because of the worlds which these two great voyagers had opened.

Official Mystic Seaport Photograph by Louis S. Martel

26

Around the World

1. MAGELLAN

It is not known exactly when the leader of the first expedition to sail around the globe was born, but Ferdinand Magellan, which is the Spanish version of his name, was the son of a rather poor Portuguese nobleman. His father managed to send him to the court in Lisbon in the latter part of the fifteenth century, and there he was lucky enough to study with some eminent geographers and scientists.

In 1505, he joined a famous expedition which spent seven years in the East Indies, where he acquired good practical experience as a sailor. He also showed personal bravery and cunning. On an excursion to Malacca in 1508–09, he saved all the Europeans there when he got wind of a Malaccan plot to surprise and kill the foreigners. Magellan warned the commander and let a counterattack.

In 1511, he heard firsthand about the Spice Islands, which we now call the Moluccas, from his cousin, Serrao, who led an expedition there and thought he had found paradise, although he wrecked his ship on the journey. Magellan was fired by this information, but he did not at once act upon it because he felt himself a little unpopular with the Portuguese Viceroy, Alfonso d'Albuquerque. In a war council, Magellan had protested against an expedition which Albuquerque planned, and when it failed, the prophet was distinctly without honor. Everyone hates a fellow who says, "What did I tell you!" So in 1512 Magellan prudently returned to Portugal.

The next year he took part in an expedition to Africa where he was wounded in the knee so badly that for the rest of his life he limped. Again he returned to Lisbon, thinking he had put on a good

225

Ferdinand Magellan.

show, but he was offered only a small position. Disappointed by court intrigues, and feeling himself insulted, he tried to bring himself forward by presenting to King Emmanuel a plan for a great expedition to find a way to the Spice Islands through a passage which he supposed existed through the land discovered by Columbus.

The King turned him down, whereupon Magellan issued a signed document informing his king, and everyone else, that he was changing his nationality. In fact, he already had turned to the Holy Roman Emperor, Charles V, King of Spain. Two others who felt they had been badly treated in Portugal went with him, a famous astronomer and mathematician, Ruy Faleiro, and a wealthy merchant.

Magellan brought with him a globe on which he demonstrated to Charles the feasibility of his plan, but he seems to have impressed the Emperor as much by his political skill. At this time there was great rivalry between Spain and Portugal in empire building. Since both were most devoted Christian countries, their sovereigns had asked the Holy See to arbitrate their claims. In 1494, Pope Alexander VI gave all the non-Christian world to these two; Spain to have everything west of a line drawn 370 leagues west of the Cape Verde Island and Portugal everything to the east. No one knew it then, but the "hump" of South America is east of the line and so Portugal got Brazil. It was anybody's guess as to whether the Spice Islands were in the Spanish or Portuguese half of the world. Magellan convinced the Emperor that they were west of Peru rather than east of Brazil. In March, 1518, the Emperor promised Magellan and Faleiro that his government would pay the expenses of an expedition to find out, but also keep most of the profit. Magellan and Faleiro were allowed five per cent. Both also were to be viceroys of any new countries they discovered and to enjoy great privileges.

The news leaked out and caused a great sensation, mostly in Portugal, whose king was believed to be architect of a plot to murder Magellan. The navigator was having other troubles. When Charles knighted him, he became the object of hostile intrigues at court by jealous Spaniards. Then the Portuguese ambassador turned Faleiro against him, and the astronomer withdrew from the project.

The Emperor kept his promise, however, and although the five ships he provided were old and half rotten, Magellan went ahead with his preparations. None of his ships was large. The *Trinidad*, of which he was captain himself, measured 110 tons; the *San Antonio*, 120; the *Concepçion*, 90; the *Victoria*, 85; and the *Santiago*, 75. The total expenses were 20,000 ducats, including provisions for two years and a lot of trade goods to barter with natives. The crew came from all parts of the world, 230 men, and none of them very dependable. From the beginning, the Spaniards sought an opportunity to mutiny because they resented being under the command of a Portuguese.

Only Juan Serrao, captain of the *Santiago*, was loyal. An Italian nobleman, Antonio Pigafetta, went along as scientist and historian. It is from his story that we have a record of what really happened.

On August 10, 1519, Magellan went on board the *Trinidad* and the expedition was off. A capable man is not always a kind man, and probably he was hard to get along with. By the time they reached the Canaries, the first argument arose. Magellan ordered the other captains to follow him blindly, and they naturally wanted to know the course, if only in case they were separated in storms. Unrest spread to the entire crew when Magellan cut rations in half because of the long calms they met around the equator. Finally a council was held on the *Trinidad*, at which Captain Cartagena of the Concepçion was so insulting that the Admiral had him clapped in irons.

Pigafetta's story of the voyage across the Atlantic tells of sharks which could swallow a man in no time, of a miraculous visitation of the Holy Body of Christ appearing as a clear fire on the mainmast to end a gale and "give consolation and to calm the evil thoughts" of those who planned mutiny, of flying fish that "rise from the sea almost like a huge wave in such a number that they squeezed in between them fish that have no wings."

Eventually they reached the easternmost point of Brazil, where fresh water and good food made Magellan popular for the moment. Late in March they still had not found a way through the continent, so he decided to winter in a well-protected harbor almost as far south as 50°, near their goal.

It was in this place that they encountered a race of giants. Pig-afetta says none of the Spaniards stood higher than the waist of these men. The giants wore a single, tuniclike garment of the skin of a strange animal, which turned out to be the llama, and their feet were wrapped in such clumsy footgear that Magellan called them Patagonians, which means big-footed. All was friendly, several of the big men being baptized, until Magellan decided to capture some of them to take back to Spain. He tricked two men into trying on handcuffs, for iron was a great novelty to them, but when he sent some of his crew to seize a pair of women, the sailors got into a fight in which one was killed by a poisoned arrow and all the women got away. Neither captured giant survived to reach Spain.

Meanwhile, Magellan found it necessary to cut rations again. Officers and crew were resentful and a little scared. Many wanted to return to Spain, but Magellan told them he would keep sailing as long as his ship could stand it. The three Spanish captains there-upon met secretly on the *San Antonio* and organized a mutiny.

With only his own ship and the *Santiago* loyal, it seemed that Magellan would not be able to prevent the other three from return-ing to Spain, but he was not a man to give up easily. He sent one of his officers with an order to Captain Mendoza of the *Victoria* to report on board the *Trinidad*. Mendoza read the message and let out a roar of laughter to show what he thought of an order from Magel-lan. At this moment, the messenger leaped forward and thrust his dagger through Mendoza's throat. At the same time, others of Magel-lan's men boarded the *Victoria*, and all resistance ceased. The other two ships gave up, too. Magellan promptly had Captain Quesada of the *San Antonio* beheaded by his own valet, and marooned Captain Cartagena and one of the priests on shore. Forty men who also deserved execution were paroled after taking a new oath, the break-ing of which would send them to a much hotter hell than a breach of their old one.

Now, although it still was winter, Magellan sent the *Santiago* to explore south for a passage. The ship ran on a rock and the waves crushed it, the crew reaching shore only through extremely good seamanship. Although they were more than 100 miles away, Magellan managed to send them provisions overland across cliffs and through thorny bushes, and all were rescued.

In the middle of August, 1520, with spring hardly begun, the Admiral put to sea with his four remaining ships and promptly ran into terrible gales. Not until October 21, did they reach the 52nd degree south latitude and there they found the opening of the strait at last, which they called the Cape of Eleven Thousand Virgins.

Magellan, cautious after many disappointments, sent the *San Antonio* and *Concepçion* ahead to see how deep the "inlet" really was. He had thought them wrecked in a gale when they returned with flags set to announce that they had found an outlet to the west. This was perhaps the happiest day of the expedition, and a little later they found that there were two outlets. Magellan ordered the *San Antonio* and *Concepçion* to try the one to the southwest.

Four days later the *Concepçion* returned, but had not seen the *San Antonio* since the start. Magellan wasted several days waiting and sending out boats to scout, but in fact, the *San Antonio* was on her way back to Spain. Her mate, Esteban Gomez, hated Magellan because he himself had suggested an expedition to find the Spice Islands by sailing west, only to find himself a mere mate under a Portuguese commander instead of at the head of the expedition. Now he and the crew overwhelmed Captain Mesquita, made him a prisoner, and headed for home, picking up Cartagena and the marooned priest on the way. In Spain, Gomez said he had tried to persuade Magellan to return now that they had found the strait so that the voyage could be completed with better ships, more adequately provisioned. Magellan, he said, swore he would go on even if the men had to eat leather from the ship's rigging, which indeed they did before very long. Just the same, Pigafetta always mentions Gomez as a traitor and deserter.

The others headed into the open ocean on November 28, 1520. The next leg of the voyage, 4,000 miles, was to take three months and twenty days, and was remarkable in several ways. They did not sight land except for a couple of small, uninhabited islands. They did not encounter a single gale, which is why Magellan fixed the name of Pacific on this body of water. Week after week they had the same calm sea and burning sun. Disease, starvation and thirst plagued the sailors and most of them were near to going mad.

Food grew worse and worse. The hardtack did not look like bread any more, being moldy and full of worms, and stank from being perpetually soaked in the urine of mice. The drinking water was stagnant and full of dead rats and mice. Finally the men were reduced to chewing leather and eating sawdust; a fresh rat, which usually is most repulsive to men, was regarded as a treat worth half a ducat. Scurvy, of course, took a big toll; nineteen men died and more than thirty were too sick to move. Many thought that God had forsaken them, and all but Magellan gave up hope of reaching journey's end. Then on March 6, 1521, looming up ahead were some small islands, fertile and inhabited, with many canoes paddling out to meet them. Unfortunately, the natives were not of the pleasantest sort. Every man was a thief. They stole with alacrity and enthusiasm and openly, even the lifeboat at the stern of the Admiral's ship. Magellan, therefore, gave the islands the name of Ladrones, which means thieves. Later on they were called the Marianas, and this particular one was Guam.

Magellan, furious at the dishonesty of the natives, went ashore with fifty men, recovered his lifeboat, collected a big pile of provisions and shot up the village, killing about a dozen men before the inhabitants fled.

With fresh food and water, the expedition sailed on at once. A week or so later, a little island with a snug harbor invited a longer stay where the men could recuperate. No natives were in sight, so the sick were brought on shore and housed in tents. The next day a canoe arrived with a dozen natives who luckily were not thieves. They had fish and bananas and coconuts and even a sort of palm wine which they happily traded for knives and trinkets. A few days later they were back with spices, the very kind Magellan was out to get, as well as gold. They let Magellan understand that further west were larger islands with any amount of these goods.

Full of hope, the Admiral set sail and soon arrived at a cluster of islands, large and small, which he named for St. Lazarus but which later were called the Philippines. Observations taken here indicated that this group, at 10 degrees north and 161 west, was just within the Spanish half of the world, according to Pope Alexander's line.

For the first time, too, Magellan could communicate with the natives. Years ago he had acquired a slave in Malacca and this man, Anrique, could converse with the Filipinos remarkably well. The islanders had a higher culture than any he had seen so far. When the king of the island arrived, he donated three large porcelain containers of rice and some goldfish, as well as other gifts. In return he received a full dress of red and yellow Turkish cloth with a purple cap, Magellan assuring him that he wanted peace.

Then he got down to business, showing the king what he had to sell and explaining what he wanted to buy. He also gave a demonstration of strength, firing a couple of cannon which badly frightened the islanders and showing how men with swords could not wound another in full armor. The king exclaimed that such a man could fight a hundred warriors, to which Magellan replied, not very truthfully, "That is true, and we have three ships, each carrying two hundred men armed as this one."

Great feasting followed. Pigafetta had to ask God's forgiveness for eating pig on Good Friday, and got so drunk on palm wine he had to sleep on shore.

Then the king of another island arrived, his weapons and even his teeth inlaid with gold. He said that in his kitchen all the utensils were made of gold, too. Both kings and many of their people were baptized at a big party, at which it was also proclaimed that peace should last forever between Spain and the islands.

The kings then piloted the expedition to another island, which proved to be Cebu, where they met a ruler smarter than the others as he had traded with ships from Siam and learned to levy taxes on them. Magellan explained through Anrique that his ships belonged to the mightiest prince on earth who would pay taxes to no one and would destroy all Cebu if war should be declared. An Arab merchant on the island had heard of Charles V and confirmed Magellan's story, so the king agreed to waive the taxes.

Here, too, the king and his subjects were baptized, an event celebrated in another feast at which young girls, beautiful and of a delicate complexion, danced and played for the guests all night. They were entirely naked, their ear lobes pierced and weighted so they hung down almost to the shoulders. Each day after that, mass was said on shore, but the Spaniards had a hard time concentrating on their devotions because all the women wore only a bit of cloth at the waist even when not dancing.

They forgot women, though, when it came to trade. Magellan had to restrain them because the natives had so much gold that the sailors wanted to sell everything they owned.

For some time they were able to convince the kings that the Christian God helped His people. When a couple of villages refused to be baptized, Magellan helped burn them and kill all who could be caught. Then one of the kings won a great victory over an old enemy, which Magellan assured him was due to the favor of God.

These successes made Magellan so confident that when he heard that the chief of a small island, Matan, refused to recognize the Emperor as his overlord, he took the case in hand personally. His officers tried to dissuade him, but he insisted he was not a man to stay behind and let others fight for him. Pigafetta, a brave soldier as well as a scientist, wrote this account of what followed: "We left eleven men in the boats so we were only forty-nine in all and the islanders were about 1500, arranged in three divisions which furiously attacked us immediately. Magellan divided his few men in three divisions as well, and those with guns spent half an hour shooting at the enemy without stopping their advance.

"Soon two of our men were killed, and that gave the islanders great encouragement. They screamed and came on against us anew, and now Magellan was hit in the leg by a poisoned arrow. At once he gave a command to retreat in good order, but his words were misunderstood, and most of the sailors fled, with only seven of us standing by our Captain.

"We were now forced backwards and were in water to our knees when the islanders came so close that they could throw a lance and pick it up to throw again five or six times. They recognized Magellan and three times managed to strike the helmet from his head with their spears. He did not surrender, and though only a few of us fought at his side, we kept the battle going for more than an hour. Finally, one of the enemy managed to hit Magellan in the forehead with his lance. Magellan, in his turn, thrust his lance through the islander, but when he tried to use his sword, his arm was so deeply wounded that he could not raise it. Then the others closed in on him —and that was the end of our illustrious leader.

"He fell over, but several times turned to see if we were able to make the boat. All of us were more or less wounded, and we had no chance of rescuing him. We headed for the boats and left him. The death of Magellan saved us, as the enemy turned their attention to him and we escaped back to the ships."

The King of Cebu and his men stayed out of the battle because Magellan had ordered them to do so. The Admiral and twelve of his men were killed. All the others were severely wounded. The Matan islanders were so elated by their victory that they would not allow Magellan's body to be ransomed. The day was April 27, 1521.

The disaster changed everything for the expedition. The officers elected Juan Serrao and Duarte Barbosa to take command. They had little opportunity to prove their abilities. Now that the natives saw these foreigners could be wounded, even killed in spite of God's protection, they reverted to their own paganism and, what was worse, were ready to listen to the slave Anrique when he urged them to kill the visitors and seize their goods. Anrique was motivated by the refusal of the new commanders to give him his freedom, which he expected after Magellan's death. The king liked this idea and invited as many as cared to come to a dinner on shore. Pigafetta writes: "Twenty-four of them went, but I did not go because my face still was very swollen from the wounds I had received.

"Juan Carvalho soon returned to the ship as he had sensed something wrong, and no sooner had he arrived aboard the *Trinidad* than he heard screams and moaning from the shore. We weighed anchor right away and sailed closer, and began to shoot at the village. Now Juan Serrao was seen. He was manacled and wounded and he shouted to us to stop shooting for if not, he would be killed. We asked him about the others, and he said everyone had been murdered with the exception of the interpreter. He asked us for the sake of God and humanity to offer all the goods we had on board to save his life. But the new captain, Carvalho, refused and did not allow the ships to come closer to land."

Only 115 men were left of the 230 who had sailed from Seville. It was decided, therefore, to burn the *Concepçion,* and then the other two ships steered southwest—discipline deteriorating fast with Magellan's firm hand removed, says Pigafetta. After visiting a number of smaller islands they reached Borneo, again on short rations, and here found a city which did not regard them as mighty men. A powerful king ruled, and the newcomers were humbled to ask permission to take on water and to trade. They were much impressed by elephants, a royal bodyguard of 300 richly uniformed men, and a magnificent dinner. They were uneasy, although everyone seemed friendly, so when they saw several hundred canoes approaching the ships one day, they hoisted sail and departed. On the way out of the harbor they fired on some large junks in their path, killing a number of persons on board and taking many prisoners. One of these they called the chief admiral of Borneo.

Unfortunately, they had left behind them a good deal of trade goods and some of their men, including Carvalho's son. They tried to exchange the admiral for him, but Carvalho had to settle for a large ransom instead; he never saw his son again. However, he kept sixteen of the men and three young women as prisoners.

By this time the ships were leaking badly, but they found a small island where, with great difficulty and admirable skill, they caulked and repaired the ships. This seems to have been the last time the influence of Magellan prevailed. The expedition virtually turned pirate, seizing and looting at least two peaceful vessels. But they never forgot that the Spice Islands was their goal, and on November

6, 1521, after twenty-seven months minus two days, they reached the Moluccas. They were well treated and traded as briskly as the amount of their goods would permit, acquiring tons of the spices they had endured so much to find. Carvalho gave the Sultan the three women he had abducted in Borneo, but the sailors all feared treachery, and finally learned that the King of Portugal had ordered their ships destroyed wherever found. At last, loaded almost beyond capacity with spices, including 800 pounds which the Sultan sent aboard the last day as a gift to the Emperor, and with new sails, they weighed anchor. Almost at once it was found that the *Trinidad* was not seaworthy. It was decided to separate, the *Victoria* going under the command of Sebastián del Cano, who had been one of the mutineers at Patagonia. The *Trinidad*, after repairs, would try to make it back across the Pacific to Panama.

On December 21, 1521, therefore, the *Victoria* set sail alone for the Cape of Good Hope with forty-six men, one of whom was Pigafetta, plus thirteen natives. At several small islands on the route Pigafetta saw strange sights. He tells of cannibals who looked more animal than human, with their beards wrapped in leaves, and whose women went to war with bow and arrow, of a race of pigmies only two feet high with ears as long as their bodies. They slept on one ear as a mattress and covered themselves with the other as a blanket.

In spite of strong winds and dangerous rocks, the *Victoria* reached Timor, where several of the crew deserted, and set a course across the Indian Ocean to round the Cape of Good Hope. It took nine weeks to reach the Cape, and once more the sailors were on a diet of moldy rice, rats, and stagnant water. They passed the dangerous Cape on May 6, 1522, and set a northwesterly course which kept them at sea for two months more before they sighted the Cape Verde Islands. Twenty-one men, including most of the islanders from the East, died on this part of the journey.

The survivors knew that they were in enemy territory, so the men sent ashore for provisions were told to say they were returning from America. They were believed, and made two trips in a small boat with food. But one thing puzzled them. They were told it was

Thursday and their calculations showed them it was Wednesday. Only later did they learn they had made no mistake but had lost a day sailing around the world to the west. They were the first men who had this problem, and the scientific world of the day was soon discussing it heatedly.

Meanwhile one of the *Victoria*'s boats with thirteen men made a third trip ashore for supplies. One of the sailors let out the secret of their real identity, and a little later those still on board saw several caravels moving out toward their anchorage. Justifiably alarmed, del Cano ordered the anchor up and hurried away, leaving the thirteen men behind.

There were no more stops now, and on Monday, September 8, 1522, the remnant of the Magellan expedition dropped anchor in the harbor of Seville. Of the 230 men who had started out three years and a month before, only eighteen were on board the *Victoria*, most of them sick. A handful of the Spice Islands natives also survived. Next day the eighteen, wearing only their shirts, barefooted and carrying wax candles, marched to church to give thanks to God for their deliverance. Then they were taken to Valladolid where the Emperor received del Cano with great honors. The *Victoria*'s last captain was ennobled and granted a yearly pension of 300 ducats.

The *Trinidad*, after being repaired in the Moluccas, had only bad luck, so that no more than seven of her fifty-three men saw Spain again, and then only after many years.

Costly as the expedition had been in lives and ships, it was a great success financially for the Spanish crown. The cargo of the *Victoria* consisted of almost twenty-six tons of spices, mostly cloves, and it brought the sum of 41,000 ducats. As the entire outfitting of the expedition had cost 20,000, the profit was more than 100 per cent. It was a return which would have delighted the practical Magellan, perhaps the greatest navigator the world has seen.

Map makers made up in decoration for lack of facts, but Magella

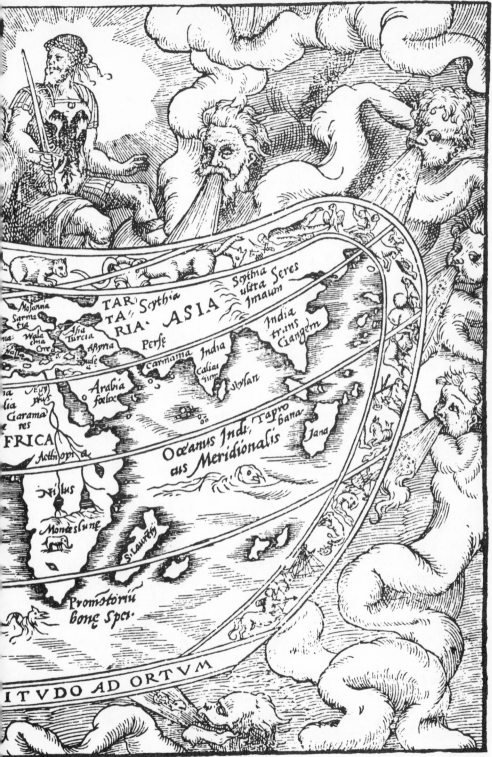

Peter Apian's *Cosmographia*, 1545

gave them their first accurate idea of the passage south of **America**.

2. AROUND THE WORLD ALONE

Years ago one was always reading a more or less foolish question put to prominent men: What ten books would you pick if you were to live on a desert island for ten years? Many times I saw the name of Joshua Slocum on the lists. I didn't know who he was but later when I got hold of his book, it revealed to me one of the best stories I have ever read about the sea. It is full of humor, facts and new views on old things, and at the same time an account of a daring trip.

The first man to sail around the world alone was no young sportsman but an old professional master mariner who had been at sea since he was ten years old. He worked up from deck hand to skipper and finally master of his own little bark, and he was proud that he came to his command "over the bows" and not "through the cabin windows." But one day his bark went ashore on the coast of Brazil, and Slocum lost everything except his good humor and his creative abilities. He worked in a shipyard in Boston for a couple of years until, in 1892, a whaling captain as a joke presented him with a little antiquated sloop, the *Spray*, which had been lying on the shore at Fairhaven, opposite New Bedford, for seven years.

People laughed at him, but Slocum said he was going to rebuild the old girl, and he did! All by himself he felled a big oak tree for a keel, and other timbers for her ribs, and hired a farmer to haul them. Slowly, a virtually new *Spray* took form, 36 feet 9 inches long, 14 feet 2 inches wide, and 4 feet 2 inches deep in the hole. She measured 9 tons net, 12 tons gross. She cost Slocum thirteen months labor plus $553.62 for materials. But he couldn't work on her all the time, and it was April 24, 1895, before he weighed anchor and sailed to Gloucester to fit out for a real voyage. At first he thought he would go fishing, but that seemed dull. So he decided to sail around the world.

He needed a lifeboat, so he cut an old dory in half and boarded up the end. This he could hoist in and out by himself and it fit nicely on deck, while a whole dory would be too heavy for him to handle. The chronometer he had used as a skipper was out of order,

Joshua Slocum's *Spray*.

so Slocum bought an old tin clock for which the owner asked $1.50 but took $1.00 because the face was smashed. He had a big lantern, and a lady in Boston gave him a two-burner cabin lamp which could light the cabin and double as a stove. At Yarmouth he took on stores —some butter, a barrel of potatoes, canned goods and six barrels of water—and on July 1, 1895, he sailed.

In the beginning the solitude was painful except when a gale was blowing to keep him busy. He fell into the habit of giving commands and answering them. When he was in his cabin, having lashed the rudder, he yelled every once in a while to an imaginary hand at the helm: "How does she there?" Then he would answer: "All right, sir; all right, sir!" At the meridian altitude of the sun he would call aloud: "Eight bells!" The sense of loneliness passed, but he continued to shout commands and answer himself respectfully.

People had heard of him, and the papers had written about this foolish, stubborn old salt, so he was well known on his travels. Eight days out a barkentine ran alongside and the captain threw over a line by which to send down a bottle of wine, slung by the neck, and very good wine it was. Exactly eighteen days from Cape Sable, Joshua Slocum cast anchor outside Fayal in the Azores. Islanders are always the kindest people in the world, and they welcomed Slocum joyously, gave him more fruit than he knew what to do with, and one of them, a fellow who had sailed out of New Bedford on a whaler and spoke a little English, even brought on board one night a damsel, innocent as an angel, who was willing to embark on the *Spray* for the rest of the voyage. She could cook flying fish and do all sorts of work besides. Here was Slocum's first real obstacle, because when he explained that he had neither room nor taste for the lady, the interpreter, who had been promised five dollars if he got her the job, demanded that Slocum pay him for his loss. The *Spray* sailed hastily for Gibraltar.

Here he was wonderfully well treated by the British who entertained him and refitted and supplied the *Spray*. They also warned him that if he took the Mediterranean-Suez Canal route as he planned, he would never get past the pirates. in the Red Sea. So

Slocum decided to go the other way, on Magellan's old route.

His first adventure was with pirates anyway, as he was chased by some off Morocco. He kept all sail he dared, but the pirate craft was gaining when he went down to the cabin to get his gun and sell his life as dearly as he could. Suddenly the main boom broke short at the rigging in a squall. Slocum forgot all about the Moors while he downed the jib and secured the boom, and by then the pirates had vanished. The squall which broke his boom dismasted them.

Life across the Atlantic was easier after that. He saw a ship once in a while, but mostly his companions were dolphins which followed him and sometimes were threatened by sharks. Slocum didn't like sharks and fed them empty tin cans which they swallowed with great appetite. His own food supply held out well, supplementing his stores with an occasional catch. One was a turtle he harpooned cleverly and then found it was too heavy for him to lift. He got it on deck finally by hooking the throat halyards to one of its flippers. So he had turtle steak, potatoes and stewed onions for several days. He wrote that never was a ship's crew so in agreement with the cook.

Joshua Slocum reached Rio de Janeiro in November and sailed almost at once. On the coast of Uruguay in mid-December he ran hard and fast on the sand. He could not get off although he worked and worked with his dory, laying out the anchor and then attaching a cable, as he could not get both in the little boat at once, until at last he upset the dory. Now he suddenly remembered he could not swim, and he was near giving up when he managed to right the little craft and paddled it ashore where he fell asleep, exhausted. He woke to find a young man trying to drag the dory away with his horse, but when Slocum shouted, the youth brought more people and they all were very kind to the lone sailor. They even got word to Montevideo, where the authorities sent out a steam tug to drag the *Spray* off the sand and tow her to the capital. Here and in Buenos Aires, Slocum had a wonderful time and received many gifts, including a better stove than he had up to now, but hungry for wood. He sailed at last on January 26, 1896, to round the Horn.

He stopped at Sandy Point, a coaling station near the Strait whose

2,000 people, he learned, were not all the Lord's best boys. But they were kind to him, and besides warning him that the natives in those parts were treacherous, so that he never should let them come close to his sloop, one of them gave him a bag of tacks.

As he sailed through these dangerous waters, Slocum hit on a trick to keep the natives from thinking he was alone. He arranged a piece of the bowsprit, which he sawed off, on the lookout, wrapped in seaman's clothing and with a line attached so he could make it move. Then when he saw a canoe he would let himself be seen, step into the cabin and come out of the forescuttle, changing his coat and cap as he went through. So the natives thought he was three men. When he anchored, he chose a place with plenty of seals which was a sign of no people. Thanks to these precautions and a friendly tow from a Chilean gunboat, the *Spray* managed to pass Cape Pillar, and Slocum was singing proudly as he navigated the Pacific Ocean.

But little by little the wind freshened until Slocum had to take in all sail, and under a bare pole the little *Spray,* sometimes riding high on the waves and at others almost submerged, was driven back into the Strait of Magellan! Her captain had to sleep sometime, and finally succeeded in anchoring in a little cove. But before he went down to the cabin, he sprinkled tacks all over the deck, making sure that quite a few were business end up.

It is a well-known phenomenon that one cannot step on a tack without saying something, and that a savage will howl and claw the air. That was exactly what happened at about midnight. The captain was awakened by yells as some of the savages jumped into their canoes and some into the sea to cool off. Every night while he remained in these waters, he sprinkled tacks on the deck, but he never was boarded again.

One day when he went ashore in his skiff for fresh water and firewood, he found wreckage and goods washed up from the sea, including a barrel of wine and barrels and lumps of tallow. He got the wine and as much tallow as the *Spray* would hold on board, although some Indians hiding on shore fired at him and stuck an arrow into the *Spray*'s mainmast. But at last Slocum worked his way out of the Strait in a snowstorm and this time steered north.

Fifteen days later he came to the island of Juan Fernández, where Alexander Selkirk, who inspired the novel *Robinson Crusoe,* spent four years, and then east for seventy-two days to Samoa, a long stretch, but his chief danger was that he nearly collided with a whale. Here he sold his tallow to a German soapmaker, and felt rich. Rough seas and gales sent him north of the Fiji Islands, but he made New Caledonia forty-two days later in a gale which wrecked the American clipper ship *Patrician* and was so bad that a French mail steamer coming into Sydney reported seeing the *Spray* in the thick of the storm and feared she was lost. But the *Spray* had dry decks while passengers on the steamer were up to their knees in water in the salon. Slocum followed on to Sydney.

Everywhere he was royally treated. The Yacht Club in Sydney even gave him a new set of sails. He made money charging sixpence to see his sloop, and when that business fell off he caught a shark and charged sixpence to see that. When he went north along Australia's east coast, he was plentifully supplied with provisions and even had some money, too. But he did not want to arrive at the Cape of Good Hope before the middle of the Southern Hemisphere's summer, so he headed for the big island of Timor north of Australia, and then to Cocos Island in the middle of the Indian Ocean. On this leg of his journey the wind was so steady that for twenty-three days he did not spend more than three hours altogether at the helm.

He set out again on August 27, 1897, glad to be alone on his own deck again. He stopped at Rodriguez Island and Mauritius on his way to Durban on the African mainland, where again he was wonderfully entertained, but in December, 1897, after a farewell luncheon he was off again. He was about 800 miles from Table Bay in a stretch of water which always has been quite rough, and so it was this time. Gales swept around the Cape of Good Hope; some blew the *Spray* along on her course; some blew her back. On Christmas Day she really was trying to stand on her head, and this was the first time Slocum seriously doubted whether the sloop could stand it. He was under water so often he feared he wouldn't be able to breathe. Just then a large British steamship passed and ran up the signal: "Wishing you a Merry Christmas!" The big ship was throwing her propeller out of the water, and the incident restored Slocum's good humor.

Two days later the *Spray* was sailing with the nicest kind of fair wind, and once around the Cape, her skipper regarded the voyage as good as finished. He allowed Cape Town to entertain him until March 26, 1898. Then, with only pleasant weather and the company of porpoises and flying fish, he proceeded toward home.

He did not know war with Spain had been declared and he was liable to capture. But he had heard rumors that war might come, so when he saw the Stars and Stripes flying from the United States warship *Oregon,* racing around the Horn from the Pacific, he thought something might be up. He was sure when the *Oregon* broke out a signal: "Are there any men-o'-war about?" Slocum hoisted a signal, "No," because he had not seen any Spanish ships, and then with his usual humor added the signal: "Let us keep together for mutual protection."

But the *Oregon* did not wait, and on Slocum went alone. On May 18, 1898, he wrote in his log: "Tonight for the first time in nearly three years I see the North Star." He paused a week at the island of Dominica, then headed for Cape Hatteras, which he reached in three days, and fought a gale from the southwest until he rounded Montauk Point at the end of Long Island. Here was more peril: Newport Harbor was mined for fear of Spanish warships, but Slocum did not care and on a fair wind entered Newport on July 3.

The *Spray*'s voyage still is unsurpassed for distance and the number of places visited by a man alone in a sailing vessel. Joshua Slocum was fifty-one years old when he started this three-year journey; he never stayed home for long again. He went to Australia where he married, and he and his wife sailed 6,000 miles across the Pacific. Fourteen years after the start of his famous trip, he was longing for loneliness again. Once more he rigged up his old sloop, the *Spray*. He sailed her out of Bristol, Rhode Island, meaning to make the Oronoco River in South America his first port of call. But neither the *Spray* nor Joshua Slocum ever was heard of again.

27

Northeast Passage

A sea has been called after Willem Barents, and a fine big sea too, but the thing that makes him more important than many other navigators who left their names on various parts of the ocean is that he was the first European who learned how to winter in the Arctic. After more than 350 years, this amiable Dutchman seems much closer to the Arctic and Antarctic explorers of our own day than he does to Columbus or Drake or Magellan who were much more nearly his contemporaries.

We aren't sure about the date of his birth, but it was at or a little before the middle of the sixteenth century on the island of Terschelling in the North Sea. He went to sea as a cabin boy and rose to the command of an Amsterdam merchant ship. Then he became a seal hunter and learned more about the waters of the north than almost any other navigator of his day.

He was more or less retired, a stocky fellow with a square beard and a great reputation for good sense and good humor and for taking good care of his crews, when the merchants of Amsterdam set out to find a trade route of their own to the Indies. As subjects of the Spanish King, they had trafficked with the East along the routes pioneered by Magellan and da Gama (for Portugal was temporarily absorbed into Spain) but a long quarrel with King Philip had culminated in 1581 in a Dutch declaration of independence, and by 1594, it looked as if they would win it. But the Dutch ships were not very safe if they had to put in at ports where Spanish officers were in charge, and even before their rebellion they had been restricted in their trade, so that they were all the more ready for a free route of their own—free, that is, from the tolls and exactions of Spain.

The city employed its best captain to find such a route, speculating that if it was possible to go south of Africa to the East, it should be equally practicable to go north of Europe and around to China. This was the Northeast Passage Barents was to find.

He sailed in June, 1594, in a ship not very much different nor any more seaworthy than the ones in which the great Spanish and Portuguese explorers had achieved their successes. But he ran into such heavy pack ice before he had gone beyond territory already known that he could not get through. He returned to Amsterdam, counseling an earlier start next time, and the city prepared for him over the winter an expedition of seven ships.

In 1595, therefore Captain Barents led his flotilla around the top of Scandinavia, past North Cape, past the present site of Murmansk, and around the Kola Peninsula into the White Sea. This turned out not to be a passage reaching down toward China, but the expedition encountered some friendly hunters, Laplanders they were, who were dressed in strange skins, the hides of reindeer. These hunters were no encouragement in the quest for a water passage to China. They said the sea froze in winter so hard that men could pass over from the peninsula into Russia. Barents went no further than the White Sea for fear of being trapped in the ice, and sailed back to Amsterdam.

For 1596, the city fathers equipped two ships, and for some reason, decided they wanted another commander, perhaps a man of more gentlemanly ancestry than Barents. Anyway they selected Captain Jakob van Heemskerk, an experienced sea captain of a family so influential that usually it did not send its sons to sea. He had a good scientific education for that day, and was much interested in the Arctic. He and Barents proved to be congenial shipmates, for van Heemskerk treated the older man as the real head of the expedition. Barents actually was called navigator and chief pilot. There was a second smaller ship commanded by Jan Corneliszoon de Rijp.

The story of this expedition comes down through the doctor, or

The Barents Expedition catching Polar bears.

barber-surgeon as he was called in the ship's crew list, a very cheerful young fellow who in some things was ahead of most of his profession. He was Gerrit de Veer, and his story of the year on which he now embarked was one of the most popular books of its generation.

The two ships sailed in May, but at North Cape, instead of sailing straight east as Barents suggested, van Heemskerk and de Rijp decided they should proceed further north first. After struggling through ice floes for some days, they came to an island, which no one had ever suspected before, and a party of men went ashore to search for food. They met a lean, fierce polar bear which killed two of them before Barents led rescuers to shoot the animal. The place has been Bear Island on the maps ever since.

Still holding on the northerly course, the expedition discovered Spitsbergen, which means jagged mountains, and which Barents supposed was part of Greenland. However, the Dutchmen solved

249

one age-old mystery, for they saw wild geese nesting in the crags of Spitsbergen, and no one ever had known before where these birds came from. At last Barents got his way, and he and van Heemskerk headed toward the east, although the smaller ship of de Rijp was sent back to Amsterdam to report progress that far.

In July, the explorers sighted the long island of Novaya Zemlya about halfway along its western shore. They followed the coast north and east but after they rounded Cape Mauritius and entered the Kara Sea, the weather turned bitterly cold, while the sea was full of icebergs and large, menacing floes. It was only August, but already the Arctic winter was approaching. "The wind blew so uncertain that we could hold no course but were forced continually to wind and turn by reason of the ice and the inconstantness of the wind," de Veer wrote.

They made little progress toward their goal, therefore, and were still on the northeast coast of Novaya Zemlya in September when heavy snowfalls began. Barents suggested that they take refuge in a snug little harbor, which later they called Ice Harbor, in the hope that they could beat their way east into what he hoped would be warmer waters after the storm passed. But in the morning their ship was frozen fast in the ice.

There was nothing for it except to plan to winter here, the first Europeans faced with the prospect of surviving through the long Arctic night, and they went at it with good sense and good spirits enough, according to de Veer's account. Fortunately, Barents and van Heemskerk remained always in cordial agreement, for some of the men were sick and none of them quite sure what was best to do. However, under the guidance of the ship's carpenter, they began to construct a sizable house of driftwood, of which they found plenty lying about on beaches and rocks, and some timbers from their ship.

The carpenter was the first man on Novaya Zemlya to die, and the floor was not yet laid, but they carried on the plan he had made, although many of the men were barely up to the task of hauling heavy timbers around. They had no trouble getting the walls up, but when it came to a roof they were stumped for a while. Then they hit on the trick of covering their house with one of the ship's sails and weighting it down on the outside with sand. This made a very snug roof indeed, because it soon was covered with a thick layer of ice and snow, which is a fine insulation as every Eskimo knows. To keep warm they burned wood in a ship's stove set up in the center of the house—it was just one big room—and let the smoke out through a hole in the roof, using a barrel with the bottom knocked out as chimney. Bunks were built along the walls, and all the ship's supplies they could handle, including the trade goods of the Amsterdam merchants, were stored around and between them.

Barents was one of those who got sick before the winter was very far advanced, and the men rigged up a special bed for him near the fire. Young de Veer tried to keep them healthy by making every man take a hot both once a week; he contrived a bathtub out of half a barrel, and melted snow on the stove. He insisted that they take regular exercise, and those who were strong enough got plenty going outside through snowdrifts to collect wood for the fire.

Food, of course, was not very good, but they had plenty of biscuits and pancakes and some wine. They caught a great many foxes in traps, and had fox stew (not very tasty), and used the skins to make coats and caps and shoes. In spite of blizzards and some depression, they celebrated Three Kings Day on January 6 with as good a party as they could. De Veer furnished music and everybody enjoyed such skits as electing one man King of Novaya Zemlya for the day. In spite of all de Veer's efforts, one of the sailors died in January.

As the sun came back and the ice began to break up in March, Barents and van Heemskerk consulted on how they might make their way back to Holland. Their ship was smashed up in the ice, but there was enough left of her timbers to make two open boats in which to sail along the coast of the island, across to the Russian mainland, and back along the route of Barents' 1595 voyage. It would be a hard trip for open boats, but there was no other hope for them.

The voyagers did not start until June, and even then the ice was so thick that they had trouble forcing their way through the floes, and once they were frozen in for a little while altogether. Before they

Barents' own map of the Arctic,

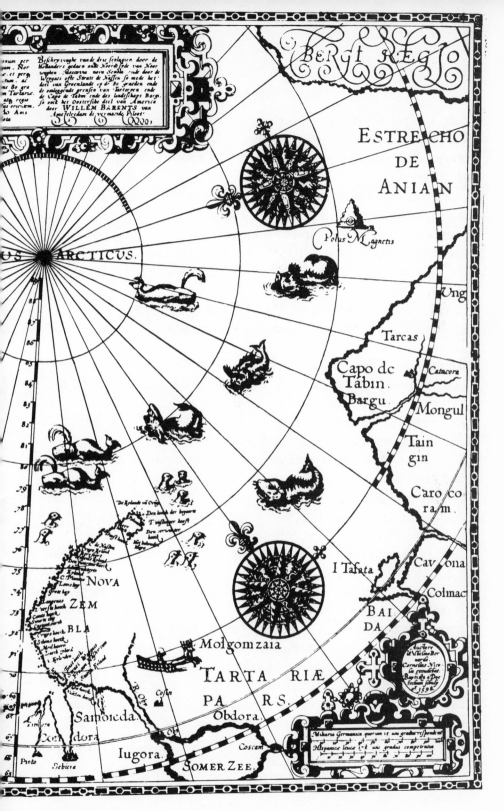

left, Barents wrote out an account of their experiences and left it hanging in a powder horn on the wall of their hut. If all of them were lost, perhaps someone else would explore that way and find their record.

Barents was too weak to walk, and he was taken down to one of the open boats in a sled. Once in a while the men landed and built fires to warm themselves and cook a meal. But Barents grew worse all the time, and on June 28, 1597, he died "with a sudden qualm," de Veer wrote. The boats were off the mainland just south of Novaya Zemlya.

For three months the survivors struggled westward. The boats sprang leaks, but they were afraid to land because of the savage polar bears which would attack them on sight. Mostly it was cold, but one summer day when they came to a small island which was not inhabited by polar bears, van Heemskerk made the sailors unpack all the boxes of trade goods which they were carefully carrying back to the merchants in Amsterdam. The cloth was taken out and aired and dried, and everything well packed up again.

At last they reached some fishing villages inhabited by Russians, and there to the intense surprise of both parties they were found by de Rijp and his men. Their ship had been blown down from the Arctic into the White Sea, and the men had wintered there comfortably enough with the help of the Russians, and now the two parts of the expedition were reunited. At the end of October, they got back to Amsterdam.

There is a curious postscript to the story. Nobody, so far as can be told, went to Ice Harbor on Novaya Zemlya for the next 274 years. But then in 1871, a Norwegian hunter passed that way and found the hut of the Netherlanders just as they had left it, preserved by the cold and undamaged. The bunks looked as if the men had just left them. There was the half barrel which de Veer had made into a bathtub, a musket in one corner, and hanging on the wall the powder horn with Barents' last letter. These relics are all in the Naval Museum at The Hague now.

254

28

All for Science

During the years when England's American colonies were quarreling with the mother country and finally asserting their independence, one English sailor stood out as an entirely new figure, not only among his contemporaries but for all time. The very first man to introduce humane relations with primitive peoples, he also was a captain who took care of his crew and had other intentions than just to conquer land or win fortunes. He was James Cook.

Cook was born in 1728, in Yorkshire, England, one of the many children of a poor workman. When the boy was thirteen years old, his father apprenticed him to a local haberdasher. But James ran away to sea. A deck boy at this time was the lowliest of the low, but this one seized every opportunity to learn and spent his few coins on books about navigation and astronomy. Soon he was an able seaman earning a little more money, so he could buy more books, and at twenty-seven, serving on board the *Eagle* in the British Navy, his knowledge won him promotion to petty officer. Assigned to Canada, he surveyed and mapped waters of Newfoundland, Labrador, and St. Lawrence Bay. He also produced an accurately detailed work on an eclipse of the sun observed in Newfoundland in 1766, which brought him promotion to lieutenant and to the attention of the Royal Society, most influential group of scientists in the world. It was so unusual for a sailor to show any special interest in astronomy that when the Society and the British Admiralty equipped the bark *Endeavour* for a scientific expedition to the South Seas to observe an eclipse of Venus across the sun, Cook was selected as skipper.

Before his preparations were complete, Admiral Wallis returned from the South Seas with stories of an earthly paradise, Tahiti. That there was something to the tales was seen when eighty men of Wallis's crew applied for berths on the *Endeavour* just for a chance to revisit this wonderful island where the astronomical observations were to be taken.

Cook had some novel ideas about equipping the *Endeavour*, and his insistence on taking live sheep and goats caused some comment. He had a theory that fresh food would prevent scurvy—terror of all sailors—regarded as inevitable on long voyages. Some brilliant scientists joined the expedition, mostly botanists, but Cook arranged also for two artists to go along.

The first Cook expedition left Plymouth, August 26, 1768, and reached Cape Horn, January 21, 1769. The first task was to survey Tierra del Fuego, and several scientists went ashore to encounter a most extraordinary experience. They climbed a mountain where it suddenly was so deathly cold that even the Swedish botanist, Daniel Solander, who had traveled in Lapland, was quite stiff. The cold was so intense that it took the party two days to come down the mountain, and two Negro servants died of exposure.

After this nothing remarkable happened until they reached Tahiti, in May. They received a most cordial welcome, especially after the inhabitants recognized several of their friends from Wallis' visit. The complete harmony lasted, too, for the whole three months of the *Endeavour*'s stay. Tahiti was blessed with a wonderful climate and the observations of the transit of Venus were excellently performed, giving valuable data on the distance between earth and sun. Besides, the scientists also had a marvelous opportunity to study the habits and daily life of the people, and the entire group of islands was surveyed and mapped.

Here Cook for the first time showed the quality of his mind by retaining native geographical names wherever possible. That most unhappy custom of giving new names often led to much misunderstanding. Many times an explorer arrived not knowing that someone else had been there before him. He would give a name of his own, usually to honor a king or statesman of his country, as Wallis had called Tahiti "George the Third's Island." But Cook asked the natives for the proper names of places and put these on his maps. As there was no name for the entire group of islands, he called them the Society Islands in honor of the Royal Society, sponsor of his voyage. In spite of his work, they belong to France and consist of an archipelago of eleven islands, estimated at 637 square miles, of which Tahiti covers about 600.

Cook eventually had to go on with his voyage, much to his and his men's regret. The women had shown themselves gracious and lovable, and real friendships had been established. One of the chiefs, a holy man named Tupia, was willing to accompany the expedition with his young son. They proved of the greatest help.

Cook sailed due south until he reached 40 degrees south without seeing any land but the isolated island of Tubuai. He turned west and came to New Zealand, earlier seen by a Dutch explorer of these parts, Tasman. Like Tasman, Cook wondered if New Zealand could be the mysterious Terra Australis Incognita, the unknown continent which map makers imagined extended from the South Seas to the South Pole. Cook decided to find out, and spent the next six months circumnavigating what turned out to be two islands separated by a strait later named for him.

The natives at first were unfriendly, but Tupia soon found that the Maoris could understand him, and as an interpreter and go-between he managed to improve relations. Cook's natural mildness and desire for peace were interpreted by the Maoris as a hostile gesture and they attacked the Englishmen, who were obliged to shoot a couple of warriors in self-defense. Then Cook got the idea of catching a few natives, showing them great friendship and letting them go to assure their countrymen that the sailors meant no harm. In capturing three men out of a canoe, the English killed four, but then Tupia took over and the three soon forgot their fright and their dead friends. They were overwhelmed with gifts, laughed and sang and promised to tell their people what nice folk these visitors were. Next day Cook and a number of others went ashore; the three young men told about the treatment they had received, and Tupia explained that Englishmen never ate human flesh, which helped most of all.

After that Maoris visited the ship freely, a peace slightly marred when some of them suddenly tumbled Tupia's small son into a canoe and made off with him. The English fired at the paddlers, wounding some, and in the commotion the boy jumped overboard and was rescued. The incident convinced the English that the Maoris really were cannibals, which few believed until then, but Cook forbade reprisals. However, the point off which the *Endeavour* was anchored at the time is called Cape Kidnapper.

Forbearance worked, and the expedition proceeded. Natives met the whites with confidence, and soon it was possible to spend whole days and nights among the villages to study their daily life. Cook describes the women as coquettish. They painted their faces with red ochre mixed with oil. As the paint was renewed every day, it was always fresh and many sailors walked around with red noses, as the proper way of showing affection for a girl was to rub noses. Although the Maoris sometimes stole and even attacked the foreign ship in canoes, Cook did not allow his own men to mistreat a native. He insisted they respect the property and persons of the people they were visiting. He ordered three sailors flogged for helping themselves to some sweet potatoes. Two received twelve strokes of the cat-o'-nine- tails. The third, who protested he could see nothing wrong in taking what he wanted from a mere wild man, got an additional twelve to teach him that his attitude was wrong.

Not only was Cook the first European to rise above race discrimination in remote places, but he was an excellent surveyor, and his maps are very minute and well designed. Those he and his assistant, Charles Green, made on this trip are wonderfully exact, and Joseph Banks and the Swede, Solander, and their helpers gathered valuable notes on natural history of the region and the ethnology of the Maoris before European influences eradicated many native customs.

Completing his work in New Zealand in March, 1770, Cook was minded to sail straight west to find out if Terra Australis Incognita really existed. But he realized that his ship was not in the very best

Cook at Botany Bay.

condition and winter was coming to this part of the world. So he decided to make for Tasmania, follow the coast of Australia or New Holland, as it was called, still rather unknown, and return home around the Cape of Good Hope. One of the places at which they anchored they called Botany Bay because the naturalists found many previously unknown plants. England used it later as a convict settlement. In 1770, the natives were so shy that they would not even touch gifts left for them on the beach.

Having taken a wealth of plant specimens, the expedition sailed more than 1,000 miles up the east coast of Australia. This alone shows Cook's masterful seamanship, for his route was a channel filled with rocks and dangerous reefs. Finally, in June, the ship struck on a coral reef. Cook ordered cannon and much of the heavier gear thrown overboard and got the vessel off at high tide. But she was leaking so badly they could not keep her afloat even by manning both their pumps all the time. One of the petty officers proposed an old trick of letting the leak plug itself by lowering an old sail filled with sawdust and sheep manure so that it would be sucked into the hole from the outside. This device enabled Cook to get the *Endeavour* into a cove where they could beach and repair her.

Now for the first time scurvy showed itself on board, Tupia the Tahitian being one of the worst affected. He went into the forest, gathered plants and fruit, caught fish in the sea and soon he and the other sick men were cured, all except the astronomer, Green, who refused to "lower" himself to "go native" and finally died.

With the *Endeavour* seaworthy again, Cook continued north, claiming the entire country for the English crown and calling it New South Wales. Turning west through the strait already seen by the Spaniard, Torres, in 1606, he reached New Guinea, which he thought had been sufficiently explored by the Dutch, so he decided his mission was fulfilled.

On their way home, the expedition stopped at Batavia, where every member except one contracted a fever which killed ten men, including Tupia, his son, and the ship's physician. Curiously enough, the one not infected was an old salt who was constantly drunk. He enjoyed perfect health. As his age was seventy or eighty, the doctors both then and later in Europe argued whether his immunity was due to his age or to alcohol. It was three months before the survivors were strong enough to leave Batavia, just after Christmas, 1770. On the next leg of the voyage, scurvy returned and a few men died on their way home. In all, thirty out of eighty-five were lost.

The *Endeavour* was back in London in July, 1771, after a forty-three months' cruise. The scientific results stimulated interest all over the world, and the British government decided on a new expedition to solve the riddle of Terra Australis Incognita. Captain James Cook was the logical man to command, this time with two ships, *Adventure* and *Resolution*.

After a year at home he was ready. He realized that on his first trip fresh fruit and vegetables helped prevent scurvy. This time he would be in the Antarctic, and it was a matter of dispute then as to whether or not cold aggravated scurvy since it was known the disease was most common among Arctic explorers and whalers. Cook planned his expedition so he would be able to get fresh vegetables from time to time. He started with 118 men of whom he lost only four, and the very few cases of scurvy were easily checked.

All for Science

Cook's second expedition began July 13, 1772, and at the end of October, passed Cape Town where more scientists joined the distinguished group already on board. He kept the course due south but as early as 50 degrees south ran up to such heavy floes combined with thick fog that further progress was extremely dangerous. He put a small party out on the ice to explore it, but nearly lost them and did not venture this again. He sailed northeast and then south again. On January 17, 1773, he became the first of all navigators to pass the Antarctic Circle. Heavy ice prevented him from going further than 67 degrees south, and he also lost contact with the *Adventure*. According to plan, they rendezvoused at New Zealand, and after sailing eastward for some time spent the southern winter in Tahiti, as welcome as on the previous voyage.

In the spring the two ships loaded a great store of food, including no fewer than three hundred pigs besides poultry and coconuts. They completed provisioning in New Zealand before heading again into the Antarctic. Once more they were separated, but this time failed to meet. The *Adventure* eventually gave up and reached London just two weeks before the *Resolution*.

Meanwhile Cook once more passed the Southern Polar Circle, this time at 147 degrees west longitude, and again was stopped at 67 degrees south by ice floes, gales and freezing temperatures. He attempted a southern route further east, and this time reached down to 71 degrees. It was many years before any other seaman duplicated this feat. Cook himself met here an impenetrable ice barrier; his rigging and sails were frozen so they could not be manipulated; the expedition could call itself happy to escape.

Cook knew his men needed sun and fresh fruit, so he went to Easter Island, arriving March 9, 1774, and for three weeks he and his scientists studied this strange place, especially the remarkable high stone monuments found all over the island.

In 1774, the fine plantations of coconuts, grapefruit, and yams cured the Englishmen's scurvy, and from Easter Island they went to the Marquesas and Tahiti where they saw the entire Tahitian Navy preparing to fight against a neighbor island. The fleet consisted of 160 double canoes, 100 feet long, carrying the warriors, and 170 smaller double canoes serving as transports. There were hospital canoes fitted with beds of banana leaves.

Leaving without waiting for the outcome of this war, the Cook expedition sailed west and found a small group of islands now called Cook Islands. The population here was Melanesian, not at all like the amiable Polynesians. Four days later, Cook came to a huge island which he called New Caledonia. The people here had neither pigs nor goats, nor dogs nor cats, and Cook presented them with a pair each of pigs and dogs. Then he sailed to New Zealand for a last try at meeting the *Adventure,* but she had long since left. After three weeks, Cook set out for home, eastward across the Pacific to South America. He reached Cape Horn in January, 1775, continuing east to a little island which he named South Georgia. He dipped southeast to find out if land existed, but no further than 60 degrees south, where he found a small group of ice-covered islands which he called the New Sandwich Islands. He pushed on to the latitude of the Cape of Good Hope, so that he had sailed all around the South Pole without finding any great continent—the real object of his expedition. In July, he was again in England after three years and eighteen days.

The expedition brought back more scientific and geographical information than any before it, and Cook was hailed as a hero by the nation and elected a member by the Royal Society. The government also had another job for him. It had long been a favorite dream of many to find a passage between the Atlantic and Pacific north of America. Now, James Cook, the great navigator, was assigned the job, exploring from west to east. With two ships, *Resolution* and *Discovery,* he sailed out in the summer of 1776.

To get to his starting point, he had to go into the Pacific around the Cape of Good Hope. He had taken with him livestock, cattle, sheep, goats and horses, for the South Sea Islanders, to be distributed on his way. In November, he rounded the Cape, steered east so that he passed south of Australia and Tasmania and from there to his old anchorage in New Zealand. Turning north, he visited several islands before arriving in July, 1777, at his favorite Tahiti, where he persuaded his good friend King Otu to stop the practice of sacrificing human beings to the gods in exchange for Cook's gifts of cattle.

Cook left the Society Islands late in the year, and came on Christmas Day to a small uninhabited islet where there were more turtles than he ever had seen in his life. He called it Christmas Island, and headed north to begin the main task assigned to him. Late in January, he sighted a group of islands which had been visited by Spaniards more than 250 years before but had been forgotten. Cook called them the Sandwich Islands; we know them as the Hawaiian Islands. He thought the people more advanced than most islanders, with well-organized farming, and very anxious to learn. They had a few iron tools which showed they had been in touch with Europeans sometime—actually these were survivals of the long-forgotten Spanish visit.

Sailing on, Cook sighted the coast of North America just south of the Columbia River, at the place Sir Francis Drake had been during his round-the-world trip of 1577-80. Cook overhauled his ships on Vancouver Island, and in April, followed the coast to Alaska, and in through Bering Strait. He became the first sailor to cross both the northern and southern Polar circles, but it was impossible to go further. Heavy ice blocked every lead to the north. After mapping some of the Aleutian Islands, Cook turned back to Hawaii.

He anchored nearly a year after he first saw these islands, in a bay called Karakagua. People thought he was a god who had gone away many, many years before, promising to return on a floating island filled with coconuts, dogs, and pigs. Their king, Tiriobu, gave Cook beautiful coats and feather helmets and exchanged names with him, the highest honor he could bestow. The rest of the stay lived up to this promise for the expedition, but at last in February, 1779, both ships weighed anchor. Overtaken and damaged by a furious gale, they put back to Karakagua to repair. Everything was changed, no canoes to offer food and souvenirs, no people at all. The king had declared the bay "taboo" and no one was allowed to go near it. The superstitious order was fatal to Cook.

Some of his men had persuaded a few Hawaiian women to break the taboo and go with them to Karakagua. The Hawaiians were aroused, and in the morning the lifeboat in which the men had gone ashore was missing. Cook went ashore himself to persuade the king to have the boat returned. He took a few armed men with him, and was winning the king's agreement to come aboard the *Resolution* to discuss the problem when one of his wives admonished him not to go with the foreigners. As he hesitated, someone else shouted that a high-ranking chief had been killed. Instantly fighting broke out; warriors donned their battle dress; the boat in which Cook landed was attacked with the loss of four men killed.

In the midst of the turmoil, Cook was not attacked as long as he stood face to face with the king. When he turned to signal his men to cease firing, one of the Hawaiians leaped at him and stabbed him in the back; others yelled victoriously and dragged his body from the water into which it had fallen, stabbing it over and over.

Cook had instilled so well into his men his ideas of how to treat natives that they did not try to avenge him. They asked only for his body, but it already had been burned, and they could obtain only a bit of his ashes. Hawaiians regarded Cook as the reincarnation of their god, and for years his ashes were the object of much veneration.

Without Cook, the expedition once more tried to find the northwest passage, and failed. Captain Clerc, commander of the *Discovery,* led the expedition to Kamchatka, where he died, and Lieutenant King brought the ships home around the Cape of Good Hope more than four years after they had started.

James Cook must be for all time honored among the most daring and courageous and able sailors of the British Empire. In such a short time as ten years, he achieved more than any man had done before or after him in the extent of new waters explored and territory mapped. He was the first and one of the greatest of the truly scientific leaders of great voyages. It is one of history's ironies that he, who wanted more than any other explorer to be fair to the natives, should have been killed by them.

29

North to the Pole

The story of exploration at the top of the world is more than an account of the dashes northward which ended when Robert Edwin Peary reached the Pole itself. Ever since Willem Barents sailed into the Arctic, brave men and, it must be admitted, foolish men too, had been adding to knowledge about the northern ocean and its lands of ice and snow. The full story is one of science as well as adventure. It may be possible to give an idea of the whole by relating a few of the significant parts.

As long as men lived in Greenland they used gratefully the driftwood which wind and tide and currents deposited on the shores of that treeless country. Where it came from was no concern of theirs. Only later on did scientists begin to think about the route it must have taken, for much of it was known to be of Siberian growth. And then one of the most tragic events in Arctic history prepared the way for an expedition that was to give an entirely new concept of many phenomena in the high Arctic.

The tragedy began when a young American naval officer, Lieutenant Commander George Washington DeLong, interested James Gordon Bennett of the New York *Herald* in an idea he had for reaching the North Pole. Bennett, who had sent the famous traveler Stanley to find Dr. Livingstone in Africa, was not the man to count expenses if a sensational story for his paper was in the making. He promised DeLong to finance his voyage.

DeLong was full of enthusiasm but not sufficiently careful in selecting his crew, although he had some very good men, nor his ship. The three-masted bark *Jeannette*, fitted with an auxiliary steam engine, had come around the Horn into the Pacific. At Mare Island, California, where she was examined, naval contractors and engineers said DeLong was deceived in her, that she never would do for such a trip as he proposed. But Bennett persuaded the government to approve her.

At St. Michael, Alaska, DeLong engaged two Indians, Alexey and Anequin, as hunters and dog-drivers, although why he preferred Indians to Eskimos, who are more experienced in this work in the Far North, is not known. There was a great store of provisions and equipment, but too little coal.

They did not get very far past Bering Strait when on September 6, 1879, the ship froze fast in the ice east of Wrangel Island. They did not worry, however, for they had found a new island which they named Herald for the newspaper. But when summer came again, they got almost no nearer their goal.

December, 1880, found them again in the grip of ice with the temperature at 50 degrees below zero. January brought gales along with the bitter cold; by the end of the month the ice with the ship in it had drifted to 74° 41′ North and 173° 10′ East, north of Siberia. This was no record; in Greenland explorers had been up to 83° North, but DeLong made a number of observations and was satisfied, for he still expected to get out of the ice.

In the summer of 1881, DeLong decided not to use his engine because of the shortage of coal, which would be needed during the coming winter. He relied on sails, but even into June the pressure of the ice grew worse and worse.

The men urged DeLong to leave her and try for shore in the boats but he refused. Ice actually pierced the hull, but when DeLong went below to look, the pressure eased and the openings in the ship's timbers closed. The ship was heeled over at 23 degrees, but DeLong simply ordered Chief Engineer Melville to photograph her as it would make a sensational picture for the *Herald*. But that night as they ate, they could hear the ship shrieking and moaning as the ice squeezed her timbers. All that night they watched, and when the ice came through the sides, they knew the *Jeannette* was lost.

The crew unloaded boats, sledges, pemmican, supplies of all kinds in a haphazard way. Incredibly, no orderly preparations had been made for abandoning ship, and at the last no one could find the casks of lime juice, chief guard against scurvy in those days, although one sailor even dived into the icy water of the forehold.

Thirty-three men gathered around the pile of equipment on the ice. One was too sick to stand, one half-blinded some days before in an explosion, and several suffering from cramps. They had three boats, weighing four tons, and three and a half tons of food and supplies. The Lena Delta, nearest mainland point, was 500 miles away, and the temperature ranged from 10 to 25 degrees below zero.

From this moment, DeLong showed himself a different man with a firmness new to his men. For four days they camped on the ice, sorting supplies and nursing the sick. DeLong ordered the three boats with provisions for sixty days loaded on sledges. Firmly he forbade carrying nonessentials although the men grumbled at leaving their clothing. Only the ship's papers and scientific records were added to the load.

On June 17, 1881, as they were about to eat supper, one of the men shouted that they had better look out of their tents if they wanted to see the last of the *Jeannette*. The ship had been crushed by the ice until it did not look like a ship any more, and now the ice seemed to be content. It opened suddenly, and the remains of the vessel sank within a few minutes.

Next morning they began their terrible journey over the ice. Even after stripping the load still more, they made only five and a half miles in eight days, and when DeLong took his bearings he found that the drifting ice had put them twenty-five miles further north than they started! He did not tell the men. Soon the drift turned south and by July 28 they had covered 180 miles, and saw land which they named Bennett Island. At Kotelni Island, the largest of the New Siberian group, they wasted time looking for provisions around the long-deserted hut of fossil-ivory hunters. At last they could launch the boats. DeLong commanded in one, Melville in another, and the second mate, Cripp, in the third.

They had not gone far when a gale blew up, and suddenly the second mate's boat failed to top a wave. There was nothing the others could do and soon, on September 12, they were parted, too, ninety-two days after the loss of the *Jeannette*. Melville reached the mainland four days later, met some natives, and was saved. DeLong and the eleven men with him did not make it; their bodies were found the following March with the commander's diary beside him. The last entry read: "October 30th, Sunday, 140th day, Boyd and Goertz died during night, Mr. Collins dying." DeLong could not have survived long after that. He had proved himself a brave man who paid for his errors with his life, and provided the impulse for the systematic Arctic exploration of modern times.

The initial quiver of this impulse came in 1884, three years after DeLong died, when an Eskimo seal hunter from Frederikshaab in West Greenland, out in his kayak, saw a confused mass of objects spread out over an ice floe. He helped himself to some, which he showed to the manager of the colony. Later the ice floe was located again, and was found to be bearing supplies from the DeLong expedition. They had drifted across the top of the world, and for one daring explorer this was a challenge to solve a riddle of the North.

The man who saw in the *Jeannette* tragedy a key to Arctic mysteries was Fridtjof Nansen. The year DeLong was dying off Siberia, he was twenty years old and had left his studies at the University of Christiania for a voyage on a sealer, the *Viking*, off the east coast of Greenland. That spring of 1881, he gathered specimens of animals, and collected scientific data on them, at the same time envisaging what later was his first triumph, a trip across the Greenland icecap.

After completing his scientific studies at the University, he was able to prepare for this trip. A sportsman as well as a scientist, he proposed to make the youth of the world conscious of the exciting possibilities of skiing, up to then exclusively a Norwegian device for moving across soft snow. In 1888, he used skis for the first crossing of the icecap, and he proved to be right about the boost it would give to skiing all over the world, so much so that it is now, of course, a great international sport.

When Nansen returned, he had ready a plan for a polar expedition which he laid before the Geographical Society. Although it was strongly criticized, the Norwegian government agreed to pay one-third of his expenses, if the rest was obtained by private subscription.

Nansen's plan was to seek what DeLong had fought against, getting trapped in the ice. The Norwegian proposed to enter the floes at a point where the winds and currents would drift the ship across the top of the world from one side to the other. He expected to pass right over the Pole or very close to it. For his purpose, he needed a ship such as never had been built before, one that would ride with the ice instead of being crushed by it. He and Colin Archer, a Norwegian shipbuilder who must share the honor of the expedition's achievement, designed and built a vessel of great strength, pointed at both bow and stern and with sloping sides so angled (after figuring and refiguring many times) that ice pressure would lift the vessel out of the water instead of cracking the hull. This ship was named *Fram* which means "forward."

With Otto Sverdrup, a great explorer in his own right, also on board, the *Fram* left Christiania (now Oslo) on June 24, 1893. On September 22, Nansen made fast to an ice floe at 78° 50′ North and 133° 37′ East, not far from Bennett Island, the same pack ice which had crushed the *Jeannette*.

Now came the test of the *Fram*'s ability to withstand the deadly thrusts of the ice. The rudder was hauled up, the engine taken apart and oiled for its long rest. When ice pressure on the ship began, everyone rushed up on deck to see how the *Fram* would take it. Slowly the ship was lifted up, just as her designers had intended. Soon the crew grew so indifferent to the deafening noise of the ice pressure that they did not even get up to look at what was happening, let it thunder ever so hard!

As Nansen had calculated, the *Fram* now started drifting northwest, although she was fixed in the ice with her bow pointing south. Because his expedition was so well prepared, there were none of the usual exciting but tragic stories to tell of it. They just drifted, and after nearly a year and a half she was at 84° North, 101° 55′ East.

This was not fast enough to suit Nansen. By now also he knew that the *Fram* would not drift across the Pole; he realized that he should have entered the ice pack further east for that, he said later. So he decided to leave the ship and make a dash for the Pole with one companion, Hjalmar Johansen. On April 14, 1895, they got to 86° 14′ North, the highest latitude yet reached by man, and then came home by way of sledge to Franz Joseph Land where they found a ship.

Meanwhile, Sverdrup was bringing the *Fram* safe home and reached Norway only a week later than Nansen. They had drifted as far north as 85° 57′, then west to Spitsbergen and then southward. Sverdrup knew it was no use to stay longer in the ice because the drift from here was too well known. So in June, 1896, the engine was reassembled and Sverdrup, an old ice navigator, jockeyed the ship free over a course of 180 miles, and in August the *Fram* passed the last of the floes after being fast in the ice for thirty-five months.

Her voyage stands out as one of the most important contributions to oceanography. Six huge folio volumes on the results were published, and Nansen is hailed as the first man in his line. He has been outstanding in everything he did, and when the Nobel Peace Prize was added to his many honors for scientific achievement, the whole world could see that the hero of the *Fram* was a man of many parts—all of them great.

The fact that Nansen had not reached the Pole, however, left an opportunity for another Norwegian, Roald Amundsen, who already had made a name for himself and was to become the only man to reach all four major goals of the aspiring explorer—North Pole, South Pole, Northwest Passage, Northeast Passage.

Roald was born July 16, 1872, on a tiny Norwegian farm. His mother, who wanted him to become a doctor, died shortly after Roald entered the university, and he himself has told me that she was spared a bitter disappointment, because he would have left to be an explorer; nothing could have stopped him. First he had to go through his compulsory military service, which he enjoyed because it hardened him for his later work. Then in 1894, he signed on as a deck hand on a sailing ship to get experience. While the rest of the crew idled away the time between watches, he studied about the sea and navigation and made a nuisance of himself asking questions of the officers.

After three years at sea he was able to take his examination for ship's officer, and at twenty-five he became first mate on the Belgian Antarctic exploration ship *Belgica* under Captain Franz de Gerlache, a fine man but unfortunately more of a scientist than a sailor. The expedition spent a month at Tierra del Fuego studying marine and land life and mapping the rugged coast. Then they sailed south, and it was here that the Captain's shortcomings were felt. At one point, Roald knew they should be heading north out of the ice and forgot himself when Gerlache kept the course south.

"It's a mistake, Sir," he cried. "We'll be smashed to pieces."

Gerlache told him to mind his place and go aft. But the mate was right, and the ship froze fast. The Captain lost his head and his health, and Roald and the ship's doctor really took over and managed the expedition for the thirteen months their ship was frozen tight. The doctor was Frederick A. Cook, whose future was miserable but who was an able traveler and a man of courage.

In later life, Amundsen used to laugh and tell funny stories about this expedition, but at the time it was not so easy. The expedition had not been fitted out for an Antarctic winter, for example, so that there was not sufficient clothing for all the men to be on deck at one time. Amundsen got out his needles and sewed garments for the crew out of extra red blankets. The men were very conspicuous but they were warm. Roald also proved his theory that fresh meat would prevent scurvy—he had them all eat seal, and sick men recovered. In the end, he and Dr. Cook finally got the *Belgica* out, and Gerlache slapped Amundsen on the back in the presence of all the men and said: "You did a fine job, my boy. I shall recommend you." Back home, Roald set himself to study with several scientists to whom he was recommended by Nansen. What he wanted to do was find the Northwest Passage, which had cost so many lives and taken the best years of many daring men. So while he studied, he worked at odd jobs and saved as much money as he could until he found a little old ship, the *Gjoa,* which he thought capable of the voyage.

Nobody else agreed. The *Gjoa,* forty-seven tons, had been a fishing boat in North America for twenty-seven years. But Roald was happy that his ship was the same age as himself. He washed it and scraped it and worked on it himself for two years, supporting himself part of the time as waiter in a water-front restaurant. He gathered friends as enthusiastic as himself, willing to toil at getting the ship ready after a day's normal work. They took short cruises to familiarize themselves with their vessel. But financial backing they could not get. In June, 1902, his creditors, who had been hounding him for some time, served him with a bailiff's bill, which seemed to mean that he would lose his ship and stores.

But Roald would not give up. He went to some dealers he still had not done business with and got some provisions and gear on credit, then got his crew of seven men together, and in a frightful rainstorm, when even the harbor master's men were not out, they slipped away to sea without saying good-by to anybody.

Amundsen proved on the way across the Atlantic that his ship could take gales and waves. Then he re-provisioned, before he set out to negotiate a Northwest Passage. He thought that other ships had been too deep in the water to find it; the little *Gjoa,* just seventy feet long, drew little more than six feet. Even so, he was grounded once but got off, and in King William Land found good winter quarters. Here he stayed for two years, because he had in mind to locate the magnetic pole, too, which he did after a long sledge trip. In 1953, when new observations were taken with instruments much superior to anything he had, the magnetic pole was found to be not far from the place he put it. In his long stay, too, he made collections of plants and animals and studied Eskimo life. At last, in August, 1905, he started the *Gjoa* on her voyage again, and although there were several points in Simpson Strait where there was only an inch of water under the keel, he saw open water ahead on August 26. He returned to Norway with cash enough to pay his creditors, but many of them refused to accept it because they were honored to have

Admiral Robert E. Peary on the main deck of the steamship *Roosevelt*.

had a share in so great an achievement. Amundsen had no trouble getting financial backing now, and he set about preparing an expedition to the North Pole when suddenly a telegram announced that his old friend, Cook, had reached the Pole. Roald was disappointed for himself but glad for his friend, when another telegram gave credit for that exploit to Robert Peary, who also denounced Dr. Cook as a fraud. The actual conquest of the Pole, of course, was achieved by sledge and not by ship. Peary, who had been coming into the Arctic since 1885, was an experienced traveler and a fine organizer.

Peary went by ship, the *Roosevelt* skippered by Captain Bob Bartlett, who later was to become my close friend, as far as Cape Sheridan on the northern end of Ellesmere Island. They spent the winter of 1908–09 on the ship, hunting and preparing for the sledge trip. This started February 15, 1909, and by March 1, Peary had established and pushed on from an advanced base at Cape Columbia, ninety miles away and the last land he would encounter. A series of advance parties prepared the way further north, the last of them under Bartlett turning back at nearly 88°, on March 30. Peary, Matthew Henson, and four Eskimos with two strong dog teams made the final dash. They reached their goal on April 6.

He was loaded with honors and medals and promoted to Admiral when he got home. But meanwhile, Dr. Cook was for a time feted in Copenhagen, where Amundsen came to see him and offered to leave at once for Etah, Greenland, where Cook said he had left some notebooks. I, too, was there, having entered upon my journalistic career for the newspaper *Politiken* to write about the Cook expedition on the basis of my own experience in the Arctic. As a matter of fact, both Amundsen and myself suggested expeditions to Etah, but Cook himself opposed them—it should have made everyone doubt him—and so neither of us made the trip.

At this point in his career Amundsen faced a crisis. His backers cooled to the idea of trying to drift across the Pole, and withdrew their support. Roald had to do something clever, and as usual he did. If the North Pole was no longer unconquered, there remained the South Pole! But as yet he told no one of his plans.

30

South to the Pole

Just one hundred years before Roald Amundsen changed his destination from one end of the world to the other, the first hint that conquest of the South Pole was a land and not a sea operation was discovered by a young American skipper from Stonington, Connecticut, named Nathaniel B. Palmer. Captain Nat, who became one of the most famous masters of sail in the great days of the clippers and the Atlantic packets, was looking for seals, not fame. He found both.

In the New England ports of those days, boys became men very fast. Nat Palmer went to sea when he was fourteen. At seventeen he was a mate, at eighteen he got his first command, but she was just a little coastal schooner, and he was a deep-sea sailor. So when he got a chance to serve as second mate with one of the Stonington sealers, he took it gladly, and at nineteen was sailing to the Antarctic.

Already in those years the relentless slaughter of seals in the known rookeries had thinned out the animals alarmingly from the islands just south of South America. There was no thought as yet of limiting the kill so the seals might survive; the idea of the Stonington men—and of many more from Europe and America—was to find a breeding ground which no hunter had seen before. On his first sealing voyage in 1819, Nat Palmer won the respect of his captain by cleverly figuring out where a British ship, met in the Falkland Islands, was likely to be heading. It turned out to be the South Shetlands, discovered by mistake only that year when another British vessel was blown off her course. The Stonington men followed. They brought back such a load of prime skins and such glowing accounts

275

of the rookeries that an expedition was fitted out for the year 1820.

One of these craft was to be used exclusively for scouting, a handy little sloop of only forty-five tons drawing no more than six feet, specially built for this trip, which would cruise about locating the rookeries so the five brigs and two schooners which made up the rest of the expedition would not have to risk exploring unknown waters and islands. At twenty-one years of age, Nat Palmer commanded this vessel, named *Hero*.

By the time the little fleet reached the South Shetlands in November, 1820, the rookeries had been so thoroughly looted that only a few seals were to be seen. The other captains were glad they had a scout to locate some new beaches, and Captain Nat promptly set off for the south. He found a nice harbor and some eggs on Deception Island but no seals. Since it was a very clear day, he could distinguish the hazy outline of more land about fifty miles further south. He headed for it and on November 18 saw the perpendicular, icy shores of the Antarctic Continent, the first man to discover the long-sought *Terra Australis Incognita*. He sailed along far enough to appreciate its inaccessibility and absence of seals.

He did find seals on other islands, and while the animals were being clubbed on the beaches, he explored some more of the mainland. On the way back he ran into fog, and when it cleared he was surprised to see two warships, which ran up the Russian flag. He was invited on board the larger one, and there met Captain Fabian G. von Bellingshausen, who for a year and a half had been on a mission to find or forever disprove the southern continent. The Russian, surprised that such a small vessel as the *Hero* was cruising around so far from home, was delighted with the news Nat gave him of the mainland. In many books of reference, in fact, Bellingshausen later was credited with the discovery although he never claimed it for himself, and in fact it was he who gave to the land the Americans told him about the name of Palmer Peninsula.

Of course, no one then knew how big this continent was, nor how rugged and filled with glaciers. In the next century some of these things were learned. The Gerlache expedition on which Amundsen and Cook became friends was the first to winter in the Antarctic. After that, wintering was done on shore, not on ships. Men built huts and were left with their supplies, their ship returning for them the next summer. From then on it was well known that the South Pole could be reached only overland.

Back in Norway after the Peary-Cook controversy of 1909, Roald Amundsen refused to be stopped by insufficient funds. He rented a small bakeshop, and he prepared there his own pemmican, canning it himself, and personally storing it on board the *Fram*. And at last he sailed, but not until he reached Madeira on September 10, 1910, did he call all hands on deck to tell them where he was going.

That Amundsen had the South Pole in mind from the start was plain from the fact that he had about a hundred Eskimo dogs on board. Friends wondered why he wanted to bother with them for a long sea voyage, and why he wanted them at all if he intended to drift in his ship across the North Pole. A few suspected he had another plan, and now all the world heard about it. In England the news was received with bad grace because the English explorer, Robert F. Scott, already had started for the same goal.

The *Fram* sailed south. She had a hard time getting through the Antarctic ice, quite different from that which Amundsen had fought in the Northwest Passage, and the southern gales for which she had not been built. But the stout ship stood it all well, and Amundsen, who had been here before, mastered the difficulties again. He never had set foot on the Antarctic Continent, but he felt no fear.

He brought his ship up to the rearing walls of the Ross Barrier, a most inhospitable spot where frequently gigantic pieces of ice a mile long break loose. The Barrier itself is afloat and shifts its position in the ocean. Then Amundsen began to unload his supplies to establish a camp, so the *Fram* could get provisions in Buenos Aires and come back for him and his party after he made his dash for the Pole.

While he was at work on this, one of Scott's ships, the *Terra Nova*, called by. The commander, Lieutenant Hugh Pennell, informed Roald that Scott was one of the foremost experts on the Antarctic and advised strongly against trying to use dogs. Even Sir Ernest

Shackleton, who really was a much better traveler than Scott, preferred ponies. Amundsen replied by offering Scott half his dogs, an offer which was refused.

The story of how Roald conquered the Pole has nothing to do directly with the Seven Seas. But it should be said that with four companions, fifty-two dogs, and four sledges, he left camp October 19, 1911. They reached the Pole December 14, thanks to the leader's fine strategy and the skill of his fellow travelers, including the dogs. The round trip took the party ninety-nine savage days.

Scott, slower in his progress and inferior in his preparations in every way, reached the Pole on January 12, 1912, almost a month after Amundsen left. He had not had much luck with his ponies, and he had not had the moral courage to turn back while he still had a chance. He and his companions died on the way back tragically, and it might be mentioned here that Shackleton, too, perished at Enderby Land in 1922 because he had no dogs. That Scott's name is held in high esteem is not due to his talent as an Antarctic traveler but to his tragic fate which evokes a pity stronger than the sentiment for a man who shows how the job really ought to be done.

Amundsen reached his own camp while Scott was struggling back from the Pole. To his dismay, the *Fram* had not returned when he reached his hut. However, there was plenty of food, and the five men settled down to wait. Their ship arrived the very next day, only twenty-four hours late for the rendezvous made months before; she had been delayed by a terrific gale which taxed her to the limit.

Roald sailed at once to Hobart, Tasmania. Here he went to the telegraph office to inform the world of his discovery, and at least one official would not believe it—"The Scott Expedition must have done that," he said. But he could not reject Amundsen's message, and soon from all over the world telegrams of congratulation poured in. Only not from the Royal Society in England. They were critical and wanted to hear from Scott. They never did.

Amundsen had not forgotten his plans for the North Pole. He spent much time lecturing and receiving honors, but all the time he fitted out the *Fram* for an Arctic drift. At the same time there were possibilities in this newfangled invention, the airplane, and at forty-two years of age in 1914, Roald bought a secondhand Farman biplane and learned to fly. He had everything in order for his expedition, too, when war broke out. Although Amundsen was a citizen of a neutral country, German U-boat warfare, with its gunning of helpless sailors on rafts or in lifeboats, did not fit into his conception of humanity. He had been highly honored by Kaiser Wilhelm, but now he took all his German medals, testimonials and scrolls, packed them in a briefcase and dumped them on the desk of the German Ambassador to Norway.

For the time, his expedition was impossible. He went into ship-building to earn enough money for a future one, and by 1917 had acquired a quarter of a million dollars. That was enough for him, and he ordered a new ship which embodied all that he had learned both north and south. *Maud* was her name and it took a year to build her. She was 120 feet long, forty feet in the beam, made of the best timbers, and food supplies expertly chosen. Amundsen left Tromsoe in her on July 15, 1918, for the Barents Sea.

The *Maud* seems to have been one of those cursed ships which every sailor knows. At first, though, everything went well. The Germans, no doubt, would have liked to sink her because they were desperate by then and torpedoed everything they could, neutral or belligerent. But the *Maud* slipped through, and negotiated the Northeast Passage, passing Cape Chelyuskin early in September. Then the ice thickened and the channels between floes narrowed, so the expedition had to prepare for winter—they spent almost a year here—and Amundsen was not too satisfied with the place. He had hoped to be fast in a floe which would drift across the Arctic Ocean but was not in the current. To make matters worse, he fell and broke his shoulder; then when he walked out in darkness just as it was mending but with his arm still in a sling, he was attacked by a polar bear. He was clawed badly and the fractured shoulder broke again. This time he was two weeks in his bunk.

Bad luck held and three years passed with nothing done. He immediately began to plan another expedition, this one to combine

279

Fotograf Osl

Roald Amundsen.

a ship with a plane which could stay in the air for a full day or longer. But his own fortune had shrunk in the depression to $75,000, and although he was surprised and delighted to hear that the Norwegian Government had appropriated 400,000 kroner to enable him to go on with his work, there was barely enough for his project.

Just at this point, when he was fifty years old, a doctor whom he consulted for a checkup told him his heart was bad and he was through with exploration. Amundsen's answer was to join a mail carrier in Alaska on a trip of 500 miles, walking through deep snow at the rate of fifty miles a day. Then he loaded seven years' provisions on the *Maud* and, leaving for Norway, gave instructions for his business agent to get a plane. When he returned, he found that the agent had bought three, and he could not pay for them. All of a sudden people began to talk of how Amundsen had fled from his creditors in the *Gjoa*. His achievements were forgotten. He was adjudged bankrupt; the *Maud* was put in the hands of receivers, and Amundsen returned to Norway a disappointed but by no means a broken man.

He could raise no money here, only advice to earn money by lecturing in America. He did, but soon found out that it would take him several hundred years at this work. Then, just as he was thinking of taking a job as mate on a merchantman, his telephone rang. He had a mind not to answer it, but he did and a voice said: "My name is Lincoln Ellsworth."

That night changed everything for Amundsen. Ellsworth was a man with enthusiasms and money, too, one of the finest men I ever met. He was without fear, an excellent athlete, a wonderful comrade and friend. He belonged to the new time, and he took Roald Amundsen away from the sea, and so away from this book, into the air. They almost flew over the North Pole in 1925; actually did it with General Umberto Nobile in an Italian airship the next year. Then Nobile tried to do it alone and was wrecked. Amundsen at once fitted out a plane to rescue the Italians, stranded on the ice, and left Tromsoe on June 18, 1928, with Leif Dietrichsen as pilot. They never were heard of again.

No greater man in his own right ever has figured in exploration. No more beautiful death could come to one who, daring to the last, enhanced the fame of himself and his country. But time flies as fast in the Arctic as anywhere else. The feat which was a sensation a few years ago is the commonplace of today when planes fly across the North Pole as a matter of routine. The Northeast Passage is traversed by great fleets of merchantmen every summer, bringing goods and passengers to Siberia.

Even the Northwest Passage, completed only four times since Amundsen did it, is now being examined sharply to see if it can be practicable for cargo ships. The reason is that the line of weather stations, "Distant Early Warning," called the DEW line, has a large crew which must be supplied expensively by air. More money is spent this way than on all Arctic expeditions put together. So the sailors are looking for a feasible ship route, and no doubt they will achieve it. Already buoys which ice cannot damage are marking many of the shoals Amundsen passed, and the Northwest Passage will join the other seaways which men of daring pioneered for the benefit of the entire world.

31

The New Unknown

The heroic days of exploration are over. There is no more undiscovered land to find, no more hidden seas. But that does not mean that we will have no more great voyages. For now the goal of the explorer is changed, and he is a scientist looking for the answers to the age-old riddles of the sea which never could be found by even the most adventurous men sailing to the most remote places.

The great unknown now lies beneath the surface of the waters. The vast uncharted deeps and shallows, mountains and valleys, volcanoes and canyons have only been glimpsed so far. The mysteries of life in the depths of the ocean, of the behavior of tides and currents are still to be unraveled.

In the early days many great scientists had the urge to explore remote parts of the Seven Seas. But they usually were not in good enough health or otherwise were not sufficiently rugged to undergo the hardships of the strenuous voyages of their time. But now with the airplane and the well-appointed ships at their disposal, they have come into their own. They can fly anywhere in a few days, and within three weeks come back after having learned more than ever was found by men of the old style expeditions which sailed out into the ocean and were not heard from again for several years.

Of course the old voyagers made important scientific contributions, too. We have only to remember Magellan trying to find out how deep was the ocean, and Captain Cook making his minute observations, and Charles Darwin on the *Beagle*. But most scientific men were interested in the land, its life, and geography. The first really modern expedition to concentrate on the phenomena of the Seven Seas sailed only eighty-five years ago.

It was called the *Challenger* expedition, from the name of the 2,300-ton corvette on which the scientists embarked. Their leader was Charles Wyville Thomson, a forty-two-year-old professor of natural history at the University of Edinburgh. He and his companions were equipped with the best scientific instruments of the time. Just to follow on a globe the pattern of their voyage is to understand something of their achievement—they took soundings and gathered samples of ocean bottom and noted surface and underwater phenomena all along the route.

The *Challenger* sailed out of Sheerness, England, on December 7, 1872, down to the Canaries, across the Atlantic to the West Indies, up to Halifax, back across the ocean to the Azores and past the Cape Verde Islands, St. Paul's Rock, and Fernando de Noronha to the coast of Brazil. From here by way of remote Tristan da Cunha, she rounded the Cape of Good Hope, and sailed on to Crozet and Kerguelen islands, into the Antarctic, and back to Melbourne and Sydney in Australia. She cruised to Fiji, Hawaii, Japan, then south to the Tropic of Capricorn and east to Valparaiso in Chile, through the Strait of Magellan to Montevideo, Uruguay, across to the Canaries again and so home, reaching Spithead, England, on May 24, 1876, after three and a half years of the most important discoveries.

The *Challenger* had cruised 68,890 sea miles, taken 363 deep soundings, brought back so much marine information that it took thirteen years to arrange and publish it. Professor Thomson, knighted by Queen Victoria, died in 1882, and the work was completed by his colleague, Dr. John Murray. Almost all writings about the sea ever since, including this book, are much indebted to the great *Challenger* expedition.

Not all the scientific exploration has had to cover as much of the Seven Seas as the *Challenger* did. The great Swedish oceanographer, Otto Pettersson, worked out an important theory of the tides and their influence upon mankind without using any scientific observations except those he could take in the fjord where he was born. He already was an old man when I visited him at his home in Bohuslan, looking out over the Baltic—he was ninety-three years old when he died in 1941—and all his life he had been setting his instruments and making his calculations as the tides rolled in and out of the fjord.

What he learned in his studies has explained many things in the history of human beings and of the seas themselves that were until then mysterious. Why were the first colonies of the Vikings in Greenland abandoned? Why were the Middle Ages such a time of storm and terror? Was there any connection between the terrible winds and rains which killed the crops in Southern Europe in those times of famine and the year the Baltic Sea froze so thick that men drove horses and wagons across in places where this never was possible again? What was there about this time that brought so many herring into the Baltic Sea that for many years the herring fishery was a main industry of Danes and Swedes?

As he watched the tides and his instruments, and compared his facts with what already was known, Otto Pettersson thought he found the answer. First he learned that deep down in the sea were tremendous movements of great masses of water which were set off by the tides, so he called them "moon waves." These tide waves rolled into the Baltic Sea from the great ocean below the surface where the much less salty water of the Baltic itself was flowing out. His instruments traced the fluctuations on a paper automatically.

Since the waves grew and subsided with the tides, Pettersson began to wonder if they would not also grow and subside in relation to the strength of the tides, too. This was true, and since astronomers can calculate the position of the heavenly bodies at any time in the past or future, Pettersson could get the dates at which the sun and moon would be in a position to cause the greatest possible tidal pull upon the waters of the sea. He found that this was the case about every 1,800 years.

The period in which we live, Pettersson calculated, is just a little more than halfway from the last time of maximum tide to the next period of minimum tide. The maximum tides should have occurred, according to the position of earth, sun, and moon, in the first third of the fifteenth century. The gentlest period will return at about the year 2350. Of course, these are not reached suddenly. Like the ebb and flow of the tides themselves, there is a gradual increase toward the maximum and a gradual fall toward the minimum.

Working backward from the fifteenth century period of highest tides and strongest "moon waves," Pettersson figured that the previous era of mildness should have been around A.D. 550 and the highest tides again about 900 years before that. If his theory is correct, the many years before and after the maximum tides should be a time of storms; the years around the mildest tides an era of calm and gentle weather. What actually were the facts? Well, indeed for a century before and after the Middle Ages point of highest tides, the old records speak of unprecedented storms and floods and cold. This was the time that the Baltic ice was so much thicker than later, although I have seen it solid enough to walk across. These were the years when Pettersson's ancestors in Sweden were getting rich on the herring fisheries around their shores because the enormously strong "moon waves" were sweeping the herring in from the North Sea and leaving them there. These were the years when the Norsemen no longer sailed straight west to Iceland and Greenland but detoured far south to avoid the ice. In fact, these were the years when the Greenland colonies disappeared, and snow and ice covered their once fertile pastures. And all over Europe old men told their grandchildren that winters weren't so cold when they were boys.

As far back as he could go, Pettersson found that the records backed up his theory. When the Vikings first started on their great adventures in northern seas, there was much less ice than later, if one may believe their sagas. The grass in Greenland was more lush, and other vegetation more plentiful than at any time since. Going back still another nine centuries, Pettersson caught hints of another era of great storms in legends and literature, all the way from Iceland to the Mediterranean.

This long-range cycle, taking 1,800 years to complete the full circle, is made irregular by the fact that there are smaller cycles within it running in multiples of nine years, Pettersson said. These account for the fluctuations from cold to warm seasons which we all can remember. But in the long run they do not interrupt the steady progress of the "moon waves" in creating a milder or a more severe climate.

The new explorers are finding out new facts about the currents, too. At the Oceanographic Institution in Woods Hole, Massachusetts, it had been suggested that many of the major ocean currents such as the Gulf Stream, Humboldt, and so on have a return flow in a countercurrent along the bottom. A new instrument which for the first time makes it possible to measure deep ocean currents has shown that this theory is a fact.

The instrument was constructed by Dr. Swallow, a British oceanographer. It is a strong aluminum tube, closed at the end and weighted on a minutely graduated scale so that it will sink to any desired depth in the sea and then remain at that level. The weight of sea water increases the deeper one goes because of the pressure, so that the aluminum tubes, which resist pressure much better than water, could be precisely regulated. Each tube carried a battery-powered transmitter which could send ultrasonic messages for miles.

It had been easy, of course, for ships to take samples of sea water from the surface right down to the bottom. Differences in temperature, salinity, and oxygen content were the factors which made scientists think of deep countercurrents. Now Dr. Swallow released his deep water floats—if such an expression may be used—one after another. They were regulated to sink to various depths off the South Carolina coast where the Gulf Stream runs northward at its fastest. With submarine detecting apparatus, Dr. Swallow could follow the course of his tubes by picking up the ultrasonic signals. It was found that for a couple of thousand feet down, the Gulf Stream flows to the north. Between 4,500 and 6,000 feet there is virtually no motion in either direction. But deeper down there is a definitely detectable countercurrent flowing southwards at as much as one-third of a mile

Piccard's bathysphere.

an hour. Up to now the Gulf Stream is the only current examined in this way, but probably the same conditions exist everywhere.

As the scientific adventurers in the sea get more ingenious, and stronger equipment, they are discovering all sorts of wonders about the deep ocean. Some of them even get to look at it with their own eyes. They do it in a modern version of Alexander's glass barrel which is called a bathysphere. The latest ones are heavy steel bubbles with portholes of new synthetics, powerful searchlights, good air-conditioning, cameras, and other instruments.

William Beebe, the American scientist and author, was the first to reach any great depths in one of these devices. Off Bermuda on August 15, 1934, he let himself down to a depth of 3,028 feet, and then wrote a book about it, *Half Mile Down*. He was the first man to see what the ocean was like at such depths. His record was broken by one of his own colleagues, Otis Barton, who took the bathysphere down off California, in 1949, to a depth of 4,500 feet.

Now, this has been greatly exceeded by two French naval officers who went down to 13,287 feet, or more than two and a half miles, in a bathysphere built by the French Navy to specifications drawn up by Professor Auguste Piccard, a Belgian scientist more noted for setting altitude records over the Alps than for depth records in the sea. The Frenchmen, Georges Houot and Pierre-Henri Willm, tested their bathysphere several times in the Mediterranean and established the fact that it had enough oxygen to last them for thirty-two hours. They made their record dive in the Atlantic off the west coast of the "hump" of Africa on February 15, 1954.

Many men in universities and institutes and government departments all over the world are working to expand our knowledge of the Seven Seas. It is possible only to give some idea of the enterprises on which they are engaged, not even to list them. I am sure every student of the ocean will think that many important researches are omitted here, and that indeed is the case. But we might speak of one or two interesting examples with the understanding that they are by way of illustration, not with any intention of slighting the achievements of so many others.

In the United States, Professor W. Maurice Ewing of Columbia University has been for many years engaged in notable research which adds to our knowledge of the ocean's depths. Some of his earlier acclaimed studies were measurements of the sediments deposited on the ocean floor, and the rocks beneath them. He used sonic instruments to record the intervals of sound echoing back after an underwater explosion. He got one echo from the bottom and a second one from the bedrock underneath the sedimentary deposits. Using the known speed of sound, he was able to measure the thickness of the sediments. Dr. Ewing made the first of these studies on board the *Atlantis* of the Oceanographic Institute at Woods Hole. Other measurements taken in the same way were made by the Swedish *Albatross* expedition, and so many deposits were known in

289

a relatively short time. The thickest of them was 12,000 feet.

More recently, as head of the Lamont Geological Observatory of Columbia University, Dr. Ewing has combined instrumental observations taken in laboratories on shore with those he and his associates get on their floating laboratory, the three-masted schooner *Vema*. At his headquarters on the Hudson River Palisades, Dr. Ewing has seismographs so delicate that spiders tramping about can cause them to register, and they also record undersea earthquakes anywhere in the world. From the *Vema* it has been possible to collect a great many samples of the ocean bottom in the form of "cores" which can be studied, and also the Ewing people have devised a technique for lowering cameras and taking pictures at a greater depth than any others I know about. It was from such data as this, supplemented by the records compiled by other scientists all over the world, that Dr. Ewing traced the vast trench in the bottom of the oceans which I have described in an earlier chapter.

Another famous continuing exploration of the ocean is one led by the French scientist, Jacques-Ives Cousteau, on board the laboratory ship *Calypso*. These *Calypso* Oceanographic Expeditions, as they are known, have done especially interesting work in and on the Indian Ocean.

There is still one more route for the modern explorer to take, and in some ways it is a return to the adventures of the past. It is provided by quite a new science, marine archaeology, a way of studying the relics of the past to develop new information and understanding of earlier civilizations. It seems to open up as rich a field for this research as the "digs" which attracted older archaeologists and excited the wonder of the world in deserts and jungles, at the sites of long abandoned cities and remote villages.

Since the men of these earliest civilizations went down to the sea in ships, they unfortunately were wrecked every so often. If that happened to them on an open coast, their vessel would be pounded to pieces, and all traces would soon disappear. But ships which foundered in water too deep to be affected by the waves, and this need be only a few fathoms, would be preserved better than if they had been in a dock. From such remains it should be possible to learn as much about the life of those times as has been discovered from the careful excavations of tombs and houses and palaces on land. But the wrecks must be approached with just as much care.

The Mediterranean, of course, is supposed to be the greatest storehouse of such sunken ships. It was the great trading highway of the ancient world, and the records tell of many wrecks. From time to time divers have seen them and even brought up statues and pieces of pottery from some of them. But this is not the same thing as serious study of the vessel itself by learned men, and until a few years ago there was no way for an archaeologist to get down to one of these wrecks.

In the last few years the invention of self-contained diving equipment permits the scientist to do his work on the bottom of the sea—anyway, down to 100 or even 150 feet—with the same care that he can in digging out an Egyptian tomb. The older diving suits with heavy helmets and air pumped down were for expert craftsmen. The so-called free diver with a tank of compressed air on his back, goggles or mask on his face, flippers on his feet and some lead weights in his belt can swim around under water for as much as an hour at a time.

One man who has done it and has written the first books in this new science is a Frenchman named Philippe Diolé. In his two books, *The Undersea Adventure,* and *4000 Years Under the Sea*, I have learned most of what I know of undersea archaeology. No one yet has done one of these submarine "digs" with all the scientific precautions which M. Diolé would like to see, but he tells of some remarkable discoveries.

The one which struck me as most interesting was the wreck of a big Roman cargo ship of the year 86 B.C., loaded with Greek art—marble columns, statues, bowls, candelabra, busts, decorative cornices, and so on. She had gone down in a storm off the North African port of Mahdia, a little southeast of Tunis. We know it must have been a storm, M. Diolé tells us, because the crew had put out five anchors in an attempt to hold the ship from being blown out to sea.

Photograph by G. Beuchat-Borelli from *Undersea Adventure* by Philippe Diolé. Courtesy of Julian Messner,
The undersea archaeologist.

For two thousand years the ship rested in about twenty fathoms of water. Then in June, 1907, a Greek sponge diver reported seeing some odd looking mounds which looked like big guns covered with silt. The news happened to reach a skilled scholar, Alfred Merlin, the Director of Tunisian Antiquities. With government and private backing, he was able to conduct five exploring expeditions to the wreck between 1908 and 1913. He had to use professional divers, of course, and M. Diolé notes that the inability of the scientist to see the wreck in position was the one drawback. Otherwise the expeditions, which overcame many difficulties with great ingenuity, were a brilliant success. Some of the greatest of the world's present treasures of antiquity were brought up from that wreck. Also the recovery of ordinary implements used on board added to the knowledge we have of life on these ships.

Not all of the heavy columns could be raised then, and it is an exciting second act to the story that thirty-five years later, after two world wars, another expedition was sent out to explore the Roman wreck. This one could have the "free divers," and they were able to work more gently than the heavy-footed, helmeted divers of a generation before. Four of the big columns were raised—one weighed three tons—and the ship itself studied. She had been 126 feet long with a beam of thirty-six feet, obviously one of those round and clumsy Roman cargo ships. The columns had been placed across her deck; the smaller objects stored in the hold below. It seems obvious

292

that the weight of the freight must have contributed to the wreck.

It is part of the interest of marine archaeology that modern science can read a lot into a few simple objects. For instance, a chemical analysis of one of the ship's nails proved that they were of a certain age, made of copper which had been handled by very skilled metallurgists, and much purer copper than any refined nowadays.

M. Diolé describes the researches which have been conducted at the site of other wrecks. One was a ship which had carried a cargo of pottery and wine in the clay jars which the ancients used. Many of the jars were intact, with inscriptions which enabled scholars to establish the name of the man who had owned them—and he lived in 240 B.C. There are other wrecks of about the same era where the wine is still preserved in the jars.

The marine archaeologist does not have to limit himself to the study of wrecks, of course. There are the very interesting remains of old harbors. There is much evidence that on many coasts the land has sunk—or the sea has risen—and that the vestiges of old, drowned cities could still be found preserved under the sea at least as well as Pompeii was under volcanic ashes and lava. Nor is it likely that these cities were overwhelmed with sudden disaster. They would rather have been abandoned as the waters slowly encroached upon the land. But they may tell us about the ways in which prehistoric people met the irresistible demands of the ocean.

The defeat of the Spanish Armada.

Part VI

Battles at Sea

The Battle of Salamis, detail from the celebrated painting by William Kaulbach.

32

The Battle of Salamis

Xerxes, King of Persia, the Great King, the King of Kings, was a mighty conqueror, as everyone has read. On September 28 in the year 480 B.C., he sat on a hill in Attica to watch a drama which no man since then has seen from so fine a stage. He had a panoramic view of one of the big, decisive naval battles of all history from an eminence high enough to look out over the whole scene and close enough to distinguish the movements of individual ships. There were a thousand of them down there in the Bay of Eleusis—an island which formed the outer shore of the bay was called Salamis, someone told him.

The ships already were the development of hundreds of years of naval warfare. No one knows how long men had been fighting each other on the water. But by the time of Xerxes, the warship was as different from the merchantman as a modern destroyer is from a cargo carrier.

Both the Greeks and Persians fought in solidly built craft as much as 150 feet long, nearly twice the length of the biggest of Columbus' ships. Their triremes, as they were called from the fact that they were propelled mainly by great long oars arranged in three tiers, were about eighteen feet in beam and almost flat-bottomed so that they drew no more than four feet of water. Their bows, heavily reinforced to serve as rams, curved up and back; sterns were curved only a little less. A stumpy mast and square sail helped move them when the wind was right. With oars alone they could make ten knots for a short spurt.

A trireme could carry as many as 220 men. Most of them tugged at the long oars. Forty or fifty infantrymen armed with sword, axe, and dagger, were the fighting force for close quarters, and that was what decided battles as a rule. Half as many archers and javelin throwers might be aboard, too, loosing their missiles as the trireme came within bowshot of the enemy. The only weapon capable of doing any damage to another vessel was the ram. Of course, the first attempt always was to crash into the side of an opponent, but if that did not work, and usually it did not, the vessel would be attacked by actual boarding, and captured in hand-to-hand battle.

Triremes seldom ventured out of sight of land and were beached or anchored close to shore every night, although merchantmen were capable of long voyages. Triremes were unseaworthy in rough weather, and so crowded that it was remarkable when one of them carried enough provisions to last her crew for three days. There were no sleeping quarters; oarsmen and soldiers camped on shore at night and even went ashore to prepare meals. So they had to be attended by fleets of smaller sailing ships carrying food, weapons and gear. (The Persians in this campaign had five supply vessels or transports for every two of their fighting ships. The Greeks, being closer to home, did not need so many.)

Strategy was fairly simple in these days. Naval commanders tried to maneuver around enemy ships so as to be able to ram them in the side, and if that failed, ships closed with each other and fought it out on the decks. The ships fought in close ranks, no more than ten ship lengths apart and often no more than two.

We can picture the mighty Xerxes in his grandstand seat waiting for the show his fleet had arranged for him. His black hair and beard would be oiled and perfumed. He wore a great deal of splendid jewelry and was wrapped in gorgeous robes of purple or white. He expected his Navy to complete for him this day a great project on which he had lavished all the strength of his empire for five years— the conquest of Greece.

The whole campaign had been a triumph for the strategy and forethought of Xerxes. He had led his army overland, building a bridge across the Hellespont to do it, through Thrace and Thessaly in a march wonderful for that time. He had been delayed for two days at the pass of Thermopylae by Leonidas, King of Sparta, with a mere handful of soldiers, but the heroes of this forlorn hope—every one of them had died in the pass—had provided the one bit of glory gained by the Greeks so far. The fleet, which had covered the sea flank for the guardians of Thermopylae, had fought for two days. Then, the pass lost, the ships withdrew south to the Bay of Eleusis.

Meanwhile the Persians had swept into Greece; they occupied undefended Athens on this September day. As soon as the Greek fleet was out of the way, the conquest of the rest of the peninsula would be easy. In fact, Athenian refugees on various islands, including Salamis, were talking about crossing the sea to found a new home as Trojans founded Carthage after the destruction of their city.

Greece, then, was at bay in these narrow waters between the island of Salamis and the Attic coast. The fate of classic civilization rested with the 375 Greek ships and their 80,000 men who, forced to retreat once, now faced a considerably larger number of Persian triremes—600 or 700, manned by 120,000 men.

Xerxes was quite sure that besides his superiority in numbers, he enjoyed a superiority in morale. He had received a message from the man who was the soul of the Greek alliance, Themistocles the Athenian. A shrewd man, said to be not very scrupulous, he had inspired the coalition of Greek states formed when word of Xerxes' grand preparations began to circulate through the world. Themistocles was a big navy man, too, and his eloquence and political tricks had added 200 triremes to the fleet. In the beginning he had shared command with Eurybiades the Lacedaemonian. Now he was ashore, leaving Eurybiades in sole command, but he helped the cause by words which led Xerxes to suppose that the Greek fleet had no stomach for another fight.

Already the Greeks had a reputation for trickery which should have made even a confident conqueror suspicious. But the news was too near to the Great King's desires to be doubted. His reliance on what Themistocles said dictated the Persian tactics. Before entering the Bay of Eleusis from the east, they detached the Egyptian squadron to block the west, and these ships, nearly two hundred of them, were seventeen miles from the scene of the decisive action, just as Themistocles had planned.

The main Persian force would not have attempted to attack if it had expected serious resistance. It had to come through a narrow strait where no more than nine ships could keep in line. Then the whole column must make a sharp turn to the right, through an angle of at least 45 degrees, before it could deploy on a broad front. A few ships were sent by way of an even narrower channel, either as a diversion or to come at the Greeks from another quarter.

Themistocles had foreseen this maneuver, and naval experts say his plan of battle was the first in which a fleet prepared to defeat an attacker by taking up a position which flanked his advance. The Greek triremes were drawn up in a massive column, fifteen ships in line and twenty-five deep with an interval of 100 yards between them. As the Persians wheeled their vessels around out of the straits, the Greeks came on at full speed, the oarsmen straining every muscle as they heaved at the great sweeps. Before the Persians could form any sort of ordered line, the Greek rams crashed into their sides.

Dozens of Persian triremes were destroyed then and there. The others, although they succeeded in getting into the bay, never did manage to recover a solid formation, and were left at a fatal disadvantage in the in-fighting which followed. The Greeks always had superiority in boarding anyway because their infantrymen were more powerfully armed and wore better armor than the Persians. No one knows how great was the loss, but so little of the attacking fleet survived that Xerxes on his hill knew that the invasion of Greece was ended. He needed control of the sea to supply his army, and the remnants of his fleet were still in sight, fleeing for safety through the straits, when he began his withdrawal to Thessaly.

The Battle of Salamis freed the Greeks from their most serious foreign threat. Athens went on to the Golden Age of Pericles, who was about twenty years old when Salamis was fought, and the development of a civilization which has remained the pride of mankind.

33

The Battle of Svoldr

Before the year 1000, Scandinavians had developed the arts of navigation and shipbuilding far beyond the rest of Europe. This gave them a formidable advantage over farmers and fishermen wherever they sailed, and always they came as enemies.

The fact was that they were forced to the sea because at home they had not the resources for their fast-growing population. Only the coasts of their countries were inhabitable; the interior was impenetrable forest. They could live from their own land only by fishing or tilling a miserable soil. Then their seafarers brought from foreign nations some samples of a more luxurious standard, and soon the demand for a share of such things rose insistently. It became every man's duty to go "Viking" for a few years to procure the means to keep him for the rest of his life.

This habit made them all warriors, and their religion led them to glory in battle, too. They were hardy and courageous anyway, and it was an advantage to them in their chosen trade that they had no fear of being killed. They wished only to preserve their kinfolk. For their religion taught them that if relatives avenged those who died, the slain warriors were guaranteed perpetual joy and luxury in Valhalla.

At first each man built his own vessel. Later specialists took over, and big shipyards produced navies of many strong, long ships. Some of the mightiest chiefs made themselves kings, and if their kingdoms seem tiny in our eyes, a ruler's real sovereignty was in a big fleet with strong crews living abundantly over the winter on his bounty so they would be prepared to follow him in the summers to any coast where booty could be had. Denmark, Norway, and Sweden were divided into smaller kingdoms of this kind, and of course each ruler was eager to enlarge his territory. Some succeeded although they were restrained in part by the laws of so-called "honor," which forbade some practices, and sometimes by family alliances since they often were related to each other and intermarried in family treaties which helped keep the peace.

The Danish King of this period, Sweyn Forkbeard, son of Harold Bluetooth, as a young prince had plundered in England, and when he became king he looted there on an even greater scale. The weakling monarch of England, Ethelred the Unready, undertook to pay 10,000 pounds of silver, the so-called "Danegeld," as tribute to avoid raids, and agreed to allow the Vikings to live free in England.

This, of course, only invited new forays, and Sweyn joined with the Norwegian King Olaf Tryggveson for another expedition. With about 100 ships they tried to capture London, already the biggest and richest city in England, but the brave citizens drove them off. They plundered the countryside, however, until Ethelred paid a new tribute of 16,000 pounds of silver. Sweyn returned to Denmark, but Olaf remained until he got 22,000 pounds, in return for which he agreed to be baptized, and promised to defend the coasts of England even against his old friends.

For the first time there was a split between the Nordic kings, and at the time it did not seem very big because Olaf stayed in Norway, not interfering, while Sweyn Forkbeard raided England for seven years in succession, until Ethelred paid a new Danegeld, this time 24,000 pounds. Meanwhile Olaf had killed his only rival in Norway, Earl Haakon. Then, not content with having all of northern Norway, he took over the southern section which had belonged to Sweyn of Denmark.

About this time a new factor increased the enmity of the two. The King of Sweden died, leaving a rich and proud widow, Sigried Storreade. She was a good matrimonial catch, but dangerous; she had two suitors burned to death in her guesthouse. Olaf, however, won her consent to marry him, which would make him greater than ever.

Viking sea warriors.

Unfortunately, he sent her as a gift a famous ring, which once had ornamented a pagan temple. Sigried was pleased with it until she had it examined and found that inside it was nothing but copper. Her feelings were so hurt that when it came time to discuss the wedding and Olaf demanded that she be baptized, she refused, saying she would keep to the old religion although he might believe what he pleased. Olaf was not accustomed to arguments.

"Do you really think I then want you, you old hag and pagan bitch?" he cried, and flung his glove in her face.

Sigried then married Sweyn Forkbeard, and neither of them tried in the least to lessen the other's desire for revenge on Olaf. This, indeed, was heightened by another family quarrel. Sweyn had sent his sister Tyre against her will to Poland to marry Earl Boleslaw. A week after the wedding, she managed to run away, and took refuge in Norway, where she married Olaf. So far from mending the breach between the new brothers-in-law, this was adding insult to insult, and the accumulation led to the most famous naval battle ever fought in the North.

Olaf had gone to Poland to negotiate the matter of Tyre peacefully with her first husband when his enemies began gathering a fleet against him. To Sweyn's own ships were added those of young King Olaf of Sweden, Sigried's son, and some brought by Eric Haakonsson, son of the Norwegian Earl whom Olaf Tryggveson had killed. The King of Norway hurried home and took command of seventy-one long ships, with himself in *The Long Serpent,* considered the largest and most costly ship ever built in Norway.

On a beautiful autumn day, September 9, 1002, the two fleets found each other in the Baltic Sea at a place called Svoldr on the north shore of what now is Pomerania. Olaf Tryggveson defended himself valiantly for a long time. In fact, he made head against both Danes and Swedes. But then came the ships of Eric Haakonsson, and it was Norwegian against Norwegian. Eric smashed ship after ship and at last reached *The Long Serpent.* This pride of its time was attacked from all sides, bows and spears and swords being wielded by experts. One of Olaf's warriors was Ejnar Tambeskaelver, the greatest archer the North ever knew, and he killed man after man until at last his bowstring was hit by an arrow. Olaf heard the string snap. "What was it that broke?" he asked.

"The Kingdom of Norway out of your hands, Sire," replied the bowman.

Now the enemy attacked more furiously than ever, and just before *The Long Serpent*'s deck was cleared completely, King Olaf threw himself overboard, his heavy armor dragging him down to die in the sea. The victors found his widow in the hold. Eric Haakonsson tried to console her and offered to marry her, but she refused both him and all food until she died nine days later.

The consequences of the Battle of Svoldr were immense. The three victorious princes divided Norway among them. Eric got the northern part, Olaf of Sweden the middle, and Sweyn the south. But Olaf turned over his share to Eric's brother, and Sweyn gave his to Eric himself, so that all Norway was in Norwegian hands.

This was much, but the effects in England were more. The miserable Ethelred decided that the Danes had suffered so much in the battle he could free himself from them. He arranged that on a certain night all Danes in England were to be murdered, regardless of sex or age or rank. In the eastern part of the country, there were many Danes and the plan did not succeed. Elsewhere the English slaughtered their conquerors in the most terrible ways. Some Danes were buried alive. Others were buried only up to the breast, and then dogs were set on them to tear them to pieces. Still others were burned, and children had their brains dashed out on doorsteps.

The young and beautiful Gunnhild, Sweyn's sister, was forced to watch the murder of her husband and child, then was tortured horribly, her stoicism spurring her tormentors to ever more painful devices. In Guildford, only twelve daring young Danes escaped in a boat down the Thames, captured a ship at sea, and sailed to Denmark to bring the news to their King.

Sweyn gathered ships and many of the most ferocious Vikings from all Scandinavia to wreak his revenge. For five years he plundered England, suffering only one defeat at Thetford in all that time, until in 1007, Ethelred paid 36,000 pounds Danegeld, and promised to let all Danes live free in England. Sweyn took the money, but did not keep the peace. In 1012, Ethelred tried to buy him off with 48,000 pounds, but again the Danish King accepted the cash without bothering about the terms. Now there was no more money to be had in ravaged England, so in 1013, Sweyn decided to take over the country permanently. He sailed with a mighty fleet and his son, Canute, and by midsummer established himself as King. The next year he died of a heart attack while preparing a meeting of his chiefs at Gainsborough; punishment from Heaven, it was said, because he had seized all the money which was formerly sent to the Pope in Rome. Canute, who later was credited with the story of how weak man is against the sea because he cannot command the tides to stop, succeeded his father.

And so the Danish conquest of England can be traced to the Battle of Svoldr. Many Danes settled in England under Canute, but as always when the Vikings took homesteads, neglected their ships and forgot about the sea which had made them great, they degenerated slowly, and they were not able to hold the new kingdom.

Official Mystic Seaport Photograph by Louis S. Martel

34

The Battle of Lepanto

The Vikings' successors as the terror of the seas, at least of the southern European seas, were the Turks. It has been a long time since anyone thought of them as a particularly dangerous naval power, but in the first half of the sixteenth century they were supposed to be unbeatable. Their Sultan Solyman, who came to his throne at the age of twenty-four, in 1520, was called "The Magnificent" as much for the prowess of his navy as for his warlike exploits on land or his patronage of arts and sciences.

Venice, the strongest Christian naval power of that day, hardly tried to do more than defend her own islands and canals, although in an earlier age her ships had offered battle in the eastern Mediterranean. The coasts of Italy, France, and Spain were raided periodically and systematically by Solyman's auxiliaries, the Barbary pirates.

Through most of Solyman's long reign, naval battles were chiefly raids by or against the pirates. No one dared challenge the Turkish fleet in its own waters. Then, in 1565, the world began to hear that the venerable Sultan was assembling the biggest fleet ever seen upon the seas. Every Christian port in the Mediterranean was alarmed for fear of being the target. But there was little secrecy about government plans in that age of easy gossip and small security precautions. Pretty soon it was known that the Turks were aiming at Malta because they didn't like any pirates except their own.

Malta's ninety-five square miles were the haven of what the West said was a religious order, the Knights of St. John of Jerusalem.

Only Moslem heretics would be so impious as to brand these warriors of the Cross as pirates. However, they had been raiding Turkish commerce ever since the Crusades with the thoroughness of the Barbary corsairs, and Solyman proposed to put an end to them and their Order once and for all. In 1530, he had succeeded in driving them from their original home on the island of Rhodes. Emperor Charles V then presented the refugee knights with the island of Malta, and they had gone on seizing or sinking Turkish ships with a strong fleet of galleys manned by war-loving adventurers from all over Europe.

For five months the garrison, which had five thousand men to start with, rolled back wave after wave of Turkish assaults. On a very thin diet, the knights fought by day and rebuilt shattered fortifications by night. Finally a Spanish fleet fitted out in Sicily, which then belonged to Spain, came to the rescue. Only five hundred of the knights were still alive.

The siege of Malta proved that the Turks could be beaten. But they still ruled the Mediterranean, and the Barbary pirates were worse than ever. Christian rulers after long exchanges of plans decided on a big effort in 1571 to destroy Turkish naval power and so deprive the pirates of the Sultan's protection. The actual contributors to the Allied fleet were Spain, Venice, Genoa, the Pope, and the Knights of St. John, who speedily recruited new members and built new galleys. The Papal State in those days had a substantial army but a very small navy, so His Holiness' chief share was to finance the Knights. Between them, they furnished one-sixth of the eventual fleet, Venice and Genoa two-sixths, and Spain three-sixths.

As the senior partner, the King of Spain was entitled to name the commander of this force. The King was Philip II, son of Charles V. Philip had a half-brother twenty years younger than himself, an illegitimate son of the illustrious Emperor Charles. The boy had been reared with Philip's own son and nephews in almost royal dignity—he was addressed as "Excellency" instead of "Highness"—and called with ostentatious simplicity merely Don John of Austria.

In 1571, Don John was twenty-four years old and already had

Don John of Austria.

made a reputation as the last of the knights of the great age of chivalry. He was no more than middle-sized, but he was a singularly handsome fellow with deep blue eyes and a lot of golden curls which he wore pushed back from forehead and temples. A dashing swordsman, huntsman, and ladies' man, the most graceful dancer at court and one of the acknowledged wits, he charmed men and women alike with his gayety, generosity and an expressive voice.

Don John's admiring older brother conferred upon him the title of Captain General of the Holy League and sent him off to sea at the head of the second biggest fleet ever floated in one body of water —300 and some odd ships into which were packed more than 80,000 sailors, rowers and soldiers. (Among them was a common soldier, Miguel de Cervantes, who was just the same age as the Captain General.) The very biggest fleet was the one they sailed east to meet. The Turks had nearly 400 ships and 120,000 men, under the command of Ali Pasha.

Except for the introduction of cannon, the vessels and the way of handling them in a fight would have been more familiar to the warriors of Salamis, 2,000 years earlier, than to the seamen who fought Trafalgar 150 years later. Oars were the main motive power, although the sails were larger and a little better handled than those of antiquity. The cannon, capable of murderous damage at close quarters, were not much for accuracy or range. Their gunners were sorry marksmen with no devices to help them compensate for the pitch or roll of their ship. The guns, which were introduced as part of naval armament a few years after 1350, fired solid shot—shells were a much later development. Naval skill consisted of getting in close to ram the enemy or come alongside in the most advantageous position for a cannonading broadside or a boarding, while preserving a formation which would prevent the foe from doing the same. The final stage of a battle was up to the soldiers fighting hand-to-hand on slippery decks cluttered with all sorts of gear and debris.

Don John's ships assembled without interference at Messina in Sicily, which then had one of the better Italian harbors. Ali Pasha later was criticized for letting the various portions of the fleet get together without interference. Instead, he waited confidently in the Aegean Sea and there, off the small Greek port of Lepanto, only a few miles on a straight line from the scene of the Battle of Salamis, the Allies found him.

The Turkish galleys, with supply vessels behind them, stretched in a formidable line of battle right across a gulf which sometimes is given the name of Corinth and sometimes Lepanto. The extreme left, commanded by Uluch Ali, and the extreme right under Mahomet Sirocco, both experienced sea warriors, were within cannon shot of the two shores. Ali Pasha gave his personal attention to the massive center of his line.

When the Allies sailed up the gulf far enough to observe the enemy's formation, a council of war was held on board Don John's flagship. The principal commanders thought the redoubtable Turks were in too strong a position to be attacked. Such was the view of the Genoese Andrea Doria, grandnephew and namesake of one of the most famous Renaissance naval *condottiere*. Marc Antonio Colonna, another experienced admiral and member of one of Rome's most influential families, agreed as did the Venetian leaders, Barbarigo and Veniero. The Spaniard of second highest rank and most battle experience, the Marquis of Santa Cruz, admitted that the Turks were strongly placed, but he doubted that the wily Ali Pasha could be enticed into offering a better opening.

Young Don John as Captain General took responsibility for overriding the council majority. A gallant knight always was for bold action, and he reserved for himself the post of greatest danger. He instructed the Venetians to attack Mahomet Sirocco on one side while the Genoese sailed against Uluch Ali. He himself, with most of the Spanish galleys, undertook to smash the center. Santa Cruz, with the rest of the Spaniards, would act as reserve and fling his weight into the battle wherever he saw it needed.

The admirals returned to their own commands, sails were hoisted, the long oars bit into the water and the Allied line bore down upon the waiting Turks. On the deck of one of Don John's galleys, Miguel de Cervantes, like all the other soliders, adjusted helmet and breast-plate, fingered his sword, and stared across the narrowing gap between himself and the enemy. The date was October 7, 1571.

Cannon fire at first caused more noise and smoke than casualties. Cannon balls skipped across the water and here or there plunked into a hull or broke an oar. As the Allied line came within this distance, the Turkish wing commanded by Uluch Ali executed a deft maneuver. His galleys feinted inshore as if to pass around the right end of the Allied line and come in from the side. When Andrea Doria ordered his steersmen to turn to meet this threat, Uluch nimbly changed course, and the whips of his galley masters cracked as they drove the slaves to greater efforts, speeding to piece the gap widening between Doria's Genoese and the rest of the Allied fleet. It was a stroke which might have plunged the whole line into inextricable confusion. But Santa Cruz knew his business. He had watched the Turkish maneuver, and his galleys were dashing into position to plug the hole left by Doria's change of course.

Meanwhile, Don John crashed full into the Turkish center. The gunners began to get in damaging shots at close range, ships shuddered into jarring collisions, men yelled in all tongues and dialects of the Mediterranean. The fighting was fierce and deadly, one of the bloodiest of all naval battles. The Allies admitted to 8,000 killed and 16,000 wounded. No one ever knew just what the Turkish losses were, but the estimate of 25,000 dead is accepted generally by historians as falling short of the truth, if anything. Ali Pasha's own galley was captured. Of all the proud Turkish fleet, only a handful of Uluch Ali's squadron escaped.

One of the casualties was Cervantes, whose left hand was permanently crippled this day. Future generations, in fact, would remember the battle chiefly for this reason, and the creator of Don Quixote was nicknamed *el manco* (the maimed one) *de Lepanto*.

The news of the victory sped across Europe as fast as ships and horses and running men could carry it. In every Christian country

The Battle of Lepanto.

one happy statistic gave hope to bereaved families. Much muscle was required to move the galleys, and the Turks used "infidels" almost exclusively for this work. They used so many, in fact, that Don John found no fewer than 15,000 Christian slaves chained to the oars of the galleys he captured. Most of them were seamen taken by Turkish or pirate warships or strong fellows seized during raids on Christian coastal towns. Now they were to be sent home, some of them after many years, although usually the life of a galley slave was short.

Their liberator was the darling of Europe. No other such international hero arose during his generation. Englishmen, Frenchmen, Spaniards, Germans, Italians, much as they hated each other, could all rejoice in the splendor of this golden youth's victory. Men of many nations began to brush their hair in imitation of his. Te Deums were sung in fifty thousand churches.

These were the first fruits of the greatest battle fought in the memory of living men. It would be nearly 350 years before naval powers would be able to bring as many men and ships together for a fight as were involved at Lepanto. The supremacy of the Turks at sea was ended forever.

313

The control of sea-borne trade and therefore of the development of modern civilization shifted from the East to the West, from the Crescent to the Cross. Thanks to their sea power, the successors of Solyman the Magnificent were well on their way to domination of commerce which the Phoenicians once had held. Victory at Lepanto might have opened the larger seas to them as they expanded their shipping interests. The prizes of trade and empire for which English, Dutch, Scandinavians, Germans and French competed in the next centuries might well have been seized by Turks.

Lepanto also was a turning point in the history of naval warfare. It was the last great battle between oared ships; galleys never again played any considerable part in a major sea fight anywhere.

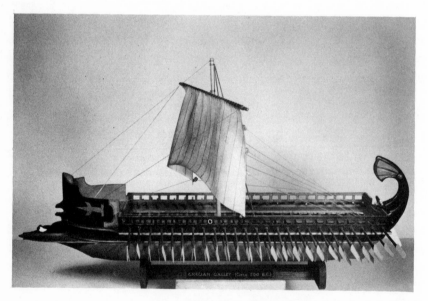

Official Mystic Seaport Photograph by Louis S. Martel

35

The Defeat of the Armada

It was called the "Invincible Armada." Sailors ought to have known that such a name doomed it because the sea does not look kindly upon proud boasts of men. The one who ordered her built, King Philip II of Spain, and the one who did the building, his best admiral, the Marquis of Santa Cruz, were not so arrogant themselves. They called it "the enterprise of England," but history has preferred the more picturesque and ironical title.

The reason for the "enterprise of England" was the same as that which sent Don John against the Turks. The Turks had been raiding the coasts of King Philip's dominons in the Mediterranean. The English had been raiding his dominions in America, and capturing his treasure ships on the seas, too. He proposed to invade and conquer their island, setting up a government he could control, and he had an army for the purpose in his domains in the Lowlands, almost in sight of the Dover cliffs. The job of the Invincible Armada was to be no more than protecting this army while it crossed. The fleet was less than half the strength of the one which had sailed under Don John's banner at Lepanto. The Armada which actually sailed for England on July 23, 1588, on one of the craziest adventures in the history of battle fleets, consisted of 128 ships carrying 30,000 men.

Santa Cruz was not with them. He died a few months before the expedition sailed, and his successor was Alonso Perez de Guzman, Duke of Medina Sidonia, appointed partly because he was son-in-law to Philip's best friend and to the one-eyed beauty recently

315

portrayed on the American stage by Katharine Cornell in *That Lady*. His chief interests were farming and his family. His chief antipathy was ships because he invariably was sick at sea.

Mild, dull, plump, and easily confused, he was a most reluctant admiral. Notable personalities among the Spaniards of his day were called such things as "the proud," "the brave," "the wise," "the splendid," "the conqueror," and so on. Poor Medina Sidonia was called "the good." He also was wise enough, though, to do his best to beg off from being a Captain General.

The King refused to listen to his excuses. He himself knew no more about naval warfare than Medina Sidonia, but he drafted complete instructions to cover every contingency—how the fleet should sail (in half-moon formation), how to fight (grapple with the English ships), how to make a landing (in the Thames, using flatboats), how to behave (worship God and punish any sailor caught swearing).

For all the confusion of absentee orders and a seasick commander, the Invincible Armada probably could have whipped any English fleet foolish enough to fight her on Philip's terms. But the sailors of Queen Elizabeth invented a new style of sea warfare for the occasion. With it they destroyed Spanish rule of the seas and substituted their own.

England's Lord High Admiral was Lord Howard of Effingham. His principal subordinates were Sir Francis Drake, Sir John Hawkins, Sir Martin Frobisher and Sir William Wynter. All of them were great names at sea even then. They had practiced but not perfected their new tactics in smaller sea fights all around the world in the course of raiding, trading, and exploring voyages.

The ships they had available to repel the invasion were mostly raiders or merchantmen. Compared to the Spanish vessels, which were clumsy and quite incapable of sailing close into the wind, they were fast and handy. So instead of coming to grips with an enemy hand-to-hand—the strategy of naval action since Salamis and before —they dodged around, firing at a ship rather than at the men in her, and came in close only when she was disabled. It sounds ob-

The Spanish Armada coming up the English Channel.

vious today, the proper use of cannon, but nobody had thought of it earlier, or at least nobody had the ships capable of doing it.

Ever since 1588 the English have enjoyed telling each other and the world how their brave, outnumbered little ships outfought the Spanish giants. But there wasn't all that difference in size or numbers that the stories indicate. In fact, the English had more ships, 193, although sixty or more, including about forty little coasting vessels, never got into the fight. The biggest ship on either side measured 1,250 tons, and the Spaniards had seven of more than 1,000 tons. The English had two bigger than 1,000 tons and six of more than 600. Both fleets counted ships of no more than twenty tons. The English carried about the same number of guns as the Spaniards, and had much better gunners.

Most naval battles of that age were affairs of a day or two. The repulse of the Invincible Armada was a running fight which lasted for ten long summer days, beginning on a Sunday, August 1. Howard had only a part of his fleet with him as the Armada approached Plymouth, but he attacked at once. The new style of warfare was unveiled for the first time in a major engagement as the handy English ships sailed circles around the slow Spaniards, peppering away at the bigger targets and avoiding close quarters. The Spaniards cursed their enemies as cowards, but Medina Sidonia had no intention of attempting a landing at Plymouth as the English feared, and sailed on up the Channel. That was the story of the whole action, with a few variations.

On the second day, Drake, in the 500-ton *Revenge,* battered and captured the 1,150-ton *Nuestra Señora del Rosario.* Showing how the English packed power into small space, Drake's *Revenge* had almost as many guns as his enemy, forty-three to forty-six. The capture of the big galleon was a wonderful exploit, but Drake almost lost the battle to do it. He was supposed to guide the whole English fleet with his lantern as he followed the Armada through the night. But he saw that the *Rosario,* damaged in Sunday's fighting, was falling behind. To keep her for himself, he put out his lantern so that no other English ship could follow him and share the prize. Drake still was at least as much pirate as patriot. With his beacon extinguished, no captain could tell just what course to steer, and the confusion was as bad as anything in the Armada. It was so serious that the English fleet couldn't get into action again until Tuesday except to capture another big ship, the *San Salvador,* which was put out of commission by an internal explosion. She was the paymaster's ship, but the Spaniards took off all the coin before they abandoned her, a fact which generations of treasure hunters refused to accept.

Tuesday, the two fleets fought again in the familiar pattern off Portland, and Thursday off the Isle of Wight. Friday and Saturday saw a running battle as the Spaniards headed for Calais where Medina Sidonia expected to pick up help from the Spanish army in the Lowlands—he still knew so little about fighting at sea that he supposed soldiers would help somehow.

Sunday was quiet, the Spaniards crowded at anchor near shore, the English spread out, also at anchor, a cannon shot away toward the Straits of Dover. Howard had decided to send fire ships against the enemy; it took all day to get them ready, and Sunday night they came down upon the Spaniards, eight great blazing torches borne on a strong breeze. In a panic Medina Sidonia ordered the cables of his flagship cut. His example was followed by the rest of the Armada, and on the English ships they could hear the great ugly chorus as ropes squealed in pulleys, timbers creaked, ships banged in collision, men shouted in anger and despair—the King's orders against swearing were violated grandly that night—and the fearsome fire ships floated harmlessly by.

On Monday morning the Armada was scattered over a good deal of the North Sea with the British in formation behind them, firing as they came. Forty of the bigger Spanish warships managed to recover their discipline, and all that day they fought their ships as best they could against the frustrating English pursuers. Tuesday, the tenth day since the fleets met, witnessed a final hot battle off Gravelines in which two Spanish ships were sunk, the first actually destroyed on either side by direct enemy action—and the last. There was no hope, Medina Sidonia recorded, of fighting a way back through the Channel even if the wind had been favorable. The only chance left was to sail north, around Scotland, in spite of dangerous rocks and shoals, pass to the west of Ireland, and pray to reach home.

That voyage, for any sailing ship of the day—battered, short of food, water, and gear—was bound to be terrible. Up to this point the English had parried the blow of King Philip's "enterprise of England" with skill and courage. But the Invincible Armada was destroyed by a greater power, the sea. The defenders of their country had captured two Spanish ships and sunk two. Five others were wrecked, perhaps through battle damage, on the European coast. But fifty-four ships and most of the men died on the miserable flight around the British Isles.

If the sea was more powerful than man, it was not so cruel. It did take a tremendous toll in men drowned or battered to death on the rocks. But more Spaniards were murdered for their clothes as they came ashore from wrecked ships in Scotland and Ireland (both countries then were regarded as being at least as savage as Borneo), or died of disease or starvation as the result of the rotten food supplied by Spanish victualers.

Sixty-five of the 128 ships which sailed so bravely in July, straggled back in October, leaking and jury-rigged, with fewer than 10,000 men left alive—and these were miserable walking skeletons, sick, wounded, and starved, clad in tattered rags. They were as broken as Spain's proud command of the ocean, which had seemed so absolute after Lepanto.

A few survivors, more fortunate than the ones who made the long trip to Spain because they were wrecked on some of the less savage British shores, remained where they landed to give a definite Spanish cast to some remote British and Irish families and neighborhoods.

The new mistress of the seas began now the steady rise to preeminence as a world power which enabled her to inherit the Spanish boast of ruling an empire on which the sun never set. Naval supremacy took and held it. Of course, before this full development could take place, England would have to settle the rivalry of the Dutch and the French.

Back in Spain, the sailors who crawled ashore from the floating wrecks were more bitter about the food and pestilence than about the English or the storms. But in that age, no one seems to have been able to provision and maintain a large fleet at sea for a long cruise. A year after the defeat of the Armada, England launched an "enterprise" of her own. It was designed to invade Portugal, which Philip had conquered, and set a Portuguese pretender on the throne.

It was not, however, a government undertaking. English naval operations such as the expeditions of Drake and Hawkins had done well as the ventures of joint stock companies. Queen Elizabeth, a notably thrifty woman, saw no reason why private capital should not finance her revenge on Philip, so she chartered another stock company to carry the war to Spain. She and her chief ministers subscribed to shares, but the royal treasury was not burdened.

The fleet assembled by this warlike corporation consisted of 200 ships, none of them as big as the larger Spanish vessels of the Armada, carrying 20,000 men. Drake commanded the sailors, and Sir John Norris, a tough, experienced general, commanded the soldiers. There was no Spanish Navy left to hamper fleet operations.

But the most that Drake and Norris could do was burn and loot the undefended lower city of La Coruña. They failed to take the upper city, and were beaten back from Lisbon after a short siege.

Drake, certainly one of the accomplished sea warriors of his time, lost exactly the same number of ships to enemy action as had Medina Sidonia, who was no sea warrior at all. It happened because there was a dead calm when the soldiers started to re-embark after the failure at Lisbon, and while Spain could gather no defensive fleet, there was one good, well-armed galley at hand. Taking advantage of the fact that not a single one of Drake's ships could move in the breathless air, the galley dashed out of the harbor, captured three English ships and burned another before a breeze rose.

The remaining parallel with the Armada—a tremendous casualty list—was completed on the way home. Rotten food, foul water, and overcrowding did to the English what the same evils, plus storms and battle, had done to the men of the Armada. Fifteen thousand of the slightly more than twenty thousand recruited by the joint stock company died, disease taking greater toll among them than it had among the Spaniards because the English of that day were more laxly disciplined.

36

The Battle of Trafalgar

If you went to Portsmouth, the big English naval base, before World War II, people used to ask if you had seen the *George*. If you asked what it was they would tell you it was the inn where the great Lord Nelson ate breakfast before he sailed to beat the French at the battle of Trafalgar. Then they would even show you the back door through which their hero went in order to avoid the crowd waiting to cheer him.

Nelson has been the top naval hero of England and perhaps of all the world ever since. To fighting men of the sea he has been a symbol of all that they would strive to be—wise and brave and generous and a master strategist. It was his good fortune, too, to win a glorious victory which not only finished the only rival England had as a sea power but established his country as the mistress of the seas undisputed for more than a century after him.

His last and greatest battle has been studied by naval men and historians so carefully because it ended the threat of invasion from his day to Hitler's. England's enemies often have gathered great armies across the Channel and waited for their fleets to open a passage for them. Spaniards, Frenchmen, and Germans have waited there at one time or another.

In the year 1805 it was Frenchmen. Napoleon, supreme in Europe, had encamped a big invasion force at Boulogne. All he needed was for his navy to give him a few days to ferry his men across. His navy hadn't done it, and in fact his most favored admiral of the moment, Pierre Charles de Villeneuve, had taken most of his fleet to Spain. England could not be safe until those ships were put out of action.

322

The great thing about Nelson was his grasp of a situation; that even more than his cleverness in planning or carrying on a battle. Nothing could divert him from the simple fact that the only way to be sure of Napoleon's fleet was to destroy it. It would not be enough for him to drive it into port or chase it from one place to another; as long as the ships floated they were a threat to England. Nelson was above all else a fighting man, and he had proved that in many battles. In one he had lost his right eye, in another his right arm. He was not much more careful of the men under his command than he was of himself, but they admired him just the same and trusted him, too. When he went down from Portsmouth to Cadiz on his flagship to lead the fleet which was gathered to oppose Villeneuve, he worked out the plan by which he proposed to make England secure.

Fleets had fought ever since the defeat of the Spanish Armada with their biggest ships in great lines drawn up in rather regular formation one against the other. They were called "line of battle ships" and then "battleships." But Nelson argued that in a line of some thirty ships, the commander had to be out of touch with most of his captains, and maneuvering was bound to be clumsy. So he proposed to attack Villeneuve's combined French and Spanish fleet with his own vessels in columns which would cut through the enemy line and overwhelm the enemy a few at a time.

Nelson explained to his captains that what he wanted was not an orderly contest of lines of ships solemnly maneuvering around each other but a general melee in which everybody would be at close quarters. In order to bring this about, and at the same time to give some strategic advantage to the English, he planned the battle so that his second in command, Admiral Cuthbert Collingwood, with fifteen ships, should break the Franco-Spanish line in front of its last twelve ships and overwhelm these. Nelson himself, with most of the rest, would try to break the line nearer the center, but in any case would prevent anyone from going to the rescue of the cutoff twelve.

When the two fleets came together on October 21, 1805, off a low cape at the western entrance to the Strait of Gibraltar on the Spanish side—it was called Trafalgar—the French Admiral had his ships in a curved line at right angles to the approach of the two English columns, the curve being concave from the English viewpoint. This gave Villeneuve the advantage of being able to fire whole broadsides from each of his ships into the approaching English, concentrating his shots on one after another. The English would be able to fire only their guns which pointed forward—most ships' cannon were on the sides and could be aimed only a few degrees in either direction. Furthermore, the ships at the rear of the column would hardly be able to fire at all for fear of hitting the leaders. Nelson, however, deliberately took on this disadvantage so that he could bring the French and Spanish ships into a fight at close quarters. He counted on two things. One was that his men were better trained both as sailors and as gunners. The other was that the French had a fixed belief that if they could disable an opponent's ship they had done enough, and so they shot at masts and rigging instead of the hull.

The wind was very light, west northwest, as the English slowly got into their two columns and from a distance of about ten miles began heading for the objectives Nelson had given them. Progress was slow and uneven, because some ships did better in the light breeze than others. Everyone knew there would be a longer interval than the Admiral planned between the time the first ship in column hit the enemy line and the time the others could get in close enough to help. But Nelson did not alter his plan, and shortly before the first shot was fired he hoisted his famous battle signal: "England expects that every man will do his duty."

The sailors cheered dutifully. But Admiral Collingwood was heard to mutter: "I wish Nelson would stop signalling. We all know what we have to do."

Collingwood did it very well, too. A few minutes later, just before noon, the French *Fougueux* fired the first shot of the battle at Collingwood's flagship, the *Royal Sovereign*. Then half a dozen ships were shooting at him, and as he sailed doggedly on right between the *Fougueux* and one of the biggest ships of all, the Spanish *Santa Ana,* he let each of these have a full broadside from his eighty-four guns, and all three ships disappeared for a moment in smoke. It took more than half an hour before the last seven of his own fifteen got within range, and then Nelson's *Victory* hit the Franco-Spanish line

The Battle of Trafalgar.

too, actually bumping into the 74-gun *Redoubtable,* close alongside Villeneuve's flagship, *Bucentaure.* In these close quarters, and with the rest of the English ships slow in coming into action, the day was saved by the better training on which Nelson had counted. The English could fire their guns two or three times as fast as the French, and so they held their own even though heavily outnumbered in guns and men.

Then at last the slowest ships in the English fleet came up, and Nelson had what he wanted, a confused mass of ships engaged in single combat with each other. He himself was no longer on deck. The captain of the *Redoubtable* decided that his best chance was to board the *Victory* and while he got gun crews on deck to swell the boarding party, marksmen in the rigging were shooting down on the English ship. One musket ball struck Nelson, cutting an artery in his lung and lodging in his spine.

There were 478 other Englishmen besides Lord Nelson killed in the battle, and 2,800 French and Spaniards. Of the British ships, the *Temeraire* was most badly damaged, having all her rigging shot away and floating almost a hulk. Both the *Victory* and the *Royal Sovereign* lost all but one mast apiece, and were almost unmanageable after bearing the brunt of the French and Spanish fire.

They could be repaired and replaced. The 24 French battleships destroyed or captured could not. Napoleon's resources were not enough to rebuild a navy and keep up the army, too, and after Trafalgar he had no taste for new naval adventures anyway.

It is possible to wonder how well the British Navy would have come off in a test with another rival as formidable as the fleet of Villeneuve. The question comes up because within a few years the crews of British warships seem to have lost some of their superior skill and gunnery. When war with the United States broke out in 1812, and the successors of Nelson did not take it very seriously because they knew that the Americans had only sixteen warships capable of navigating the ocean, and not one of them could class as a line of battleship. The biggest were frigates which carried fewer than half as many guns as the smallest battleship.

These frigates, however, were something special in design and construction. The three newest were called the *Constitution,* the *United States,* and the *President.* Their timbers and planking were much heavier than those used for British frigates of the same general proportions, and although they carried only a couple of guns more, they had much heavier fire power. A ship's strength then was as much in the weight of the shot she could fire in a single broadside as in the number of cannon. The *Constitution,* for example, threw 684 pounds of metal at a time. The British frigate *Guerrière,* which she met in the first American victory of the war, fired only 556 pounds. The American vessels, besides, had faster and cleaner lines so that they could run away easily from any battleship, and with a good skipper in command, outsail their own class.

All this was shown on August 19, 1812, when the *Constitution* sighted the *Guerrière* at sea directly east of New York and south of Newfoundland. The first shot was fired at five o'clock in the afternoon, and for an hour the two ships maneuvered toward each other, exchanging shots but doing little damage. Then they closed as if by mutual consent, and in fifteen minutes the *Guerrière* had lost her mizzenmast and mainyard and had a big hole in her counter, then her mainmast and foremast. At 7 o'clock the ship surrendered.

Americans like to remember the story of this fight, which was won by the stronger ship and men better trained by the *Constitution*'s famous captain, Isaac Hull. Englishmen prefer to tell about how their frigate *Shannon* beat the *Chesapeake*, which had an untrained and undisciplined crew of pickup volunteers, in just fifteen minutes outside of Boston on June 1, 1812.

The *Constitution*'s victory was proved no lucky accident, when Captain Hull battered the frigate *Java* into submission on December 29, 1812, and the *United States*, commanded by Stephen Decatur, took the frigate *Macedonian* on December 4. But the little American Navy could not defeat the British numbers, and at the end of the war, most of the sixteen warships were sunk or had been blockaded in their own ports. Only five of them—the *Constitution* was one— were still at sea.

The *Victory*.

37

The Merrimac and
the Monitor

Ten years after the battle of Trafalgar, all the ships engaged there, and all the other navies of the world, were obsolete, only nobody knew it. By 1815, that inventive American artist, Robert Fulton, had combined new marine wonders of iron and steam into the greatest revolution in warfare at sea since cannon were lugged on board a ship.

Ever since he had tried to destroy British sea power with his submarine, Fulton had been talking and writing against the domination of the ocean by a single nation. In 1814, he thought he had what he wanted, a torpedo boat which could not be damaged itself and could sink all Great Britain's wooden vessels. The War of 1812 was on, and Fulton's idea was a boat so low in the water her deck was just about even with the surface. That deck was armored so heavily that any cannon ball of the day, especially as it would have to be fired downward at her, would bounce off harmlessly. Down below, the crew drove the boat toward her target by manpower, turning an armored paddle wheel, and when close enough, fired torpedoes.

Fulton actually built an experimental version, which he named the *Mute,* and in June, 1814, twelve men took her to sea. They were promptly driven ashore on Long Island by a gale, and here the British warship *Maidstone* found her. Captain Richard Burdett of the *Maidstone* doesn't seem to have realized that he was seeing something new in his profession, but he scattered some militia gathered to protect the *Mute,* and sent marines ashore to blow her up.

Meanwhile, Fulton was adapting his steamboat to naval warfare. The first fighting ship driven by steam was projected by him in March, 1814, and launched in October. Fulton persuaded a group of New York citizens' who had formed a Coast and Harbor Defense Association, to finance the construction with a Federal Government promise to pay them back if the thing worked. But it was so hard to get materials in wartime that the ship wasn't completed until September, 1815, and meanwhile she had killed her inventor. Fulton was in poor health, but insisted on leaving his home against advice to iron out troubles in fitting the ship, which he called the *Demologos*, in bad February weather. He got much worse as a result and died on February 23.

The ship was finished as the *Fulton the First*. She had twin hulls 167 feet long with the paddle wheels in-between to protect them from enemy fire, and was fifty-six feet in the beam. Her sides and deck were five feet thick, a wooden wall proof against most of the cannon of that day. Although she was a clumsy, heavy ship with thirty big guns, her 120-horsepower engine drove her at five knots, and also worked a couple of hoses which were supposed to knock enemy sailors off their decks when the *Demologos* was ready to board. Too slow for offensive action and probably not very seaworthy in any sort of weather, Fulton had supposed she would be a sort of floating fortress mainly useful for harbor defenses, which is what the New York citizens wanted.

The war ended before the world's first steam warship could get into a battle, and she served out her days as a receiving vessel at the Navy Yard in Brooklyn. The use of both steam and iron by any navy had to wait for a long time. Until steamboats could go as fast as sail, naval officers would have small use for them. Also the steamboat for years was much more likely to be knocked out of commission by a single shot than a sailing vessel. And, of course, admirals always are conservative fellows when it comes to taking up something new. As one of them, Sir Charles Napier, who served with the British Navy in American waters during the War of 1812, put it to the House of Commons one day: "Mr. Speaker, when we enter His

Majesty's naval service and face the chances of war, we go prepared to be hacked to pieces by cutlasses, to be riddled with bullets or to be blown to bits by shot and shell. But, Mr. Speaker, we do not go prepared to be boiled alive."

The brave Admiral Napier lived long enough to see sailors take even that chance. In fact, in the next forty years steam was put to use in the navies faster than iron armor. Like the merchant ships, most steam warships had auxiliary sail. But they were otherwise much like the vessels which fought at Trafalgar.

Armor plate came into its own when it first was used by the British and French in the Crimea on floating batteries. But just what a combination of iron and steam could mean in battle was demonstrated only on a March Sunday in 1862, when the American Civil War was not quite a year old.

The demonstration took place in Hampton Roads, Virginia. It is a very curious thing that the great offensive power of uniting steam to armor plate should have been devised at exactly the same moment as was the best answer to it. This was the famous struggle between the *Merrimac* and the *Monitor*. It was one of the decisive naval battles of the world for when it was over, every navy afloat was obsolete, but nobody won, nobody lost, and nobody was hurt.

The *Merrimac*, one of the United States Navy's newest steam frigates, with two tall masts fore and aft of the single funnel, was in the Virginia port of Norfolk when the war broke out. Her officers, loyal to the Union, scuttled her when they had to abandon the navy yard, but the Confederates raised her and turned her into the world's first fighting ironclad. They removed the masts and almost all the superstructure. Over the rest they built a sloping roof and covered this with iron thick enough to deflect any cannon ball that could be fired at her in that day. The funnel rose out of this armored roofing like the chimney of a house, and ten square openings were cut in the sides as ports for ten big guns, four on each side, one in the bow and one in the stern. Just under the waterline a tremendous sharp iron beak was fastened to the bow to be used as a ram.

While this work was being done in Norfolk, John Ericsson, a

Swedish engineer who had helped improve ship's engines and the propellors which enabled warships to dispense with vulnerable paddle wheels, was working on a novel kind of fighting craft. It was not too different in appearance from Fulton's *Mute,* but it was a lot more efficient. Ericsson, too, was combining the virtues of steam and iron. His little vessel was almost awash in the water. She was narrow and easily maneuvered. Her deck was as heavily armored as the *Merrimac's,* and her pointed bow was strongly reinforced to serve as a ram. Sticking up off the low deck was a funnel aft, a pilothouse made of nine-by-twelve-inch iron beams forward, and a round gun turret with eight- and nine-inch iron plates amidship. This gun turret was one of the big strides in naval design. It was turned by men working below decks so that the two eleven-inch guns could be aimed in any direction. For the first time, a whole ship did not have to be swung around to bring guns to bear on a target.

Wonderful as they were, neither the *Merrimac* (which the Confederates renamed the *Virginia*) nor her rival (which Ericsson called the *Monitor* because he hoped it would show that all wooden ships were useless) could go out into the open ocean unaided.

The Union authorities knew about the *Merrimac* before she was ready, and were badly frightened. On March 6, 1862, they dispatched the *Monitor,* whose final touches had been made by mechanics working all night, to Hampton Roads, where one of the most effective units of the naval blockade of the South was stationed. These were all wooden ships, of course, and the new Confederate ironclad might be able not only to smash the blockade but steam up the Potomac to attack Washington, or break into New York harbor and shell the city.

The *Monitor's* strange voyage and the fight which followed are most dramatically described in a letter written to his family at the time by her first lieutenant and commander during part of the battle, S. Dana Greene, who was only twenty-one at the time. The letter, owned by Mr. Warren C. Shearman of Los Angeles, has only recently been published.

The *Monitor* couldn't carry enough fuel to make the trip under her own steam, so she was towed by the steamer *Seth Low* once she passed Governor's Island. All that first day went well, but soon after Lieutenant Greene turned out on the second day, Friday, the ship was in trouble, "and from that time until Monday at 7 p.m. I think I lived a good ten years," he wrote. The difficulty was that the sea got rough and the new craft, while proof against shot and shell, wasn't waterproof. Waves broke over the deck, and the hawsepipe, turret, and plates just over the berths all leaked while water streamed down the smokestack and blowers into the engine room. This could be handled by pumps as long as the engines worked, but with the blowers out of commission, the engine room filled with gas. Lieutenant Greene writes:

"Then, Mother, occurred a scene I shall never forget. Our Engineers behaved like heroes, every one of them. They fought with the gas, endeavoring to get the blowers to work until they dropped down apparently as dead as men ever were. I jumped into the Engine room with my men as soon as I could, and carried them on top of the Tower to get fresh air."

Finally they signaled the tug to move closer to shore where the sea was calm, and for the rest of the day all was well with "the old tank going along five or six knots very nicely." Not until next day, though, did she reach her destination.

"At 4 p.m.," writes Greene, "we passed Cape Henry, and heard heavy firing in the direction of Fortress Monroe; as we approached, it increased, and we immediately cleared for action."

The firing heard on the *Monitor* was the last stages of proof that wooden ships never could stand up to the ironclad. All day the *Merrimac* had been pounding two of the best ships of the Union Navy and destroyed both of them. She had come into Hampton Roads attended by five little gunboats and commanded by Captain Franklin Buchanan. The Union frigates *Cumberland* and *Congress*, either of which outgunned the ironclad, were waiting, and the *Merrimac* bore down on the *Cumberland*, ignoring the heavy fire from both her enemies. The *Cumberland* was a sitting duck, having turned in the accepted tactics to fire a broadside, so the *Merrimac* simply plowed right into her and through her. Only after she had backed out, leaving the water to rush into a huge ragged hole in the wooden ship's side, did the *Merrimac* bother to open fire. In forty-five minutes the *Cumberland* was at the bottom in fifty-four feet of water, along with 121 of her 376-man crew.

As the *Merrimac* turned to attack the *Congress*, the Union captain decided his only chance to escape ramming was to run his vessel aground. He did, while three other frigates—*Minnesota, Roanoke,* and *St. Lawrence*—sailed out from the protection of Fortress Monroe only to get themselves stranded on a shoal a mile away. With the shots from the *Congress* still glancing off harmlessly from her armor, the *Merrimac* steamed closer and her shells soon had the frigate on fire with several guns disabled and many men killed. About half her crew of 434 escaped to the shore as the colors were being hauled down; the rest were either killed or captured.

It was now seven o'clock, and after turning toward the grounded frigates as if to attack, Captain Buchanan steamed slowly back toward Norfolk. He said later the light was failing too fast for effective action, and he had no doubt about finishing off the other three ships next day.

Two hours later the *Monitor* arrived. The *Roanoke* and *St. Lawrence* had floated but the *Minnesota* still was aground. The *Monitor* took up a position to protect her, while at a little distance the *Congress* burned brightly until her magazine blew up in a grand display.

At 8 o'clock Sunday morning the *Merrimac* came back, and the first battle of ironclads began, the Confederates a bit scornful of what they called this "Yankee cheesebox on a plank." But Ericsson's newfangled turret worked. The *Monitor's* captain, Lieutenant John L. Worden, directed the turning of the turret from the pilothouse through a speaking tube to the chief engineer at the machinery while the second in command fired the guns. This last was Greene, whose account reads: "After fighting 2 hours, we hauled off for half an hour to hoist our shot into the Tower. At it we went again as hard as we could. The shot, shell, grape, canister, musket and rifle balls flew about in every direction, but did us no damage. Our tower

The *Monitor* and the *Merrimac.*

was struck several times, and though the noise was pretty loud, it did not affect us any. Stodder [next in rank] & one of the men were carelessly leaning against the Tower, when a shot struck the Tower exactly opposite to them, and disabled them for an hour or two."

The only other injury on board was to Worden, temporarily blinded when a shot from the *Merrimac* struck the pilothouse. Greene took over, but the *Merrimac* already was withdrawing to Norfolk, and at noon the battle was over.

Neither ironclad was much damaged. No shot penetrated the armor of either, in spite of what Greene thought. The *Merrimac* did not come out for another round with the *Monitor,* and the Union blockade was saved. And the wooden warship was finished.

Two months later the Confederates had to abandon Norfolk, and since the *Merrimac* could not safely go to sea, they destroyed her. The *Monitor* foundered off Cape Hatteras on the last day of the same year. Between the two, they brought the machine age to the navies of the world.

38

Battles of Our Time

Once the machine age got to work on warships, the sailors had to be as good engineers as they were fighters. Everyone will have his own ideas of the most important steps in the progress toward the modern ship which can hit a target further away than her crew can see it. But we can list some of them here.

It wasn't long after the *Merrimac* and *Monitor* failed to damage each other seriously before the technical experts could make shells which pierced the thickest iron armor. Then the protecting plates were made of steel, but the gunners got shells which would pierce that, too. Electrical machinery turned the turrets, worked the ships, even sighted the big guns. Ships became faster and bigger.

But for a long time there were no big fleet actions. The countries with the biggest navies and most ships were fighting "little wars" in the nineteenth century. There was no chance to see what the mechanized men-o'-war could do to each other until in 1898, the United States, which had a navy ranked as third class, declared war on Spain, which was overestimated by being considered as in the second class. By this time battleships were as heavy as the old *Great Eastern* had been, and could make as much as twenty-one knots in spite of armor plating a foot and a half thick in places. They had guns fired by electricity which threw a half-ton shell five miles.

The first meeting of two fleets of major warships anywhere on the Seven Seas since the battle of Trafalgar took place on May 1, 1898, when Commodore George Dewey led six United States warships—*Olympia* (the flagship), *Baltimore, Raleigh, Petrel, Concord,*

The annihilation of the Spanish fleet at Manila.

and *Boston*—into Manila Bay. Two Spanish battleships, two cruisers, and six smaller destroyers and gunboats were anchored there under the command of Admiral Patricio Montojo. In six hours forty-nine minutes, according to Dewey's timing, all ten Spanish ships were sunk or burning and had ceased fire. They lost 167 killed and 214 wounded. On the American fleet only seven men were wounded and none killed. The result was due almost entirely to better handling of ships and guns.

Two months and two days later, on July 3, a bigger United States fleet, which had blockaded another Spanish squadron in the harbor of Santiago de Cuba, had its chance when five big armored cruisers and two torpedo-boat destroyers tried to escape, led by Admiral Pascual Cervera. The American fleet, under Admiral William T. Sampson and Commodore Winfield S. Schley, destroyed them in less than four hours.

The rise of Japan as a big naval power showed again that bravery is no substitute for good shooting. When Japan went to war with Russia in 1904, many people in the West thought she would have no chance, but she scored victory after victory, and in one of them, Admiral Heihachiro Togo destroyed six Russian battleships and seven cruisers, with a loss of 10,000 men. The Japanese lost three torpedo boats and suffered fewer than 1,000 casualties.

Ten years later, navies were bigger and stronger and even more highly mechanized. Submarines had become effective fighting ships, and there was even some use of aircraft for scouting. Guns were so long-ranged that when the big ships got within less than three miles of each other, some chroniclers of their fighting speak of them as "slugging it out toe to toe."

During World War I there were only two fleet actions. In the first, on December 8, 1914, a British squadron found five German cruisers off the Falkland Islands east of the southern tip of South America, and sank four of them. But the really big fleet battle was on May 31, 1916, when the grand fleets of England and Germany fought for an afternoon and night in the North Sea. The English call it the battle of Jutland after the Danish province on the mainland of Europe, a finger pointing north to Norway. The Germans speak of it as the battle of Skagerrak, from the body of water which opens from the North Sea into the Baltic.

It surely was the biggest sea fight since the Spanish Armada in point of men and ships involved. Admiral Sir John Jellicoe commanded twenty-eight battleships, nine battle cruisers, eight armored cruisers, twenty-six light cruisers, and seventy-eight destroyers. The Germans under Admiral Reinhard Scheer put into the fight twenty-two battleships, five battle cruisers, eleven light cruisers and sixty-one destroyers. The British lost more ships and men—fourteen ships and 6,097 men—because through all the daylight hours the Germans had the best of it. They were taking heavy punishment in their turn at night, though, and turned back to port. Eleven of their ships were sunk and 2,545 men killed. Naval historians haven't stopped arguing yet about who really won, if anybody. But of one thing there is no doubt. This battle was the first in which an airplane launched from a ship took part.

By World War II, of course, the airplane was a major part of all

337

navies, and improvements in everything else had been made in great quantity. There were no fleet actions, though, before the United States entered the war. Neither the German nor Italian navies nor both together were strong enough to take on the British, so the war at sea for more than two years was confined to battles between a few ships at a time—and, of course, submarine warfare, airplane raids and commerce raiders. Two of them were:

The fight between the German pocket battleship *Admiral Graf Spee* and three much smaller British cruisers, *Ajax, Achilles* and *Exeter,* December 13, 1939, in the South Atlantic off the River Plate. The *Spee,* only slightly damaged, was scuttled on Hitler's orders December 17.

The sinking of the British battleship *Hood* by the *Bismarck* off Greenland, May 24, 1941. Three days later British ships and planes caught the *Bismarck* before she got home and sank her off Brest.

After the attack on Pearl Harbor there were several major sea battles in the Pacific, and in some of them there were about as many men engaged as had fought at Lepanto. But the one which seems to provide the clearest demonstration of naval tactics in the machine age as well as being in overall strategy perhaps the most important was the battle for Leyte Gulf, sometimes called the Second Battle of the Philippine Sea, in October, 1944. In this one, fought in and under and over several seas, bays, and straits around the Philippines, the newest planes, ships, and submarines were involved.

Just to list the composition of the two armadas gives some idea of the scope of this battle. The United States engaged thirty-two carriers, twelve battleships, twenty-three cruisers, 100 or more destroyers and other small craft, submarines, more than 1,000 planes. The Japanese threw in nearly all that was left of their navy—four carriers, seven battleships, two battleship-carriers (battleships converted into partial carriers), nineteen cruisers (mostly heavy), thirty-three destroyers, more than 500 planes.

The Japanese wanted to knock the Americans out of the Philippines, where they had just landed on the island of Leyte, before they could dig in to reconquer the archipelago. The first part of their plan was a trick. One Japanese fleet which included all the big carriers Japan had, but with very few planes on board, would come out from Japan itself and offer itself as bait for an attack several hundred miles north of Leyte, and then its commander, Admiral Jisaburo Ozawa, would draw the Americans still further away. The ships it hoped to divert from the main scene of action were those of the Third Fleet which included the major American strength.

The second part of the plan called for Admiral Takeo Kurita's squadron, the most powerful single section of the Japanese force with five battleships and ten heavy cruisers as well as lighter warships, to hit the great accumulation of American landing craft and supply ships in Leyte Gulf from the north. To get there he had to come from far to the west by way of Borneo, cut through the Philippines in the Sibuyan Sea and emerge into the Philippine Sea through San Bernardino Strait north of the island of Samar.

The third part of the plan contemplated the arrival of a third squadron under Admiral Shoji Nishimura, striking into the Americans from the south. The two battleships, heavy cruiser, and four destroyers of this squadron were based, like Kurita's fleet, at Singapore, but were to be joined by several other cruisers and destroyers from Japan. Nishimura was to pass through the Mindanao Sea and up through Surigao Strait which leads right into Leyte Gulf.

The Japanese hoped that Kurita and Nishimura, helped by land-based planes from Philippine airfields, would overwhelm whatever protecting force was left to cover the landing, and destroy the hundreds of supply and landing ships crowded into the Gulf. The attack was scheduled for October 25, which was only five days after the first American troops landed on Leyte island. But actually the two Japanese squadrons combined would not have too much superiority over the Seventh Fleet at Leyte commanded by Admiral Thomas C. Kincaid. Kincaid had six old battleships, sixteen makeshift carriers converted from merchant vessels, only eight cruisers, but a great many small warships such as destroyers and destroyer escorts. His weakness was this: his ships and ammunition were designed to assist a landing, not to fight another fleet.

Two days before Kurita was due in Leyte Gulf, he was seen by two United States submarines. Well to the west of the Philippines and north of Borneo in the South China Sea, the submarines launched torpedoes, and three Japanese cruisers were put out of action. Two of them sank quickly; the third was so badly damaged Kurita sent her back to Borneo.

Next morning, October 24, both attacking fleets were spotted by scouting airplanes at almost the same time, Kurita in the Sibuyan Sea, and Nishimura nearing Surigao Strait from the Mindanao Sea. While the scattered forces of the United States Third Fleet were being drawn together, airplanes from both carriers and the land opened the battle for Leyte Gulf. Only slight damage was done to Nishimura's ships, which had not been joined yet by the squadron from Japan. But destruction was heavy further north. A Japanese plane scored a hit on the carrier *Princeton*, which sank after almost a day of fire-fighting. An explosion on the carrier killed or wounded 650 men on the cruiser *Birmingham*, which was trying to help the *Princeton* put out the flames. But the American planes hit more targets. One of the two biggest Japanese battleships, the *Musashi*, was sunk by a combination of bombs and torpedoes—it is estimated it took a total of twenty-five direct hits to do it—and another heavy cruiser was crippled so badly she had to head for a repair port. The airplane attack was so severe that Kurita turned back toward the west in midafternoon.

About an hour later, American planes discovered the Ozawa squadron, the "bait," coming slowly from the north, and Admiral Halsey set off to destroy it.

Meanwhile Kincaid's Seventh Fleet waited for Nishimura. The strategy was to harass the enemy with PT boats and destroyers in Surigao Strait while the battleships and cruisers opened up when the Japanese column of ships reached the wider waters where the Strait becomes Leyte Gulf. This gave the Americans the advantage of position, what naval writers call "capping the T" for they were in line firing broadsides at the enemy, who remained in column and could use only his forward guns.

Japanese shells striking around a U. S. carrier in the Battle of Leyte Gulf.

It worked perfectly, although this phase of the battle was fought in the dark of the night, October 24-25. In the Strait itself, destroyers got Nishimura's flagship, the battleship *Yamashiro,* and a destroyer. Two other destroyers were damaged. The big American ships then finished off the other battleship of this squadron and a cruiser. Only one destroyer of Nishimura's squadron escaped.

While this fight was taking place in the night, Kurita had turned his fleet back on its original course. He rounded the shoulder of Samar island before dawn. At almost the same time, in the morning of October 25, the two final stages of the battle took place hundreds of miles apart as Kurita came into conflict with Kincaid's ships, and Halsey's planes found the decoy fleet of Admiral Ozawa.

The northern phase of the battle was a running chase as the Japanese turned north according to plan and drew the Third Fleet after them. Without protecting aircraft, the "bait" was easily taken.

In the southern phase, although it lasted only about two and a half hours, it appeared for a time that the Japanese would reach their target—the shipping and supplies in Leyte Gulf. The Kurita fleet was seen first by planes from some of Kincaid's carriers and de-stroyers off Samar island. The entire fight was between these craft with their airplanes against Kurita's heavy ships, including the *Yamato* which, since the sinking of her sister ship the day before, was indisputably the biggest warship afloat.

As shells began to hit the carriers, planes and destroyers attacked the Japanese in their turn, the planes carrying ineffective bombs, and the destroyers trying to get close enough to score torpedo hits. They managed to land some blows, but none was strong enough to stop the Japanese ships. The Americans lost one carrier sunk and two badly damaged, three destroyers sunk and two badly damaged. The hit, but surviving, carriers were saved because they had no armor plate and the big armor-piercing projectiles of the Japanese went right through them without exploding. For these carriers were not the massive fighting ships specially built for their purpose; they were converted liners and cargo carriers fixed up enough to carry two or three dozen planes and called "baby flattops."

Meanwhile Kincaid in Leyte Gulf prepared his six battleships and few cruisers for a last ditch fight. He was going to be outgunned by Kurita's bigger and newer vessels, and he had to hurry to get his own restocked with ammunition after their night fight. Suddenly, when the Americans thought the day looked darkest for them, Kurita or-dered his ships to fall away and make for home. The explanation given later was that he thought the carriers braving his heaviest fire were the big ones of Halsey's fleet, and he feared he could do noth-ing without air protection of his own. But he did withdraw, and except for pursuit by aircraft, the battle for Leyte Gulf was finished.

So was the Japanese fleet for all major offensive purposes. There wasn't enough left to meet even a fair-sized section of the American Navy. But it is more interesting to speculate that this may have been the last battle between great surface fleets. With planes and submarines and guided atomic missiles and what new wonders, it does seem that any concentration of ships such as is needed to begin one of these naval battles would amount to suicide. So perhaps this has been the story of the end of fleets fighting on the Seven Seas.

39

The Irregulars

It is impossible to write about all the adventurous people who roamed the Seven Seas. Every seafaring country has its heroes, and quite often mixes the facts about them with fancies. Episodes are omitted or changed to glorify the men in one age or nation and vilify them in the next. To none has this process been applied so much and so often as to those guerrilla maritime warriors, pirates and privateers. For what is legal in some centuries will be piracy or betrayal later.

A man like Francis Drake is forever established as one of the heroes of England. That he was a great adventurer there can be no doubt, but many events in his life would hardly meet the moral standards of our days. Even in his own, half the world called him pirate. Either way we look at him, his energy, bravery, and wonderful deeds put him on the list of men who never can be forgotten.

Francis Drake was born around 1541 and sent to sea when he was barely ten years old. He was fortunate in getting a berth with an old skipper who sailed between England, Holland, and France. In him, the boy found a fatherly friend who taught him to work, to go without sleep for days, and to navigate a ship. When he died, his will left his ship to young Francis.

Not much is known about Drake until 1565, when he was in partnership with a Captain Lovell running a load of slaves from Africa to Mexico. In the West Indies they were attacked by Spanish naval ships, since Spain did not allow foreigners to bring slaves to her colonies, and their vessel and cargo were confiscated. This was the beginning of Drake's lifelong hatred of Spaniards.

He was without funds, but obtained command of the *Judith,* a fifty-ton bark, in which he returned to the slave trade and did so well that he came to the attention of his government, which then was engaged in what we would call a "cold war" with Spain, which was trying to overthrow Queen Elizabeth. She was using every device to harass her enemy, which was too powerful for her to fight openly. One way was to give secret help to raids such as Drake and his uncle, John Hawkins, also a slaver of experience, offered to conduct. The Queen put a ship of 700 tons at their disposal in return for a big share of their profits. She could do this the easier as the ship, which boasted the name *Jesus of Lübeck,* was condemned to be scrapped, so it cost her nothing. She let the adventurers have the *Mignon,* 250 tons, also reported by the Admiralty as rotten and unfit for sea duty. Drake borrowed against everything he owned to get two smaller ships, one of which was the *Judith.*

The frankly buccaneering expedition left England in October, 1567. On the way to pick up slaves in Africa, they sighted two Portuguese ships, and to please his crew, Drake gave the command to attack them. Portugal was neutral in the "cold war" but Drake had a talent for overlooking formalities. He took both and to show his gratitude to the Lord, renamed one of them *The Grace of God.* Drake was accused of piracy for this, but he defended himself by saying his devotion to the Queen, who was a partner, and his devout Protestantism, which included a flaming hatred for the Catholic Church, justified him.

When they reached the island of Dominica, the Spanish Governor would not allow Drake to sell his cargo nor even exchange it for food and water. Drake saw no other way than to force the Governor to trade. He went ashore with 200 men, conquered the fort with a loss of only eleven men, then turned to the peaeceful pursuit of selling his slaves.

He started to return to Africa for more, but a gale forced him to run into a small harbor, where a few days later thirteen Spanish warships appeared and attacked immediately. Only the *Judith* with Drake and the *Mignon* with Hawkins managed to escape. However, the Spaniards lost 500 men killed and four ships sunk in the battle.

This deplorable result of the expedition roused a great cry for revenge in England, but Elizabeth refused to make open war on Spain. She satisfied herself with sending Drake out as a pirate, with the blessing of the government but without its protection, so if he should be caught he would be hanged. Drake accepted this condition and sailed to the West Indies again. He captured several cities, and property he could not take he burned. On this voyage he lost two of his brothers—captains on ships of his squadron—but had the good luck to meet a caravan of 100 mules loaded with silver. He also undertook several excursions into the interior, and in 1573, climbed a tall tree from the top of which he saw the Pacific Ocean. Sitting there aloft he hatched a plan by which he hoped to deal his arch enemy a really hard blow.

Drake went back to England with a rich cargo of loot so the Queen was willing to listen to him. She had profited much from his expeditions while all the risk had been his. Now he proposed to take advantage of the knowledge Magellan's circumnavigation had brought to the world. By following Magellan's route, with five ships, he would be able to hit Spain in her most vulnerable spot, cutting her trade in an ocean where she had few warships.

The secret was well-kept from Spanish spies until after he left late in 1577, with five small ships, the biggest being the *Pelican*, 100 tons, and the smallest a thirteen-ton bark, the *Marigold*. The crew consisted in all of 160 men, who were told where they were going only after they reached Morocco. But first Drake could not resist a little piracy. He captured several Portuguese fishing and merchant vessels, and on board one of them was a sailor named Nuno da Silva. Drake formed a great friendship with him, and his knowledge of South American waters made da Silva a valuable pilot for the expedition. Drake let the Portuguese ships go free after stripping them of their cargoes. But he saw to it that they had enough water and provisions to reach home, and he himself started across the Atlantic.

By a coincidence, he selected for winter quarters the same harbor Magellan had found, still rich in seals and fish, and met the same tribe of natives although none were as gigantic as those Magellan had described. In fact, some of the Englishmen were as tall as the tallest Patagonians. Here some of Drake's officers and sailors entered into a conspiracy to return to England after killing the Admiral. Drake heard of it but would not believe what he was told because the head man among the mutineers was a gentleman, Thomas Doughty, mentioned as a wonderful speaker, a learned man who spoke Greek and Hebrew, and loved to read and study nature. Drake liked him very much and had confided in him during the first part of the voyage.

Some of Drake's real friends exposed the plot, and Drake, much against his will, had Doughty arrested. A council was called; Doughty confessed, and was sentenced to death. Drake offered the prisoner the choice of being left on shore, being sent back to England to be hanged, or being beheaded on this very spot. He chose the last, and asked for the favor of receiving the Holy Sacrament together with his Admiral. Doughty and Drake knelt side by side and were blessed by the ship's chaplain. Then they had their last meal together, with the other officers, and chatted merrily as though nothing had happened, even drinking toasts to each other.

Meanwhile a scaffold and block had been erected. Doughty on his knees said a prayer for the Queen and the expedition, and asked Drake to forgive everyone he suspected of taking part in the attempted mutiny, which Drake did. Then Doughty put his head on the block with a joke about his short neck, and his head fell at the first blow. At the same place, they found the ruins of a gallows with the skeleton of a man, supposed to be the remains of one of Magellan's mutineers, a remarkable coincidence that two gentlemen should die in this small, remote harbor for the same crime.

The Irregulars

When winter ended, the *Pelican, Elizabeth,* and *Marigold* were made shipshape, but the other two vessels were burned as not fit for further sailing. The three remaining ones passed through Magellan Strait in spite of terrible winds and blizzards; when they reached the big ocean to the west, Drake realized that the name Magellan had given it was absolutely a mistake. One gale after another battered them.

The little *Marigold* disappeared forever; the *Elizabeth*'s captain, driven back into the strait, decided to head for home, and did so. He reached England in July of the next year, and was jailed for having deserted his chief.

Drake sailed on with his one ship, but was so disturbed by the way the fates were treating him that he thought to change his luck by renaming his vessel the *Golden Hind.* It did not do much good. At first he was driven down to 55° south before he could sail north again and reach his goal—loot. The first ship he took was anchored in a harbor with only eleven men and 37,000 ducats on board. In the town, the inhabitants ran to the mountains, and Drake collected several objects of solid silver, lots of good wine, and some valuable cedar boards. Still further north he sent fourteen men ashore in a boat, but 300 Spanish horsemen came out against them, and they retreated with the loss of one man, whose head and right hand were cut off, his heart cut out, and the body turned over to the Indians for target practice.

Elsewhere on shore, where they landed for fresh water, the Englishmen had better luck. At one place they found a sleeping Spaniard who had thirteen silver bars, which they liberated from him. On another occasion they ran into a Spaniard with an Indian boy and eight llamas, each of the animals carrying two leather bags with eighty pounds of pure silver in each. They took twenty barges laden with silver bars and a bark with extra canvas, which pleased them as their own sails were well worn.

In Lima's harbor, they found no fewer than twelve large and twelve small ships at anchor, all of which were plundered and set adrift. Another prize yielded ropes and rigging, as well as eighty pounds of pure gold and a golden crucifix set with precious stones. One of the richest hauls was the *Cafuego* carrying diamonds and other gems, thirteen chests of gold coins and twenty-six tons of silver.

Incensed as the Spaniards were by this magnificent plundering, even the Viceroys in their reports mentioned Drake as a most amiable man who did not retaliate on his prisoners the brutality inflicted on his own men. These prisoners describe him as being about thirty-five years old, rather short in stature, with a beautiful beard. One of the greatest sailors who ever sailed the seas! The Spaniards who were taken on board the *Golden Hind* were impressed by his kindness to his men, estimated at 100, and by the fact that he dined in great state off silver plates with golden rims, to the music of violins. When Drake fought, he fought hard, but he set his prisoners free after throwing overboard their maps and nautical instruments, if they were sailors, to prevent pursuit.

By the time he reached Mexico, where the Portuguese pilot da Silva was captured on shore and spoke very well of him, Drake thought he had loot enough to avenge all the injustices he attributed to the Spaniards, and anyway his ship would hold no more. He thought Her Majesty would be content with her share of the booty, and decided to go home.

That might not be so easy. Undoubtedly, the Spaniards were waiting for him with more than superior forces if he returned the way he came. Before trying to cross the Pacific and go home around the world, he looked for a passage through America further north. He was a friend of the English sailor Martin Frobisher who, in 1576, returned from an American voyage convinced that there was a passage like Magellan Strait in the north, for he thought America must narrow to a point there as it did in the south.

Drake was disappointed, of course, and his reports of this part of his expedition are a little exaggerated. He sailed the *Golden Hind* as far as Vancouver, spent a month in California, probably San Francisco Bay and finally came home across the Pacific and Indian

Drake at the River Plate.

Oceans, around the Cape of Good Hope and north to Plymouth, where he arrived twenty-seven months after leaving.

The *Golden Hind*'s treasure was valued at two million pounds sterling, much more than Parliament appropriated for the government's annual running expenses. Queen Elizabeth looked upon Drake with marked favor although she could not show it publicly because the Spanish Ambassador was protesting violently against Drake's ravages and demanding that he be hanged, a demand which some Englishmen of high standing were inclined to think was reasonable. Elizabeth saw her accomplished captain several times, always in secret, until one day she went on board the *Golden Hind* and knighted him.

A man of Sir Francis' taste for adventure and exploration does not stay at home long. War between Spain and England broke out

Book of the Seven Seas

formally at last, and in 1585, Drake led a fleet of twenty-five ships to the West Indies where he destroyed many Spanish ports and captured many Spanish ships. In 1587, he succeeded in destroying part of the Invincible Armada, preparing for the invasion of England in Cádiz, and next year took part in the victory over that fleet, as has been told.

In 1595, the great pirate-privateer-admiral fitted out his last expedition. With twenty-seven ships he sailed against the Spanish West Indies, but when he tried to march across Panama, he met defeat and retired to his ship, a sick and disappointed man. He called his officers together, made his will, donned his armor so he could end his days as a warrior. In January, 1596, he died. So many men had been lost that the expedition had to abandon two ships, and they served as the Admiral's funeral pyre. One of the most famous heroes of the seas was gone, but Britannia's rule over the Seven Seas was due in great measure to the deeds of this man.

For many years both before and after Francis Drake, the seas were full of bold men, some good and some bad, who combined what they called patriotism and what the world called greed to harass their enemies—and all the world was an enemy. There were the Malay and Chinese pirates of the Far East, whole Arab kingdoms of corsairs among whom the brothers Barbarossa ranked high for power and cruelty, buccaneers of the Spanish Main, and many more. But the most fearsome raiders in history were the Norsemen.

Beginning in the eighth century, they sailed their wonderfully built "long ships," which no other craft could match, against the peaceful and the warlike. They were cruel and ruthless, but they had a good reason for their voyaging. Their lands would not support their population. Many a "king" ruled over what was no bigger than a good-sized Scandinavian farm today. For such a man there was no choice but the life of a sea raider. The stories of the Vikings are without number. The softer civilizations to the south of them reviled them as pirates and murderers, but in their own world they were heroes, too.

350

The Irregulars

The sagas tell of Ragnar Lodbrok, to mention just one among many, who ended a life of highly successful piracy by being captured in England and thrown into a pit of poisonous snakes. He sang there until he died, interrupting his chant only to say: "The little pigs would grunt now if they knew how it fared with the old boar." He referred to his four sons, and indeed one of them exacted the classic Viking vengeance of tearing the living lungs out of his father's executioner with his own hands.

During the fifteenth century, a new sort of ocean-going fighter appeared, devised by nations with plenty of ships and sailors but short of cash with which to build and man a navy. This was the privateer, a warship owned, armed, and operated by private individuals with a government license to capture enemy vessels. The license, called a "letter of marque" or "letter of reprisal"—the second term used if the excuse was that the idea was to get revenge for losses inflicted by the enemy—authorized the holder to sell any prizes he took for his own account, and protected him from being treated as a pirate if captured. At least that was the theory; privateers often were executed in spite of their papers.

Before long the business of privateering was so profitable and popular that even countries with large navies got into it. In some of her wars, England had a hard time getting men for the Royal Navy because experienced seamen preferred signing on with a privateer. Instead of small Navy pay, he got a share of the profits, and on a good cruise this might be enough to set a common sailor up in a small business ashore. Also because the men were partners in the enterprise, the old-fashioned brutal Navy discipline was not so severe on a privateer.

The United States had privateers before it had a navy at all, several of the New England states issuing letters of marque to shipowners before 1776. Before the war ended, more than 2,000 American privateers had been commissioned, and some handsome fortunes were made; the peak strength of the Continental Navy was thirty-four vessels.

351

ARUCH En CHERIDYN BARBAROSSA
Koningen van Algiers.

The Barbarossa brothers.

The Irregulars

Privateering was a wonderfully cheap way to run a navy, but the maritime nations began to find that it was more costly to commerce. The trouble with privateers was that sometimes they were not too fussy about the flag of the ships they attacked; they were known to loot neutral vessels or even those of their own country. Between wars they hated to give up the booty and the excitement of the chase, and so many of them turned pirate.

The War of 1812 was the last in which the United States issued letters of marque, but Congress authorized plenty then, as the fitting out of forty privateers from the port of Salem alone testifies. A generation later, all the maritime powers were agreed that privateering was more of an evil than a good, and in what is known to diplomatic history as the Declaration of Paris, in 1856, they abolished it so far as they were concerned. Even the countries which did not sign abided by this international ruling, and no privateers have been licensed since.

Out and out pirates were more colorful if not more greedy than the privateers. Almost every sea and every nation has contributed its bad men to the roster, and from time to time certain ports were noted as refuges for the trade. The West Indies were full of good hideaways among the reefs and islets. The word buccaneer, in fact, comes from "boucan," the dried meat which the robber bands from what is now Haiti used as the staple of their diet. At one time New York City was a favorite resort for pirates, and a good many New York merchants and some English colonial officials got rich by doing business with them.

As the wealth and power of Spain declined, and the rich trade with the Far East swelled in the seventeenth century, the center of pirate activity shifted from the Spanish Main to the Indian Ocean. The chief participants in the trade of the East were English and Dutch ships, so gradually the English and Dutch governments began to frown on piracy. It was a long haul around the Cape of Good Hope to New York, but after the English took the place away from Holland in 1664, the merchants were found to be as hospitable to the buccaneers as London had been to Drake. Pirate ships outfitted here and sold their booty at prices which gave everyone a nice profit.

The traffic reached its peak in the administration of Governor Benjamin Fletcher, an army colonel sent out in 1692, with instructions from King William to suppress piracy. William was both Stadtholder of the Dutch and King of the English, so he was more anxious than most to make honest shipping safe. But he selected as Governor what they called in those days "a necessitous man," and Fletcher wanted to get rich.

One of his pets was Edward Coats of the *Jacob*. He had done so well in the Indian Ocean that he paid Fletcher £1,300 for his "protection" and made the Governor a present of the *Jacob* which brought £800 next day. But Fletcher's prime favorite was Captain Thomas Tew, who had been even more successful than Coats. When the Governor finally was dismissed, and brought up on charges after a very lucrative five years, one of the points against him was that he always was in Tew's company, driving or strolling or dining. Fletcher's defense was that he spent so much time with the pirate only "to make him a sober man and in particular to reclaim him from a vile habit of swearing."

By 1697, when he was recalled, Fletcher had become such a connoisseur of piracy that he took a dim view of Captain William Kidd, who arrived in New York with a commission under the Great Seal of England for fitting out a ship to battle pirates in the Indian Ocean. Kidd was known as yet only as a middle-aged retired merchant skipper of wide experience in New York and the East. In London he had told great men at court that he could clear the seas of pirates without putting the government to any expense. All he needed, he said, was backing to outfit a good, well-armed ship and man her with a fighting crew stimulated by a promise that instead of pay they could share the proceeds of whatever loot they recovered. As a reverse twist on privateering, this appealed to wealthy, influential landlubbers. A syndicate put up £6,000 to finance the venture.

The Lord Chancellor of England, the First Lord of the Admiralty, and the Earl of Shrewsbury, one of the leading noblemen of the country, were in it. So was the Earl of Bellomont, the chief promoter of the project, already selected to replace Fletcher as Governor of New York.

They acquired for Kidd a ship which mounted more guns than the toughest sea rover ever carried. It was called the *Adventure Galley,* and the Captain took her to New York to recruit a crew, the Navy having rounded up most able British seamen at that time. He sailed on his adventure in February, 1697, and Fletcher's report on him ran: "When he was here many flockt to him from all parts, men of desperate fortunes and necessitous, in expectation of getting vast treasure. He sailed from hence with 150 men, as I am informed great part of them from this province. It is generally believed here they will have money *per fas aut nefas,* that if he miss of his design intended for which he has commission, 'twill not be in Kidd's power to govern such a horde of men under no pay."

The *Adventure Galley* arrived off the coast of Madagascar in July and promptly fulfilled Fletcher's prediction. Ever since, Kidd has had his defenders, who say he was forced to turn pirate by his crew. They preferred to get rich by seizing defenseless merchant ships than by fighting the fierce freebooters of the Indian Ocean. Others insist he planned the whole thing this way.

It took a year for the news of his exploits to reach London. They lost nothing in the telling. Once he had chosen piracy, it seems Captain Kidd flung himself into the work with enthusiasm. His victims said he had them tied up and beaten with the flat blade of a cutlass to make them tell where they had hidden money or jewels. He had prisoners killed, and set fire to ships, and made terms with other pirates to exchange ammunition. He was the terror of the seas from Madagascar to the coast of Malabar for two years. By then he had accumulated such quantities of silks, spices, jewels, and money that even his men were satisfied. They burned the *Adventure Galley,* and

355

while most of his crew took service with other pirate chiefs, Kidd and some of the less adventurous found passage for New York. ·

The Captain had every right to suppose that his share of the two years of piracy, presumably transferred into portable form, would make him welcome in Fletcher's province. But it was his bad luck that Fletcher no longer was Governor. He had been recalled while the *Adventure Galley* was sailing to the East, and his successor was that enemy of pirates, the Earl of Bellomont. By the time Kidd reached America, Bellomont was furious with him, and his anger was increased by his many frustrations in trying to suppress the business which New Yorkers were doing with the freebooters.

The theory of generations of treasure hunters is that Captain Kidd prudently buried his treasure before he got to New York. He wanted to find out how much he would have to pay for safety before he risked his loot. It is known that he stopped at Gardiner's Island, and legend has him hiding chests of fantastic value along a thousand beaches. But the best argument for his defense, which was that he had no treasure and was a victim of his piratical crew, was the fact that no New Yorkers appeared to help him when Bellomont had him arrested and sent to England for trial. Kidd was tried, convicted of the murder of one of his crew and hanged at Execution Dock, still protesting his innocence. Ever since, he has been the prototype of all brutal pirates.

Actually, when the fiction is taken away from the facts we can prove, Kidd seems to have been a kindly soul compared to "Blackbeard," as they called Captain Edward Teach, a very good seaman but a man who liked to see people suffer. He lived up to his reputation and his very frightening appearance. This last he helped by braiding his long black whiskers, and wearing six pistols, a couple of daggers, and a sword at the same time. He got his protection from the Governor of North Carolina, who was said in an early book on pirates to have been gracious enough to attend the wedding when Blackbeard married his fourteenth wife. Teach flourished until Virginia got a governor named Spotswood, who hated pirates as much as

Bellomont and was more belligerent. In 1718, he sent an armed ship to take Blackbeard, and after a long fight off North Carolina, the Governor's men triumphed and brought back Teach's head on a pole.

A more attractive pirate was the most literary buccaneer of whom we know anything much, William Dampier, who was born in 1652 and went to sea when he was seventeen. After some service in the British Navy, he joined the pirates in 1679, and for a dozen years sailed in gradually increasing posts of command with various chieftains, including Davis of the *Bachelor's Delight* and the almost equally notorious Captain Swan of the *Cygnet*.

Dampier was an odd fish for a pirate; he did not drink, and while his companions were carousing in port, he was off on nature studies, bird-watching and enjoying the beauty of tropical flowers. Then he would come back and write about them. He was also much interested in everything about the sea—the winds and tides, the birds and fish— and he made some very shrewd observations about them. (His map of the winds is in Chapter XII, of this book.) He sailed all around the world on his piratical cruises, mixed with a little legitimate trade here and there.

Returning to London in the early 1690's, Dampier had only his notes and a tattooed East Indian prince to show for his adventures. He exhibited the prince for a living, but apparently he did not make a fortune. Then in 1697, he published a book on his voyages and became an immediate success. He was taken into the society of such men as Samuel Pepys and John Evelyn, who were much impressed with his scientific observations. Thanks to his new friends, he was commissioned a privateer, but this lover of nature was such a hard master at sea that he was court-martialed on his return. Later he served as pilot of another privateering expedition, and it was his ship that rescued Alexander Selkirk, the original of Robinson Crusoe, from Juan Fernández Island.

The other literary pirate of that age was a Dutchman named Esquemelin, who, in 1678, published in Amsterdam what is believed

Anne Bonney and Mary Reade as a contemporary print maker saw them.

to be the first book by a buccaneer, but he is not the literary crafts-
man that Dampier proved to be. The first English edition of his book
attracted attention, though, because it carried a frontispiece of Sir
Henry Morgan who at that time—1684—had made piracy romantic
in high places. At least King Charles thought him a fine fellow and
knighted him. Morgan had sacked enough Spanish towns to make
up for his crimes against Englishmen. And as Blackbeard enjoyed
the protection of the Governor of North Carolina, Morgan always
had a safe haven with the Governor of Jamaica.

The popular stories of the pirates teemed with men tortured and
cut to pieces, of women ravished, and even children dashed to their
deaths. They could be true, too, but not all of these deeds were the
work of men. Two of the most bloodthirsty villains ever known in the
West Indies were Mary Read and Anne Bonny, who joined their
husbands on a pirate vessel, wore pantaloons, and wielded a cutlass
with the best of them. They were said to be without mercy except as
they were accused of "carrying off struggling and tender young males
as well as loot." When their ship was captured in 1720, the entire
crew was promptly condemned to be hanged by a Jamaica court.
Whereupon, the two women "pleaded their bellies," as the saying

then went, which meant that they invoked the law which forbids the execution of a pregnant woman.

The crusade against pirates, which brought about the downfall of Captain Kidd and Blackbeard and many lesser pirates, did not put an end to freebooters. Almost a century later the United States was fighting a war against the Barbary corsairs, and won it, too.

Not that there were no buccaneers nearer home. Jean and Pierre Lafitte were so successful in the Gulf of Mexico that they had their own community ashore and called it Barataria. In the War of 1812, the British thought so much of their prowess that they tried to bribe the Lafittes to join in the attack on New Orleans. Instead the pirates helped to defend the city and were a valuable part of Andrew Jackson's army which defeated the invaders. Their services earned them a pardon from President Madison.

In the end, it always seems that navies and arguments do not suppress piracy anywhere. One great discouragement to the practice has been the fact that powerful men on shore found it was not safe to protect pirates or even do business with them. Then the opportunities for great gain in legitimate trade drew off a lot of these greedy fellows, and at last the police work could be effective.

Official Mystic Seaport Photograph
by Louis S. Martel

The *Golden Hind.*

A Spanish treasure galleon.

Part VII

Treasures of the Sea

Portuguese fisherman mending nets.

40

Food from the Sea

In 1498, Columbus' compatriots, John and Sebastian Cabot, sailing across the North Atlantic for King Henry VII of England, brought back only bad news, they and their employer thought. They had supposed they would find a short route to the gold, spices, and silks of Cipango, and all they saw were rocky, icy coasts which the Vikings had explored before them. It was as a mere afterthought that they mentioned the mildly interesting fact that at one place, near what they called the New Found Isle, codfish were so plentiful that the sailors lowered baskets into the sea and brought them up full of squirming silvery bodies.

The Cabots had discovered the Grand Banks, greatest fishing grounds in the world. The bigwigs at court and the merchants did not care, but before very long a lot of simple fishermen were making a good living, and improving the diet of folks at home, by sailing to the Grand Banks of Newfoundland for fish. After a while the rights of fishing here were considered more valuable than all the treasure of the fabled East. When the United States succeeded in getting independence recognized, the one thing old John Adams insisted on getting into the treaty of peace besides that recognition was the right of New Englanders to fish the Grand Banks.

The sea always has furnished so much of men's food that it has been calamity when the supply moved away. When the great earthquake of 1923 drove the fish from the northern Japanese islands, hundreds of thousands of people starved to death before it was learned that the schools had migrated to Korff Bay in eastern Siberia. Even more recently the slight warming of Arctic waters has induced

363

cod to move further north, so that the fisheries around Iceland now claim the biggest catch of any in the world.

The principal salt-water food fish are the cod and others of its family (haddock, hake, and whiting), salmon, sardines, herring, and flatfish—mackerel, plaice, sole, flounder, and tunnies. All of them are pretty widely distributed in the oceans and have formed the basis of large industries since the earliest times. Oysters, which are one of the most if not the most valuable commercially of all sea foods, and clams, crabs, and lobsters are extremely important in the world's diet.

Japan for a long time has been the chief fishing nation but hardly any country with a seashore fails to make something of its position. In the tropics, of course, the problem of keeping the fish restricts their use in national diets. Where it is so hot that the catch must be put in the hands of the consumer within five hours of the time it leaves the sea, there is a terrible problem of refrigeration. The ordinary commercial processes make the fish too expensive for people of these countries. The older methods of drying and salting are impractical in that climate. So some of the rich fishing grounds of the world, such as those created by the cold Humboldt Current, cannot be used to the full for the benefit of man. But new techniques of freezing and preserving may solve this problem.

Fishing, of course, is an old and respected occupation. It is almost always an occupation of peaceful, gentle people, too. When seafarers like the Vikings began to use their ships to look for something else than food, they developed more violent habits.

There are three ways to catch fish commercially. One is with hook and line, but when the trawlers do it they are not equipped like sportsmen. There may be as many as 10,000 hooks on the ground line or trawl, which may be several miles long. Another system is netting, and the third is trapping. Each, of course, is designed for a particular fish.

There are many odd stories about fish and fishing, which is hard, dangerous work when the men have to go out in rough, foggy weather far from shore. Some people used to have a special regard for haddock because they said this was the fish from whose mouth Saint Peter took tribute money. Haddock have a black spot on either side of the head, which was caused by the finger and thumb of the Saint when he held the fish to open its mouth, according to the legend. Peter was a fisherman in fresh water and the haddock is a salt-water fish, but of course, the Saint could have got around that difficulty by a miracle.

A much more practical feature of haddock was discovered by the sensible Scots. This fish smokes well, and one of the widely used European foods is "finnan haddie," which takes its name from a place called Finnan or Findon, in Scotland, where the process was supposed to have originated.

The great popularity of cod for centuries was that it could be dried or salted, and was tastier than most fish when salted. The oil from its liver has been much used in the last hundred years because about a century ago it was discovered that this is the most easily digested of all animal fats.

Sardines are not the same thing to the scientist that they are to the housewife. Technically, the sardine is the name of a species of the genus Sardinella. Commercially, it is the young of quite a few fish which are packed in oil. The idea of thus using a catch of little fellows which otherwise would be too small for reasonable sale first occurred to the French, but the fishermen of other countries soon copied them. There are thriving sardine industries now in Italy, Spain, Portugal, the United States, Sweden, Norway, and Japan. Young pilchards, herring, and sprats are used extensively, but a great many others also are packed and sold as sardines.

By contrast, the biggest of the commercial fish are the tunnies, which belong to the mackerel family—in fact are called horse mackerel in some places and tuna in others. These and salmon are the two commercially sought fish which also interest sportsmen. Tunny have been known to reach a length of ten feet, and a fish of that size may weigh as much as 1,500 pounds.

International food experts have been trying for a long time to improve the fisheries of countries with poor nutrition and easy access to the sea. The good health of the Japanese on an otherwise skimpy diet has been attributed to the fact that they are the biggest fish eaters in the world—seventy-two pounds per capita per year. Since this means more than three million tons of fish, it is easily seen why fishing is a major Japanese industry. It compensates for the comparatively small amount of meat and cheese in Japan. England, where the average consumption is forty-four pounds a year, is another big fish-eating country, and of course the Scandinavians and Dutch are about the same. In the United States, people eat only about eleven pounds apiece on the average. It is becoming more popular with diet-conscious people, however. Halibut and salmon, for example, have as much protein as beef, or more, but much fewer calories because they have very much less fat.

Before the discovery of America, the great northern fisheries were in the North Sea, which is sometimes called the German Ocean. Here there are banks very nearly as rich in marine life as the Grand Banks, and the fishermen of many nations have trawled there for centuries. Since 1882, fishing there has been regulated by international agreements, starting with one to which Denmark, Great Britain, France, Belgium, Germany, and the Netherlands were parties.

All the fisheries, of course, are governed by the presence or absence of a food supply for the fish. So the most fertile spots are those where the water is cold, teeming with the protozoans which make up the basis of plankton, and where the bottoms are covered with starfish, periwinkles and shrimps.

Shellfish are not as important in the world's food supply as the finny fish, but they make up a disproportionately valuable part of the catch. Oysters are by far the most important. There are about 100 species of oysters, most of them edible, and all of them gregarious. They live in great colonies called beds, and reach maturity usually at the age of four years. This comparatively slow growth is one reason why a great many oyster beds have been exhausted, and nowadays they are cultivated scientifically. They are fussy animals, very selective in the choice of habitat, which is why it has been found impossible to colonize the Atlantic oyster in Pacific waters. New seed oysters have to be planted every year. They are seldom found in water shallower than fifteen feet or deeper than 120. The reason for the old saying that they should be eaten only in the months with "R" is that, while not harmful at other times, they become very emaciated as they approach the breeding season, which usually is May and continues until September.

Lobsters are second only to oysters in commercial value. The common American and European varieties are the ones best known to us, but there are others eaten with relish in many parts of the world. Caught in traps or pots baited with flesh, they are now cultivated, too. Lobsters have a strange life cycle. As soon as they are hatched they rise to the surface, and for several weeks they swim vigorously on the surface, feeding on any tiny animals they can catch. In this period they molt no less than six times, finally acquiring the form of an adult. Then they sink to the bottom and spend the rest of their lives crawling about, in shallow water during the summer and in deeper water in winter. Old lobsters are quite nomadic animals.

Clams, which have been called the poor man's oysters, live in sandy or muddy bottoms and make their way through the sediment in search of food. The biggest known bivalve is the giant clam of the South Pacific, which sometimes weighs 500 pounds.

Crabs and shrimps and prawns are of less consequence in the market, but perhaps more so in the diet of other sea animals. They are shallow water dwellers, and the crab particularly is a scavenger. The so-called soft-shelled crab is not a different species but, usually, the ordinary blue crab of the American Atlantic coast which has just shed one shell and is caught before the new one has hardened.

There are a great many other varieties of food in the sea. Far more fish than have been mentioned are caught and eaten. Sea turtles and tortoises are important to many peoples, especially island dwellers. Seal and walrus were the basic meats of the Eskimos. Shark meat, whale meat (especially in Japan), squid or cuttlefish, flying fish, and others are consumed and even esteemed as delicacies.

That the sea can provide a great deal more food than ever man caught there in the past is plain from many studies of the richness of marine life. The cultivation of species which seemed to be on the point of extinction proves that there is a vast potential here. As long ago as the golden ages of Egypt and Greece, men fenced off enclosures in the sea where fish were nourished until they reached a size suitable for serving on the table.

But there is a new possibility even more far-reaching than the potential to be gained from improved methods of preservation. This is the suggestion made by a number of learned scientists that the greatly increased human population which they expect in future centuries will be nourished from the very source of all life, the little one-celled plants of the sea, without bothering with the "middlemen" of fish or cattle.

It has been proved that algae, which can be grown in sea water in virtually inexhaustible quantities with nothing more than sunlight, contain all the essentials for the nourishment of man. The more sober workers in this vineyard, however, do not propose to feed us on the stuff right away. First they will use it as animal feed, fattening endless herds of cattle with it on the theory that steers are not as fussy eaters as human beings. But this does not eliminate the possibility that still another step will take them into growing algae of different flavors to tempt the appetite of man. If that ever happens, farmers and ranchers and fishermen will have to go out of business, but by that time it is supposed there will be so many people on earth that there will be no room for farms and ranches anyway. And then everyone will depend on the great ocean for everything he eats.

Cod fishing after a Currier and Ives print.

41

Mining the Sea

There is so much mineral wealth in the ocean that many men have grown dizzy just calculating how rich they would be if only they could separate these minerals from the water. The actual amount is so great that scientists have figured that if all that are dissolved in the sea could be removed in their solid state and spread evenly over the land, they would form a layer more than 400 feet thick.

The gold alone is enough to make everybody on earth many times a millionaire, for there is $90,000,000 worth in each of the ocean's 329,000,000 cubic miles. Naturally, ever since this was discovered, there has been a great interest in trying to extract the gold. Processes for doing it have been worked out, too, the most practical being an electroplating type of machine. Gold, however, collects in colloidal or suspended form instead of in a solid layer, and then the colloidal gold must be worked into its more usual form.

One of the men who came closest to a commercial success was a famous German chemist, Fritz Haber, shortly after World War I. I remember how everybody in Germany was excited about him. They were going to pay all their war debts and reparations and have plenty left over so that no one would worry about anything ever again. The people had great confidence in Haber because during the war he found out how they could get nitrogen from the air to make explosives. This kept Germany going because her old supply of nitrates from Chile was cut off. In theory, it seemed to the nonscientific world that it ought to be as easy to get gold from the sea as nitrogen from the air.

In 1924 Haber sailed in the *Meteor,* a floating laboratory. She cruised back and forth across the Atlantic for four years while Haber took samples of the water and tried them out for their gold content. Actually it seems a lot when one says $90,000,000 worth. But a cubic mile of water, in which this sum of gold is dissolved, is a formidable amount to put through any man-made machines. Actually, it seems, Haber had calculated that there was more gold in the sea water than really is the case. He got gold, but it cost about five times as much as it was worth. Haber's experiments were unable to cut the cost further, and no one has done much better since.

The big difficulty was handling the enormous amounts of water that were necessary. Assuming that one wanted to use a cubic mile of water to get the $90,000,000 in one year, it would be necessary to fill and empty every day a tank as big as a city block square and about twice the height of the Empire State Building. That is why chemists have not been able to make gold as common as sand.

Of course, that does not mean that there is nothing in the sea which is worth mining. Actually people have been taking minerals out of sea water for a long time. First of all, probably, was simple salt from the evaporation of the water, especially in places where there is a very hot, dry climate. And, of course, it is supposed that the great salt deposits on land were originally part of the ocean which dried up. However, taking salt from the sea never was a very romantic occupation nor any way to get rich quick.

The next sort of mining operations were done at secondhand, so to speak, by utilizing the chemical talents of marine life to get at the minerals. Bromine, which is used nowadays in making the so-called antiknock gasolines among other things, was first found useful to man through the ability of a little purple snail, murex. This animal extracts bromine from the sea in considerable quantities, and perhaps not with very much difficulty because bromine is one of the sea's most abundant minerals. The Phoenicians gathered the snails and made from them a famous dye, Tyrian purple.

Then men discovered that they could produce bromine themselves, and American corporations started doing it commercially only a little more than twenty years ago. The first plant for this purpose was opened near Wilmington, North Carolina, by the Dow Chemical Company, in 1934. About all that is needed, except for some rather elaborate machinery, is a place where sea water can flow in on one side and flow out on the other, well away from the intake.

For centuries the sea also was the sole source of iodine. It was made available to men through seaweed; virtually all living organisms have to have it, but the seaweeds accumulate it most. Actually, the sea itself gives off a certain amount of iodine of its own accord, for the air around the shore has faint traces of it, and at one time there was some belief that this helped make what old-fashioned doctors called "the tonic property" of seashore vacations. Seaweed got a rival as a source of iodine when the Chilean nitrate fields were discovered, and that was a better source.

One of the newest mining operations in the sea is for magnesium, that wonderfully light and strong metal for which an enormous demand has been created by the airplane industry. Before 1918 there were only a few unimportant uses for magnesium compounds, and the only people who wanted the pure metal at all were photographers who exploded it in powder form as a flash for taking pictures. Then chemists of the Dow company developed a metal of which magnesium was the base and called it *Dowmetal*. They got the stuff from brine or from dolomite rocks.

Success with bromine plants led to experiments for getting magnesium from the sea when World War II created a big demand from airplane manufacturers. There is more magnesium in the ocean than any other mineral except sodium and chlorine—3.7 per cent of all the minerals are magnesium. This means that a single cubic mile of sea water contains 4,555,000 tons of the metal. By 1941, the company had the process perfected so that a big plant was built in Texas on the Gulf of Mexico. It gets about a ton of magnesium out of each 800 tons of water. Another bromine plant is here, too, and if there wasn't so much water available it would be possible to use the same supply for both minerals.

During the war, virtually all the magnesium used came from the sea. Other companies are in the field, too, the Kaiser Aluminum and Chemical Corporation being one. It recently doubled the capacity of its big plant in Moss Landing, California, where great tanks hold sea water which is treated so as to form milk of magnesia.

Just now the richest mining of the sea is the offshore oil, a subject of much political controversy because of the great wealth of this "liquid gold" in deposits under the continental shelf. No one knows just how petroleum is formed, but it has been established that even the inland pools were the creation of undersea forces and chemical changes when such places as Texas and Oklahoma were submerged. In recent years delicate instruments have been developed which locate promising spots by sound waves, started off by exploding dynamite under water.

The Gulf of Mexico has been the favorite proving grounds of this expanded industry recently, but there are plenty of other likely areas, including perhaps part of the Arctic Ocean. But getting the oil still is a difficult task. No one ever has been sure about oil until he drilled for it, and drilling under such waters as the Gulf of Mexico is not the easiest thing in the world. The drilling platform has to be strong enough to survive storm waves and hurricanes, so the piles which hold it are driven into the bottom of the sea sometimes as much as 250 feet.

The latest progress in getting useful minerals from the sea that I have seen myself was just this year in Iceland. This island never has had any limestone, and so it was not able to make its own cement. Now limestone, which was sedimentary deposits in old seas once, is constantly being washed out and sending its calcium into the ocean where it is taken by all sorts of animals to make their shells. If it were not for this use, calcium would be much the biggest percentage of mineral in sea water instead of ranking fifth. Recently the Icelanders have taken advantage of the fact that along their shores were such good conditions of life for shell-making animals, that there are huge deposits of the shells within easy reach. So cement plants have been built to use these supplies, and it is estimated that there are enough for many years of full-speed operation.

Mining the Sea

The tricks men have discovered for getting bromine and magnesium give us some grounds for believing that in time we may achieve the chemical abilities of some of the marine animals. If we could do as well as lobsters, we would have unlimited amounts of copper and even cobalt, for although copper is relatively plentiful, sea water contains less cobalt than any other mineral except tin. But lobsters use it in considerable quantities. An even less complicated form of life, the sea cucumber, takes vanadium from the sea; it was only because the blood of these sluggish animals was found to contain it that men discovered vanadium was present in the ocean at all. In fact, it is possible that there are more elements in solution than have been listed, and that chemical studies of the sea will reveal them.

There is much talk from time to time about exhaustion of the world's mineral resources. But if the chemists give us the answer to puzzles of extraction from sea water, there hardly will be any problem in the future.

TABLE V
Wealth in the Waves

Forty-four elements are in solution in virtually inexhaustible quantities in sea water. They could be sources of untold wealth if only man was as clever as a lobster or a sea cucumber in extracting them. Here they are, listed in order of the amount of each held by the sea:

1. Chlorine	16. Lithium	31. Cerium
2. Sodium	17. Phosphorus	32. Silver
3. Magnesium	18. Borium	33. Vanadium
4. Sulphur	19. Iodine	34. Lanthanum
5. Calcium	20. Arsenic	35. Yttrium
6. Potassium	21. Iron	36. Nickel
7. Bromine	22. Manganese	37. Scandium
8. Carbon	23. Copper	38. Mercury
9. Strontium	24. Zinc	39. Gold
10. Boron	25. Lead	40. Radium
11. Silicon	26. Selenium	41. Cadmium
12. Fluorine	27. Caesium	42. Chromium
13. Nitrogen	28. Uranium	43. Cobalt
14. Aluminum	29. Molybdenum	44. Tin
15. Rubidium	30. Thorium	

42

With Harpoon and Club

Whales and seals are the really big game of the sea, but no one hunts them just for sport. It is a serious business, and the men who engage in it successfully have had to be excellent seamen but good businessmen too.

The first who had courage and skill enough to kill a whale were the Eskimos and the Norsemen, probably the Eskimos a little earlier. However, some Scandinavian sea warriors were spearing whales offshore in the ninth century. Eskimos in their kayaks hunted the whale in open lanes among the ice. When they got close enough, they lanced the beast just behind the ear, then hurried ashore. From there they watched the whale's death struggles and followed it until it died. If the wounded animal got into the open sea, it was lost. But if they got it ashore they had a wonderful prize. A good-sized whale yields two and a half tons of meat very much like beef—it brings half the price of beef in Japan now—and enough oil to keep whole families in fuel through a hard winter.

The next known hunters of whales were Basques, who harpooned and lanced the animals in boats in the Bay of Biscay and then towed the bodies ashore. By the thirteen century this was a major industry. After the design of ships improved, builders made a sort of floating factory so that the whale's blubber could be "tried out" or boiled down for its oil, which could be stored in the hold in barrels, and then whales could be hunted in the open ocean. The Dutch and the

Whaling in the far South.

Danes predominated in this branch of industry until early in the seventeenth century when the English and later their American colonists began to compete very seriously.

In the nineteenth century, before the use of kerosene, whales were a major source of artificial light, of oil for soap, of whalebone for corsets and umbrella ribs. The best whalebone came from the Greenland whale, and Americans did not hunt there very much as most of their fleet sailed to the Pacific. Just before 1850, there were 680 American whalers, all but forty operating in the Pacific from the Antarctic to Bering Strait. Whalebone was chiefly a European product, and at one time the price was as much as $10,000 a ton. It is not bone, of course, but the hard plate from the roof of the whale's mouth. Its main use now is for brushes.

In the great days of whaling, described so eloquently in *Moby Dick*, the whaling ports were busy towns, and the young men who felt a call to the sea came from all over the country to sign on for a cruise, which would last three years. The law required sailing ships to put in at a port every six months, but in between the hardships could be terrible and the dangers great.

Nowadays it is hard to imagine what it meant to be six months at sea. Small but modern steam vessels have replaced the old sailing ships; a heavy harpoon fired from a gun in the bow of the ship takes the place of the hand-thrown harpoon and the long pull at the oars; quarters for the first time give sailors an opportunity to lead a life as dignified human beings, and an attractive life, too. But in the old days provisions consisted mainly of salt meat and hardtack; if there was flour on board it soon was filled with worms and insects, so good bread could not be baked. Butter or fat turned rancid in no time. But worst of all was the water. Nothing was known except wooden casks, and in them grew all manner of bacteria. It did not take fourteen days before the crew stopped drinking more water than they had to, and even so it was rationed, so much for the cook and then a little for the sailors.

As the salt meat always had to be soaked in water to soften the taste of the brine, and the taste of the water grew worse, the sailors welcomed every rain with enthusiasm. When no whales were at hand, most skippers allowed the crew to plug up gutters to collect water enough to wash their clothes. Every pail and container also was filled, but soon the taste was as bad as ever. Added to this were the rats and mice, always on board, which were found floating in the drinking water from time to time.

In the days of sail, the dangers of dietary disease, gales, and rocks were complicated by the risks of harpooning the whale. Boats often were smashed and men drowned in the battle, and in some cases maddened sperm whales even sank the whaling ship itself—the wooden hulls were no protection against ramming by an enraged animal almost as big as some of the ships.

Such a fate overtook the *Essex* of Nantucket, Captain George Pollard, Jr., three months out on November 20, 1819. One of her boats had harpooned a sperm whale, but had to cut loose from it to avoid being crushed. The whale made for the ship and rammed her just forward of the fore chains. The timbers cracked and water poured in. While the men were at the pumps the whale struck again and this time stove in the *Essex*'s bows. In ten minutes Captain Pollard knew his ship was sinking, but he managed to keep her afloat for two days while the crew built up their two biggest boats and provisioned them for a long voyage. Then on November 22, they had to leave her. They were just south of the equator in Longitude 119° West, more than a thousand miles from land. In four weeks, suffering from thirst, they found a small uninhabited island and there three men insisted on staying. The others decided to try for Juan Fernandez Island, 2,500 miles away. Fifty-two days after they started, three survivors in the mate's boat were picked up by an English brig, and a day later the Captain and one sailor. In both boats, the survivors had been reduced to eating the flesh of those who died. A Nantucket legend has the sailor, asked years later about the cabin boy, replying, "Did I know him? I *et* him!" Captain Pollard recovered from that ordeal but retired from the sea when his next ship was wrecked on a coral reef. He ended his career as a member of the Nantucket police force.

The advent of iron ships and steam reduced these hazards. At one time sizable old ocean liners were used in whaling, cut down so that the whales could be dragged up a ramp to heavy machinery which did most of the processing. Smaller vessels proved more efficient, however, and the modern whaler is a tight little craft which, in the last three years, uses an electric harpoon which will kill whales instantly.

In between the romantic era of the New England whalers and the improvements of our own day, the whalers were hard put to it to find crews. Voyages became less profitable; crew members became harder and harder to find. Experienced salts no longer wanted a three-year voyage, and the decline of the American merchant marine reduced their numbers anyway. Owners had to put advertisements in the papers for "green hands" and tempted the unsuspecting with talk of an adventurous life and comfortable ships. Often there were barely enough able seamen to man the whaler in emergencies.

Such were conditions on board the whaler *Pedro Varela* when she sailed out of New Bedford early on an April morning in 1910. The crew presented a miserable sight. Quite a few were jailbirds—pickpockets, pimps and shoplifters—and one was a victim of periodic attacks of delirium tremens. Most of the experienced sailors were deserters from the British Navy, who were safe as long as they were on an American ship. One of the green hands was a youth with a bit more education and gentle background than the rest, Walter Hammond, who wrote the story of his voyage some years later when he settled down in New England, having had enough of whaling in one voyage for all his days.

His introduction to whaling was to be lined up with the rest of the crew and told to remove hats. The third mate, a huge Negro named Nikolas P. Cruz, who could roar like a bull and was obeyed very quickly, dragged them over one by one to the first mate, a Cape Verde mulatto who usually had a New Testament in his hand but on this occasion wielded a scissors. Every sailor had a close "crew cut" to get rid of vermin, but the hair was allowed to blow about the deck and washing was not compulsory, so by the time they had been at sea thirty days, everyone was infested with lice and fleas.

The crew's quarters were entered through a two-foot square hatch in the foredeck, and below, each man had a bunk with a space only two feet between it and the bunk above. No one could sit up and read, but that was not expected and there was not enough light.

The officers had better quarters, of course, although the space was not lavish. The Captain, Antonio Corvelho, was a Portuguese from the Azores, and the second mate, also Portuguese, was an old man suffering much from rheumatism. The petty officers were the boat steerers, so-called because after they had harpooned a whale from the bow of one of the ship's boats, they changed places with the mate and steered. The mate's task was to kill the whale with a lance.

A tug took the *Pedro Varela* out of the harbor, and then all sails went up and they were left alone. It was to be a three-year voyage with the men on the regular ship watches, twelve to four, four to eight, eight to twelve repeated through the twenty-four hours. Those off watch were supposed to be on hand for meals at six, twelve and six, and everyone was on duty from 5 to 6 P.M.

Days were uneventful for some time. Meals were monotonous, with the first day's diet repeated constantly. Duty as lookout at the masthead was the chief trial for the green hands, whose stomachs could not take the pitching and rolling of the ship accentuated by their station eighty feet up in the air. Some were so sick that not even the fists and threats of the big third mate could drive them aloft.

But when the first shout of "Blow-ow! Blow-o-w!" came from the lookout off the Azores, all of them were excited. The boats were lowered, and the usual battle with a sperm whale followed.

No one can deny the stirring inside him as the boat gets so close to a whale that the oars are not used any more, but the men take to the paddles. As one comes alongside a whale, indifferent to the boat being near, there always is a strong urge to go elsewhere. But the calm with which an experienced harpooner drives his harpoon deep just behind the fin is reassuring; apparently this monster can be handled if only everybody works together.

The mate gives quick commands: "Stern all!" or "Pull three!" or "Pull two!" to maneuver the boat as the whale takes its first dive and rope is paid out. When it comes up it will try to get away on the surface, and then begins the "Nantucket sleighride" which can take the boat's crew for miles and miles, until the whale gets tired. Then as the line slackens, it is taken in, and as the whale lies quietly, up goes the boat, keeping clear of the flukes but close to the body and not far enough forward for it to see what is coming. The mate then raises his long lance and hurls it into the animal's side, penetrating to two feet or more. At once comes the command to pull away, tugging the lance out, too. The whale brings his huge flukes out of the water, rolls his body, tries to smash the boat.

Here is displayed the mate's skill, maneuvering the boat so that as the whale misses, he can drive home another lance. The whale may try to sound, but it cannot stand the pressure of deep water if badly wounded, and soon surfaces, perhaps trying another tactic by coming at the boat head on, mouth wide open. The boat remains steady until at the last moment, "Stern all!" and the big jaws close on nothing, but not before the mate has had a chance to thrust his lance down into the lungs. The whale is done for but still dangerous. He spouts blood—one can hear it gurgle in his lungs and the water is red all around—but he still lashes out although he has difficulty keeping his balance. This is the first sign of his final defeat. Usually sharks will have gathered by this time, but they stay out of range, and as the mate keeps lancing mercilessly, the whale rolls over and dies. The boat is tied up to the body; a red flag is raised to guide the *Pedro Varela* which will come along to pick up the boat and crew, who lash their prize to the ship's hull.

All hands will be busy now. Sails are down; under the tryout where the blubber will be boiled, a basin of water will be set to prevent the ship from catching on fire. Cutting spades and other tools are brought up, double set blocks hoisted aloft, and a cutting platform rigged over the side. This is so placed that men can stand leaning against the platform's rail, facing the ship, which is the best position for "cutting in." It requires some skill with the long handled spades, exceedingly sharp and about six inches broad in the blade.

A first hole is cut through the blubber at the neck down to the red flesh. A large hook is attached to the blubber through the hole and eight men, four on each handle of the windlass, start raising the hook as the men on the cutting stage carve out a broad strip of blubber. As the strip rises, another hole is cut for another hook and so on until the blubber is stripped off from head to flukes, the whale's body

The first step in whaling is to plant the harpoon firmly.

rolling over and over and the sharks gathering, sometimes by the hundreds, to tear at the exposed flesh.

Then comes one of the grimmest jobs in whaling. The head is cut off and secured to the ship so that it rests nose down in the water, the exposed portion about flush with the surface of the sea. On the *Pedro Varela* it would be the task of captain and third mate to step out on the cutting stage and cut out a piece about three feet in diameter from the head, a chunk called "the case," which is a mass of bubbles filled with oil thrown at once into the tryworks. Then one of the boat steerers steps down into the head itself.

The hole left by the case is an entrance to a complete oil tank which gives the head of the sperm whale its characteristic shape—and value. The man has to submerge himself in the liquid, which has enough body warmth to remain fluid; a little colder and it will be the consistency of lard. The tank is divided vertically by a thick membrane, and the boat steerer has to dive down into the oil, knife in hand, and cut his way through the membrane. He holds a chain in his other hand, which he drags through the hole and then loops onto itself. The dive itself is grim enough, but if the man slips as he comes out, he slides right out among the sharks. The sperm oil is dipped out and stored directly in special hogsheads.

As the head is cast off, the "trying out" begins. Fires will have been lighted under the big kettles and the blubber melted, with a little precious fresh water in each at the start. The men cut up the strips of blubber into relatively small slices, once called "Bible leaves," and throw them in the kettles. The rich, brown, crispy pieces of scrap which float to the surface are strained out and used as fuel for the fires, which always are fed exclusively from the whale scraps. Enough is kept from each whale to start the fires for the next. As the kettles fill, hot oil is ladled out, and put to cool in iron tanks before being hand-pumped down into the barrels in the hold.

This, of course, was the old-fashioned way of whaling, already out-of-date when the *Pedro Varela* put to sea. The first excitement soon dies out. After that the monotony and hard work, the bad food and lack of hygienic facilities were torture to the men of this particular crew, accustomed to clean quarters and regular meals in various prisons. When each of the boats get a catch, as sometimes happened, the crew would have several days of work with no sleep and a bare minimum of food. They cursed and grumbled that each man's share, one one-hundredth, was not worth the labor. But for the third mate's merciless fists they would have dropped down on their bunks and left the whales to the sharks.

They were in this mood when the *Pedro Varela* met another whaler, a big square-rigged, three-masted bark, the *Morning Star,* also out of New Bedford. It was calm weather, and the ships hove to about half a mile apart for the customary "gamming." This meant a boat and crew from each ship would spend the day visiting the other. Captain Corvelho allowed his crew extra water for washing and shaving, had them put on shore clothes, and went himself with the third mate's boat and crew to the *Morning Star.* These men speedily discovered that the *Morning Star*'s water was nectar compared to theirs, the food ambrosia. Captain Corvelho got drunk, and when the men rowing him back commented on the *Morning Star*'s food and water, he told them they deserved no better than they got, and the worse the food was the less they ate, so he profited from their vanishing appetites. And finally, that very night as they parted from the other ship, a dipper in the drinking water brought up two very dead and decayed rats.

The crew of the *Pedro Varela* had not been living in happy harmony, but they agreed they should protest, and picked young Hammond as their spokesman. The result was short rations. The Captain put them on a diet of one square of hardtack and one cup of bad water daily for three days, and Hammond as extra punishment had two hours additional masthead watch each day. The crew were logged as "mutinous dogs."

It so happened that the next day was the Fourth of July, and

Corvelho was still so angry with the crew that he refused to let them hoist a flag to the masthead, much less celebrate in more merry fashion. This gave their hatred of him a holy justification in their eyes, and for two days they plotted at night the strangest mutiny on an American ship. Maybe it was not mutiny in the strictest sense because no man refused to obey an order, attacked an officer, or planned to take the ship by force. But what they did was more successful than violence. They simply destroyed or threw overboard everything that was needed in the business of whaling—the working parts of the windlass, the trywork gear of boilers and skimmers, the spades, knives, harpoons, lances, and even the grindstone.

There was no question of taking any more whales, and the Captain was furious. He put six of the men he suspected of being ringleaders in irons—Hammond was one—and kept them manacled in the hold on top of the oil and water barrels so that they could neither sit nor lie comfortably. He sailed to Fayal in the Azores to refit.

In the harbor was the whaler *Charles W. Morgan,* which still can be seen, fitted up as she then was, in Mystic Seaport, Connecticut. Captain Corvelho thought to send his oil and his mutineers back with her, but she would take only the oil. Corvelho had to take the six men back to sea with him after he had bought new gear. But he could stay out only three months. After he had taken nine whales, he needed new supplies, and this time members of his crew refused to stay on board.

Hammond, who had been released from irons to work, jumped overboard and appealed to the American Consul. After an investigation by this gentleman, Corvelho agreed to discharge any crew member who desired it. The six then worked their way home, where Hammond was allowed to return to his family unmolested, but the other five were sentenced to terms in the Federal penitentiary.

That whalers did not have to be as bad as the *Pedro Varela* is plain from the diary or "log" of a New England schoolteacher, who kept it on board the *Merlin,* also a ship out of New Bedford, on a

The whaler *Charles W. Morgan.*

voyage that lasted a week less than three years from June, 1856, to June, 1859. The schoolteacher was Mrs. John S. De Blois, bride of the *Merlin*'s captain, a whaling skipper of much experience and not too much worried by danger.

Mrs. De Blois was plain scared, and sick too, when the *Merlin* sailed out of New Bedford. Her husband was heading for the Pacific by way of Cape Horn, and it took her most of the long voyage around the Horn to get used to ship's ways and ocean weather. But there were no such hardships as Hammond complained of. The *Merlin* sailed close enough to land that she could put in every few weeks for fresh food and clean water.

By the time they rounded the Horn, Mrs. De Blois was contentedly domestic, except when storms blew, and her "log" is full of

385

entries about baking a plum cake or a peach pie, doing a little personal washing and ironing, mending clothes for herself and "Blois," rejoicing over a gift of a few unripe apples after weeks at sea. When they reached actual whaling grounds, she became very clever and quick at getting her washing and ironing down below before the chase began. She couldn't stop worrying about the crew's sin of working on Sundays, but eventually figured that the Lord must understand, since no harm seemed to come of it.

The big tragedy of the voyage was when her little dog Sailor died. There was a much more active and interesting social life than she had expected. Every time they saw a ship—and there were enough American whalers in the Pacific that this was often—ceremonial visits were exchanged, and if the other captain had his wife along, there could be a good exchange of gossip. So with shore excursions, where she was royally entertained, and celebrations on board, with roast pig at holidays like Christmas and Easter, Mrs. De Blois was almost sorry when, with 1,998 barrels taken from forty-nine whales, the *Merlin* headed back around the Horn for New Bedford.

Sealing voyages never could be as idyllic as Mrs. De Blois made her whaling adventure sound. Sealers have to go into the cold waters where seals breed, and send their men ashore to club the animals to death. And in the course of seeking new rookeries, they have done some of the world's notable exploring.

Whether they pursued the fur seals or the hair seals, the men in this business did not have to worry that the animals they hunted might sink their ships, but they more than made up for it by the peril of the ice. The record of their losses is grim. Major William Howe Greene, who spent much time among the Newfoundland sealers, and even went on a voyage with them, compiled a list of what happened to the fifty-eight wooden ships in that fleet from 1863 to 1925. By then only ten were left. For the rest, the notation runs "crushed in ice" or "foundered in Arctic" or "lost on rocks in snowstorm" or just plain "missing."

Courtesy of the Mariners Museum, Newport News, Virginia

Sealing on the northern ice.

In those days the disaster to be feared most was to be caught fast in the ice, frozen helplessly in a big floe and drifting with it to be released at last if the ice, floated far enough south or to be carried by it over rocks which would tear the bottom out of any ship, or perhaps to be crushed if storms piled up the ice so it ground up the imprisoned vessel like meat in a grinder. Every sealer carried dynamite to blast the ship free, and enormous ice chisels to chop a passage. The crews were trained in the tricks of freeing a trapped craft—everybody running in unison from side to side to roll her free, or getting out on the ice with a hawser to pull and haul so she might pitch herself free.

Aside from gambling their lives, the great chance sealers take is the finding of the seal herds on the moving ice floes or the discovery of new beaches. The harp and hood seals, which breed on ice floes, may be found almost anywhere. The luck of the *Walrus* still is spoken of by old-timers in Newfoundland. In the season of 1880, she was damaged at the start of her cruise and had to put back to St. John's. But hardly was she there than a succession of gales floated the

387

seal-bearing ice almost up to the harbor. Hastily patched, the *Walrus* took two full loads of pelts and part of a third in a matter of days, while the rest of the fleet was miles away getting very slim pickings for their trouble. Part of the luck of the *Walrus* was that a ship then could take more than one load; to prevent extinction of the seals, more than this was forbidden by law in 1895.

The life on board sealers and whalers has changed now, and very much for the better, too. Great improvements have been made so that the longest voyages may be without most of the old hardships. Only last year (1956) I went north on a sealing ship from Denmark, and had my place in the forecastle with the crew. Here were no more of those cramped bunks, but plenty of room even for my length to stretch out. At breakfast every man had half a grapefruit and eggs cooked to his taste. There was a bottle of good Danish beer for each sailor every day, and fresh water for them to use not only for drinking but washing. They do not regret the "good old days."

Bettmann Archive

Cross-section through an eighteenth-century whaler.

43

Jewels from the Sea

Anyone who ever opened an oyster and wondered if he would find a pearl inside feels a little of the excitement that keeps some men always making "my last trip" to one or another of the world's great pearl fisheries. Always there is a chance that the next mollusk will have a jewel finer than ever was seen before and worth a fortune. Or the pearler may spend his whole career at the game and find, as did Victor Berge of "Danger Is My Life," that his very first pearl was his best. Berge sold his for $7,000 cash and the lugger on which he sailed.

The pearl fisheries extend in a wide, interrupted belt all around the world, pearl oysters being found in tropical waters east and west. The oldest worked by man are off India, especially in the Gulf of Manaar, and in the Persian Gulf along the entire Arabian coast. Bahrein, an island recently notable for being involved in international oil controversies, got its first fame as the center of rich pearl fisheries. Valuable pearls also have been found in quantity in the Sulu Archipelago, off Australia, off both coasts of Central America, in the Gulf of California, in the Aru Islands, in the Arafura Sea southwest of New Guinea, and to a lesser extent around almost all tropical islands and coasts. Since the Suez Canal was opened, pearl oysters even have emigrated through it into the Mediterranean.

The pearl diver almost never keeps or sells the pearl. As far back as we know anything of pearling, and everywhere pearls were found, the diver nearly always was a simple fellow with large lungs who worked for a man who owned a boat. Excitement was less in

Diving for pearls.

the diving than in the opening of the oysters, the hazards of a voyage among dangerous reefs and currents, sometimes in poaching on forbidden grounds.

Pearls are formed by the oyster out of the same material which makes the lining of his shell, which therefore is called mother-of-pearl. The common expression that a pearl exists only in a sick oyster is not quite true. The pearl is formed around a grain of sand or the like, and is no more a symptom of disease than a callous. But the location of the pearl makes all the difference in its value. If it grows entirely free from the shell, it may attain the desirable perfect global shape. If it is attached to the shell, it may be almost worthless; and most pearls are attached. It has been estimated that one out of every thousand oysters taken from beds in the principal fisheries has a pearl, but not one in a thousand of these really is a good one.

Then—alas for romance—the real business of the pearling fleets is not pearls at all, but prosaic mother-of-pearl. This is the bread and butter of the business. For many pearlers, the pearls are only an occasional bonus in a steady trade. Mother-of-pearl has commanded prices up to $1,000 a ton or more, and when Berge began his diving career, the Chinese owner of his lugger was so intent on this part of the business that he agreed to let Berge keep all the pearls in lieu of pay, an unusual arrangement but indicating the sentiment of many owners.

Until the time of men still living, pearling was restricted to oyster beds which a man could reach on a single breath. But once the diving suit had been introduced, the native skin diver of the tropics was replaced by Japanese, and they in turn lost their monopoly so that today every race is represented in the craft. Suited divers can work a depth of 120 feet or so; thirty is about the limit for a skin diver. By the turn of the century, it was said that only three skin divers were left in the fleet which sailed from Broome, Western Australia, one of the great pearling ports. Yet at Thursday Island, in Torres Straits, Broome's Australian rival for pearling honors, islanders were diving in the immemorial manner as recently as 1925 although the Japanese were giving them hard competition.

The departure of the pearling fleet from Thursday Island was a great sight. Hundreds of luggers with their square sails catching the breeze danced over the sunlit water headed for their favorite fishing grounds. These small craft, few more than twelve tons, are among the handiest, most seaworthy of vessels. They take their name from the square "lugsails" hung obliquely from the masts (two usually, although sometimes luggers have one or three), and many in the Torres Straits had big, staring eyes painted on their bows so they could see their way among reefs and rocks.

In this part of the world, the native divers use no equipment at all. They simply jump off the side, swim to the bottom and grab as many shells as they can in the minute they stay down. If there are no shells, their employers often demand that they have a handful of sand or bit of weed to prove they really got to the bottom. After a few deep breaths, sitting on the side of the boat, they jump in again. They will work in water up to thirty feet deep.

The East Indian divers get to the bottom with the aid of a large stone, weighing forty or fifty pounds, tied to a rope. They work in pairs, one diving and one hauling up the stone and basket of oysters. There are six-minute dives on record, but the average is about a minute, as it is with the Torres Straits islanders. The divers are not long-lived, if they work regularly, a fact which led the Australian government to limit the terms of service of blacks under their jurisdiction.

Columbus saw men diving for pearls in the West Indies, and in 1579, King Philip of Spain had a pearl of 250 carats which came from the island of Margarita off the Venezuelan coast. None that big has been found in these waters since. The largest known from the Pacific side, a 75-carat beauty, was brought up in 1882 from the Gulf of California.

At Thursday Island thirty-odd years ago, Boston Harry was something of a legend among the polyglot, hard-bitten men who commanded and worked the pearling luggers. Harry Adams actually was a farm boy from Ohio who seems to have gone to sea young, but he came to the South Seas in the 1880's on a Boston ship. Because he never talked about his past, he was credited with being a fugitive from the law.

For some reason, pearls fascinated him. He jumped ship in Sydney, and made his way back to Thursday Island where he started his legend by winning enough money from a half-Chinese, half-German gambler to buy a lugger. Harry was an unusually strong fellow, medium tall but with such broad shoulders and long arms that he looked short and squat. Fights or accidents had scarred his face and drawn up the corner of one eye to give him a fierce expression. They called him an ugly customer on Thursday Island, and the case-hardened pearlers used to warn newcomers to let him alone. That part of his legend stemmed from his looks and the story of a fight he had with two sailors who jumped him as he came out of a bar one night. Harry wrapped a long arm around each and squeezed. When he let go, they didn't have enough breath in their bodies to stand, and everyone who told the story added a couple to the number of their broken ribs. Harry just walked away and left them.

After that no one bothered him, although he was known to carry valuable pearls. This was another part of the legend because Boston Harry sold only mother-of-pearl and inferior pearls. He kept his really fine ones in a little chamois bag attached to a money belt he wore.

Year by year, they said, the collection of pearls in the little bag grew, and each was a lovely, round, gleaming beauty, perfectly matched to all the others. People knew this because Harry would trade a pearl that didn't match his set for one that did, and everyone knew that he'd give two for one to get the exact size and quality he wanted.

His own fishing was successful, and the stories about a man like him would make it sound luckier than perhaps he was. No one ever saw the contents of his chamois bag, and no one could get any information out of his divers, even if they had known. Harry, like a good many other pearlers of his day, and later, used aboriginal women divers; they were more docile, didn't run off on shore and were just as good under water as the men. Harry's "gins"—as the native women are called—were able to smell good shell, he boasted. They seldom had to come up with just sand to prove to him that they'd reached bottom.

Then one day in the mid-1890's, Boston Harry sent his "gins" back to their island, sold his lugger and sailed for England as a passenger. Thursday Island supposed he had gone to retire or have a big fling, and forgot all about him. Eight months later he came back, again as a passenger. It was not considered polite to ask questions in the pearling society, and Harry never mentioned his trip. But the story around the pubs, apparently started by other pearlers who had been in London for a spree, was that Boston Harry had a daughter who never had seen him. All these years he had been collecting his famous matched pearls to make her a necklace for her eighteenth birthday. But when he got to London, she refused to believe he was her father or (in another version) found him so repulsive in appearance that she wouldn't forgive him for deserting her and her mother. He never got a chance to show her the pearls, and everyone wondered what he would do with them now.

He did not linger long at Thursday Island. He sailed out with the pearling fleet, but never came back. Some thought he must have been wrecked. But a couple of years later he was seen walking on the beach of an island in the Arafura Sea. He affably gave the pearler, who came ashore to find out if he wanted to be rescued, some good advice on nearby fishing grounds, but said he was living here and doing fine. After that he had a visitor every year or so. He lived in a native hut, and wore a Malay sarong, and didn't seem to have either cares or desires.

It took thirty years to discover what happened to his pearls. Boston Harry died while one of his old pearling friends was visiting the island, and the man naturally inquired about the little chamois bag. He found it, too, but it was empty. He searched Harry's quarters —it didn't take long—and quizzed the neighbors. They couldn't remember anything about pearls until one middle-aged Aru Islander recalled that when he was a little boy and the white man first came to live among them, Harry had tossed the kids some pretty beads to

A section of coral reef.

play with. Of course, they had lost them in the sand years ago.

The idea of giving a pearl oyster a chance to grow a pearl is said to have occurred first to the Chinese, who started off by using a tiny pearl as seed. It took several years to grow into a fine, large jewel, but it was worth waiting for, and in time the cultivation of pearls became a fair-sized business.

The Chinese also used to put tiny effigies of Buddha inside an oyster, and then retrieve the shell after the images had been coated with a thin layer of mother-of-pearl. These shells were sold at a very good price to the superstitious.

As the sea gives up one precious gem, so it has one popular semi-precious stone. This is coral, but not all the coral reefs and islands in the world are of the kind which is used decoratively. The red coral of which beads and ornaments are made comes chiefly from the Mediterranean, but is found in a few other places, too. It is brought up by dragging, the coral growing on the bottom like a small

Sponge boat in the Bahamas.

bush, so that it can be broken off by a drag and brought to the surface without divers.

Sponges are not beautiful and rare as pearls nor decorative as coral, but they are precious in their own way, and have been the objective of divers for just as long as pearls. There are a great many species of these animals, about 2,000, clinging to rocks or stones or shells, down to great depths. The Mediterranean is the center of the industry, and for as long as history records, the Greeks have been foremost in it. Like the pearl divers, they go down in suits nowadays, working on the average a little deeper as the best quality sponges come from greater depths.

When they are brought up, sponges are of a great variety of colors, like coral, but in the air they soon lose them. When the jellylike and liquid substances with which a sponge is filled are beaten and squeezed out, it dries to the dull yellow with which we are familiar. It is really the skeleton of the sponge that is sold.

Sponges were so widely used that at about the end of the last century fear was expressed in many quarters that the fisheries would be exhausted. The use of diving suits, which multiplied by several times the areas which could be fished, and the later invention of synthetic sponges has removed this likelihood.

Courtesy of the American Museum of Natural History
How the pearl is formed.

397

44

Sunken Treasure

There is a great fascination about wrecks, the poor dead carcasses of once good ships, and if it is supposed that they carried a treasure which cannot be damaged by salt water, why the fascination is all the greater. Sailors always have a lot of tall stories of sunken gold, and some of them even claim to know just where there is a wreck which would make them rich if they could get the price of a salvage expedition. Enough people have brought up lost treasures that there is a perpetual freshness to these tales.

The favorite wrecks for this purpose are old Spanish galleons because it is known that quite a few of them were lost at sea. The hunters always hope they sank in shallow water, too. Some of them did, and divers have been able to get at them. Now, although the man who got the biggest haul ever recovered from a Spanish galleon has been dead for 250 years, he has had his imitators ever since.

This man was William Phips, and he was the hero of one of the first fabulous American success stories about a poor boy who became rich. He was born on the Maine frontier on February 2, 1651, and was a shepherd until he was eighteen. Then he apprenticed himself to a ship's carpenter. As soon as he learned his trade, he went to work in Boston, and as he was an ambitious young fellow he taught himself to read and write. Within a year he married a rich widow and was able to take on contracts to build ships. He made several voyages as captain of two or three of them, and on trips to the West Indies he heard stories of wrecked Spanish treasure ships. He was very much excited by these sailors' yarns, and because he believed them absolutely, he was very convincing when he talked about them. In London, he managed to be brought before the King, Charles II, and was so eloquent that a Navy ship, the *Rose of Angier,* was put at his disposal to hunt for a wreck in the Bahamas.

This was in 1683, and Phips signed on a crew of ruffians and cutthroats who were paid no wages and even had to supply their own food, but were promised a share of the treasure. Phips seems to have been an easygoing captain when the crew got drunk or began fighting, but when some of the worst of them tried to raise a mutiny, he got really angry. He rushed among them, and with his bare hands knocked the ringleaders about so severely that the whole crew behaved well for a while.

They found no wreck off the island where Phips was sure it had sunk, and he decided to give up at last. He unloaded the ship, even her guns, to lighten her for repairs before the voyage to England. While they were on shore most of the crew got together and hatched a plot to seize the *Rose,* maroon the Captain, and go off as pirates to make up for their lack of pay. Phips got wind of the plan, had the few men loyal to him get the guns back on board, and when the mutineers started for the ship, he had the cannon trained on them. He told them he would maroon them as they planned to do to him, but after they begged and pleaded and promised to behave, he took them on board again and got safely back to England.

Phips wanted to fit out another expedition, this time to look for the richest ship of the 1642 Spanish treasure fleet, which was known to have been lost. Phips heard it had gone down off the island of Hispaniola, then Spanish. He could get no royal help this time; King Charles died about the time Phips came back, but the Duke of Albemarle believed in him, and got a few others to finance a private venture. The cost of two ships, special diving equipment, and as much provisions as the vessels could hold came to £2,712. Besides, the expedition took along £500 worth of trade goods so they should not come back empty-handed even if they found no treasure.

The two ships were the *James and Mary,* of 200 tons, and the *Henry of London,* a fifty-ton frigate. Phips was more careful in picking his crew this time, and the men were to be paid, as well as to get bonuses if the trip was successful. The two ships sailed to Puerto Plata, in what is now the Dominican Republic, and while Phips stayed there in the *James and Mary* trading with the Spaniards, his two chief assistants, named Francis Rogers and William Covell, took the *Henry* west along the coast, examining reefs and rocks. Somewhere in the neighborhood of Cape Cabron, they found the wreck.

It was, so they admitted later, due to luck. In the very clear water, Rogers saw far down such a lovely sea feather that he wanted Phips to have it. So he sent one of the divers down, and the man came up with the exciting news that right where the sea feather was growing was what looked like big guns overgrown with coral. Other divers went down and located the hull, also encrusted with coral as might be expected of a ship lying on the bottom for more than forty years. She was on a bank, sloping down from thirty-five to fifty feet below the surface.

This was just about as far down as divers in those days could work. Of course, the profession of diving was not new. The Romans had divers, skillful men who could stay under water for quite a long time, breathing through a tube which had its upper end floating above the water. Four hundred years before that, Aristotle had spoken of men drawing air from above the surface. About the only improvement from then to Phips' time was that a helmet had been invented. It had a long pipe leading upwards, and the diver got his air through this, which also had its upper end floating on an inflated bladder like a toy balloon. Of course, the men could only work on a very calm day.

Phips stopped trading in a hurry when Rogers came to tell him of the find, and the treasure hunters hurried back to the wreck. It took weeks to salvage the treasure, which turned out to be as splendid as rumors said, for a wonder. The divers worked until they collapsed, but they couldn't stay under very long, and were always getting sick from foul air. But they kept bringing up bars and ingots and pigs of gold and silver, masses of loose coins and fine pieces of gold and silver plate. They even salvaged the galleon's big brass guns.

When Phips came sailing into London in 1687, with nearly

Sir William Phips raising sunken treasure.

twenty-seven tons of treasure, nobody remembered or cared that he once had been a workman. His cargo was worth £300,000—probably as much as the income of the eight or ten richest men in England. There was a complicated system of dividing it up—the Duke of Albemarle got £50,000, the "royal tenth" which was the King's share of any such windfall amounted to £30,000, and Phips himself received £16,000, while all the other backers and officers and divers and sailors shared in proportion. (Some historians think these figures should be reduced one-third to one-fourth.)

In those days, £16,000 (or even £12,000) was a great fortune, and Phips now was richer than his wife. Also the royal tenth had been so well received that the King made William Phips a knight, and the one-time illiterate shepherd and apprentice was now addressed as Sir William. In 1692, he was appointed the first royal governor of Massachusetts, but soon was called to London to be accused of misgovernment. He died while awaiting a hearing in 1695, only forty-four years old, but a man who had achieved in real life what every boy who thinks of going to sea dreams about—finding sunken Spanish gold.

For every adventurer who got even a little bit of gold or bag of precious stones from a sunken treasure ship, there have been hundreds who failed. One of the treasure hunts which went on for years and years—and may still have its devotees for all I know—is a story of pirates and adventures which shows that if one is going to try to recover sunken treasure, it is well to be associated with trustworthy people. It is the story of the fabulous treasure of Cocos Island.

The Cocos or Keeling Islands are little dots in the middle of the Indian Ocean almost 12 degrees south of the equator. If you draw a line from Colombo in Ceylon to Freemantle in Australia it will pass right through them. As far back as the seventeenth century they were visited by pirates who refreshed themselves with the sweet spring water and plentiful coconuts of the main island. And that is when the legend of treasure begins.

The man who is said to have hidden the first great mass of it here was the favorite pirate of the pirates of that age. He was a brave and strong man, this Captain Edward Davis, who kept his men firmly disciplined. They knew what was good for them well enough to elect him leader of the biggest pirate fleet in the whole Pacific. This was at the time of Captain Kidd and some other famous pirates who were better known but not so greatly respected by their fellow buccaneers as Davis. He never killed anyone in cold blood nor tortured prisoners to find out where they hid their jewels, and so he was neglected by the storytellers.

Davis liked to command a happy ship. When he captured a Danish vessel which was much better than his own, he transferred his crew to her, scuttled his old one, and named the new, *Bachelor's Delight*. In this he cruised up and down the west coast of Spanish America as admiral of a pirate fleet, sacking towns, taking ships, and finally caching the heavier part of his loot, millions and millions of dollars worth, on Cocos, so the story goes.

He never went back for it, but not because he had bad luck. In fact, Captain Davis became respectable. At about the time Captain Kidd was being hanged, the most successful of the buccaneers bought himself a King's pardon and ended out his days either as a prosperous merchant in the Far East or a farmer in Virginia—accounts differ. He had plenty of easily portable treasure.

For more than a century this was the legendary treasure of Cocos, but no one ever found it. Then an ever greater fortune came to join it. In the early 1820's, Spanish loyalists in Peru were thinking of sending all possible treasures home to be safe from the great South American liberators, Bolivar and San Martin. A fleet was collected, said to be the richest Spanish treasure fleet in more than 300 years of such armadas, and in it was a hired little English brig with the affectionate name of *Mary Dear*. Her master was a Captain Thomson, and the Spaniards loaded his ship with all the gold and jewels of the Lima Cathedral, estimated then at $12,000,000.

It had been a long time since Englishmen made a habit of looting Spanish treasure, but Thomson and his crew seem not to have been able to resist temptation. At any rate, the next heard of them, they were pirates in partnership with a noted freebooter named Benito

Benito. It was said that they had murdered the priests sent with the Cathedral treasure, and only then realized that they could not sell it because it was too well known. While he thought about this problem, Thomson stored the stuff at Cocos.

He had not figured out a way when Spanish warships caught the pirates. Benito killed himself, but Thomson managed to get away and worked his way back to England, where he lived for a while under an assumed name. Then he sailed to Newfoundland, where he became close friends with a man named Keating. To this friend he confided his secret, and Keating obtained a ship for them to recover the treasure because maybe after years it would be possible to sell it. The story goes that they found it all right, but as the two men looked at the piles of emeralds and diamonds and pearls, the carved golden figures and the inlaid silver decorations, they became frightened of their own crew. They were sure the sailors would kill them for this treasure. So taking as much as they could carry, they sneaked off in the ship's boat one night.

Out beyond a sand bar, a big wave overturned their boat. Thomson, with his pocket full of jewels and a fortune in gold strapped to his body, sank like a stone. Keating managed to get out of his coat, which also was full of gold, and drifted out to sea on the overturned boat. Two days later a passing ship picked him up, and eventually he worked his way back to Newfoundland.

Nowadays, of course, treasure hunting under the sea has been put on a businesslike basis and has become part of the machine age. Salvage is a highly organized trade, with lots of complicated and powerful mechanical equipment. Wrecks are brought up from depths a little short of 300 feet for all sorts of reasons. But the lure of gold on board is still one of the strongest.

One might think that there was something unlucky about carrying gold across the ocean, so often do we hear of ships with such a cargo being sunk. This has happened often in our own time. In fact, the richest of all treasure ships was an English liner, the *Laurentic*, sunk by a German submarine in 1917 when she was carrying $25,000,000 in gold bars. The ship went down in 150 feet of water, and the

Taken from the book *Panorama of Treasure Hunting* by Harold T. Wilkins. Copyright Harold T. Wilkins. Reprinted by permission of the publisher, E. P. Dutton, Inc.

Buccaneer's map shows silver galleon wreck still awaiting the modern salvor.

British Navy kept divers at her for seven years, at a cost of only half a million. Although there were stormy weeks on end when no diver could go down, and they were able to work for only an hour at a time when they did, they cut through twisted steel girders and plates, and finally salvaged all but 154 of the 3,211 gold bars.

One of the most persistent salvage jobs was done by the famous Lloyd's of London a century ago. They had insured a big coin and bullion shipment on an old frigate, *Lutine*, in 1799, and she sank on a sandy shore. In 1857, Lloyd's managed to locate the wreck, and in four years divers sifted the sand and got £22,000. They also brought up the *Lutine*'s bell, and ever after Lloyd's rang it to announce the loss of a ship at sea.

These modern salvaging operations are made possible by the diving dress which was invented by Augustus Siebe in 1830. He was the first to give a diver an outlet as well as an inlet, and the suits for deep-water work have had no revolutionary changes, only improvements since then—compressed air instead of pumps, lights, telephones, and so on. But the depth at which divers can work is limited. The greatest depth at which any of them have been able to work for any length of time was 275 feet, achieved when a United States submarine, the *F-4*, was raised off Honolulu. The modern "free diver" with only his tank of compressed air strapped to his back, mask, weights, and flippers can get down to half this distance or more.

In fact, this free diving is making wrecks so accessible to amateurs that there probably will be a whole new generation of treasure hunters coming along with stories of riches to be salvaged.

Bettmann Archive

45

Black Ivory

For thousands of years slavery was a respectable part of human society. It remained respectable on land, too, long after it was despised and also illegal on ships. It enters into the story of the Seven Seas when slaves began to be carried over the ocean in the infamous slave trade after the discovery of America.

It all began as soon as the Indians were killed off faster than they could be rounded up. Spanish conquerors did not think that plantations could be worked by free men, so when the supply of natives tame enough to catch ran out, the Spaniards turned to Africa, where slaves had been an article of commerce from time immemorial.

Sailors of every European nation went into the traffic because it was almost always lucrative. Spaniards jealously forbade foreigners to trade with their colonies, but smugglers defied the law with slaves as with other merchandise, and after a while other countries got colonies, too. The first Negro slaves in what is now the United States were landed from an unknown Dutch ship in Virginia in 1619. Before long the traffic became so important that it was a valuable prize of war and diplomacy.

Spaniards called the license they gave to the slave-carrying monopoly "Asiento," which means contract. *The* contract in those days was for slaves. Spain was prevailed upon to give it to a French company at the beginning of the eighteenth century, but after the War of the Spanish Succession, England's peace commissioners demanded and got written into the Treaty of Utrecht in 1713 a provision that the "Asiento" be assigned to an English company. The contract provided that Spanish America take at least 4,800 Negroes a year for thirty years. The company could sell as many more for twenty-five years as planters wanted to buy, but must pay a duty on each head. Half the profits were to be divided between the King of Spain and the King of England.

By this time the English and other colonies on the mainland and in the West Indies were a good market for slaves, too. London, Bristol, and Liverpool were the chief home ports of the English slaving fleet, and Newport for the Americans, although the first American slave ship was built in Marblehead, Massachusetts, and named *Desire*. By 1752, there were 369 slave ships sailing out of the three English ports, and 150 from Rhode Island.

On the average, the British ships were larger, seventy-five tons with an average capacity of more than 200 slaves, against forty tons for the Americans. Even a forty-ton ship could carry seventy-five to one hundred Negroes in addition to a fair amount of other cargo. Some of the notable heroes of the American War of Independence got their naval training in this trade. John Paul Jones, for example, had served on the slaver *King George*.

One reason the slave trade paid off so well was that there always was a good market for its wares. Another was that no ship need fear having to make one part of the trip in ballast, as was the case on many runs, and owners got a profit three ways. Outward bound to Africa, the typical Newporter carried New England rum, which was traded for slaves, gold, and spices. The slaves were sold for cash in the West Indies, where a small part of the price was laid out in molasses for resale to the New England rum distillers.

Captain David Lindsay was a fine representative of the New England slave trader during the middle years of the eighteenth century. He was a conscientious man, so noted for integrity that other captains entrusted bags of gold dust to him for safe transportation. In 1752 he was in command of the forty-ton brigantine *Sanderson*, not one of the better products of New England shipwrights. She had cost only about half the amount usually spent for a new ship of her size half a dozen years before. By the time Lindsay got her to the Gold Coast "we can see daylight all round her bow under deck."

Leaks, tattered sails, and inadequate gear were no excuse for delay in those days, and Lindsay resolutely loaded his ship with slaves and pepper for the run to the Barbados. He was very busy because both his first and second mates came down with fever and "ye traid is so dull it is actually a noof to make a man creasy." Undiscouraged, and ignoring daylight visible through the deck, he set sail for the west. He made the Barbados ten weeks later with sails "alto pieces" during three weeks of squally, rainy weather.

"My slaves is not landed yet; they are 56 in number for owners, all in helth & fatt," he wrote, failing to mention if he had any for his own account, but captains usually did a bit of trading for themselves. "I lost one small gall. I've got 40 oz. gould dust & eight or nine hundred weight Malegabar pepper for owners."

The loss of only one child in the human cargo was a good but not unprecedented record. As long as the trade was legal, the comparison between slaves and cattle was a fair one, even if men were less trouble because they could survive greater hardships. Captain Lindsay even had his freight up on deck in small batches when the weather was good, and had sea water drawn up to be thrown over them once in a while. Down below, to be sure, only a fairly small child could stand upright, for the 'tween decks of a slaver often was no more than three and a half feet. There Negroes were stowed as carefully as any inanimate cargo.

One standard method was to pack them "spoon fashion," each slave lying on his side with knees slightly bent and back bowed and the next one's body fitted to the curves. Another favored practice was "the toboggan"—long rows of slaves sitting virtually in each other's laps with legs stretched out around the man in front like children on a sled.

This slave carrying voyage was the famous "Middle Passage." It was called that because it was the middle leg of the three in a slaver's round trip. It remained for a British master of a generation later than Lindsay to attempt a novel method of insuring his profit.

In 1781, owners of the ship *Zong*, Captain Luke Collingwood, master, brought an action against the underwriters. These insurers refused to pay for part of the cargo which had been jettisoned. It is standard marine risk that if some freight has to be thrown overboard to save the rest or save the ship, the insurers must pay. But in this case the cargo jettisoned had been 132 slaves, and the underwriters balked. Captain Collingwood testified that because of circumstances beyond his control, the *Zong* was short of water. In order to have enough to keep some of the Negroes alive, he swore, he was obliged to throw 132 overboard. He disposed of the weakest and brought the others safe to port. The lower court ruled that the claim was valid. But Lord Mansfield, one of England's great judges, held on appeal that while the law of insurance was on the side of the owners, there was a higher law of humanity which forbade the jettisoning of human cargo. He ordered a new trial, which the insurers won.

The worst horrors of the slave trade at sea were reserved for its closing years—years in which the traffic was outlawed but so profitable that greedy and ruthless men rushed into it in droves. The United States prohibited importation of slaves in 1807; a series of laws against the traffic followed, and in 1824, Britain declared the slave trade piracy punishable by death. Warships were sent on patrol, and the yardarms of more than one cruiser were decorated with the dangling corpses of captured traders.

The risk and the demands of Southern planters had driven the price of "black ivory" up in America and down in Africa. Before the trade was outlawed, a likely Negro cost $100 at the barracoons and sold for four or five times as much in American ports. After 1842, the price in Africa fell to as low as $8 a head, and a healthy human brought $1,000 to $1,200 on an American auction block.

Outlawing also changed the design of slave ships. Now the typical slaver either was so big that she would return an enormous profit on a single voyage, even if lost on the next, or so fast that she could outsail the cruisers—or both. Cargo was packed with new refinements of cruelty. In the legal days, a forty-ton vessel seldom carried more than 100 Negroes. When the *Maria*, thirty tons, was caught in 1847, she had 237 on board.

The mortality was incredible. No one then understood how such close quarters spread disease, and sometimes the body-snatchers suffered along with their victims. In 1819, both cargo and crew of

British warship capturing Spanish slaver.

the French slaver *Rodeur* went blind during the Middle Passage—all but one sailor. He steered the ship alone, and one day saw a sail. Changing course, he was horrified to see that what he thought at first was a tattered derelict actually was manned by blind men who when they heard him call screamed to him for help. They were the crew of a Spanish slave ship, the *Leon,* and every soul aboard had lost his sight. The *Rodeur* sheered off quickly and eventually made a West Indies port. The *Leon* never was seen again.

Slavers threatened with capture jettisoned their cargo to destroy the evidence. One of the most persistent and successful was Captain Homans of the brig *Brillante,* a tough, piratical fellow who mounted ten guns on his vessel, recruited a crew of sixty, and defied the British Navy. He had defeated one cruiser in fair fight, beaten off the boats of another, and was credited with having landed 5,000 Negroes in Cuba in ten voyages, which meant he probably had started with double the number, before four British warships trapped him at sea. They got within range only as night fell, and so stood by to board him in the morning. Homans used the interval to get all his slaves, 600, on deck and bound to the anchor chain. As he heard the British boats approaching at dawn, he ordered the anchor let go, chain and all. The men in the boats heard the screams as 600

411

Negroes were dragged to the bottom. When they boarded the *Brillante,* Homans laughed at them. Where was any evidence that he carried slaves?

Well, there was the stench, for one thing. You could smell a slaver further than you could see one on a clear day, officers on patrol said. But courts would not accept smell as evidence, nor the rings to which slaves were chained, nor screams in the dark. They had to let Homans go.

For all the horror and cruelty of the Middle Passage, it can be argued that the sea was a greater respecter of liberty than the land. There was the case which figures in United States diplomatic history as that of the ship *Creole.* On October 27, 1841, she sailed from Hampton Roads, Virginia, for New Orleans with 135 slaves, one of whom was named Madison Washington and had tasted freedom. Some time earlier he had escaped from a Virginia plantation to the North, but went back for his wife and was caught. After a fearful flogging, he was "sold down the river."

The *Creole* was ten days out when the cargo broke loose. Under Madison Washington's leadership, the slaves seized the ship in a brisk fight and sailed her to Nassau in the Bahamas. It fell to the lot of Daniel Webster, then Secretary of State, to demand that the British either return the property or pay for it. The British politely but firmly refused. They did hold nineteen of the slaves briefly on charges of mutiny and murder preferred by United States agents —one white man had been killed in the struggle on the *Creole*—but a Bahama court ruled the incident justifiable homicide.

The most famous of the slave mutinies at sea is known by the name of the ship on which it occurred, the *Amistad,* and it brought together two of the most attractive characters of the nineteenth century. One was an African slave named Cinque. The other was the sixth President of the United States, John Quincy Adams.

Cinque and fifty-two companions, surviving the Middle Passage, had been sold at auction in Havana to a couple of Cuban planters. Their new owners were taking them home on a small schooner, the *Amistad,* when somehow on June 30, 1839, the slaves broke their bonds and overpowered the crew, killing the captain and cook in the process. Their one idea then was to go home but of course they understood nothing of navigation. They trusted one of their owners, who promised to help them in return for the lives of the crew. All day the schooner headed east, but at night the white man managed to reverse the course. Nearly two months of this erratic sailing ended up off Culloden Point, Long Island, where on August 26, a United States naval vessel took them in charge.

Cinque, a bold young man with natural graces and charm, became a hero to Northern abolitionists. But the Spanish government demanded exactly what the United States would ask in the case of the *Creole*, and the administration was inclined to grant it. Abolitionists rallied around the young African chief and his companions—four societies which went on to aid the freedom and progress of his race stem from this legal fight. It was lost right up to the Supreme Court. There Adams argued that the Constitution and laws of the United States could not be perverted to condemn men who had acted solely in defense of their own freedom. The Court agreed in part; it held that the *Amistad* Negroes had been taken in violation of the laws and therefore had a natural right to defend their freedom, even by violence. For this one group of Negroes, then, the grim Middle Passage was reversed, and they went home.

From that time forward, excitement over the slave trade did a good deal to arouse Northern people against slavery in general. Southerners who defended their "peculiar institution" demanded to know by what principle it could be right to transport a Negro from Virginia to Mississippi and wrong to bring him from Africa to Virginia. A lot of people decided that this logic was unanswerable, but they said that both slavery and the slave trade must be wrong. Meantime the traffic in "black ivory" continued undiminished, and some of the traders used strange tricks. One of them might be called: "How Captain Corrie Lost His Membership in the New York Yacht Club."

Captain Thomas Hawkins, building superintendent for the James G. Baylis boatyard in Port Jefferson, Long Island, was a very proud man in the spring of 1857. Taking beautiful shape on the ways was what he insisted would be the fastest yacht afloat. His friends said he talked as if he were expecting her to fly, not sail. But they agreed

413

Cinque—leader of the *Amistad* Mutiny.

she was a lovely thing when he launched her in June. *Wanderer* was the name painted on her graceful stern.

Sleek and slim, 104 feet overall with a beam of twenty-six and one-half feet, she was a strongly made schooner, and Hawkins was giving her plenty of canvas. Her mainmast towered eighty-five feet above the deck; her main boom swung back sixty-five feet; her bowsprit swept twenty-three feet outboard. Her owner, Colonel John D. Johnson of the New York Yacht Club, a retired Louisiana sugar planter, fitted her for luxurious cruising, and had her portrait painted under full sail by the well-known artist, Warren Sheppard.

Less than a year later he sold her, reportedly for a price of $30,000. The purchaser was William C. Corrie, elected a member of the club on the same day, May 29, 1858. He was a tall, suave, handsome man of about forty. A Northern sports journal called him "a high-toned Southern gentleman, and one of the most liberal patron of sports of any and all kinds in the South." He also came well recommended to the members by some of their Southern friends. One of these, Charles Lamar, Savannah shipowner and cotton broker, actually was one of Corrie's partners in the *Wanderer*.

Lamar was a hotheaded defender of slavery, and practiced what he preached. He once wrote to the Secretary of the Treasury that "your damned saphead of a collector" detained one of his ships, which had been running blacks illegally. Lamar had the nerve to demand that the government pay him $1,320 for eight days delay.

The affable Corrie seemed to have all the leisure in the world. He said he was buying the *Wanderer* for an extended pleasure cruise. He planned to visit the West Indies first. Then he had a keen desire to see St. Helena and Napoleon's last residence. After that he might go anywhere at all.

The *Wanderer* sailed in the early summer with Corrie as her captain, according to the club rules. Her sailing master was a Captain Semmes, another amiable, popular Southerner whose brother soon would acquire immortality as commander of the Confederate raider, *Alabama*. The schooner was supplied both for comfortable living and lavish entertaining. After a fortnight in Trinidad, she sailed to St. Helena, where she was much admired.

Some days later a lookout on the British warship *Medusa,* cruising on slave patrol off the mouth of the Congo River, saw the topsails of a schooner. Any ship was suspect in these waters, so the *Medusa* altered course to intercept the stranger. The ship made no attempt to avoid the meeting, and as they drew closer the British officers could admire the fine lines of Captain Hawkins' masterpiece. She was flying the flag of the New York Yacht Club, of course.

The *Wanderer* provided the *Medusa's* officers with the most pleasant interlude of their long tour of distasteful duty. Captain Corrie and Captain Semmes were charming and in no hurry to part from their new friends. The *Wanderer's* wine and food would have done credit to a London club; the Americans were very generous with it and much interested in stories of the dull routine of patrol. For several days warship and yacht sailed leisurely in company. Shore parties were organized for hunting and sports, and there was a sailing race which the Americans won easily. But mostly the naval officers spent their hours off duty in the *Wanderer's* spacious salon. Once Captain Corrie suggested that they really ought to inspect the yacht's deep hold to make sure she wasn't fitted out to carry slaves. Everybody laughed heartily and had another drink.

Finally the *Medusa* headed north on her regular beat. Hardly was she hull down on the horizon than Semmes gave orders which sent the *Wanderer* speeding for the nearest slave barracoons up the Congo. In less than a week she had loaded 750 Negroes into the hold, filled her fresh water tanks and was vindicating Captain Hawkins' opinion of her speed. Five weeks out from the Congo she was off Savannah.

Here they waited while Corrie got in touch with Lamar. A fort guarded the entrance to Savannah, and one of its garrison's duties was to prevent slave running. Lamar got around that. He invited all the officers to a magnificent ball. Then he said it was a shame the enlisted men never had any fun, and why not bring them to a separate party which he would give? The commander thought him very generous, so that night the fort was deserted and the *Wanderer* slipped by to land her cargo on Jekyll Island, which has a different sort of sportsman's club now. From there they were distributed among several plantations belonging to friends of Lamar. Later he was very bitter because one of them charged him fifty cents a head for the accommodations.

The cruise of the *Wanderer* was not the sort of story which could be kept quiet in Georgia in 1858. Before she came down river, it was all over Savannah, and the United States authorities promptly seized the ship. Captain Corrie was not on board. He had gone to Charleston, and there he was arrested, brought before a Federal Grand Jury and charged with piracy under an act of 1820. The case attracted a great deal of attention in those days of deepening conflict over slavery, and the final decision did nothing to calm feelings.

The Act of 1820 had put the brand of piracy on any ship's officer or crew who seized or decoyed a Negro on a foreign shore and transported him to the United States with the intent of making him a slave. That seemed to fit the *Wanderer*'s captain perfectly. But Judge A. G. Magrath, who presided over the District of South Carolina, was an ingenious man. In a long technical opinion, he declared that if Congress wanted to rule the slave trade was piracy, which he conceded was well within its powers, it would have to say so. The Act of 1820 did not mention the slave trade as such. Therefore, he held, the law applied only to those who seized free Negroes with the intent of making them slaves; no man could be guilty of transporting Negroes who already were slaves. There was no evidence that the *Wanderer*'s cargo had consisted of free men; in fact, surely they had been enslaved before they were sold to Corrie.

The Captain walked out of court a free man and something of a hero in the South. The United States court in Georgia, however, declared the *Wanderer* forfeit for having been used to violate the laws against importing slaves, a decision which cut the profit of Corrie, Lamar, and their four partners to $10,000 apiece. This was so small for a successful slaving voyage that Lamar for one thought it hardly worth the trouble.

The government sold the yacht at auction, and the successful bidder was Charles Lamar! He got her for $4,000 after persuading all his friends not to bid anything, and punching the head of the only man who did dare make an offer, a Yankee who took the hint

417

and dropped out of the auction. Lamar immediately sent the yacht on another slaving cruise. Again she landed her cargo safely; again she was seized. But before she could be sold a second time, the Civil War broke out. She was pressed into government service as a revenue cutter, sold into the coconut trade after the war, and eventually piled up in a storm on Cape Henry.

Captain Corrie did not get off scot free. The New York Yacht Club was upset by the use of its flag on a slaver. A committee of indignant yachtsmen met and on February 3, 1859, William C. Corrie was expelled ceremoniously from membership. But they never blamed a ship for the sins of men. Although the name of *Wanderer* had to be erased from their squadron list, the painting of her hung for years in an honored place in the club, and is now the property of Mr. John C. Marsellus of Syracuse, New York.

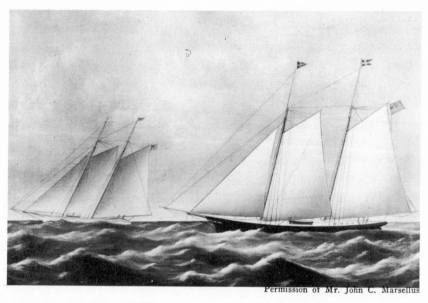

Permission of Mr. John C. Marsellus

The *Wanderer*, painting by Warren Sheppard.

46

The Greatest Treasure

For all the wealth taken out of the Seven Seas, the trade that has been carried over them has been worth everything else combined. It can be said, too, that the business of the world made much of its progress because businessmen discovered the ocean highways long before land transport in bulk was a feasible proposition. Some of the most heroic deeds have been the by-product of commercial ventures.

We have many stories of the importance of sea-borne trade, the fortunes made by men and nations, the rise and fall of busy ports. The Phoenicians were the first people to become powerful through the courage of their sailors and the skill of their navigators who could carry the products of far lands from one to another. Like businessmen everywhere, they had their trade secrets, and no Phoenician sailor would tell about trade routes and where bargaining was good.

When Rome was in her glory, those two great men, Caesar and Pompey, took as their comrade in the First Triumvirate one Crassus, a man who had grown rich and powerful in part—and the most respectable part, too—bringing corn by ship to the city. Sea traffic created the famous republics of Venice and Genoa and the Hanseatic towns of Germany. When the Netherlands took the place of these powers as the biggest merchant shippers in the world, the Dutch also became the greatest maritime power of the seventeenth century.

England took command of the sea as much by trade as by fighting, and also, it must be said, because the Dutch were weakened by long expensive wars. Spain and Portugal lost their naval eminence in large part because they did not have the merchant ships to back them up. The Scandinavian countries remained strong at sea because their

419

Old Roman port.

young men went into trading and fishing vessels in great numbers.

The saying about Britannia ruling the waves grew up as much from the tradition of the merchant seamen as from that of the fighters such as Drake and Nelson. Stronger than war fleets were some of the companies of English shipowners and merchants chartered to trade with various parts of the world—the East India Company, the Turkey Company, the Virginia Company, the Muscovy Company, and so on. The most famous was the East India Company, and so much was it the keystone of English trade that for several years at the end of the seventeenth century a quarrel between two factions in it virtually dominated English politics. For 200 years the East India "nabobs" were a symbol of British prosperity.

Trade, besides, led to most of the improvements in the design of ships and the science of navigation. Most of the great explorers were men looking for business of one kind or another—new trade routes or new sources of merchandise. Shippers and shipowners rather than police and politicians finally made piracy unprofitable. Everyone who reads knows that even a lot of the romance of the sea is in the adventures of the merchant skippers and their crews.

Every great maritime country has its special ports where the tradition of the merchant vessels is strong. Any one of them is a symbol of the benefits which have been brought to all countries by the sailors who carry goods back and forth across the ocean. One of the most interesting of them is the town of Salem in Massachusetts.

One may wonder how the young United States would have developed without its sailors before the wonderful industries were built and agriculture spread across the whole continent. But the pioneers had been brought here by sea, and the sea offered them their best opportunities. So, for many years, Americans were a seafaring people. In a hundred harbors they created better and better ships, but four places especially were famous for shipping and shipbuilding: Philadelphia, New York, Boston, and Salem.

Salem, never a big city, had become a most important one as early as 1810. Her citizens owned no fewer than forty-one full riggers, forty-nine brigs, and fifty schooners. Their captains were known as daring enterprisers. The saying went that they sailed where no other dared go, where no one else dreamed of looking for trade.

For more than a hundred years the men of Salem followed the sea. A gray-headed ship's master in each generation would be retiring from the quarter-deck to the homestead, while a boy of fourteen took his hereditary place before the mast, confronting the gale which had blustered against his sire and grandsire.

Nathaniel Hawthorne, born in Salem himself, wrote that during the Revolution his home town had fitted out 158 privateers with 2,000 guns and 6,000 men. The total population of the place then was just 2,000. These Salem ships captured 444 prizes or more than half of all those captured by the colonies during the war. In the War of 1812, Salem fitted out forty privateers and paid for and built the frigate *Essex*, which under the command of David Porter swept the Pacific Ocean clean of British commerce until she met a glorious end in the harbor of Valparaiso dueling against the big English warships *Phoebe* and *Cherub*.

As Salem symbolizes all the ports of all countries in all ages where the commerce of the sea was held in high esteem, so one man's story can be told as virtually that of the history of his city.

Richard Cleveland was born to a life of adventure. His father was quite an adventurer himself. His name was Stephen Cleveland, born in Salem. When he was sixteen years old he went on a visit to Boston where he was kidnapped by a press gang to serve on board a British frigate. This was in 1756, when the crews of the navy led a hard life. In the beginning, Stephen Cleveland rebelled so that time and again he was flogged or suffered other cruel punishments.

He was not broken in spirit, but he did realize that it didn't pay to go around with his back carved by the cat-o'-nine-tails. So he calmed down and became what was called a willing hand. In the English Channel he fought with great bravery against the French, winning promotion to midshipman. He was on the brink of being appointed a lieutenant when his time was up. He promptly quit the navy and returned to Salem, where soon he was given a chance to satisfy the hatred he had been nursing against the English during his whole naval career. The colonies fought for their independence, and Cleveland was one who outfitted privateers to harry the British flag.

His son, Richard, had been born in 1773, and while very young was put into the office of one of the shippers where he learned the trade as it looked from the desk, as was the custom. When he was nineteen years old, his father deemed him sufficiently qualified to ship out as a second mate.

This was one case where a ship's officer who "came in through the cabin windows," as the saying went, did not prove to be a failure. His first voyage was on the bark ship *Herald,* and it certainly was not a sanctuary for old men. The first mate was the same age as Richard, and the Captain was not yet twenty years old either. The shipowners of Salem had plenty of confidence in youth. For five years young Cleveland sailed as a mate, then was given command of the bark *Enterprise* bound for South Africa.

The new Captain expected to get a good share of the profits from this voyage but when the *Enterprise* put in at Le Havre, in France, Richard found new orders. He was told to take on a cargo in France and sail back to America. He was indignant at this prospect, for it meant much smaller profits, so he went ashore.

Cleveland had no money himself, but he made such an impression in Le Havre that he was able to buy a little cutter, the *Caroline*, on credit. The reputation which Salem captains already had did not hurt him. It was his plan to go to Cape Town to pick up the valuable cargo for which he left America in the first place. But it was not easy to get an able crew, and in fact he found it impossible. But he sailed anyway, with a few incompetents to man the cutter, only to meet a terrific gale as soon as he was out of port. The *Caroline* was dismasted, and only with difficulty was Cleveland able to rig spare sails on what was left of the mast and return to Le Havre. Here he succeeded in restoring his creditors' confidence, repairing the cutter, and gathering a crew which he called "robbers and pirates and entirely unfit to manage a ship." His first mate was an ignorant fellow from Nantucket, and a German sailor who was to act as second mate was afraid to go aloft.

Despite these handicaps, Cleveland brought the *Caroline* safely to Cape Town, and there began the troubles which merchant skippers had to expect in those days. They usually were on their own in making business deals in foreign ports, whether they were trading for their own account, as Cleveland now was, or acting for the owners back home. Communications across the oceans were too slow and uncertain for businessmen at their desks to arrange for cargoes and terms. All this was left to the Captain.

In Cape Town, Cleveland found that because of political conditions in Europe he was not allowed to trade at all. Nor was he permitted to sail out, either. After some shrewd Yankee negotiations with the Governor and other authorities, however, he was able to sell his cutter and cargo for $10,000. With this to finance a new venture, he took passage to Canton, where he heard about great opportunities for trading in furs on the northwest coast of North America. His funds were dwindling, but again he managed to borrow enough money to buy another small cutter and recruit twenty-one men of different nationalities, but all villains and crooks—"the worst crew that ever disgraced a forecastle," he called them.

The Captain was not yet twenty-six years old when in 1799 he sailed out of Canton with a debt of $20,000 and an uncertain gang, not only among the seamen but his officers. This showed when, hardly were they in the open sea than a full-fledged mutiny broke out, and Cleveland found he could rely only on his second mate and four hands. The rest, saying that provisions were insufficient, the voyage too long, and conditions too uncertain, demanded to put back. With his five loyal men, Cleveland managed to close the hatches over the mutineers and kept them below decks for several days while he remained anchored off an island. Every time a mutineer showed his head above the hatch, a bullet whistled over it. At last, reduced by hunger and thirst, they asked only to be put ashore. Cleveland agreed, and let them come out three at a time to be landed.

There proved to be nothing on the island and after a while the mutineers put up a sign saying they wanted to arbitrate. Cleveland went ashore and found them all willing to return to the ship and their duty. He told them he would refuse to take the ringleaders, but they insisted he take all or none. However, two of them sneaked off from the others, told Cleveland they had been forced to take part in the mutiny, and begged to be taken on board. With himself and seven men now to man the cutter, he decided he had crew enough, so he hoisted anchor and left the thirteen mutineers stranded. They never were heard of again. Certainly some of these Salem captains were hard customers.

Fifty-six days sailing brought Cleveland to British Columbia, where he spent several months trading with the Indians. He found them hostile so that he was obliged to fight several tribes, and later was accused of taking some of his cargo at gunpoint. The cutter was almost filled with furs when, heading north for more, she ran on a submerged rock. It was a dangerous moment, for Indians could be seen on shore preparing to attack, but fortunately a combination of high tide and a strong breeze from the land floated the little craft off the rock just as the canoes of the Indians drew near.

The cutter was found to be damaged so that she had to be beached, and water had got among the skins. Cleveland found a secluded spot where the furs could be spread out to dry and the

cutter repaired. He himself was handy with an axe; the forest provided excellent timber, and soon his ship was afloat again. The
cargo was restowed, and Cleveland decided he had enough. He
enjoyed a good passage back across the Pacific and sold his furs for
$60,000.

With $40,000 in his pocket after he had paid his debts, he
thought of undertaking another fur-trading voyage, but Salem
friends had told him about good business to be done in India, and
he decided to go there. Selling his cutter for $6,000, he embarked
at Canton for Calcutta as a passenger. The trip was enlivened by a
sight of eleven Malay pirate craft near Singapore, and the ship on
which Cleveland was a passenger prepared for an attack, but apparently the pirates did not see them.

In Calcutta, Cleveland bought a vessel of twenty-five tons, but
found business difficult to transact, and sailed to the Danish colony
of Serampore. Here he changed not only the flag of his ship but his
own nationality and became a Dane. The Napoleonic wars were
making it hard for traders, but the little country in the north was not
at war with anyone.

Opportunities for trade did not improve at once, so Cleveland
stole away one day into the Indian Ocean and after forty-five days
sailing arrived at Ile de France. No cargo was immediately available
and he had to spend ten months here, during which time he sold
his small craft and bought a bark. This he finally loaded with 7,000
bags of coffee. As a "Dane," flying the Danish flag, he sailed "home"
to Copenhagen, where he sold his coffee at great profit and had a
lovely time. He also met Nathaniel Shaler of Connecticut, who became a lifelong friend.

Together they went to Hamburg, which then was Danish, and
bought the bark *Lelia Byrd* with the idea of taking a cargo to South
America. On the toss of a coin, Shaler became Captain and Cleveland the supercargo. For two and a half years, their adventures were
typical of the sea-borne commerce of the time.

At their first port of call, Rio de Janeiro, they were not allowed to
trade, so they sailed around the Horn to Valparaiso. Here they
learned that four American captains had been arrested when three

of them protested the confiscation of the fourth's cargo, which consisted of guns. Cleveland and Shaler promptly forgot they were supposed to be Danes, and went at once to the Governor General. They actually succeeded in winning the freedom of the four captains but on condition that all five ships leave port at once.

Their next attempt was San Blas in Mexico, where they were limited to $10,000 in trade, so they sailed for San Diego on the California coast where, they heard, was the best place to get sea otters. There Cleveland set up tents on the beach to trade with the Indians. He had not asked permission, and when the Spanish coast guard came to investigate, trading was so good that he played for time. Telling the men to continue to trade, he asked the coast guard to take him to the Governor. Cleveland dragged out the talk with the Governor as long as he could, finally promising not to land more trade goods and to pay duty on what he already had brought ashore. Meanwhile, Shaler and some of the crew were busily trading for sea otters and doing a brisk business, until they were arrested.

They were in the harbor master's prison when Cleveland got back to their ship in the evening, and at daylight he saw them being taken inland. He promptly armed his crew, went ashore and liberated the captives. That, of course, ended the sea otter trade for them, and as they left hurriedly they exchanged shots with the harbor fortress, doing little damage themselves and suffering little although one shot hit the hull and five the rigging of the *Lelia Byrd*. This was later known as "the Battle of San Diego."

From California they sailed to the Sandwich Islands, causing a sensation, as they brought the first horse ever seen there. The local ruler was quite interested when he saw sailors riding the animal up and down the beach, but refused to buy it. Cleveland finally managed to sell the horse to one of the chiefs, and then the *Lelia Byrd* set sail for Canton, which they reached in August, 1803.

It had been a profitable voyage, but Cleveland had a longing to see his home again. Parting from Shaler in friendly fashion, he took passage around the Cape of Good Hope for Boston, and at the age

426

Danish merchantmen starting out for the East Indies, painting by Christian Mölstad.

of thirty, after being away seven and a half years, he returned to Salem. He was a rich man, bringing $70,000 with him. He built a house, a beautiful house which still stands today, married, and settled down to be a Salem businessman. But he was not as successful in his native city as he had been in dealing abroad, and soon lost his fortune. He had to go to sea again and sailed, sometimes as mate but mostly as skipper, for the next fifteen years with ups and downs of luck. Finally he applied for a small post in the Boston Customs House, and this man who had taken part in so many adventures around the world was happy when he received a letter telling him he was accepted for the job.

In many ways, his career was that of Salem. Competition from larger ports had some effect, but Salem really began to fade when the Indian spice trade ended. Its harbor began to fill up just when ships began to be larger and larger, and little by little the busy port contented itself with a smaller role in the commerce of the sea. At last it was left with only the homes of such men as Richard Cleveland and its museum as reminders of its glorious and dignified past.

427

Trade, of course, was not always so profitable as Cleveland found it, and his experience did not include all the problems which piled up around the old sailing skippers. Several letters from some of these men have been collected in Denmark in an excellent book, *Til Osten under Sejl,* from which many items which illustrate life in the merchant marine of those days may be extracted.

The *Kongen of Denmark,* for example, left Copenhagen in June, 1798, with a cargo transferred from another vessel which had bad fortune in Norway and returned home in a disabled state. On June 26, the *Kongen of Denmark* was ready to depart from Elsinore, but that was not so easy in those days. The difficulties are plain when it is said that about 200 ships, including six Russian men-o'-war, were waiting in the roads for favorable winds for four days.

At last on the last day of the month the *Kongen of Denmark* sailed into the North Sea. Contrary winds and bad weather met her all along the way and it was February, 1799, before she reached the Portuguese colony of Macao at the mouth of the Canton River. On the way, the Captain had signed on nineteen Chinese sailors at Batavia, through an agent who assured him everything was on the level, but now the Chinese demanded to be put ashore, saying that the agent had cheated them. The Captain was willing to pay them off, but they belonged to the Chin Churs, a people not tolerated in Macao. After some dickering with the shore authorities, the Chinese were paid and allowed to hire three sampans.

A Chinese pilot now was engaged to take the ship to her anchorage, whereupon the coast guard came aboard to arrest him because there was a new rule, in effect only two days, that no ship could pass until the Ho Po, highest Chinese customs official, had given a permit. The poor pilot had not heard of this, but on the theory that it was the duty of every subject of the Chinese Emperor to know the law, he was bastinadoed anyway. The Danish ship then was taken to her anchorage, and the Captain began his dealings with Chinese merchants for the sale of his cargo and the purchase of a new one. The pace of business in those days may be seen from the fact that it was considered unusually fast time that all this was completed in less than two months.

At last, in April, the *Kongen of Denmark* started for home, towed across the mudbanks by a fleet of forty-three sampans. The chief incident recorded in the log was a dispute over food—"some of the officers who eat in the Captain's mess are dissatisfied with the fare or the refreshment of which they partake there." They accused the skipper, it appears, of enriching himself from the food allowance made him by the owners.

It was a year before they reached home by way of Falmouth, England, where they put in for water and provisions, and Humbersund, Norway, where they waited early in April, 1800, until they got news that the ice had broken at Elsinore.

So it can be seen that in gathering the greatest of the treasures of the Seven Seas, its trade, there were perils not found in other enterprise associated with the ocean.

Courtesy of Peabody Museum of Salem and Bettman Archive

Crowninshield's wharf—Salem.

Fritz Hen[

Hawaiian fisherman.

Part VIII

The Islands of the Seven Seas

The Romantic Islands
The Rugged Islands
The Lonely Islands

"Religious Procession" by Castera Bazile.

47

The Romantic Islands

If one goes by the dictionary, the land is nothing but islands since all of it is completely surrounded by the ocean. But mostly when people speak of an island they mean one that is not big enough to be a continent and, although they may not say so, possessing something different which the sea gives to even the biggest, Greenland and New Guinea, or the thickly populated British Isles and Japan.

Just as islands have their special plants and animals, partly evolved through their isolation, so the people of islands are distinctive, too, having an affinity with the encompassing sea which is not quite the same as that of seafarers from the mainland. Coming from a country which is mostly islands and having lived in others for many years, I have experienced the feeling of this distinction more clearly than I can describe it.

The physical facts are not enough. Some islands have been formed by the rising of the sea to cut them off from the continents or the falling of the water level to expose the land. Others are built up by submarine volcanoes or earthquakes or the industrious action of coral. And, of course, more than one factor may be involved, as when a rising land or lowering sea level brings a large coral formation above the surface.

I suppose it would be possible to count the islands of the Seven Seas, and maybe it even has been done. But it is a profitless enterprise, and by the time the job is finished it would be out-of-date. New islands appear and old ones vanish, sometimes in the manner of Krakatoa, between Java and Sumatra, which blew half of itself right

433

out of existence in 1883, killing 35,000 people and leaving nothing but a hole a thousand feet deep which in 1929 was filled up by a new island deposited there by another eruption. Anyway, a purely statistical approach to islands is not a good way to understand them. They are of an infinite variety, and for most people they have a great lure, especially those lush tropical isles which have been associated with so much romance ever since the first Europeans saw them.

Millions of continentals who never will cross the sea have very firm ideas about them. They see in their imaginations the Samoa of Robert Louis Stevenson, the Tahiti of Paul Gauguin, or the mutineers of the *Bounty*, the West Indies where Columbus found a gentle, friendly people "without clothing and without law." For the romance of islands seems to have associated itself intensely with two great groups. One is the vast concourse of islands, sometimes called Oceania, which dots the Pacific all the way from 30° north of the equator to 30° south. The other is the great arc which, swinging around from Florida to the northeast coast of South America, encloses the Caribbean Sea.

On both sides of the world, the nations of Europe sought out likely islands to annex, especially so far as the smaller countries were concerned, in the interests of trade. So Denmark, the Netherlands, and Portugal were as competitive as England, France, and Spain in occupying islands wherever they could. Later Germany, Japan, and the United States joined in the game. Wars and revolutions knocked Spain, Germany, and Japan out of the picture; Denmark sold her islands in these areas; the territories of the Dutch and Portuguese are much reduced. New island republics take up some of the former colonial space. The first was Haiti, now occupying one third of the island of Hispaniola, which won its independence from France in 1804, second independent country in the Western Hemisphere. The most recent was Indonesia, spreading over the largest archipelago in the world, which was freed from the Netherlands after World War II. In between came the Dominican Republic, Cuba, and the Philippines.

One can find almost every kind of government in the islands.

"I Raro te Oviri" by Paul Gauguin.

There are self-governing dominions such as New Zealand. There are colonies in the old-fashioned way ruled from the owning country entirely. There are islands which technically never lost their independence but became protectorates of European powers, such as the aptly named Friendly Islands, a native Polynesian kingdom under the protection of Great Britain. There are a great number governed by United Nations trusteeships, with Australia, New Zealand, and the United States as trustees. There is the Condominium of the New Hebrides by which a group of islands are ruled jointly by England and France. There are islands which even have a say in the government of the home country, as Martinique in the West Indies sends deputies and senators to the French Parliament, and as Hawaii may be admitted as one of the United States.

The Europeans who saw these islands first set the pattern for our opinion of them. Over and over again they told of the beauty which nature lavished on these islands, "remote and mysterious like constellations of the sky," as Joseph Conrad said. Sometimes they found the natives, as Columbus did, gentle and friendly; sometimes they were suspicious and hostile, but mostly that last turned out to be after they had some experience of the Europeans. There were among them the well-made, bronze Caribs, the tall and handsome Polynesians, the shorter and darker Melanesians. Long before the philosophy of Rousseau made some Europeans think well of "the noble savage," most of the islanders had been destroyed or corrupted. The Caribs had disappeared from the West Indies almost without a trace. The Polynesians to this day have never recovered from contact with white men, which reduced their numbers from more than a million to perhaps a quarter of that number.

In the West Indies the fate of the aboriginals was very simple. Enslaved, tortured or killed to give up secrets of treasure they did not know, overworked and afflicted with new diseases brought from Europe, the race died out. They were replaced with slaves from Africa, and a new chapter in the West Indies romance began.

In Polynesia, the story was more complicated. The people were tall; it is said they averaged five feet ten inches at a time when Europeans were three or four inches shorter. Their regular features, straight hair, and very light brown, almost golden skins made them the handsomest race of the islands in the eyes of whites. They were friendly and well ordered, but not altogether as peaceful as the storytellers made out because when the white men first came there, Tahitians were said to be able to raise 68,000 warriors and 7,000 war canoes. If they did not do a good deal of fighting, why all this force?

The Maoris of New Zealand, the Society Islanders, Samoans, and Hawaiians all are Polynesians. Their numbers were reduced more by new diseases than by mistreatment.

The peoples of Malay stock survived better. They are shorter, tougher than the Polynesians, and often very good seamen. They were the most active pirates of the South Seas, and ruled a great many of the islands. Many of them were converted to Mohammedanism early and were fanatically pious. They are the dominant population of the Philippines and Indonesia, both republics having a Malay tongue as official language.

In the Philippines alone there are more than 7,000 islands but two-thirds of them are so insignificant that they do not even have names. The original population, a pygmy race called Negritos, apparently were conquered by the Malays and then pretty nearly wiped out by civilization.

There aren't so many Indonesian islands, only about 3,000, but much larger on the average and peopled by many interesting races—Achinese, Papuans, Balinese, Javanese, Dyaks and so on. In their native state, some of these islands developed a fairly high order of government, with rajahs and chiefs and sultans of more or less recognized authority over wide areas. The romance of later days gave a somewhat rosier appearance to this society than perhaps it deserved. The warlike races made life miserable for their neighbors, and the wonderful fertility of the soil, artistic talents of the people, and mildness of climate could not of themselves convert the islands into Gardens of Eden.

At least one island, in the opinion of many, did become such a paradise. This is Bali, the smaller island just east of Java, where a succession of European lotus eaters have found the peaceful delights which romancers so long associated with the South Seas. The Balinese themselves, extraordinarily talented weavers of cloth and graceful interpreters of ceremonial dances, inspire lyric praise. A few phrases from the painter and traveler, Carl Shreve, are typical—"irresistible charm," "blessed children of nature who live in freedom without degeneration," "without ambitions or wants."

In Hawaii, as Captain James Cook found, the idyllic life in a perfect climate was not always perfectly peaceful. Hawaiians before then had developed a feudal system not unlike that of Europe in the Middle Ages. It was not any more ideal, and when white men established big fruit and sugar plantations, the new and the old did not mix too well. Hawaii had been remarkable for a number of able women rulers, mostly regents for weak men, but in 1891, big, handsome Liliuokalani succeeded her brother, Kalakaua, and became the last Queen of the Hawaiian Islands. It is hard to say whether she or the American who married her, John Dominis, a Yankee who won a Queen, provides the stranger tale. But the big planters were not happy with the Queen's government, and in 1893 they started a rebellion which a year later deposed Liliuokalani and set up a republic with Stanford B. Dole, whose name is now attached mostly to pineapple juice, as president. The islands were annexed to the United States in 1898. The deposed Queen lived on contentedly enough until her eightieth year in 1917.

The romance of the South Seas extends to the more primitive islands of the Melanesians, called Papuans, of which the biggest is New Guinea. In fact, New Guinea is the biggest of all islands, after Greenland, and a teeming jungle which got a bad name for its climate long before American troops fought there in World War II. Hot and sticky as its lowlands can be, there are mountains with perpetual snow. A haven for exotic birds, New Guinea was explored in part by hunters for western zoos who trapped here the best birds of paradise.

Probably no one ever realized more completely the romantic dreams of Western youth in the South Seas than James Brooke, who was born in 1803, and went out in the service of the East India Company as a young army officer of twenty-three. Badly wounded during a war in Burma, he was invalided home, but after his recovery spent several years traveling among the islands. In his thirties, he inherited a substantial fortune, with which he bought and equipped a ship, the *Royalist,* for a long cruise. In Borneo he met Rajah Muda Hasim, heir to the sultanate of Brunei, who was having difficulty putting down a rebellion of Dyak tribesmen. Brooke helped him, and in gratitude the Rajah presented him with a kingdom. This was Sarawak, the size of England and Wales put together, with perhaps half a million inhabitants, mostly Malays and Dyak head-hunters.

In September, 1841, Brooke took formal possession, and as "the white rajah of Sarawak" became a legendary figure. He spent a good deal of his time fighting pirates and suppressing the practice of head-hunting. He was successful in the second. In 1857, he actually was chased out of his capital by an attack of Chinese pirates, but gathered his own forces and won it back. Rajah Brooke spent most of his last years in England where, after a Royal Commission found charges made against him in connection with his operations were "not proven," he was very popular and was knighted by Queen Victoria. An estate in Devonshire was bought for him by public subscription, and he died there at a ripe old age, having returned to his island domains only twice, both times to suppress rebellions. His successors made Sarawak a British protectorate, and it was occupied by Japan in 1941. After the war, it became a crown colony by agreement with the last "white rajah," Sir Charles Vyner Brooke, the founder's grandnephew.

On the other side of the world, the West Indies yield nothing in the way of romance and adventure to the East. In any book of rare derring-do, a slave who becomes a black king is worthy of as much space as an officer who becomes a white rajah. This was the improbable lot of Henry Christophe. Born a slave, he was one of the two principal generals of one of the most attractive characters in history, Toussaint L'Ouverture, also born a slave, the real author of Haitian independence who was betrayed into Napoleon's hands.

Haiti was not only the first American republic after the United States but the only example of a slave revolt which established a new nation. Christophe was elected President in 1806, and proclaimed himself King in 1811, but he ruled only the northern half of the country. Napoleon's court was no more splendid nor more bizarre than his. King Henry created a nobility—such titles as the Duke of Marmelade and Duke of the Limonade were from place names actually—and built at least nine palaces and eight chateaus.

One of these palaces and a tremendous fortress are the chief architectural wonders of Haiti to this day.

Outside of Cap-Haitien, his capital, on one of the loveliest sites in the Caribbean, he built a palace patterned after Saint-Cloud in France, only bigger. Ornate but graceful, floored and paneled with the most exquisite hardwoods, it was "air conditioned" by piping water from a cold mountain stream under the floors. Half a mile up in the air, and four and a half miles along a path which still takes a horseman nearly two hours to ascend, the King constructed what has been called the world's greatest monument to vanity and fear, and is certainly one of the wonders of the West. Some of the walls are 100 feet high, none of the outer ones less than seven feet thick. Perched on this inaccessible height, it was built to accommodate 10,000 troops and the royal court, with water and provisions to withstand a siege of at least a year. It became only its builder's tomb.

The royal ex-slave was not popular any more. Only fear kept him on his throne and when he was struck with paralysis in 1820, he knew he would be overthrown. Rather than face such an end, he shot himself with a silver bullet. His family dragged his big body up to the Citadel where it was buried in a lime pit.

The West Indies offer romance in less tragic form, too. The people have stories much brighter than their history. Like everyone else, they reveal themselves in their art, and here again it is most plain in Haiti. One has only to walk into the Centre d'Art in the capital, where the works of now well-known primitive painters can be seen in wonderful variety and charm, to understand the real spirit of the country. They tell me that every Haitian paints as naturally as he breathes, but breathing does not tell the story of a unique nation nor reflect its problems. Their painting does that.

The whole great arc of the West Indies has inspired some lyric names. "The emerald necklace of the Antilles" is one. Cuba was long "the pearl of the Antilles." But the romance which such titles high light was clouded by the colonial plantation system, a system which it must be admitted continued even after some of the islands

440

The Citadel—Haiti.

were independent. Sugar and slavery, it was said, were twins, and the Antilles were the world's sugar bowl. No one paid much attention to the people who produced the cane. It is not a nice thought that only a few years ago Puerto Rico and the British West Indies were called a laboratory for the study of starvation.

They are, of course, more than that, and even the food supply is improving. Jamaica, where the great buccaneer Sir Henry Morgan took his ease, has a large population of refugees from less pleasant climates. But then the West Indies as a winter resort need no advertising in America.

It is said that once you have lived in one of these enchanted islands, you never can be the same again. Such surely was the case with a young fellow named Robert Browning who went out to Saint Kitts of the Lesser Antilles in the 1790's.

He was nineteen years old, a full-faced handsome youth, full of excitement because he was going out to take over the rich Tittle family plantation left him by his mother, who had died when he was a small child. It was a place he had dreamed of in chilly English schools, and it lived up perfectly to his imaginings. Lush and lovely and languid, Saint Kitts floated artistically, the boy thought (he had a painter's eye), on a marvelously blue sea. He fell in love with the island, of course, and supposed he never would want to leave.

Actually he wasn't there very long. Slavery, on closer acquaintance, did not appeal to him. Without consulting anyone, he emancipated all his slaves and divided up the plantation among them. After that it would not have been safe for him to linger in white society, and besides he was quite penniless, so he sailed home to England. For the rest of his life he worked as a bank clerk and never was heard to lament his loss; he had had a taste of paradise, and it kept its good flavor for him for the sixty-five more years he lived. We know this about him, not because he was at all famous or pointed out as unusual but because he had a son, named for him, who became one of England's greatest poets.

48

The Rugged Islands

Scattered over 23,000 square miles of the Pacific Ocean, right on the equator almost 600 miles from Ecuador, are the least hospitable of tropic islands on which men have attempted to live. They are the Galápagos group, twelve major islands and a great number of smaller ones totaling perhaps 3,000 square miles of dry land, of which about half is in the one island of Isabella.

Of volcanic origin, the group are peaks of undersea mountains. The larger ones rise two to three thousand feet above the surface, but at the south end of Isabella an active volcano 5,540 feet high is a constant reminder of how this land was formed. The surrounding seas provide some of the best fishing in the ocean; the scarcity of water makes for some of the worst living conditions on the land.

The excellent fishing is due to the two currents which pass the islands, as described earlier. The Humboldt Current turning westward from South America runs through all the Galápagos islands except the northernmost. El Niño brings tropical waters from the Panama-Ecuador coast, and runs parallel to the Humboldt at varying latitudes so that the whole sea around the islands is fed irregularly by cold and warm water. The result is a churning movement that causes a constant upwelling of plankton. Plankton flourishes on the rich minerals of the Humboldt Current, and feeds greater numbers of sardines than can be found anywhere else in the world. This attracts an abundance of sea birds, penguins among them, which indicates the close connection with Antarctic waters. Seals flock here, too, to take advantage of the ample food supply.

The land fauna are rather primitive, although numerous. An edible land iguana and the giant tortoise, which has been of great importance for both visitors and settlers, are notable examples. The vegetation is sparse for the tropics, the outstanding specimen being a giant cactus.

The scarcity of fresh water, both along the shore and inland, is the most marked feature of the islands. The cold Humboldt Current creates very heavy fog, called "garua," which often hides the island peaks, and heavy rains, especially from December to February or March. But the rain disappears into the porous volcanic ground so that scarcely any streams or springs are formed.

The first European visitor to the Galápagos was a Bishop of Panama who, in 1535, drifted west in six days of calm when he wanted to sail south. His men spent several days in a futile search for water on one of the major islands. Then they sighted another island and took three days to cross over to it. Here were seals, turtles, iguanas, and many birds, so tame they could be caught in the hand, but not a drop of water. The Bishop ordered a well dug, but the water proved to be as salty as the sea. After his party lost two men and ten horses through thirst, they discovered a little water in a ravine, enough to gather eight hogsheads.

The next visit was in 1546, when a Captain Rivadeneira stole a ship in Chile and went to sea without instruments or charts. He sailed north for twenty-five days before he sighted one of the Galápagos islands and sent twenty-two men ashore to look for water. They gave up in a few hours and came back on board, afraid their comrades would desert them in this desolate spot. A rainstorm enabled these men to quench their thirst, and they sailed away. Other Spanish caravels saw the islands, looking in the fog as if they floated mysteriously on the surface, and the name of "Las Islas Encantadas" was given to them.

About a hundred years later, British buccaneers used the islands as a base and changed the name to Galápagos after the giant tortoise. Captain Davis in the *Bachelor's Delight* came here to divide up the loot of three Spanish merchant vessels. His men explored the group and found one place on Santiago Island where there was excellent sweet water. A French expedition in 1700 found former buccaneers still living there.

In 1793, Captain Colnett of the British ship *Rattler,* searching on behalf of his government for ports where whalers could put in for repairs, found the old watering place of the pirates, but the water had dried up. Old daggers, nails, and implements showed that the freebooters had spent much time here. Colnett located other fresh water, however, and the islands were used sufficiently by whalers that at the so-called Post Office Bay there was a barrel where homeward bound ships would pick up letters left by vessels outward bound. During the War of 1812, Captain David Porter of the American frigate *Essex* captured a number of British ships through information he obtained when he sailed in and confiscated the barrel.

At that time the Galápagos had their first permanent resident, an Irish sailor who quarreled with his Captain and asked to be set ashore. He found a patch of soil sufficient to raise some potatoes and pumpkins which he sold to whalers. Later he tricked four sailors into coming ashore, and he kept them virtually as slaves for some time. But finally, after a good many years, he had enough, and with his men managed to steal a ship's boat to take them to the mainland.

Up to 1832, no nation claimed the Galápagos. Then the newly independent Republic of Ecuador took possession, sending eighty soldiers who had been condemned to death after a rebellion, along with a number of women. A good but small spring was found and some farming was done, but the experiment was not a success. Ecuador converted the islands into a penal colony, which increased the population by a couple of hundred. Discovery of water on other islands brought some voluntary settlers, but this only led to strife. The officers and guards of the penal colony were murdered and the remaining population fled the islands altogether.

A third attempt to colonize the islands was made in 1893. Four years later the settlement moved to Isabella to mine sulphur from the volcano's crater. A small garrison was established in 1902, and a small town named Villamil grew up. In the 1920's and 1930's, some Norwegians and Germans immigrated, but most of them left because of water shortages, although a few still live on the second largest island, Santa Cruz, where water is gathered in tanks in the wet season. They have been joined by a few other Ecuadoreans and Europeans, and a small garrison is stationed here, too. During World War II, American engineers built a line to carry water to Villamil from a small waterfall, but living conditions are not pleasant. The rest of the Galápagos group remains uninhabited and unexploited.

In the same year Ecuador took over the Galápagos, England occupied a group of very different but equally unwanted islands, the Falklands, 300 miles east of the Strait of Magellan. East and West Falkland are the two biggest, but there are about a hundred others. All of them are rocky moors with plenty of lakes and streams. The bleak countryside is excellent for sheep, and a good deal of wool is raised, mostly by Scots herders. It is also a center for the whalers, and there are more than 2,000 people living on the islands now.

Formerly sealers went from the Falklands, called in Argentina and Chile the Malvinas, to even more desolate isles in the Antarctic, where some very fine catches were made until the hunters had destroyed the animals. In both the far south and far north, the islands are covered with ice and snow, but the Antarctic ones never were inhabited by men. In some of the northern islands, Eskimos learned to live happily with the conditions imposed by a long, cold winter and a minimum of plant life.

The largest island in all the Seven Seas is Greenland, and most of it is rugged indeed. On the west, of course, life can be good, as I who have lived there for years in my time can testify. But on the east and in the interior where the great icecap is hundreds if not thousands of feet thick, Greenland is as inhospitable as the Galápagos. Of course, that is only to man. There is a life of birds and seals and plants which have adjusted themselves to the rigors of the land and the climate. They are in far more danger from the oil and

Galapagos Island group.

fumes and wastes which are brought in with the new white man's settlements than ever they were from snow or low temperatures.

Eric the Red is said to have been the first European to settle in Greenland, and he gave it the name to entice other settlers. But late in the tenth century, it would appear that the climate was milder, the growing season longer. Then, as has been said earlier, the settlements of the Norsemen disappeared, and the winters grew harsher. But at the same time there were found in Greenland at least 400 kinds of flowering plants, so that it is quite a mistake to consider it nothing but an icy waste. This impression is due to the fact that so many Atlantic icebergs have originated here.

When I first went to Greenland as a young man, the Eskimos still retained their own way of life, and a wonderful one it was, too. In their loose, warm garments, their houses made of ice, their skin boats and sledges, they had achieved comforts which Europeans who would not learn from them never knew. At that time they were getting some tools of metal from explorers, especially Peary, and from

447

A seal hunter at Disko Bay in northern Greenland.

whalers to replace the crude knives from the only iron they saw—
meteorites. The only wood they had was what drifted to them on the
currents, and it was very special lumber since it had been soaked
so long in salt water that it would not split. There was enough of it
and enough variety that the Eskimos distinguished between the
different kinds and had names for them. They well understood the
principle of quick-freezing meat, and the use of oil for heat and light.

Their family and community customs were admirably suited to
the life they led, and in many ways their ideas of right and wrong,
although sometimes apparently quite different from those of Europe,
were more intelligently suited to their needs. But of all this I have
written earlier. The point about Greenland as the largest and perhaps
most rugged island of the Seven Seas is that it has not only great
natural beauty but has nurtured a population who found in the
island's very difficulties and obstacles some of the means of creating
for themselves a good and happy life.

448

The "Bastion" rocks in Greenland fall 3000 feet vertically into the sea.

49

The Lonely Islands

In the year 1506, Tristan da Cunha, one of those bold Portuguese sailors who did so much to expand men's knowledge of their world, was sailing far out in the Atlantic, 1,400 sea miles from the African coast and 1,700 from South America, when he saw a volcanic peak rising more than a mile into the cloudy sky. In latitude 30° 6′ south and 12° 17′ west longitude, this peak proved to be the most isolated in all the world, and Tristan appropriately named it "The Lonely Island."

We know now that it is one of the highest points of the great mountain range running down the middle of the Atlantic. Two smaller outcroppings, called "Inaccessible" and "Nightingale," are quite close. The nearest land is another of the lonely Atlantic islands, Gough, 220 miles away.

The very steep walls of the mountain rise almost sheer out of the sea for anything from 900 to 1,800 feet, then slope more gradually upward to a volcanic cone. At the very top a small, clear lake several hundred feet deep fills the extinct crater. The whole volcano, measured from the ocean bottom, is enormous—twenty-five times the size of Mt. Etna, Europe's largest. To the south and the northwest a little comparatively low, level land, eroded in deep trenches by heavy rainstorms, is covered with enough soil to support vegetation. The whole island never can be seen at one time for fog always hides part of it.

The name of Lonely Island did not take with the world, which preferred to call it after its discoverer. Occasional ships visited it, but

The cloud-capped peak of Tristan da Cunha rises 6700 feet above sea level.

for 300 years it was inhabited only by a strange population of birds —no one knows how they got there—and some smaller animals. Then Napoleon changed the history of Tristan da Cunha as he changed that of most of the world.

This particular change came only after his downfall. The British government feared that his friends might try to rescue the deposed Emperor from St. Helena, using Tristan da Cunha as a base. So in 1816, a party of colored soldiers was sent there, and to their surprise they found a single lonely settler already in residence, Thomas Curry. The soldiers did not fare very well in this rugged setting and soon were withdrawn. But William Glass, who came from New London, Connecticut, asked and received permission to stay with his wife and family. Curry died shortly before the troops left in 1817, but five unmarried men wanted to remain with Glass, and on November 7, 1817, they all signed a Constitution (now in the British Museum) which set up a communal society. It reads:

451

We, the Undersigned having entered into co-partnership on the Island of Tristan da Cunha, have voluntarily entered into the following agreement:

1st. That the stock and stores of every description in possession of the Firm shall be considered as belonging equally to each.

2nd. That whatever profit may arise from the concern shall be equally divided.

3rd. All purchases to be paid for equally by each.

4th. That in order to ensure the harmony of the Firm, no member shall assume superiority whatever, but all to be considered as equal in every respect, each performing his proportion of labour, if not prevented by sickness.

5th. In case any of the members wish to leave the Island, a valuation of the property to be made by persons fixed upon, whose valuation is to be considered as final.

6th. William Glass is not to incur any additional expenses on account of his wife and children.

The little settlement got along with no additions for two years, but there seems to have been general satisfaction when at the end of that time a passing whaler promised to bring some women to the lonesome unmarried men. He was as good as his word, and soon returned with five prostitutes from St. Helena. They posed on the beach, and each of the love-starved quintet on the island picked one. Strangely enough, there was less peace after than before they arrived. It does not seem that their past was held up against them, but they fought with each other, and many quarrels developed which had not been the case as long as only one woman was present.

Later some shipwrecked sailors joined the colony, but it always has been difficult to get women to come there, and Mrs. Glass and the five St. Helenites are the great-grandmothers of the approximately 200 people who live on Tristan da Cunha now. John Glass, William's son, grew up to be a well-known whaling captain, but most of the people always preferred to remain in their isolated home despite many offers to move them. They are a kindly people, very clever in handling their small canvas boats. They eat mostly fish and potatoes. At one time they grew oats and wheat, apples and peaches, but the arrival of rats on the island put an end to these crops. Cattle and pigs were raised for income, being sold to passing ships. Nowadays there also is a meteorological station, which is fortunate since the ships no longer need to buy produce at the island, and recently an occasional cruise ship has brought tourists to the island. There is a school, a church, a doctor, and regular communication with Cape Town. Crime is unknown and the climate seems to be healthy; although toothbrushes are as nonexistent as robberies, the teeth of the islanders are excellent.

The sea is always eating away at the island, waves digging into the cliffs until millions of tons of lava and boulders tumble down into the water. At the same time it is plain from lines on these islands that the sea level has lowered some fifteen to thirty feet in the last three or four thousand years. Since similar conditions are noted in Samoa and other Pacific islands, this is believed to be due to the lowering of the sea rather than a rising of the land. Between this on the one hand and the erosion on the other, it is calculated that if there is no great eruption in the meantime, the wind, rain, and waves will whittle all of Tristan da Cunha down below the surface of the sea in about ten million years.

Some unique birds were found on these islands, no fewer than five species not known anywhere else. One, the Tristan cock, has been exterminated by rats, which were introduced from ships and have been a scourge of this and many more islands. The Tristan cock was a wader, and in spite of good cover in almost impenetrable masses of fern and grass, was unable to survive. Rats also were believed for a time to have eaten the last thrush, called the "starchy," but it now is known that this bird remains on the two smaller islands.

The starchy, which looks like a young blackbird, is one of the most curious and troublesome birds. Although unfamiliar with man, they have no fear, and will explore everything in a tent, getting into every opening, and fighting with each other for the privilege of looking into the barrel of a gun.

Another unique bird here is a canary called the Wilkinsi because the explorer Sir Hubert Wilkins, who spent a few days on Tristan da Cunha, was the first to notice it. Although little bigger than the ordinary one, it is called "the giant canary," because of a large beak and powerful legs. It is very shy, and even islanders seldom see it.

The prize rarity, called the rarest bird in the world today, is a little bit of down, black with red eyes, which is fast as a mink, and small enough to be held in the hollow of a hand. It is the Atlantisia, and is found only on the single island so appropriately called "Inaccessible." Like the kiwi of New Zealand and the famous dodo, the last specimens of which were on the island of Mauritius, the Atlantisia has lost its ability to fly, and indeed all its feathers. It is a wonder how it ever reached this lonely spot in the middle of the ocean.

The *Challenger* Expedition saw this rare bird, but it was not recognized as unique, and not until 1923 were there any to be classified by scientists. Then four were caught, and the world had three skins and a bird preserved in alcohol to study. More recently the Norwegian scientist, Erling Christophersen, has collected and studied more of them, but never could keep one alive for more than fourteen days, seldom for more than four. The one which lived for two weeks he took to Tristan da Cunha, but it died there within twenty-four hours.

Inaccessible lives up so well to its name that it probably never will be possible that man will kill the last of the Atlantisia. But rats are another matter. As yet they have not reached this smaller island, but if they should get to Inaccessible, and it seems impossible to keep them out forever, this unique little bird will certainly go the way of the dodo.

If Tristan is the loneliest of the lonely islands, Juan Fernández off the coast of Chile is the most famous. For it was here that the sailing master of a British privateer, Alexander Selkirk, was marooned for four years and four months, and inspired Daniel DeFoe with the idea for "Robinson Crusoe." Juan Fernández had been a very ordinary place up to then, visited occasionally by ships (especially pirates and privateers), and Selkirk was not the first man to spend some time there. In fact his ship the *Cinque Ports,* had called in there in September, 1704, to pick up a couple of men who had been left by accident several months before. Selkirk had been having trouble with his captain, Thomas Stradling, and was so fed up that he asked to be put ashore. Stradling was quite willing and when Selkirk wanted to back out, the Captain just dumped him and his effects on the island and sailed away.

Selkirk had many of the adventures which are ascribed to Crusoe, catching goats for food and clothing, building a hut, settling himself quite cozily. He lacked only a man Friday. He was rescued in January, 1709, and after several years of privateering and merchant seafaring—and telling of his great adventure—he died in 1721.

The modern rival of Juan Fernández among the lonely islands is Pitcairn, a dot of land two and a half miles long and a mile wide about halfway between Australia and South America, just south of the Tropic of Capricorn. Here the most celebrated mutineers in English literature took refuge, and here more than a hundred of their descendants still live. They were men who in 1789 set William Bligh of the *Bounty* adrift in a twenty-three-foot boat with eighteen companions and buried themselves from sight with six Tahitian men and twelve Tahitian women at Pitcairn.

Motion picture audiences think of "Breadfruit" Bligh as looking like the actor Charles Laughton, and from surviving descriptions, they are not far off. He got his nickname because he had been sent on his famous voyage to collect breadfruit plants in Tahiti and transplant them to the West Indies as food for slaves. Bligh had been Captain Cook's sailing master on his second voyage and knew the islands well. He had not learned humanity to his men from Cook, and the old brutal navy discipline which he enforced did not go well in the South Seass. The *Bounty* had collected her cargo of breadfruit plants and was headed back with them when the mutiny took place on April 28, 1789.

One of the world's great feats of seamanship was Bligh's navigation of his little boat, without a chart, over 3,618 miles of ocean to Timor by way of a few small islands, he and his men subsisting largly on fruit and shellfish. The voyage took nearly three months,

Captain Bligh.

and by then the mutineers were safe on Pitcairn. They destroyed the *Bounty* and before another ship came there, all the mutineers except one were dead, and no one wanted to bother him. After all the trouble, the experiment of transplanting breadfruit to the West Indies did not work; the people preferred plantains.

Shipwrecks account for the population of many a lonely island in the best Robinson Crusoe tradition. Until recently they were isolated by distance and the fact that they were not on any shipping lane, but now of course they have wireless and are sought out as weather stations. Some of them even become summer resorts. They say that is what has happened to Lord Howe Island, and I suppose it can be reached in a couple of hours by plane, but thirty-odd years ago it was as remote from the world as any inhabited place on earth.

Lord Howe is 436 miles northeast of Sydney, Australia, and by a freak of politics is within the Sydney electorate, so that in the 1920's, of which I am speaking, the exact election figures had to wait a couple of weeks at least until the once-a-month little steamer came in with the Lord Howe returns. There were all of ninety-six adults on the island then.

Their story was that the well wooded speck of land of volcanic origin, about as wide as Pitcairn and twice as long with a 2,840-foot mountain at the southern end, was discovered around 1788 by the crew of the *Lord Howe,* when their ship was wrecked there. For a long time they were marooned, and had set up housekeeping so comfortably that when they were found, they sent for their wives instead of asking to be taken off. Later still, the captain of an American whaler arrived looking for an out-of-the-way place to settle because he had acquired two wives at Pitcairn, offspring of the mutineers, and needed a place where not too many questions would be asked.

A century later the island, where the small interisland steamer called once a month, was an interesting study in sociology. The English and American factions were as distinct and separate as if they had lived on different islands all this time. They didn't even observe the same Sabbath because the whaler had been a Seventh

Day Adventist and so were all his descendants. They kept crossed British and American flags on their walls, which also were decorated with chromos of Lincoln, Washington, and Grant. They preserved a few "real American recipes" and served green peas cooked in milk and a sort of pumpkin pie. The descendants of the Englishmen were just as fiercely British.

For all that the two factions did not mix socially, they had a good working co-operative, communal arrangement. In those days many if not most of the Kentian palm seeds that were sold all over the world came from Lord Howe, and this was the island's main industry. Almost all the level ground on the island was sand and coral with groves of palm trees and so-called roads of sand along which big draft horses hauled sledges—there were only one or two wheeled vehicles on the island. For each child born, the community set aside a certain amount of land, the area varying with the population, and until the child was of age a member of the family developed it. At the owner's death, the land reverted to the community.

The governing council of Lord Howe was chosen equally from the two factions. All the men co-operated in gathering palm seeds at harvesttime, and had to devote a certain number of hours each day to this work. Seeds were carried by sledge to a storehouse at the little harbor, sacked and weighed. Each inhabitant was credited with the share from his trees.

Women took no part in the palm harvest, but raised the fruits and vegetables and took care of the chickens and cattle. Men did the hard labor, mended fences, kept houses in repair, and so on. There was no money on the island then—people bartered things, such as part of a newly butchered hog for vegetables or whatever. The proceeds of their industry were banked in Sydney, and anyone could draw on his share to buy anything he wanted. If a youth left the island and stayed away for anything except schooling for more than a year, his land reverted to the community. He could get it back only by working three years after his return.

While there was no doctor on the island, the women were very skillful with home remedies, mostly herbs, at mending broken bones or bad cuts, and midwifery. Their rare visitors were advised to offer soap, toothbrushes, toilet water, or dress material for their board and lodging. Lord Howe was a striking example of a co-operative that worked even when not all the people were friendly with each other.

That these lonely islands cannot remain forever so secluded as one might think is plain from the history of Cocos, which also is called Keeling for one of the first legitimate ship captains to visit it. After the days of the pirates and treasure hunters, a Captain John Clunis-Ross went there to settle with his wife, family, and eight sailors who liked the idea of island life. When they got there they found Alexander Hare, who had been governor of a wild part of Borneo. He had plenty of money and could have established himself anywhere, but he also had acquired a harem of forty Malay women, so he thought the lonelier his island the better.

The force of forty women and one man were not sufficient to resist the advances of eight sturdy sailors—and perhaps the women were not all hostile anyway. Little by little, Hare retreated before the sailors until he and his harem were occupying a little atoll known to this day as Prison Island. The channel between it and the main island was shallow and narrow—and the sailors wore long boots. Hare tried to distract the sailors by giving them the makings of a big party, but the day after their celebration he saw them wading across.

"I thought when I sent rum and roast pig to you sailors that you would stay away from my flower garden!" he protested.

"You, Hare!" they called back. "Don't you know that rum and roast pig are not a sailor's heaven?"

After a time, the women themselves deserted Prison Island for the sailors, and Hare went to Batavia where he died. Many years later when Joshua Slocum touched here on his solo trip around the world he was amazed by the number of children. There seemed to be hundreds of them. All were offspring of the forty Malay women, although the identity of the fathers was not so certain. But, as Slocum said, everything seemed to be more or less in common on this no longer lonely island.

INQUIRY

INTO

THE SOMERS MUTINY.

WITH A FULL ACCOUNT OF THE EXECUTION OF

SPENCER, CROMWELL AND SMALL.

NEW-YORK:

GREELEY & McELRATH, TRIBUNE BUILDINGS.

PHILADELPHIA: BURGESS & ZIEBER.

BOSTON: REDDING & CO.

Tribune Print.   160 Nassau-st.

Title page from U. S. Court of Inquiry into the *Somers* Mutiny.

Part IX

The Law of the Seven Seas

The Rights of Men and Property

Commander Mackenzie of the U. S. brig *Somers* at his court-martial.

50

The Rights of Men
and Property

In the forecastles of the old-time ships, it was no measure of popularity when one of the crew was called "a sea lawyer." In the cabin it was a term of abuse. A sailor who argued for his legal rights was regarded with suspicion by his comrades and downright dislike by his officers. At sea, for the most part, the law was what the captain commanded.

In practice this generally was true up to our own times. However, there was no hard and fast rule because one basic principle of sea law is that the ship in effect is territory of the country whose flag she flies, and the captain is the representative of the national authority. That gives him the power to marry couples at sea, for instance.

Anyone on board, passengers or crew, disobeys him at some peril. It is his obligation to obey and enforce the law, so he has the authority to put disobedient or dangerous persons in irons, even to take life if necessary to suppress mutiny. When it often was impossible to get in touch with his owners, he could dispose absolutely of his ship, actually selling her in a foreign port if he thought best.

In theory, his actions are reviewable later by courts on shore. In practice, passengers always were safer from arbitrary orders than the crew because the captain had to account to his owners, who would not want their ship to get a reputation for abusing people who paid cash fares.

Of course, captains could go too far in mauling their crews. In 1828, Captain William Stewart of the brig *Mary Russell*, homeward bound from Barbados to Cork after delivering a cargo of mules, went a little crazy on the subject of mutiny. He had nine men and four boys on board. After having all headsails furled and the main top close-reefed so he could handle the ship alone, he tied up all the men, including his mate. His mania growing on him, he butchered seven of them with a crowbar as they lay bound on the cabin floor, and wounded two others, one with a pistol and the mate with a harpoon, but they managed to get away and hide. An Irish court found Captain Stewart not guilty by reason of insanity, and he died twenty years later in an asylum, a very gentle, penitent inmate.

In one particular it is lawful (if not always bright) to disobey the captain. Sailors may refuse to work a ship if she is not seaworthy; they may decline to take her to sea, abandon her at sea or compel the captain to return to port. How far they might go was decided in two famous United States cases as long ago as 1834 and 1844.

In the first one, a crew forced their captain to put back to Boston because they thought the ship not safe. The sailors were indicted, and there was much testimony as to the seaworthiness of the ship, very confusing because it was completely contradictory. One of the greatest American judges, Joseph Story, decided the case, however, saying that with so much doubt the sailors hardly could be guilty. Some of his words became a bill of rights for seamen.

"I am aware of the dangers of not upholding with a steady hand the authority of the master," he said, "but I am not the less aware of the necessity of having a just and tender regard for life. Seamen, when they contract for a voyage, do not contract to hazard their lives against all perils which the master may choose they shall encounter. They contract only to do their duty and meet the ordinary perils, and to obey reasonable orders. . . . Unlimited submission does not belong to that relation."

Few sailors probably knew about this, and few captains, either. The skippers of that age did not act as if there were limits on their authority, and ten years later when fourteen members of a crew in a foreign port refused to take the ship to sea because they believed it unsafe, they were jailed and sent home for trial. Neither their captain nor the American Consul would heed their appeal for a survey to determine if the vessel was seaworthy. The men were acquitted, the court quoting Judge Story and explaining that if they reasonably believed the ship unsafe they were within their rights.

That this was a strange notion to shipowners was clear from the fact that for many years after this, in ships of all nations, the spirit of these decisions was lost. Unscrupulous owners sent out "coffin ships" and counted on luck or the skill of the master to bring them to port. Many owners were happy if the vessel never came back at all because the insurance more than paid the loss. In England there were instances when seamen, jailed for refusing to serve on a ship they said was unseaworthy, were not released even after a second crew was lost with the vessel. In fact, things got so bad that a long struggle went on in the British Parliament to enact laws to curb shipowners. The leader of the fight was not a sailor but a brewer, Samuel Plimsoll, and he got his law through in 1876. The "load line" on ships which shows anyone how far it is safe for the vessel to be laden is called by his name, the Plimsoll mark. My old neighbor, William McFee, that seafarer and writer of sea stories, says that the first American legislation to do anything to ameliorate the lot of the sailor was passed only in 1913, the Nelson Bill. Among other things, it abolished jail for desertion, and provided that a man could get on arrival in any port half the wages then due him.

Additional legislation, and the formation of unions which insisted on better conditions, established further rights for seamen, and helped teach them what they were. In fact, often they thought they had more rights than they did. This was the bad luck of half the crew of the United States Maritime Commission ship *Algic* who staged a sitdown strike while at anchor in Montevideo harbor because they would not let nonunion lightermen unload the cargo. They also complained that there wasn't enough hot water and that they only got lettuce leaves while the hearts were saved for the officers. (No one could make them understand that Uruguay only had leaf lettuce so there weren't any hearts.)

In the old days a Captain would have used his judgment, and maybe his fists. The *Algic*'s skipper telephoned to Washington and the then head of the Maritime Commission, Joseph P. Kennedy, told him to put the men in irons if they refused duty. They were brought back, tried, convicted, and lost an appeal.

At the same time, there are many things besides the condition of the ship which may make a vessel unseaworthy in the legal sense. A violent, dangerous member of the crew is one, as the Supreme Court has held in a notable case. The theory is that, as the Court put it, the crew with such a member "was not competent to meet the contingencies of the voyage."

On navy ships, of course, the rights of men are another matter. In the old days, where a sailor on a merchant ship would be punched by a husky mate, the naval rating would be ceremoniously flogged by lashes from a cat-o'-nine-tails which left his back a mass of raw flesh. But of course the most heinous crime was mutiny. As the *Bounty* is the classic example in British annals, so is the *Somers* in the United States, although otherwise the two cases are not very much alike. In fact, we know as much about the *Somers* as we do mostly because the son of a Cabinet member was involved, and two of the most popular writers of the day, James Fenimore Cooper and Richard Henry Dana, took opposite sides in the resulting controversy while a third, Herman Melville, based a book, *Billy Budd*, on it.

Commander Alexander Slidell Mackenzie, skipper of the *Somers*, a brig of the United States Navy, was not a maniac in the manner of Captain Stewart, but when his ship reached New York on December 14, 1842, twelve of her crew were in irons and three had been hanged at sea. One was Midshipman Philip Spencer, son of John C. Spencer, President Tyler's Secretary of War. The others were Boatswain's Mate Samuel Cromwell and Seaman Elisha Small.

At Mackenzie's court-martial this story emerged: Midshipman Spencer, a nineteen-year-old of bad habits whom we would call a juvenile delinquent, had been sounding out members of the crew on a plan for mutiny. He proposed to kill the officers and everyone else who would not join, turn pirate, and enjoy a glorious life of murder and rapine on the high seas—he seemed especially keen on the delights of carrying off beautiful girls. The purser's steward, who was one of those approached, tipped off his chief, who reported to the Captain.

At first Mackenzie did not take the plot too seriously, although he clapped the Midshipman in irons at once. But as several days passed, the uncertainty and responsibility of his position reacted upon each other until the Commander was sure a horrible crime was imminent. First he had Cromwell and Small confined, then others. Finally, he asked his four officers and three midshipmen to form a council to advise him—it was by no means a legal court-martial—and after long deliberation, and apparently a good deal of urging by the Commander, they recommended death for the three chief culprits. The sentence was executed little more than an hour later with due formality, the Captain in his full dress uniform, the crew all on deck to witness the punishment and pull on the ropes which would snatch the mutineers to the yardarms. As befitted his rank, Spencer was hanged from the port yardarm, the others to starboard.

On the key legal point as to whether the Captain was justified in his belief that it would endanger his ship to bring the three ringleaders to port—he was only three days out from Charlotte Amalie and had been worrying about the plot for five days—the court-martial disagreed. A majority, however, acquitted Mackenzie, but the twelve men he brought back in irons were released.

The extralegal results of the case were important. Hanson Baldwin, one of the modern writers who has told the story of the *Somers* mutiny, says that the attention it directed at political influence in appointments of midshipmen was a leading factor in the establishment of the Naval Academy three years later.

*   *   *   *

"The sea is the common property of all nations. It belongs equally to all. None can appropriate it exclusively to themselves; nor is it 'foreign' to any."

In this judgment of John Marshall, Chief Justice of the United States, was stated the fundamental rule of the sea that no one, and therefore everyone, owns the ocean. This means that outside terri-

467

torial waters the law is what nations can agree upon in peace and what the strongest naval powers can enforce in wartime. Attempts have been made to assert national rights, but they fail.

After the United States purchased Alaska in 1867, American authorities began to seize Canadian sealers in Bering Strait outside Alaskan waters. The excuse was that seals there "frequented" American shores and so remained American property. International arbitrators said "no," and sealing regulations were adopted by agreement. On the other hand, nations do recognize rights acquired by usage in the open sea—Tunisian sponge fisheries, Gulf of Manaar pearl beds, oyster beds in St. George's Channel. International conferences and treaties established the sea's rules of the road, maximum loads, inspection of ships, conditions for whaling, sealing, and fishing. All this is so important that maritime law is often considered part of international law.

But the more complicated and much larger business of admiralty lawyers concerns private property at sea. This is because mercantilism supplied the climate in which sea law developed. The business of carrying goods across the ocean, of cargoes and freight and the ships themselves was what inspired the legal mind ever since the days of the Phoenicians and Greeks. This led to some fine salty terms—barratry, the crime of destroying a ship deliberately; bottomry, a loan floated on the security of the ship itself so that she can continue a voyage, usually made by the master for repairs or stores; demurrage, which involves delaying a vessel; flotsam, goods thrown or swept overboard from a ship and found floating.

But the main concern of the law as regards property usually involves insurance. While maritime law goes back to the ancients—Rhodes, more than 2,500 years ago, had the first ones we know about, and Demosthenes as a lawyer is known to have pleaded admiralty cases—insurance as we conceive it in shipping was begun by the Hanseatic cities. The other shipping nations soon copied it. William McFee says that the oldest marine policy still in existence is one dated February 15, 1613, for the ship *Tiger* of London sailing from that port to Patras and Cephalonia.

468

Lloyds' Coffee House in 1798.

The business of an insurance broker in the seventeenth century was to run around among moneyed men inviting them to take a share of the risk in insuring a ship. There were no insurance specialists; the underwriters were rich goldsmiths or merchants. The first of what became a more organized system was a London advertisement in 1692, announcing that an inventory of three ships to be hold at auction could be seen at Edward Lloyd's Coffee House in Tower Street. Soon this place, run by a shrewd Welshman, became a center for all sorts of nautical business. A little later it was the favorite resort for marine insurers, and the fame of Lloyd's of London was on its way. It was a loose association of individuals until 1871, when Parliament forced its incorporation, but the principle that the risk he undertakes is the individual underwriter's alone was not changed. The corporation is not responsible for a member's losses.

Lloyd's gained its fame as much by the accuracy and speed of its shipping news as by the integrity of its payments. From time to time insurance companies more regularly organized were started in England, but few of them survived. Lloyd's standard policy, hardly changed from the first form printed in 1771, was not altogether liked by lawyers then or later—it was too simple and direct—but it seems to work. Eventually insurance became so much a matter of course that most litigation over property on ships ends up by being a dispute between two underwriters.

A section of the law which often interests seamen more than any other is the one relating to salvage. This is the award to those who save a ship or cargo from any of the perils of the sea. In most countries the award is made by admiralty courts, and may be as much as half the value of whatever is saved, or more for a derelict safely brought into port.

The operation of the law of salvage in actual practice seems based more on common sense than technicalities. Usually the reward is reasonably adjusted to the service. But there are some neat legal points. One of them is that no ship can be considered derelict while there is anyone on board. This seemingly obvious stipulation was the crux of a case in France fifty-odd years ago. The crew of a ship, dismasted and believed to be sinking in the Mediterranean, was taken off by a passing liner, all except one man who was thought lost in the storm. But this sailor had calculated that the ship would not sink, and if he remained on board the owners and underwriters would not be subject to salvage charges. For thirteen days he stuck to the wreck, refusing to be taken off, but when another ship finally offered a tow, he accepted. Thanks to his presence, the court rejected the claim of salvage, awarding the rescue vessel only towage charges. The sailor got his reward from the owners.

The readiness of admiralty courts to be guided by the facts of life at sea has been demonstrated many times. In the United States, the first case the great Chief Justice Marshall heard when he joined the Supreme Court in 1801 concerned salvage. There was an undeclared war with France going on at the time. In the course of it, Captain Silas Talbot of the frigate *Constitution* took what he supposed to be an armed French ship, only to find it was a German merchantman, the *Amelia*, which the French had seized on her way back from Calcutta and were sending with their own prize crew on board to Haiti. Navy men shared in prizes they took—this practice was ended only in 1899 when they got a raise in pay to compensate for being deprived of prize money—but Talbot could not claim a friendly ship as a prize. So he altered his demand to salvage. Agents of the owners refused to pay, arguing he had saved the ship from no peril as they would have got it back from a French court. The case got to the Supreme Court which held that under the French decrees and practice of the time, the Germans would have lost their ship, so Talbot was entitled to compensation.

Splitting up prize money gave a lot of work to the courts until it was abolished. One of the most protracted disputes anywhere started in America during the War of Independence. Captain Gideon Olmstead and three men captured a British sloop, *Active,* and were heading to New Jersey with her when two privateers, one Pennsylvanian and one Continental, took her away and carried her to Philadelphia. A Pennsylvania court gave Olmstead only one-fourth the value, taking one-fourth each for the State, the Pennsylvania privateer, and the Continental ship. For thirty years Olmstead dragged the case through various courts, right up to the Supreme Court, losing in State tribunals and winning in the Federal ones. At the very end the State called out the militia to defy the Supreme Court order; the United States Marshal swore in a posse of 2,000 men to enforce it. A real battle was averted when President Madison persuaded the State to surrender. Captain Olmstead, who by now was eighty-two years old, finally got his money.

Bettmann Archive

Superintendent of the Rooms at Lloyds.

Catching of a sea monster, after a mural by Guilio Romano.

Part X

Strange Tales of the Sea

Supernatural Stories
Wonders and Marvels
Mystery and Adventure

An illustration by Doré for "The Rime of the Ancient Mariner."

51

Supernatural Stories

Since men first went venturing upon the ocean, it has been well known that sailors returning from places no landlubber ever sees will tell tales of the sea and ships, of other people and other lands, of portents and monsters. After his hardships and dangers, the mariner enjoys being the center of a circle of admiring or spellbound listeners. Besides, they might even reward the storyteller with drink or food.

Sailors often misunderstood most of what they saw. Furthermore, a yarn would change a little with each telling and retelling until in the course of the ages, seafarers began to be regarded with doubt even before they opened their mouths. On the other hand, audiences often disbelieved the truth because sometimes it sounded more fantastic than the most elaborate lie. Finally, of course, both kinds of stories were taken up by great writers and became part of the world's most treasured literature.

Coleridge's *The Rime of the Ancient Mariner* is a classic of this combination of the poet's genius with the sailor's imagination. Also it is very characteristic not only that the old salt was the sole survivor of his strange adventure, but that he went on talking in spite of the listener's obvious desire to get away.

The ghost ship which has had the honor of the most literary attention is the *Flying Dutchman*. She has been sailing the Seven Seas for 300 years now—often seen and plainly identified right down to our own days. Since this spectral ship has inspired so much talk all over the world, it is natural that there should be many versions of her story, or rather the story of her captain, because it is he who was the object of supernatural punishment, not his vessel.

This Captain Fokke—or Vanderdecken or Van der Straaten, as some of the tales have it—was such a wicked man, we are told, that he sold himself to the devil. He was a terrible blasphemer, a great drunkard, and sinfully lustful. He had no respect for God, the saints, nor man, and people told stories of his dragging young women aboard his ship against their will. If anyone protested against his ways, he would roar with laughter or curse furiously.

One day he was driving his vessel through a storm toward the Cape of Good Hope, cursing the maker of all weather and blaspheming in horrible jests which no one dared repeat, when the crew objected that he would bring the anger of Heaven down upon them all. Suddenly one of the black storm clouds parted and a stately Being descended from it to the deck.

"Captain," said the Being, "you are a dirty-mouthed pig-head."

"And you are an impudent scoundrel," shouted Fokke. "Get off my ship or I'll blow you off."

Whereupon the Being pronounced a solemn curse upon Fokke and his crew, poor fellows. For all eternity they would have to wander through the storm, forever trying to round the Cape and never succeeding, or alternately making for Cape Horn and never getting there either. Some say that the curse condemned the Captain to wander over all the Seven Seas, but all agree that he must always be hungry and thirsty and never know the solace of beer or tobacco again. It was such an awful curse that merely to sight the ship, which was now called the *Flying Dutchman* because it always was scudding before the gale, was misfortune. Many seamen believe that the first man to see her must die, and in the navies and merchant marines of all the world they can cite examples to prove it.

The *Flying Dutchman* on her endless patrol changes color and rig and even shape with almost every telling. She has the miraculous power to change herself into a schooner or a sloop and back into a high-pooped, rounded merchantman of the seventeenth century.

Sometimes sailors get close enough to see bent, white-haired men with long beards hauling at her ropes, and they seem to be calling frantically for help. But before anyone can get within hailing range, the ship disappears in the storm.

Not all the supernatural intervention is so tragic. Hans Egede, that holy man who became the apostle of Greenland after some very immoral earlier adventures, tells how his prayers stilled a storm which took him to the faraway island in 1721. The wind was so fierce and the waves so strong that the crew gave themselves up for lost until Hans addressed the Lord with what strikes us as a surprisingly worldly argument.

The expedition was going to Greenland, Hans informed God, in His service to convert the Eskimos, and it would give Christianity a bad name if people could say that Heaven did not protect its own servants. Hans argued that he did not so much want to save his life as to preserve God's reputation with the heathen. This common-sense appeal, he said, was very effective, because the gale calmed at once, and the ship went on safely to Greenland.

We have records, too, of friendly personal apparitions on ships. Joshua Slocum, quite early in his amazing journal, alone on the *Spray* around the world, saw one to which he swore to his last days. Slocum had left the Azores, his first stop, for Gibraltar, carrying with him some of the delicious island fruit and a big white cheese which the American Consul had given him. He spent one whole day feasting on the cheese and some plums until he got such painful cramps that he could hardly move.

At this moment the wind blew up strong and in spite of his agony, Slocum had to work hard getting reefs in his sails. Sick as he was, he managed it at last and then, there being plenty of sea room, he lashed the helm and staggered into his cabin. Though he tells us that his seaman's conscience protested this negligence, he threw himself on the floor, writhing in pain, and it was so bad that he became delirious. Then he fainted, and when he came to, his sloop was plunging in heavy seas. He went up on deck and there to his

477

amazement he saw a tall man in odd clothing at the helm. The man doffed his cap and bowed to the Captain and actually smiled as he said:

"I have come to do you no harm. I am one of Columbus' crew. In fact, I am the pilot of the *Pinta*. Lie quiet, sailor Captain. I will guide your ship tonight!"

Such was the state of mind of Joshua Slocum that he took the man for granted and told him to stay on until next day.

"But just give her sail!" he cried.

The mysterious man bowed again.

"You did wrong, Captain, to mix cheese with plums," he said kindly. "White cheese is never safe unless you know whence it comes."

Many people will think that this makes more sense than a great many superstitions of the sea. These are of great variety and endless numbers. Yet they all have a basis in an almost childlike simplicity of mind. One example is as good as a dozen to make this clear. The old-time sealers from Newfoundland never would have dared miss the ceremony of wetting the first seal's tail each season; it would have been bad luck and ruined the year's catch. So the little stub was cut off carefully and firmly suspended from a bit of wire. Each man on board solemnly dipped it into his glass of grog and toasted the success of the voyage. The well-wetted tail then was nailed up above the cabin table, a talisman of luck not to be taken down until the next year's first replaced it.

Whalers believe in luck, too, as who does not, and the luckiest whaler who ever lived, no doubt, was John Tabor of Nantucket. Supposedly lost in the Pacific—so goes the story on his home island— he climbed up on the back of a friendly whale, and was given a free ride all the way home around the Horn, probably the fastest trip ever made until the invention of the airplane.

It is possible to hear strange sounds from the sea, too, and on days when the stranger might think that the sea birds are making a great deal of rather strange noises on the shore of Iceland, the people may explain the story of Paul Rasmussen. He was a clergyman in a small

John Tabor's ride.

village many, many years ago when a party of English raiders landed from three ships. Everyone in the village fled from them, Paul Rasmussen last, carrying his seven-year-old son on his back.

He ran as fast as he could, but with the weight of the boy he knew that the Englishmen soon must catch up to him. So while he was out of their sight for a moment, he pushed the boy into the opening of a cave, warning him not to come out until he saw his father returning. Then Paul Rasmussen ran on as fast as he could.

Now he was hampered by his long cassock, so he took it off and dropped it. The Englishmen could not catch him, but one of them picked up the cassock and for a joke put it on. As they passed the cave, the little boy, thinking he saw his father, came running out, and was taken by the raiders back to their ship. Rasmussen saw them from the beach, and with a grim face he set about making black magic over three shells which he picked up on the shore, each shell representing one of the English ships. He muttered and drew his signs and then set the three shells afloat in the water. One drifted out toward the open sea; the other two turned over and sank. Sure enough, as they got under weigh, two of the English ships ran onto the rocks of the harbor and were broken up.

479

Paul Rasmussen had his revenge, but while he was still standing on the beach, the body of his son washed up at his feet. People say that the clergyman looked at his dead child for a moment and then laughed—a horrible laugh. He went on laughing, and walked up and down the beach, and the echoes rolled back from the cliffs. Even after he died, they say, he has gone on laughing, and that is what you hear when you think it is just the sea birds calling to each other.

Ghosts on board ships also make very nerve-wracking noises from time to time, although sometimes it is possible to quiet them. When the biggest steamship of her day, the *Great Eastern,* was being built, one of the riveters working on her plates was killed, and there was a thoroughly believed story that his body remained in the space between the inner and outer hull. His poor ghost no doubt often was heard, but the time that it created real excitement was when the ship was being repaired in New York after ripping her bottom on Great Eastern Rock in Long Island Sound. Every day a diver went down to inspect the new plates being put in, and on one occasion he signaled to be hauled up almost before he got down. The long-dead riveter was hammering on the inside of the ship, he declared, and neither he nor any of the workmen would go on with their work.

The *Great Eastern*'s skipper, Captain Walter Paton, could not persuade them, and finally he went down himself. Sure enough, there was a hammering which he could hear plainly. But the skipper did not believe in ghosts. He got a little boat and started rowing around the ship. Soon he found a heavy swivel which had come loose and was banging rhythmically in the waves against the side.

Ships as well as men become ghosts, and that is because the ships have personality, as every sailor knows. This is why no seaman speaks of a vessel as "it." The spirit which animates the craft has been breathed into the wood, metal, and rope sometime after they were put together in the shipyard. Sometimes the spirit is malign. Sailors always tell one story at least of such a perverse craft which seems to delight in maiming and killing.

But mostly the personalities of ships are benign. They watch over the welfare of the men on board, so that even sailors who lived through the hard days of uncomfortable quarters and bad food felt an affection for the ships on which they served. Joseph Conrad, who had the sensitive feeling for this sort of thing which comes from being both a seaman and a great novelist, tells of a good, true bark which always answered her helm like a charm except on one single occasion. She refused that time and saved a disastrous collision. If ships cannot see where they are going, says Conrad, how can one explain this?

It is this sentiment of the sailor for his ship that leads him to give her a certain immortality, to believe that even after she is dead she can go on sailing the Seven Seas, perhaps making herself visible to the eyes of man, perhaps not. Sailors can report actual cases with an air of great authority. I remember one story of a Portuguese schooner which was seen to go down by her own crew, who had taken to their boats. Yet the ship was seen days later floating quite calmly although on her side.

There was an explanation for this which avoided the supernatural if not the wonderful. The schooner had been carrying a cargo of salt. When the salt melted, the ship simply floated again, a curious phenomenon which was later to be repeated on the other side of the Atlantic. Off the Carolina coast, the schooner *A. Ernest Mills*, also loaded with salt, went down in a storm, and when the cargo dissolved she too came back to the surface, and the unsuperstitious eye of the camera recorded the event.

So, very often, there is a prosaic and practical explanation of the visions which sailors see. A derelict may be converted into a ghost ship, and sea birds may cry or laugh like dead men, but always there will be a little touch of something more supernatural to give spice to the stories which come back to us from the sea on the lips of mariners who have watched the mysteries of the ocean far from the solid, reassuring bulk of the land.

52

Wonders and Marvels

No one should be surprised that sailors have peopled the ocean with creatures of their imagination. Or perhaps not altogether of their imagination. Especially in the old days when lack of sleep, a long spell of bad weather, and great anxiety for the safety of the ship had stretched men's nerves, the strange sights which really were in the sea might easily take on a new aspect. To the man with his head full of fear or dreams or longing for home, what might not the wonders of the deep resemble?

One of the commonest and most welcome was a mermaid. The alluring form of a damsel with a fishtail instead of legs was seen by many through the centuries, and if the mermaid population seems excessive as compared to mermen, it is hardly fair to blame the sailors whose thoughts after all center much more around women than anything else.

Greek mythology included the fifty beautiful daughters of Nereus, the wise, kindly god of the sea who had the gift of prophecy. His Nereids inherited this talent, and if a fellow could catch one of them —they were to be found riding about the waves on tritons and dolphins—she could be forced to foretell coming events as the price of being allowed to dive back into the sea.

The first time we hear of a mermaid with a fishtail is in the works of Alexander ab Alexandro, a learned Greek of the first century B.C. She was cast up on shore, a lovely girl with a fair face but scales up to her middle. She was so distressed by the curious crowd gathering to look at her that she burst into tears. King Gaza, the ruler of the place, considerately ordered the people to withdraw, and when they did so the mermaid dived back into the water. She came to the surface, shouted some words which nobody understood, and disappeared. The Roman historian Pliny knew of a triton or merman who lured ships to destruction by his song, but Pliny could not tell what he looked like because everybody who had seen him immediately vanished. In his time, too, came the first indications that mermaids really were only seals, because they are described as crying like humans when caught and nursing their young.

The famous Bishop Pontoppidan of Norway describes a mermaid who was caught in a net at Hordaland in Bergen Fjord. Brought before King Hiorleif, she was asked to sing for his amusement, but her tones were not melodious. She was put overnight in a bathtub and in the morning had turned into water, which was thrown out. Busseus, a Dane, writes of a merman who spoke fluent Danish. Two noblemen netted him, but when they got him up on deck he threatened to sink the vessel unless released, and they liberated him at once.

Around 1700, a great debate was started among learned men by reports that Negroes of Angola in Africa were catching mermaids and eating their flesh. The problem for the learned men was whether or not this was cannibalism which should be punished. It must be said that they never reached any conclusion.

So much interest was aroused in these marvelous creatures that in 1723 a Danish Royal Commission was set up to investigate. If the commission found that no such thing existed, it was to be against the law to talk about them. Fortunately for free speech, the members of the commission spotted a merman off the Faroe Islands floating like a log. When their boat came seven or eight fathoms length from him, he sank, but reappeared immediately. He turned and stared at the men for seven or eight minutes, until they became alarmed, in fact, and started to pull away. The merman now puffed out his cheeks, emitted a deep roar and dived. The commissioners saw that his eyes were set deep in his head and his long black beard looked as if it had been cut.

The mermaid legend died out, but an equally ancient myth, the great sea serpent, has persisted right down to our own times, as witness the Loch Ness monster, which created such a sensation and was not neglected by innkeepers. Belief in these monsters goes back further than history. The Midgaardsormen of Scandinavian mythology is a good example—a worm at the bottom of the ocean so long that he encircles the entire world. After the Scandinavians were baptized, the story faded out for a while, but soon popped up again.

The inimitable Hans Egede saw not only mermaids and mermen but also the serpent Hafgusa or Kraken. He wrote cautiously of this last, however, as "so terrible and frightful that I do not know how to describe it." As for its length and bulk, it seemed to "exceed all size and measure." But he tells a little about it, how it spewed some sweet-scented matter which perfumed the sea all around it and attracted all sorts of fish and even whales. All these it swallowed at once, enough to live on for a whole year.

Hans Egede's countryman, Bishop Pontoppidan, describes the Kraken more exactly. He assures his readers that the monster is beneficent toward men because the codfish are afraid to stay deep in the sea when he comes near and swim to the surface where fishermen can catch them. But the Bishop warns that if the Kraken emerges too, it is time to get the boats away because he might swallow one, men and all, without realizing it. No one ever has seen his entire body, which is a mile in circumference. His back looks like a row of small islands. Bright points or horns as high as the masts of a medium-sized ship protrude from his head.

Sea serpents, which must not be confused with the much more enormous Kraken, were seen in all ages and seas, although Bishop Pontoppidan does assert chauvinistically that sea serpents were exclusively Norwegian and truthfully could be said to exist only there. The Swedish writer, Olaus Magnus, confirms this to the extent of saying that it lives under the cliffs about Bergen. He describes it as

484

The Kraaken.

200 feet long, twenty feet around, with a mane of hair two feet long on its neck, scales on its body, and small fiery eyes. It can raise itself straight as a mast and is known to snap men off the decks of ships or cattle pasturing on the islands. Hans Egede saw a sea serpent at about 64° north latitude. It was three times as long as his ship and could reach its head to the top of the mast.

In 1751, a man named Kopper took an oath in Bergen that he had seen a sea serpent in 1746 from his boat six miles from Molde. The water was calm and the serpent paid no attention to him until he fired a gun at it. It then dived. It had a head like a horse with a white mane and black eyes but was of a grayish color. He could not estimate the length, as only seven or eight folds of the serpent were above the water.

An Orkney Island surgeon, Dr. Flemming, took issue with Bishop Pontoppidan on the exclusively Norwegian character of sea serpents. The Doctor said he saw one sixty-five feet long and twelve feet in circumference at Stronsay. Its head was small, its neck long, its skin smooth without scales. It had a bristly mane and three pair of fins.

485

Perhaps this was the same serpent seen by the minister of Egg and the crews of several fishing boats.

Penobscot Bay seems to have been a favorite place for sea serpents, almost as good as Norway. During the American War of Independence, the Rev. Abraham Cummings saw one there "quite often" and reported it as sixty to seventy feet long and big around as the mast of a sloop. Some British naval officers said they saw it, too, and it was 300 feet long, but Mr. Cummings said that was an exaggeration. In 1780, this or another sea serpent leaped right over a ship whose crew saw it.

The most frequently seen sea serpent was one that appeared off Cape Ann near Gloucester, Massachusetts, in August, 1817. It was reported by so many trustworthy men that the Society of Naturalists in Boston undertook an investigation. The Society's ambassadors declared that the serpent indeed was there. They had been within 130 yards of it. The head resembled that of a turtle and was raised about a foot above the water. Its color was dark brown; it was about fifty feet long and big around as a man's body. They saw it lying still and also moving at a rate of twenty to thirty miles an hour. One of the scientists, Solomon Allen, saw it three times and put its length at eighty or ninety feet, and the thickness "about half that of a barrel." Odd protuberances stood out in bunches on its back. Allen shot at it but missed and it immediately disappeared.

After the serpent vanished—it lingered around Cape Ann for about a month—a snake such as no one ever had seen before was killed on shore and taken to the Linnaean Society in Boston. There was a good deal of excitement among members and the public because they thought it was a baby sea serpent. The discussion died down when somebody pointed out that it was just a diseased black snake.

The next great furore over a sea serpent came in 1848, when the captain of the British frigate *Daedalus* reported officially to the Admiralty that his ship had passed a sea serpent at 24° 44′ south latitude and 9° 22′ east longitude, several hundred miles off the coast

The Gloucester sea serpent.

of Southwest Africa. It held its head, which had a mane like a horse, some four feet above the water, and was fifteen or sixteen inches in diameter just behind the head. Sixty feet of the body could be seen clearly. When his report was doubted by a professor, the Captain wrote an indignant open letter insisting he had been close enough to see the snake, and several other English officers came to his support, saying they too had seen the creature.

So the stories went on and on until at last the great sea serpent became a joke. After all, no one ever saw any remains of such a beast, and it is true that porpoises playing in the sea can give the impression of a big undulating chain. Great floating strips of brown seaweed bobbing up and down, or the hulk of that great fish, the basking shark, or a huge boa constrictor swimming from one island to another may start the stories. Or maybe they needed nothing to start them.

Of course, people are not always so credulous as these stories make them sound. The great naturalist Humboldt could not get them to believe him when he said that he "does not remember ever to have received from the discharge of a Leyden jar a more dreadful shock" than that which he got from an electric eel!

This sounded too fantastic. It was easier to regard as fact stories about cuttlefish or squid. Such as the one of the beast which in 1610

487

snatched two sailors from their perches where they were placidly scraping paint from the hull of their ship. Or the monster which in 1639 drifted ashore at Tingoe in Iceland. It had a hairless, scaleless body, no head and tails like a woman's corset stays!

Finally we must come to the whale. Few stories have stirred so much argument through the ages as the one from the Bible, of Jonah swallowed by a whale and eventually being thrown up again in good health. Scientists and laymen have tried to find a whale which could accomplish this feat. Many explanations have been put forward, but up to now nothing satisfactory.

Just the same, men return from whaling trips with many mysteries to relate, although most of the strangest ones are made up by people who never saw a live whale themselves. Usually one can spot the flaw in some false detail of whale hunting or whale behavior or in the surroundings.

As recently as June, 1957, an American magazine, *Stag*, told a story of a man swallowed by a sperm whale and brought out alive after sixty hours so he could describe later his terrible ordeal in the whale's belly. The story was carried under the subtitle of "True Adventure," too.

The scene is laid in the year 1891, when hand harpoons still were used, and the good ship *Star of the East* was down near the equator. At the cry of "Thar she blows!" men tumbled into their gear and rowed with every ounce of strength, each boat crew wanting to be first. In one of them James Bartley stood in the bow, harpoon in hand. They got close enough to see "the seaweed and barnacles around the whale's piglike eyes," but so that it should not be too easy for them the beast sounded in a flurry of spray more than 100 feet high. Some of the men thought they had been seen, but the experienced boatman assured them it had just gone down to "shake off a load of lice" for it was too big to be afraid of anything. (This, of course, is to tell what a large monster it was.)

Sure enough, the whale resurfaced and the hunt was up. The mate's boat planted the first harpoon in its humped back. Then it

488

was up to Bartley, and as he prepared to hurl his harpoon the whale made straight for them, "insane with pain." Bartley sank his harpoon into the whale's body all right; it sounded, it came up again gnashing its white teeth with an expression of tortured fury. Right at the boat it came, and everybody jumped. But Bartley never hit the water for in that moment the whale made an incredibly quick turn, opened its mouth and received the falling sailor. His comrades, to their horror, saw him disappear down the whale's throat.

Other boats picked up the survivors and, of course, the whaling went on, the men more eager than ever so they could avenge poor Bartley. They got some more whales and next day the lookout spied a huge carcass floating off the port bow. It was a huge bull sperm, not long dead, fat with blubber. They got a big loop fitted over its tail and, says the story, the 100-ton body was "taken up on deck" with the winches, although one supposed it must have been brought alongside and the strips of blubber hoisted on board as the flensers cut them. This work continued for forty-eight hours until the blubber was all stowed away and the carcass lay stinking in the heat.

Then the ship's boy asked whether this might be the whale that had swallowed Mr. Bartley. Someone had noticed that it had a harpoon just where Bartley's had struck, so after much talk the flensers began to cut down through the mountain of bloody flesh. Sweating and straining, they finally exposed the immense stomach. When they cut through the retaining membrane, a hundredweight of red shrimps spilled out and the flensers could see clearly the outline of a man's body. It was then only a matter of minutes to get Bartley out. His body was purple, dripping with whale's blood, and his face was contorted in an expression of agony.

Well, after five hours of hard work they brought him to, but he was insane and had to be lashed to his bunk. For a long time he was too scared to be left alone, and forever after he shook with fear at the approach of sunset. But he lived, although no power on earth could force him to board a ship or even look at the ocean. The scientific world investigated later and heard his version of how he felt when he was swallowed and suddenly found himself in a sack much larger than his body, completely dark, and then with full comprehension of his awful fate he lost consciousness.

The magazine *Stag* gives the story in Bartley's own words, and many people might believe it. It is known that the average temperature in a whale's body is 104 degrees Fahrenheit. This is not very comfortable but it can be supported. But how Bartley could have survived the lack of oxygen for sixty hours is past anybody's understanding. Still, as I have said before, sailors have time to make up yarns and people on shore often like to believe them.

Sea monster seen by Hans Egede, a missionary to Greenland.

53

Mystery and Adventure

When people talk about the mysteries of the Seven Seas, someone is sure to mention the *Mary Celeste,* and it is possible to start hot arguments around this nice little girl name. Yet the *Mary Celeste* was just a commonplace brigantine of 282 tons, well enough built, seaworthy and comfortable as ships went in days when sail was holding its own against steam.

The mystery is what happened on board between November 24 and December 5, 1872. On the first of these days her log said she was a little more than 100 miles west of the Azores. On the second of them she was found drifting deserted in the Atlantic on the path between the Azores and Portugal, 500 miles or more from the previous position.

When she sailed from New York on November 4, with 1,700 barrels of alcohol for Genoa, she carried her skipper, Benjamin Briggs, his wife and two-year-old daughter, two mates and a crew of five. When she was seen by an old friend of Briggs, Captain David Reed Moorhouse of the British brigantine *Dei Gratia,* on December 5, she was a derelict, holding an oddly jerky course with only the jib and foretop-staysail set. Obviously no one was at the wheel, and when Moorhouse put men on board, they found the ship completely deserted. Her only boat was gone, and seemed to have been launched because the section of rail which would have been removed to put the boat over the side was lying on deck.

Everything was in good order, although there was no hot food cooking on the stove nor meals set on the table as later romancers said. A good deal of water had got into the cabins and pumps, and clothes were hanging up to dry. All the ship's papers, except the logbook, and the captain's navigating instruments were missing, but the crew seemed to have taken nothing else.

Captain Moorhouse brought the derelict into Gibraltar. A court of inquiry could make nothing of the evidence but awarded him and his crew £1,700 for salvage, and talk of sailors and landlubbers at once began to speculate on the mystery of the *Mary Celeste*. Fiction writers have been using it ever since a young fellow named Arthur Conan Doyle published *J. Habakuk Jephson's Statement,* which many readers believed was a solution to the mystery instead of a fiction story. So-called factual accounts which have just as many imaginary happenings have been published in numbers. Until it wasn't possible for a survivor to be alive any more, sailors all over the world were telling stories which they called "confessions" of how they were on board and what happened. But in fact none of those who sailed on the *Mary Celeste* ever was heard of again.

What really did happen? One version popular for a while was that it was a piratical plot hatched by Moorhouse and some of his crew who were put on board to murder Briggs and seize the ship. So when the *Dei Gratia* came along these men simply transferred to her and all told the story of the deserted ship. This version explains the hot food (which wasn't there) and has the names of all the *Mary Celeste* sailors quite different from those of the official record. Then there was the version that the crew got into the alcohol of the cargo and in their drunken fury killed the captain, his wife, and child, and made off in the boat. Another explanation is that the brigantine ran into heavy weather, took water and frightened everyone so badly that they abandoned ship and were lost in the boat. Finally it is deduced that there may have been a slight leak in one of the barrels of alcohol; fumes escaped and perhaps there was a slight explosion. Briggs may then have ordered all hands into the boat in case the whole cargo exploded, but would have kept a line to the ship so they could go back on board if it proved safe. A sudden gust of wind may have jerked the line hard enough to break it, and the men in the boat could not row fast enough to catch their ship. Then they must have been lost at sea.

Various other versions of mutiny and piracy have been put forward and much ingenious calculation applied to the mystery, but no one today knows any more than the crew of the *Dei Gratia* did when they first sighted the *Mary Celeste*. But it must be said that the mystery brigantine was a bad luck ship all the rest of her days, and in 1885 her newest skipper piled her up on a West Indies reef. He died before he could be tried on a charge of purposely wrecking her for the insurance.

In the stories of sailors, derelicts figure often because there is no more terrifying peril to meet on the Seven Seas than the almost invisible hull of a dead ship which can itself kill the living. There have been thousands and thousands of derelicts—even in recent years the United States Coast Guard has tracked down and destroyed more than two hundred a year. Some of these deserted and ghostly hulks seem to be almost immortal, so long do they haunt the shipping lanes. Or perhaps they make long, incredible journeys.

Such a one was the *Dalgonar*, a British sailing ship whose crew was saved in one of the heroic rescue stories of modern times after the vessel had been dismasted and capsized. They were taken off by a brave French boat's crew from another sailing ship, the *Loire*. The rescue was achieved during a storm in the middle of the South Pacific in 1913. More than two years later, the hulk of the *Dalgonar* stranded at the Society Islands two thousand-odd miles away.

There are sea mysteries with solutions. A favorite of mine is the fate of a French steamer which would have ended up among the ghost stories of the sea but for one small piece of luck. This steamer was one of the first ships fitted up with refrigeration equipment, and her owners renamed her the *Frigorifique*. In a dense fog off the French coast in 1884 she collided with the British collier *Rumney*. Struck amidships, the *Frigorifique*'s engine room and holds began

The *Mary Celeste.*

to fill with water, she listed steeply to starboard, and her captain gave the order to abandon ship. He and his entire crew, unhurt, were taken on board the collier.

The fog remained so thick that the *Rumney* groped along at no more than two knots. Suddenly out of the fog loomed a ship heading straight for her and only by the quickest maneuvering did the *Rumney* get out of the way. The French sailors stared in fear as the other ship vanished in the fog, for there was no doubt in their minds it was the *Frigorifique*. Some tried to say it was imagination, but again a big ship rose apparently out of the night itself and before the *Rumney's* captain could maneuver, the two rammed each other. At these close quarters there could be no question that the refrigeration ship had risen from the bottom to hunt down the vessel that had sunk her!

The collier, much the smaller of the two, was stove in and sinking fast. Fortunately her boats could hold the French sailors as well as her own crew. In a few minutes all of them were rowing away from the *Rumney* as she settled to the bottom. The ghost ship had disappeared again, of course.

Then the fog lifted. The ships had collided close enough to the coast that land was visible. The *Rumney* was gone, but the *Frigorifique* reappeared out of the gloom, not quite so supernatural as in the dark. She was steaming slowly, a little smoke coming from one funnel, and the propellor was turning. One of the men climbed on board as they got to her, and of course the mystery was quite simple. She had not sunk; the water stopped coming in her engine room, and the wheel had been lashed so that the ship kept turning in a wide circle. This had brought her across the *Rumney*'s course twice. The second collision had started the water coming in again, and this time the crew waited until they saw their ship sink for sure before they started rowing for the shore.

For sheer adventure, I think no one has surpassed the renowned Pleville Lepelly, who had enough extraordinary experiences on sea and land to crowd many lifetimes. He never had to resort to lies to enrich his stories with excitement as he worked himself up from simple sailor to admiral in the French Navy.

The most notable fact about him, though, is that probably he is the only man in the world who lost three legs in battle! It is true that only one of them was flesh and blood, but twice after that his wooden leg was shot away. His culminating adventure from his own point of view was that Napoleon made him Secretary of the Navy, a post in which he showed as much ability as he had at sea. He died before the Emperor set out to his defeat in Russia.

Of unusual adventures, the sea still supplies plenty. Sailors are men with time to dream, and in the old sailing days when a ship rode peacefully before the trade winds they had more. Magnus Andersen was such a man, a common Norwegian sailor, or perhaps not so common because he never dreamed of the impossible.

The son of a sea captain who had been drowned, Magnus shipped out himself at fifteen, was a first mate at nineteen and a captain at twenty-two. But his ship was too small for him, so he went to

America and took a job as first mate of a sailing ship bound for Japan. In 1883, when he was twenty-six years old, he saw a photograph of a decked boat which had crossed the Atlantic, and thought to himself that such a voyage might be made in something smaller, in fact in one of the lifeboats which all ships carried and to which sailors often had to entrust their lives.

Andersen was a well-paid mate for those days, fifty dollars a month, and he saved his money. By 1886, he had enough, and went back to Norway to have a boat built to his own specifications. He regarded the Norwegian "sjaegte" as superior to all other types. It was an old design, developed out of experience, and he modified it some more. His—he called her grandly the *Ocean*—was nineteen feet long with a keel four feet shorter than that, five feet three inches broad, one foot eleven inches deep, built of the finest lumber, pine on oak. He fitted her as a lifeboat should be fitted, with waterproof tanks for water, food, and equipment. She was designed to right herself with very little help if upset. Air spaces along the gunwale and floats of reindeer hair on the outer side were supposed to make her unsinkable. Actually these floats were not as good as he expected. It has been calculated that reindeer hairs, which are hollow, lose only twenty per cent of their air when soaked in water, but Magnus found that it really was fifty per cent. For additional buoyancy, though, he had an airtight compartment in the bow. The sleeping place was under the thwarts, and the boat carried one mast with mainsail and jib.

The great invention of Magnus Andersen was a sea anchor made of a strong wooden frame with thick canvas stretched over it, rigged in such a way that it would drag after the boat to reduce speed and keep the bow up into the wind and waves.

Andersen found just the right man for a companion. This was Christen Christensen, a year older than Magnus, who had been mate on the same ship for nine years under three different skippers, which showed he could obey orders. They packed the *Ocean* with food for sixty days, and water, in a tank with twelve separate compartments, for fifty. They figured they would catch rain in their tarpaulin.

By the time they sailed on May 28, 1886, they were a sensation, in England and America as well as Norway. The newspapers spoke of the daring men, but lots of experts said they were mad and could never make it.

On June 9, the venturers reached Leith, Scotland, where they were entertained very well, and exhibited their boat to make some money. One of the parties was quite special, or had a special guest, because the papers reported that someone fired a revolver in the course of the festivities "and hit a lady in her hip." There was a court hearing, but the judge said he would not detain the two Vikings. Rather he asked them please to leave at once.

The *Ocean* stopped in Ireland, too, and then on June 26, headed into the open Atlantic. July 6 was their furthest north, 56° 41′ north, 12° west. Here they ran into their first storm, but the boat rode it out well. The sea anchor worked admirably, and they kept the waves from breaking over them by trailing an oil-filled bag which spread a thin film of oil. No wave which has not already started to break will do so when it runs into oil. A boat like the *Ocean* rides the sea like a gull if she is not filled or smashed by a breaking wave. With a bit of the mizzen set to keep her into the wind, the two men stood watch and watch, slept quite well and let it blow. But one day they misjudged just one wave, and it turned the *Ocean* right over. The two men scrambled up onto the keel. They had arranged it so that they could reach their oars from here, and by using them as levers they brought the boat upright. They pulled themselves on board, bailed her out, and found that their preparations for such an accident had been all right; they lost hardly anything.

Fine weather came again, and they made good progress. They saw several ships; one gave them fresh bread and water and took mail. Then thirty-six days out and about 600 miles from Newfoundland, which they hoped to reach in two weeks, they were hailed by a German steamer. The captain, who liked their sea anchor and had his mate make drawings of it, offered to take them and their boat on board. He warned them that the barometer stood very low and was falling. But they determined to go on.

Then the gale came. Great walls of water rolled up to the *Ocean*, and all through the day only the men's strength and seamanship kept them afloat, for they had to use oil sparingly. All that night and into the next day, the boat held up, but suddenly when their little craft was standing almost on end along the side of a wave, the men felt a sudden jerk and knew the sea anchor rope had parted. The very next wave seized the boat as if it had been a nutshell, tossed it into the air and down into the water.

For the second time, the men sat on the keel, but this time when they managed to right the boat, it promptly filled with water and they had lost much of their equipment. Only the airtight box in the bow kept them afloat. They managed to get out some bread, sugar, and coffee, light a primus stove and get a meal. But for thirty hours they were very cold and wet. A day of good weather enabled them to bail out and almost restored their good humor, but then it started blowing again. They realized that if they had a chance to be taken on board a ship, they had better take it.

On August 6, they ran alongside an English bark, the *Mary Graham,* and admitted defeat. The captain took them aboard and hoisted the *Ocean* up on deck, and then they found they would not get to America at all, because the ship was bound for Newcastle upon Tyne with a deckload of lumber. Andersen and Christensen were within 270 miles of Newfoundland, 2,300 from Norway.

Their adventure was not ended, though. The night after the *Ocean* was picked up, the *Mary Graham*'s deckload shifted in a gale; the captain was killed as the lumber crushed him, the second mate and four sailors swept overboard, and others injured. The first mate, hysterical and crying, would not give orders; he thought they all were lost, so the two Norwegians took command and brought the ship safely to port. Her owners rewarded them with a sum which translates into our money at $22.50—it was worth a little more then, but no great fortune.

Many people think that the perils of the sea were much greater even then than they are now, but actually they are only different.

Time and again in recent years the great qualities of the master mariner have been called forth, his loyalty to ship and shipmates, his ability to command, to accept responsibility, his courage and calm. One of the most sensational examples ended on January 10, 1952, when the good ship *Flying Enterprise* went down off Lizard Head, the southernmost tip of Great Britain.

She was a frieghter of the Isbrandtsen Company, a good reliable ship, insured after the usual inspection. Her captain was a Danish sailor, Kurt Carlsen, thirty-seven years old, an able, conscientious skipper. His adventure began when in a rough December gale the rudder stem broke and the cargo shifted so that the freighter listed to an angle of fifty degrees. Captain Carlsen was a fighter, and rigged up an emergency rudder but the list was so great that the engines went out of commission and Carlsen sent out a call for help.

It was December 11, 1951, and there were not too many ships about. Carlsen, taking stock of his situation, realized that the *Flying Enterprise's* only chance was a tow, but there was no reason to risk his crew, so he ordered them to abandon ship when another vessel came along. Some of the men objected, but Carlsen was not a man to argue with, and at sea an order is an order. All were taken off except the Captain, and he was adrift alone on a helpless ship.

Fortunately for him, his private hobby was wireless, and he had his own battery set, which he knew how to use. So although the ship's radio was dead, he could communicate with the outside world. Soon every newspaper in the world was discussing the fate of this crazy skipper who refused to leave his ship. Day after day went by with no news except that Captain Carlsen reported all well, although no one could locate the *Flying Enterprise*.

Finally, right after Christmas, the Overseas Towage and Salvage Company undertook to have its best tug, the *Turmoil*, under command of Captain Parker, take over. By now it was not only a question of saving ship and cargo but of rescuing a man who was no longer considered so crazy but as a hero for his lone stand against the sea.

It took two days to find the hulk in the immensity of the ocean.

499

She was seen at night, and it was possible to get a line to her only in daylight. The first broke, and they had to try all over again.

This time Captain Parker maneuvered close under the stern of the *Flying Enterprise,* so close that the two ships actually bumped as a big wave lifted the tug. In that moment, Kenneth Dancy, the *Turmoil's* mate, who was holding the line ready to throw, leaped with it to the stern rail of the freighter, and as the tug slid away, he and Carlsen without a word grappled with the rope, Dancy paying it out and the Captain making it fast to the mooring bollard. Only after that was done did Carlson grasp the hand of the mate and remark casually: "Welcome to the *Flying Enterprise.*"

So the tow began. Dancy was surprised that Carlsen's first question was whether the bump had caused any damage. The mate thought it no time to worry about a little bump, but this was a part of Carlsen's makeup. He also apologized for being able to offer Dancy nothing but fruitcake and beer. Then, when they went down to the ship's slop chest to get dry clothing for Dancy, he was very careful to make note of what was taken and to lock the doors.

Meanwhile, the whole world was cheering the rescue. As the weather moderated, a tug full of journalists and photographers came out, but found Carlsen not very responsive.

"Nothing the matter here!" he shouted at them. "I am just doing my duty. What is funny about that?"

The journalists and photographers departed; the weather calmed further, and the towing proceeded. But the fifth night Dancy had been on board a storm blew again, and all of a sudden the towing gear broke. They were only sixty miles from Falmouth.

Day dawned, January 10, 1952, and the sea was worse than ever. On the *Flying Enterprise* the two men rested and waited, but the ship was getting lower and lower in the water. At last Kurt Carlsen, who had stuck to her for a full month, knew it was no use. He was ready to obey the cry of his owners and the world to save himself.

This was not so easy. If the men jumped to leeward, the ship would drift down onto them; they had to leap into the wind, and the best place for that was from the funnel. The *Turmoil* came as close as she dared as they crawled out precariously on the almost horizontal stack. Then Dancy plunged overboard, missing a crest so that he fell twenty-five feet before he hit water, and a moment later Carlsen followed—last man to leave his ship in the old tradition. In that tossing, roaring sea the two men managed to keep together, grabbed the round, white life preservers thrown to them, and were pulled on board the tug. They were hardly tucked into warm blankets with something warm to drink than Captain Parker came to the cabin, saying: "She is going now." Kurt Carlsen shook off his blankets and ran out to watch his ship go down while the *Turmoil* sounded a mournful salute with her siren.

The Captain was received everywhere as a hero, municipal receptions, honors, medals. Movie companies, magazines, publishers, and many others approached him with offers of contracts which would have made this Danish sailor a rich man. He refused them all.

"I only did my duty," he would explain.

Then he took command of a new *Flying Enterprise II*, and went on sailing around the world, plowing his beloved Seven Seas.

Sailors usually are peaceful fellows in spite of the fights and violence in which they get involved; at least they do not often start wars. I know of only one war that is named for a sailor, and for only part of him at that.

In 1730, Captain Robert Jenkins was the master of a merchantman named the *Rebecca*, and before that we do not know much about him, not even whether he was a good sailor. He was, when history first tells of him, on a commonplace voyage from Jamaica to England when he was stopped and boarded by Spanish coast guards. In these years the Spanish were being very strict with smugglers, and they said the English were the worst. Their system of preventing this crime was to be as brutal as possible with all they caught.

They found no signs that the *Rebecca* had engaged in any smuggling, and Jenkins swore he had not, but the commander of the coast guards didn't want his effort of boarding the ship to be a total loss.

He cut off the Captain's ear, flung it at him, and told him to go home and tell his King that the Spaniards would do just the same to His Majesty if he came that way.

One can hardly blame Jenkins for wanting revenge. He preserved his ear in a bottle, and when he got back to London he complained to all the authorities who would listen to him, but for a long time he did not get much sympathy. He kept on talking about it, though, and showing people the ear in the bottle, and in time English relations with Spain got so bad that it was decided to regard Jenkins as a martyr. The main complaint of the English was interference with their shipping. Jenkins' ear was an example that people could understand and get properly angry about. So after seven years the Captain found himself famous. Speeches were made about his ear in Parliament and Alexander Pope wrote a poem:

> The Spaniards own they did a waggish thing,
> Who cropped our ears and sent them to the King.

Jenkins himself was taken into the service of the East India Company, where he did very well. Finally, after two years of agitation, the aggressive people in England got their way and war was formally declared. It is known in the history books as the War of Jenkins' Ear. It was pretty much of a stalemate everywhere. In America it is remembered because George Washington's elder brother fought in an expedition which failed to seize Central America and James Oglethorpe beat off a Spanish fleet which attacked Georgia.

The sea can boast of its mysteries in aristocratic life, and until a few years ago old men kept turning up in odd places to say they were the hero of the most recent of them, the Archduke Johann Salvator, better known as John Orth. Since he was born in 1852, these claims now have stopped.

The man of future mystery, son of the deposed Grand Duke of Tuscany, was brought up in Austria. He was musical, and he published a waltz, and had an opera performed. He also was in the army, and at twenty-nine years of age became a general. But since he was cousin to the Emperor Franz Josef, these successes are not to be wondered at. He was an intimate of the Crown Prince Rudolf, whose death at Mayerling overshadowed John Orth's mystery, and then he earned the displeasure of the Emperor by writing a pamphlet criticizing the elderly commanders of the army. He also fell in love both with the sea and an actress named Ludmille Streubel, which made him less welcome at court than ever.

The Archduke took seafaring so seriously that he studied navigation and actually got a master's license at the port of Fiume. By this time the Emperor was glad to get rid of him, and when Johann Salvator asked permission to resign from the royal family, the answer was an enthusiastic affirmative. The court even wanted him to take Swiss citizenship, but the young man refused; who ever heard of a Swiss sea captain? But he did take for his new name the title of his mother's Swiss chateau and became John Orth.

It was in 1889 that Rudolf died in the tragedy of Mayerling. Later in the year John Orth bought a three-master which he renamed *Sainte Marguerite* in honor of his mother, and went off to London with Milly Struebel. He is believed to have married her there. On March 26, 1890, he sailed in his ship for South Ameirca, leaving Milly to follow by passenger liner. He employed a Captain Sodich as master of the *Sainte Marguerite*, contenting himself modestly with the post of first mate. They reached Buenos Aires in June, where Milly joined him, and he announced that he would sail next to Valparaiso in Chile, which meant a voyage around the Horn in the southern winter.

Later on he was quoted as saying several odd things. One was that he would die but still would live. Another was that he would never be seen again, but that this would not mean he was dead. It was considered significant, too, that he discharged his entire crew and signed on a new one of complete strangers without one qualified officer. When the *Sainte Marguerite* sailed John Orth was the only man on board who knew anything of navigation.

She sailed right into nothingness. Neither the ship nor John Orth nor Milly nor any member of the crew ever was seen again. In the ordinary course of events, it would be presumed that they all were lost in that known graveyard of ships which Magellan was the first to see. But then what about the strange utterances? Did the man really want to make such a complete break with the past that he deliberately lost himself somewhere? Perhaps he did not seek to round the Horn at all. The questions went on for years, but there were no satisfactory answers.

That, of course, is a commonplace of the Seven Seas. They have their mysteries which they cherish. They offer man adventures and all else that he can desire. But it hardly can be said that he will ever find out everything that there is to know about the Seven Seas.

The End

Index

Index